AFRICANS
AND
CREEKS

AFRICANS AND CREEKS

From the Colonial Period to the Civil War

DANIEL F. LITTLEFIELD, JR.

*Contributions in Afro-American
and African Studies, Number 47*

GREENWOOD PRESS
Westport, Connecticut • London, England

Library of Congress Cataloging in Publication Data

Littlefield, Daniel F.
    Africans and Creeks.

    (Contributions in Afro-American and African studies;
no. 47 ISSN 0069-9624)
    Bibliography: p.
    Includes index.
    1. Creek Indians—Slaves, Ownership of. 2. Afro-
Americans—Relations with Indians. 3. Indians of
North America—Slaves, Ownership of. I. Title.
II. Series.
E99.C9L57   301.44'93'0973   78-75238
ISBN 0-313-20703-8

Library of Congress Catalog Card Number: 78-75238
ISBN: 0-313-20703-8
ISSN: 0069-9624

First published in 1979

Greenwood Press, Inc.
51 Riverside Avenue, Westport, Connecticut 06880

Printed in the United States of America

10 9 8 7 6 5 4 3 2 1

For Robert

CONTENTS

MAPS AND ILLUSTRATIONS

PREFACE

IN RECENT YEARS, there has been an ever-increasing interest in the relationship of blacks and Indians in America. In *Red over Black* (1977), R. Halliburton explores this relationship among the Cherokees during the slavery period, as does Theda Perdue in *Slavery and the Evolution of Cherokee Society, 1540-1866* (1979), the latter work being the more thorough and significant. In *Africans and Seminoles* (1977), I explore the relationship among the Seminoles during the slavery period, and in *The Cherokee Freedmen* (1978), I treat the relationship of blacks and Cherokees in the post-Civil War period. There have been, as well, nearly a score of scholarly articles on the subject. Of all the tribes treated, the Creeks have received the least attention. The work presented here puts into perspective the role that Africans played in Creek history from the colonial period to the end of the Civil War.

From the middle of the eighteenth century on, blacks played a significant, and sometimes dominant, role in Creek affairs. After 1763, contact between the races increased to the extent that by the end of the century, many Creeks had adopted the institution of African slavery modeled somewhat on that of their white neighbors. By the time of their removal to the West, the Creeks held extensive slave property, and after removal, many of their tribal members had become so committed to the institution of slavery that they became embroiled in the American Civil War.

Any study of the Creeks must take their blacks into account. The following chapters treat the Africans among the Creeks from the early eighteenth century until the Civil War, emphasizing colonial contacts between the two peoples, the development of the institution of African slavery among the Creeks, and the relationship between Africans and Creeks during the Red Stick War of 1813-14 and the years leading to the Creeks' removal to the West. There is, as well, an account of the institution of slavery in the West, of slaving activities in the Western Creek Nation, and of the involvement of the Creeks and their blacks in the American Civil War, which resulted in the emancipation of the blacks and their adoption as citizens of the Creek Nation. I hope that this study of the Creeks' relationship with and attitude toward the Africans among them will offer new insights into the extent of social discontinuity and the rate of acculturation of the Creeks before the Civil War.

Documentary evidence relating to African-Creek relations was readily available from the post-Revolutionary War period to the Civil War. On the other hand, material from the colonial period was scattered and required a search of state archival materials as well as published letters, journals, travelogues, and other sources. Secondary works, particularly those of John R. Swanton, David H. Corkran, and R. S. Cotterill, were useful in putting Creek affairs of that period into perspective. The work of Verner Crane and various colonial historians was useful in dealing with regional and international affairs. There has been no attempt in this work to present a detailed history of the Creeks; the emphasis, rather, is on the Africans and the role they played in Creek affairs.

It should be noted that the Creek blacks, unlike their Seminole counterparts, did not draw national attention and therefore appear less frequently in federal documents. As a result, there are fewer descriptions of their mode of life and fewer indications of their self-concepts. They were not literate and had no champions to present their case as did the Seminole blacks. Therefore, the documentary evidence to some extent placed limitations on interpretations of the cultural aspects of the blacks' life among the Creeks.

Like my other works on African-Indian relations, the present volume is largely the result of work done at the National Archives during my tenure as a fellow of the Institute of Southern History at The Johns Hopkins University in 1973-74. My research that year was supported by a Younger Humanist Award from the National Endowment for the Humanities. I thank that organization for the award and The Johns Hopkins University for offering the physical setting for the work. My special thanks go also to the archivists of the Natural Resources and the Old Military Branches of the National Archives, the archivists and librarians of the Alabama Department of Archives and History, and the librarians of the Oklahoma Historical Society. I am grateful to others who are too numerous to mention but who have influenced this work in some way.

Daniel F. Littlefield, Jr.

AFRICANS
AND
CREEKS

chapter 1   BACKGROUNDS

THE PEOPLE KNOWN today as Creek Indians are the descendants of a loose confederation of various peoples who, during the earliest historical times, occupied and claimed the lands that constitute the greater part of the present states of Georgia and Alabama. Their principal towns were in the bottoms of the Coosa and Tallapoosa rivers in Alabama and of the Chattahoochee and Flint rivers in Georgia. The two names by which these people were known, Creek and Muscogee, were apparently not names they gave to themselves, yet the sources of the names are debated. The Creeks were a linguistically varied people. Most were of Muskhogean stock: the Hitchiti, including the Apalachicolas, Chiahas, Hitchitis, remnants of the Yamasees, and others; the Alabama, including the Alabamas, Koasatis, Tuskegees, and others; and the Muscogees, including the Kasihtas, Cowetas, Coosas, Abihkas, Hothliwahalis, Eufaulas, Hilibis, Wakokais, Tuckabah-chees, Okchais, and others. There were remnants of the Natchez and splinter groups of Chickasaws as well and groups of other linguistic stocks, notably the Yuchi and some Shawnee. There were no geographic divisions according to language. Along the Alabama streams were the towns of Coosa, Abihka, Hilibi, Okfuskee, Atasi, Tuckabahchee, Okchai, Koasati, and others; and along the Chattahoochee and Flint were Kasihta, Chiaha, Hitchiti, Yuchi, Coweta, Eufaula, and others.[1] Europeans called the towns along these two watersheds Upper Creeks and Lower Creeks, respectively. This geographical designation persisted until it was destroyed by removal of the Creeks to the West in the nineteenth century.

Each town was recognized as either a "red" or "white" town. The colors were associated with war and peace, respectively. Matters of peace and adoption were discussed in councils held at the peace towns, which also took the lead in making laws and regulating internal affairs. War towns were the sites of councils dealing with war and external affairs. Marriage between members of opposing towns was discouraged, and great rivalries developed in the traditional ball games between opposing towns. Throughout Creek history various towns rose and declined in prominence as peace and war towns. In the early eighteenth century, Coweta and Kasihta were the leading war and peace towns, respectively, among the Lower Creeks. Okfuskee, Tallassee, and Abihka were leading peace towns, and Thewarle and Tuckabahchee were leading war towns at different times among the Upper Creeks. The micco was the leading governmental figure in each town. He sat at the head of the town council and served as representative for his town. He was advised on matters of peace by miccos and others known as henehas and on matters of war by warriors who bore titles of emarthla or tustenuggee and who were enforcers of the decrees of council.[2] Sometimes a micco or other man rose to prominence and had great and widespread influence, but there was no recognized head of the Creeks until after removal in the nineteenth century, just as there were prominent towns but none recognized as a capital.

The town square, tchokofa, and chunkey yard formed the center of social and political activity in each town. The square consisted of four shedlike buildings facing each other around a square. These buildings were used to seat the head men of the town during councils, to seat spectators or dignitaries, and to house ceremonial objects. The tchokofa, or hot house, was a circular building, sometimes forty feet in diameter, with a high conical roof. It was used for councils and other business during bad weather and winter. The chunkey yard was a level rectangular area some two or three hundred yards long, its boundaries marked on three sides by a raised bank on which spectators sat. In the yard, the Creeks played chunkey, a game in which sticks or poles were hurled at a rolling disk of stone. In the center was also a tall pole on which a target was placed as a goal in traditional ball games. The family dwellings were modeled after the town squares, with four buildings facing each other, forming a small square in the center. Each building served a specific purpose: cooking, winter lodging, summer lodging, or storage. Each family also had a rectangular tchokofa, and nearby was a small family garden plot.[3] All buildings, public and private, were supported by upright poles, and the walls were formed by poles and lathes covered with clay.

The Creeks were hunters, taking deer, bears, turkeys, and other small game from the woods, from which they also gathered wild fruits and nuts. They took fish and turtles from the streams, farmed fields of corn, and gathered wild rice. The inhabitants of each town planted a common field of corn. On planting day men and women alike turned out to plant, and though much of the labor of cultivation was done by the women, the men assisted in that labor as well. The town field was divided into clearly marked family plots. At harvest time, each family took its produce to the family granary except for a certain amount that was deposited in the town granary for public use or the common welfare.[4]

The first contact between Europeans and the peoples destined to become known as Creeks came through trade. At first, the Yamasees and other Indians near the coast were the source of trade for the Carolinians. But because they soon developed an active trade in Indian slaves, the English quickly made their way into the interior. Earliest trading activities among the Creeks proper took place at Coweta and Kasihta, the two leading towns of the Lower Creeks, among whom the English traders were operating in 1685. The Lower Creeks at that time occupied an area reaching north from the borders of Guale (the Georgia coast from the Savannah River to St. Andrews Sound) and Carolina to the headwaters of the Savannah and west to Chattahoochee. The seats of English influence among them were Coweta and Kasihta which, during the next few years, led the migration of many Lower Creeks eastward to the Ocmulgee River. Their ten or eleven new towns on Ocheese Creek, on the headwaters of the Ocmulgee, became a great English trading center for a quarter of a century.[5]

While the English were expanding their trade, the Spanish in Florida made counter advances. In the coastal areas, the English roused the local Indians against the Spanish Indians, and between 1684 and 1703 there was a general exodus of the Guale Indians to Florida. Farther inland, the Apalachee towns in north central Florida served as the base for Spanish activities among the Creeks and along the Gulf coast west to Pensacola. By 1700, Apalachee was essential to the support of not only the Spanish but also the French in their struggle against the English. But the English were persistent. In late 1685, using Apalachee as a base, the Spanish destroyed English goods in a blockhouse at Coweta, subdued eight Creek towns, and burned Coweta, Kasihta, Tuskegee, and Kolomi, but two years later the English traders were again in the Creek country.[6]

By that time, the Ocheese country was becoming a base for expanding English trade. In the later years of the century, traders from Charles Town broke over the Appalachians and the Tennessee into the lower Mississippi region, establishing a northern trade route through the Cherokee country and a southern route from Ocheese Creek to the Coosa and Tallapoosa and from there to the Chickasaw country. The major item for which the English traded was Indian slaves. From the Ocmulgee they launched many slave-taking expeditions against the Indian allies of the Spanish and later of the French.[7]

The English and their Indian allies raided the Apalachee in 1701 and 1703, completely ravaging the country in the latter year, killing many Indians and making slaves of many others. By that time, the French had allied with the Choctaws and were making overtures to the Creeks. During the early years of Queen Anne's War, the English mobilized the Creeks against the French and Spanish and against the Choctaws as well. However, internal fights among the Indians and ruthless trading practices by the English began to weaken the British influence among the Creeks. In 1712 the French made peace with the Alabamas, and in 1717 they built Fort Toulouse near the juncture of the Coosa and Tallapoosa. Although the English managed to establish trade with the Choctaws in 1714-15, the Indians were beginning to revolt against the Carolina traders in what was to become known as the Yamasee War.[8]

Although the Yamasees bore the brunt of the war of 1715-16, it was an expression of opposition to the Carolinians on the part of the Lower Creeks, some Choctaws and Cherokees, and the small tribes of the Piedmont, Savannah River, and Port Royal districts. It is generally conceded that the Creeks instigated the conspiracy and that Brims of Coweta directed the plot. The Yamasees were destroyed by the Carolinians, many were sold into slavery in Jamaica and New England, and their towns were moved to Guale and Florida.[9]

One of the most significant results of the Yamasee War was Indian migration. The Lower Creeks moved from the Ocheese country to the old sites they had occupied on the Chattahoochee before 1690. These and other migrations prompted a further amalgamation of Muskhogean and non-Muskhogean tribes into the Creek Confederation. After the migrations, the Lower Creek towns extended for forty or fifty miles below the falls on the Chattahoochee with Coweta and Kasihta as the most important northern towns. At the forks of the Chattahoochee and Flint rivers were

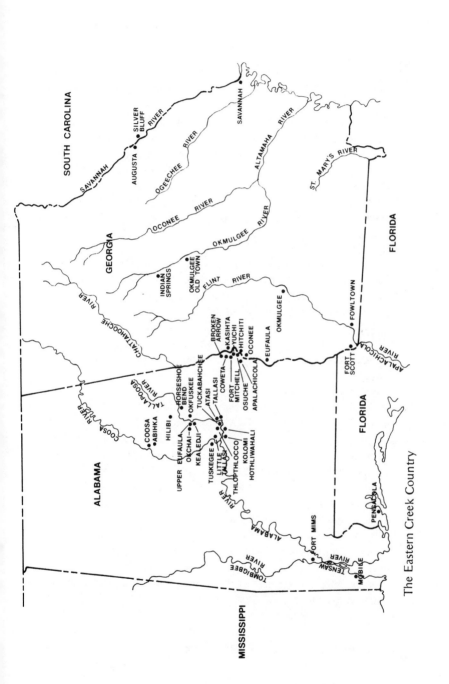

The Eastern Creek Country

some Apalachicolas who were pro-Spanish.[10] The Upper Creeks still occupied their towns along the Tallapoosa, Coosa, and Alabama rivers. The
Creeks occupied these areas until they were removed in the nineteenth
century.

By the middle of the eighteenth century, European influence on the
Creeks was great. They had given up the bow for the gun. Game was getting scarce; so they had begun to turn to livestock raising. They began to
develop great herds and raised domesticated fowls. They farmed rice as
well as corn and raised new varieties of vegetables that they had obtained
from the whites.[11] Before the end of the century, the Creeks would be
subjected to more pronounced European influences, significant among
which was the rapidly increasing numbers of persons of African descent
in the Creek country.

The first contact between Africans and the peoples destined to become
known as Creeks had occurred when the first European came among them.
Hernando de Soto's expeditionary force had included a few blacks, some
of whom had deserted and joined the Indians. One had supposedly eloped
with a Yuchi "queen." Another, named Johan Biscayan, had lived among
the Coosa for ten or twelve years.[12] One historian has postulated that
Biscayan probably fathered Creek children, thus establishing an African
ancestry for some of the Creeks.[13]

This supposition might be correct, but historical evidence does not support it. Nor does it support further African-Creek contact before the European colonies were planted. Even then, no extensive contact occurred
until after the Spanish of Florida and the English of the Carolina colony
established close trade relations with the Creeks in the late seventeenth
and early eighteenth centuries. From that time on, however, black people
became a common sight for the Creeks, and before the end of the latter
century they were a part of the everyday lives of many Creeks.

Some contact between Africans and Creeks probably occurred during
the early years of English trade with the Indians. The extent of African-
Creek contact before the Yamasee War is unknown, but it is likely that
it was slight and came more from the Spanish than from the English.
However, after the war, opportunity for contact increased as the result
of changes in the Carolina economy. By 1715 the Lower Creeks were
great consumers of English goods, yet, despite a peace treaty with the
Creeks in 1717, the English never reestablished the great prewar exchange
of munitions, cloth, and rum for the Indians' deer skins, pelts, and slaves

captured during warfare. Whereas in 1705 Indian trade had been basic to the subsistence of the colony, by 1715 rice had become a great staple.[14]

By 1700, the Carolina economy was already in transition from mixed farming and cattle raising to rice cultivation, a recent innovation. With the cultivation of rice came the development of a plantation economy and with it African slavery. During the early years of the colony, Carolinians had used large numbers of Indian slaves. Although some were artisans, they were poor field workers, and there was the ever-present danger of their conspiring with Indian enemies of the English. After 1700 the number of Indian slaves decreased as the number of African slaves increased. In 1707 the total population of South Carolina was 9,580, including 4,100 black slaves and 1,400 Indian slaves. By the 1720s, the number of Indian slaves had declined while the number of African slaves had drastically increased. In 1720 there were an estimated 11,828 slaves, and by 1724 that number had increased to an estimated 32,000.[15]

The Yamasee War had also helped make the white population static. The continued importation of African slaves resulted in an increasing disproportion of blacks to whites and caused alarm for colonial defense. Of the estimated total population of 16,300 in 1714, some 10,000 were slaves. In an attempt to counter the growing imbalance, the colonial assembly tried to stimulate white immigration through favorable legislation in 1712. An act of 1716 offered bounties for bringing in white Protestant servants and placed a check on the importation of blacks from Africa. The efforts succeeded for a while. By 1720, while an estimated 11,828 of the total population of 20,828 were slaves, the percentage they represented had declined. In spite of these efforts and an insurrection conspiracy in 1720, the percentage climbed again by 1724 to nearly 80 percent: 32,000 of the estimated 46,000 total.[16] The increase in the number of slaves made attempted escapes more frequent and Creek-African contact more likely.

Creek-Carolinian relations during the period between the end of the Yamasee War and the founding of the Georgia colony were dominated for the most part by the leadership of Brims and his successors of the Lower Creek town Coweta. Under his leadership, the Creeks maintained a more or less neutral position despite periodic flirtations with the Spanish and border conflict with the Cherokees. Creek contact with blacks increased, mainly through escape and theft. In the seventh article of the Treaty of 1717, the Creeks agreed to capture and deliver to the whites any runaway slaves that came among them. In 1721, a proclamation by Governor Francis Nicolson declared the settlements out of bounds for "uninvited Creeks" who came to the settlements apparently to trade but who destroyed cattle and encouraged blacks to run away with them.[17]

In 1724 Gogel Eyes, a head warrior of Tallapoosa, attacked the Cherokee Town of Toogaloo, where he robbed the store of trader John Sharp. He wounded Sharp and fled, taking with him a black woman and her two children. The following summer, Carolina officials sent Colonel Tobias Fitch to the Creek country to bring about an end to the Creek conflict with the Cherokees. The head men ordered Gogel Eyes to give up the stolen goods and the slaves.[18] While on his mission, Fitch encountered a Spanish delegation in the Creek country. Their interpreter was a black man who had run away from Carolina. At Coweta, Fitch had the black seized and sent to Carolina, but he escaped from his guard. Anti-English Creeks outfitted him with a canoe and sent him to San Marcos (St. Marks). Fitch heard of another black at Apalachicola town, an alleged escapee from Carolina, and sent men to take him, but the anti-English chief cut the black loose and forced the English to retreat. One of Fitch's objectives was to get Brims' successor to go against the Yamasees in Florida, but a black under the influence of the French followed the warriors and turned back a large part of the Creek war party. Fitch went to the Tallapoosa and took the black, despite the protests of the French at Fort Toulouse. On his return trip, he left the black with two men near Savannah. The black got the men's arms, shot one of them, and escaped.[19] At least in the case of these Spanish and French blacks, contact with the Creeks had been extensive enough by 1725 for them to have learned the language. Whether they learned it from the Spanish Indians or the Creeks proper is the question.

As these cases indicate, runaway blacks could not always count on the Creeks to protect them from capture. Indeed, the Indians generally cooperated with the Carolinians in taking runaways. Thus, most of the runaways looked to Spanish Florida where a standing offer of freedom awaited them, and their activities there brought about further contact with the Creeks.

Spain's policy regarding runaway blacks had been established as early as 1688, when ten Carolina blacks arrived by boat at St. Augustine and asked to become Catholics. When the English called for them, Governor Quiroga paid for them, and they were later freed. In 1699, the Spanish issued a royal decree promising protection to all slaves who fled to St. Augustine and became Catholics. This decree was repeated during the next several decades. After the Yamasee War, blacks were encouraged to run away by the Yamasees, who were then near St. Augustine. From there, joined by some recalcitrant Lower Creeks and runaway blacks, they launched slave-stealing raids into Carolina, while Creeks loyal to the English launched raids against the Yamasees. In 1722 the English warned the Spanish to end the Yamasee raids and demanded the return of runaway slaves, and in 1725 they protested the harboring of their slaves in St. Augustine. In 1731, the Spanish Council of the Indies said that runaways were not to be returned or paid for. In the wake of that decision, the Decree of 1699 was repeated in 1733 and 1736. From then until the Treaty of Paris in 1763, Spanish territory remained a haven for runaway slaves.[20] Thus for several decades blacks' attention turned more to Florida than to the Creek country. It was not until Georgia repealed its prohibition against African slavery in 1750 that extensive contact occurred between the blacks and Creeks and blacks began to look at the Indian country as a possible place of refuge.

The founding of Georgia in 1733 caused a momentary delay in extensive contact between Creeks and blacks because of its prohibition on the importation of blacks into the colony and of its conscious attempt to keep blacks out of the Indian country. Under bylaws adopted in 1733 to regulate Indian trade among the Creeks and other tribes, traders were not allowed to employ "any Negroe or other slave in the Indian Country," nor could they use them in transporting goods to or from the trading houses. The regulators of the colony were well aware of their position regarding the territories of Spain and France as well as of the extent to which the Carolinians were outnumbered by their blacks. Wanting to escape the dangers of slave insurrections and rebellions and to be able to rely on their population in time of war, the Georgians asked the trustees in 1734 to pass "An Act for rendering the Colony of Georgia more Defensible by Prohibiting the Importation and use of Black Slaves or Negroes into the same." In its final form, the act prohibited the importation of blacks after June 24, 1735; any black found after that date would be seized and sold for the support of the colony, and runaways from Carolina would be returned straight away. In 1741 the Georgia trustees, rather smug in their foresight, looked at Carolina, a colony seventy years old, yet with "scarce white People enough to secure her against her own

Slaves." It had been easy for the blacks to run away to Florida as had been demonstrated throughout the years, and the Spanish had incited the Carolina blacks to insurrection. Thus, Georgians viewed themselves as a fine buffer for the northern colonies, especially Carolina, and as "a great security against the running away of Negroes from Carolina to Augustine, because Every Negroe at his first Appearance in Georgia must be immediately known to be a Run away, since there are no Negroes in Georgia."[21] But the Georgians were not able to hold out against the prevailing economic trends of the day. African slavery, though late in coming, did come to Georgia, and between its establishment and the Revolutionary War, Georgia contributed more than did Carolina to the liaison between Africans and Creeks.

Georgia's early relations with the Creeks were for the most part peaceful. On May 21, 1733, Oglethorpe negotiated a treaty of land cession with the Yamacraws, a small band of Indians related to the Yamasees and apparently part of the Creek Confederation, whom Georgians had found when they landed at Yamacraw Bluff. Much of the credit for subsequent successful relations with the Creeks goes to Mary Musgrove, a half-white niece of old Brims of Coweta. With her husband, Mary ran a trading post at Yamacraw Bluff. With her second and third husbands, Jacob Matthews and Thomas Bosomworth, Mary maintained this post and one at the juncture of the Oconee and Ocmulgee rivers.[22] At these posts, Mary, who was very popular among the Lower Creeks, exerted great influence over the Indians during the first twenty years of Georgia's existence.

Kenneth Coleman has postulated that English relations with the Creeks were good because the Creeks needed trade to an extent that could not be maintained by the French or Spanish.[23] The Creeks had welcomed the Georgia traders, but conflict soon developed between the Georgians and the Carolinians, who already had traders in Georgia territory. Controversy over trading rights continued until 1741, when the two colonies reached a compromise and divided the trade, most of which ultimately went to the Carolinians. By the mid-1740s, the Creeks were more dependent than ever on British trade. They were becoming more settled and had begun to accumulate property in the form of livestock herds.[24]

The early trading activities of the Georgians afforded little, if any, opportunity for Creek-African contact since Georgia had excluded blacks from her bounds. However, plantation economy finally won out over any philanthropic motives for Georgia's founding or any sense of her role in international affairs. As early as 1738, petitions from the Savannah area asked for repeal of the law prohibiting the introduction of blacks. Other appeals followed in subsequent years. There were open violations of the law. One violator was Thomas Bosomworth, Mary's husband. Mary herself had been a slaveholder before the prohibition. In 1734, in the absence of her husband John Musgrove, Mary's black servant Justice was killed when angry Yamacraws tried to capture Musgrove's business partner, who had become abusive and had locked himself in the store. In 1746 it was reported that Thomas Bosomworth had sent to South Carolina for six blacks to work at his plantation at the forks of the Altamaha and that blacks had been "creeping into the Colony at Augusta and other remote places." Georgia Governor William Stephens was directed by the trustees of the colony to execute the law, but he said that it could not be done. He therefore asked the trustees to permit blacks to enter the colony under strict regulations. It was not until 1750, however, that the prohibition act was repealed and blacks were admitted legally to the colony.[25] Even then, Georgia's laws governing Indian trade forbade the taking of blacks into the Indian country. Nevertheless, the admission of blacks to Georgia put them in proximity to the Lower Creeks to an extent that had never existed before.

Meanwhile, more possibilities of African-Creek contact had developed through events in Carolina. The steadily increasing number of blacks in South Carolina had caused its assembly to pass acts in 1712, 1716, 1722, 1725, 1735, and 1740 to encourage whites to emigrate to the colony. As time passed, officials became more alarmed over the possibility of slave insurrection or over the unreliability of the blacks in case of attack from European enemies or Indians. By 1739 insurrection was the main concern regarding defense and remained a major concern for forty years.[26]

Insurrection plots had been rumored or had been uncovered in 1701, 1711, 1713, 1720, 1730, 1733, and 1737. There were several in 1738 and one in early 1739. Most of these, especially in the later years, were tied in some way by the British to Spanish intrigue at St. Augustine. But there was no insurrection until the famous Stono uprising in September 1739, in which a number of whites and blacks were killed as the blacks tried to escape to Florida. The Spanish were blamed for the Stono uprising. With the approach of the War of the Spanish Succession, the Spanish were pleased with any domestic problem that weakened the English colonies, and they welcomed the blacks as a potential buffer on the north. Thus, in 1738, the Spanish governor had promised the blacks a place where they could cultivate crops. They formed a settlement called Mosé (or Moosa) at the head of Mosa Creek, a tributary of the North River. It was here that Spanish, Indian, and black forces repelled Oglethorpe's troops in 1740. Mosé remained a threat to the English until it was evacuated after the Treaty of Paris in 1763.[27]

In the wake of the Stono uprising, the South Carolinians became convinced that their own blacks were more of a danger to them than were the Spanish, and the Georgians felt the same way. As one put it, "Had we permitted the use of Negroes, both South Carolina and Georgia might have been undone by this time." One result of this kind of thinking was the fear on the part of public officials of an alliance between blacks and hostile Indians. Historians do not agree on the reasons why such an alliance did not develop until the early nineteenth century. Kenneth Wiggins Porter believes that Brims let the opportunity pass him when he failed to cultivate the interests of the blacks before the Yamasee War and that the slaves' interests lay more with the French and Spanish, whose slave codes were more lenient than those of the English and whose societies granted a higher position to the free blacks than did English society. Chapman J. Milling has made a case for an intense dislike for blacks on the part of the coastal Indians, and it is William S. Willis's thesis that the colonists intentionally cultivated antagonism between the two races out of fear of their potential combined power in the event of their union.[28]

Whether the threat of a black-Indian alliance actually existed, it nagged at the whites and helped to shape their relations with the Indians. They used the Indians near the settlements to help control the blacks. In 1716 the Carolina government moved some of the settlement Indians closer to them to intimidate the blacks but discouraged their intermarrying with the blacks. The settlement Indians were used regularly for decades as slave catchers and were protected by the government against reprisals by the blacks for carrying out the orders of the government. Finally, the settlement Indians were used to help suppress the Stono rebellion of 1739.[29] Carolina minister Richard Ludlam summed up the colonists' attitude in 1725, when he said that the colonists used the Indians and the blacks as a check on one another lest "by their Vastly Superior Numbers we should be crushed by one or the other."[30] How much the colonial policies brought Creeks in conflict with blacks is uncertain. However, in the 1730s there were Yuchis and New Windsor Chickasaws below Silver Bluff (in present Aiken County, South Carolina) and west of the Salkehatche, and there were Creeks at Pallachuccolas and Kings Creek, all east of the Savannah River. Most of the settlement Indians migrated west to the Creeks about 1750, and by 1761 the rest appeared to have gone.[31] They undoubtedly took with them any attitude they had toward blacks.

Carolina's policy differed for the Indians in the interior. Since the Indian country represented such a potentially good refuge for runaways, the colonists sought to prevent as much contact as possible between blacks and Indians. Instructions for traders issued in 1731 strictly forbade the taking of slaves or free blacks into Indian country. Carolinians also tried to prevent Indians from coming into the settlements unless on official business. In 1742 a committee on Indian affairs warned against frequent visits, especially against the Indians' having too much intercourse with slaves in the out plantations.[32]

By mid-century, there is no evidence that the Creeks were interested in having blacks among them. Records of the 1750s show that they often raided the colonists, stealing cattle and horses, but make no mention of slaves. However, there were instances of blacks running away to the Indians. In July 1751, it was reported that three runaway slaves had tried to rouse the Cherokees against the whites, who they claimed had been joined by some Creeks and were on their way to destroy the Cherokees. Old Warrior of Keewee also said that some blacks had offered to trade the Cherokees their service for freedom. The blacks allegedly told them that "there was in all plantations many Negroes more than white People, and that for the Sake of Liberty" they would join the Indians.[33] The colonists tried to control the situation by regulating Indian trade. On May 24, 1751, South Carolina Governor James Glen had sent to Governor George Clinton of New York a "Scheme for Regulating the Indian Trade." Glen's thirty-third rule said that no trader could carry into the Indian country "any Negro, whether he be free or a Slave, or any other Person whatever, unless it be the Servants or the Pack Horse Men whose names he shall give in before he sets off for the Nation."[34]

In 1751, the Cherokees agreed in a treaty with South Carolina to do their utmost to apprehend and return to one of the traders "any Negro or Mulatto" who deserted his master. The same treaty article forbade traders to carry "any Negro or other slave" into the Indian country. And a trade ordinance passed that same year in accordance with Governor Glen's suggestion forbade a licensed trader in the Indian country to "employ any Indians, Negroes, or slaves." Traders among the Creeks were required to report all blacks found among the Indians and to hold them until they could be sent back to their masters.[35]

In August 1752, it was reported to Thomas Bosomworth, Georgia's agent for the Creeks, that two runaway slaves were seen skulking about the Lower Creek town Osuche (Oswichee), and he sent word to John Ladson, the trader there, to assist in taking the blacks. In October of the same year, Bosomworth sent a black captured at Coweta to the white settlements, but the black escaped and returned to the Cowetas. He was once more captured and once more escaped, this time taking a horse that belonged to his guard. Bosomworth sent notices for the black's recovery to all of the Lower towns.[36]

The Creeks were not always cooperative in helping capture runaways, probably because of French activities among them in the years preceeding and during the Seven Years War. Toward the end of June 1756, Mortor (Wolf Warrior) of Okchai in the Upper Creek country brought a peace talk from the Cherokees to the French and Creeks, who met at the French Fort Toulouse. The Cherokees thought that the English intended to make slaves of all of the Indians, for they had "already filled their Nation with English Forts and great Guns, Negroes, and Cattle." The Cherokees asked the Lower Cowetas and Kasihtas (Cussetas) as well to join them in war against the English.[37] In September 1756, South Carolina Governor W. H. Lyttleton sent a talk to the Creek headmen. Lieutenant White Outerbridge at Fort Augusta was charged with getting the message to the chiefs. Although the French influence was strong among the Creeks, the Indians seemed fair. Yet Outerbridge could not get a white man to go with John Petticrow, Jr., his emissary to the Lower Creeks. Thus, Outerbridge gave ten pounds to Tom, "a Negroe Fellow who has been used to the Nation to go with Petticrow." However, not all of the lack of cooperation can be blamed on French intrigue. In March 1757, Daniel Pepper, agent for South Carolina, wrote Governor Lyttleton from Okchai that traders were taking slaves illegally into the Creek country, contrary to the law and their own bonds. Traders John Brown, Daniel Douglass, James Germany, John Ross, Moses Nunes, and John Kitt had one black each, and Thomas Duval had two. Wrote Pepper, "The Carrying of Negroes among the Indians has all along been thought detrimental, as an Intimacy between them ought to be avoided." On May 31, 1757, there was a meeting of the Upper Creek headmen, attended by Pepper. Pepper demanded the return of all blacks and horses belonging to whites and being held by the Indians. The chiefs agreed to deliver them to Pepper, but after he sent for them several times, he got none of the Indians to fulfill their promises. Pepper left orders with the traders to get possession of the property, but he believed they would have no success.[38]

Georgia apparently had less trouble regarding blacks in the Creek country. It is interesting to note that in a treaty with the Georgians on November 3, 1757, and signed by the headmen of twenty-one Upper and Lower Creek towns, there is no mention of slaves or the return of runaways. However, Georgians, like the Carolinians, were concerned about liaison between Indians and blacks. Like the Carolinians, they did not want the Indians in their settlements. Persons not licensed to trade with Indians had made it a practice to encourage Indians to come to the settlements to trade. In February 1758, the Georgia governor issued a proclamation forbidding such practice. That same year, James Glen, former governor of South Carolina, told Governor Lyttelton that it had always been the policy of the government to create in Indians an aversion to blacks.[39]

With the outbreak of the Seven Years War, the Crown had felt the need for a more systematic handling of Indian affairs. The result was the appointment of northern and southern superintendents of Indian affairs. During the tenure of the first southern superintendent, Edmond Atkin (1756-61), relations with the Creeks suffered. French intrigue helped bring on the Cherokee war with the colonists in 1760. Some of the Upper Creeks joined the Cherokees, and the resulting division in the tribe's sympathy nearly led to civil war. On May 16, 1760, young warriors under the command of Handsome Fellow attacked John Ross's store in the Upper town of Sukaispoga, killing Ross and his two black servants and looting the store. Other raids occurred at Okfuskee, Okchai, and Kealedji. Eleven traders were killed.[40]

That the traders became the object of attack is not surprising. The Creeks were greatly dependent on trade goods, and the colonists were always quick to remind them how much they needed the white people. But abuses had crept into the Indian trade. The illegal maintenance of blacks by traders has been noted; in addition, "inflated prices, short measures, land schemes, and misuse of rum often created unrest." In an attempt to bring stricter regulation to the Indian trade, the Georgia Council on July 3, 1761, divided the Creek towns among the traders and restricted the traders to the towns assigned to them.[41]

Under the Treaty of Paris in 1763, France ceded all of her lands east of the Mississippi except the port of New Orleans, and Spain gave up East and West Florida. Southern Superintendent John Stuart, who had replaced Atkin in 1761, met with the Indian tribes at Augusta in November 1763 to explain the international implications of the recent peace and to secure land cessions, if possible. On November 10, the Creeks signed a treaty in which they ceded lands between the Savannah and Ogeechee rivers from Little River just above Augusta down to Ebenezer. They ceded as well a coastal area about thirty miles wide between the Altamaha and St. Mary's rivers. The English promised to continue the supply of trade goods, and the Creeks promised not to molest the existing white settlements.[42] The Augusta treaty and the Proclamation of 1763, issued the previous month, defined more clearly the boundary between the Creeks and the whites.

On April 10, 1764, the Upper Creeks met at Little Tallassee (Talisi or Tulsa) on the Coosa and sent a message to Governor Wright, belittling the Lower Creeks for ceding territory but nevertheless ratifying the Treaty of Augusta. Maintaining the treaty, the chiefs said, would depend on whether the English settlers could keep their slaves and cattle from wandering across the new boundary line.[43]

That runaway slaves were a potential point of difficulty between the Georgians and the Creeks cannot be doubted. It would become an increasing problem with the removal of the Spanish from Florida. With British control of the territory and the abandonment of the black settlement at Mosé, runaway slaves from South Carolina and Georgia could no longer look to St. Augustine for protection. That left only the Indian country, and instances of runaways going there would increase. Officials at the Augusta conference in 1763 may have anticipated such activities when they established a reward to the Indians of a musket and three blankets for each runaway slave brought in.[44]

The Creeks still did not look upon blacks as desirable property. They had killed them along with their white trader owners in 1760, and the comments of the Upper Creeks in 1764 suggest that runaways were not welcome among them. In 1763 South Carolinian George Milligen-Johnston noted "a natural dislike and antipathy" between Indians and blacks, a dislike he found fortunate: "In our quarrel with the Indians, however proper and necessary it may be to extirpate them, or to force them from their lands; their ground would soon be taken up by runaway Negroes from our settlements, whose numbers would daily increase, and quickly become more formidable enemies than Indians can ever be, as they speak our language, and would never be at a loss for intelligence."[45]

The Upper Creeks were correct in assuming that honoring an established boundary line would be difficult. In October 1765, the English honored the treaty by convicting and executing three runaway blacks who had murdered a Creek on the Saltilla River. Yet the Georgians complained that they had received no satisfaction from the Creeks for the murder of whites and charged that the Creeks protected runaway slaves.[46]

In May 1767, Stuart met the Creeks at Augusta to discuss trade regulations. While there, he demanded the return of runaway blacks. Salleche, speaking for the Indians, said that the runaways would be returned. By October, it appeared to the colonists that the Creeks would not keep their promises, for there were known runaways in the Creek country who had not been delivered. Roderick McIntosh went to the Lower towns where, with the cooperation of the headmen, he rounded up all but five whose Indian protectors refused to surrender them. Stuart believed that preventing the Indian country from becoming an "Asylum for Negroes" was "of the utmost consequence to the prosperity of the provinces," and that "any Intercourse between Indians and Negroes . . . ought to be prevented as much as possible."[47]

That fall, Stuart sent "strong Talks" to all of the Creeks concerning depredations on the whites and sent a message to the Lower Creeks demanding restitution of Georgia slaves who had taken refuge in the Lower towns. In January 1768, the Georgians demanded that all runaways be delivered, and their demands were complied with. But in April of the same year, McIntosh was back in the Lower towns to press for Creek cooperation in marking the boundary and at the same time to demand the return of runaway blacks. Seven runaways were rounded up, but nine, forewarned by Indian friends, escaped into the swamps. The Indians pursued them; one black was killed and scalped. Stuart wrote: "This cannot fail of having a very good Effect, by breaking that Intercourse between Negroes & Savages which might have been attended with very troublesome Consequences had it Continued."[48]

Border difficulties, land matters, and runaway slaves continued to plague the Creeks and whites until the outbreak of the Revolutionary War. During this period evidence indicates that there was an ever-increasing presence of blacks in the Creek Nation. During the two decades preceding the war, the rule prohibiting traders from keeping slaves in the Nation seems to have been violated more frequently. Daniel Pepper's complaint against the traders in 1757 has been noted. Most of the traders took Indian wives and had Indian families, and by their wives' rights opened plantations in the Indian country. William Frazer, trader at the Big and Little Oconee towns, had blacks in the early 1770s. In 1772, the blacks on the Tallapoosa plantation of James Germany, trader at Tuckabahchee, helped the party of British Agent David Taitt cross the rain-swollen Tallapoosa in canoes and swam their horses across for them.[49]

Traders sent their blacks on other types of missions. According to George Galphin, trader among the Lower Creeks, in 1771 the Creeks "daily" raided the settlements and stole horses and cattle. Late that year, a Creek murdered John Carey of Queensborough about two miles above Galphin's cowpens on the Ogeechee. When he got word of the killing, he and his blacks set out after the murderer, he said to save the Creeks from having to execute him. Galphin split his force, sending some blacks "on the Oconees," while he and the others kept to the Creek trading path. Galphin later split his force again, going up a stream with some of his blacks and sending the others downstream. The latter group came upon the Indian, who made for a swamp. One of the blacks shot at him, but they were afraid to go in after him. Galphin warned the Lower Creeks that if they did not keep those "Renegating fellows at home," they would involve the whole nation in trouble. The Georgia governor warned the Creeks to maintain the peace as they had agreed to do under the Treaty of Augusta or he would be forced to cut off their trade. As a result, the Creeks executed the killer at the Lower town of Cheehaws (Chiaha) in early 1772 and promised to try to keep their young men from going into the settlements.[50]

As David Taitt put it in 1772, there was "a set of renagadoes [sic] from every town in the Nation." Creeks raided plantations and settlements west of Mobile Bay. In 1771 a party of Eufaulas raided a plantation on the Pascagoula River, killed an Indian man slave and a little girl, but carried a woman and a boy into the Nation. The boy was sold to John Meally, a trader at Pallachocola (Apalachicola), who in turn sold him to George Galphin. Taitt managed to have the woman given up. At Kolomi in April

1772, Taitt found the headmen too embarrassed to talk to him because
their people had been raiding the settlements and stealing horses. Taitt
got the Upper Creeks to agree to leave the plantations in the Pensacola
area alone and not to molest what cattle the traders had in the Nation,
and he promised the Indians that no more would be brought in and that
no plantations could be made by the traders.[51]

Galphin, who was insisting that the Creeks honor the boundary line,
was himself violating it. When his range was burned off, he turned his
cattle (and doubtless his black herdsmen) across the Ogeechee on Indian
land. When the grass grew back in the spring of 1772, he rounded them
up again. Galphin also urged whites who had Indian wives and families to
ask the Indians, in the name of their families, for pieces of land west of
the Ogeechee. In 1772, at his urging, Stephen Forest asked for such land
for his Indian wife and children. After some difficulty, the Indians granted
him an area two miles square on the bay of St. Rosa on the condition that
only one white man remain on the plantation to take care of the blacks.[52]

The traders took advantage of the Indians in other ways. They got the
Creeks into debt. In 1772 the merchants at Augusta (Galphin figured
prominently here) asked for lands above the Little River as well as lands
east of the Oconee as far south as the lower Creek trading path as payment of debts. In a treaty negotiated in May, the Creeks ceded lands
between the Savannah and the Ogeechee and Oconee north and west of
the 1763 cession as well as about half a million acres between the Ogeechee and Altamaha.[53] Many Creeks opposed this cession. As whites
rushed into the new territory, conflicts developed between them and
the Creeks.

Runaway slaves also continued to be a problem. At Kolomi Square
in April 1772, David Taitt was informed that three black men, who had
been stolen, had been brought into the Nation about three years earlier
by some men from Mississippi. A reward was offered for the capture
of the men and the slaves. The latter were finally captured by Richard
Brown and Thomas Mosley, taken to Silver Bluff, and sold to George
Galphin as their own property. The next year, Taitt threatened to cut
off Creek trade unless the Indians returned such fugitive slaves. This
matter and Creek depredations on the white settlements finally led to a
trade embargo which was maintained until October 20, 1774, when, in
a treaty at Savannah, headmen of twelve Upper towns and eight Lower
towns agreed to return goods and cattle stolen and to deliver up run-

away slaves. The treaty was difficult to implement, but thirteen blacks were delivered.[54]

Thus, on the eve of the Revolutionary War, there were runaway blacks in the Creek country. There were even blacks held in servitude by the traders. But there is at present no evidence that the Indians themselves, except in the case of Mary Bosomworth, held Africans as slaves, although at times they were reluctant or uncooperative in returning runaways. Travelers made no mention of African slavery. Jean-Bernard Bossu, for instance, who traveled among the Creeks in the late 1750s, gave good descriptions of Creek life style but did not mention slaves. William Bartram, who traveled among them about twenty years later, noted Indian slaves among the Seminoles and Creeks, but he does not mention Africans.[55] In their border warfare with the whites, the Creeks only occasionally took blacks. It was not until the Revolutionary War that they began to look on blacks as property and, sometime after that, as slaves.

NOTES

1. The authoritative detailed account of the peoples who became known as Creeks is John R. Swanton, *Early History of the Creek Indians and Their Neighbors,* Bureau of American Ethnology Bulletin, no. 73 (Washington, D.C.: Government Printing Office, 1922), and Swanton, *The Indians of the Southeastern United States,* Bureau of American Ethnology Bulletin, no. 137 (Washington, D.C.: Government Printing Office, 1946). Useful general sources are Frederick Webb Hodge, ed., *Handbook of American Indians North of Mexico,* 2 pts. (Washington, D.C.: Government Printing Office, 1907) 1: 362-65; and, derived principally from Swanton, Angie Debo, *The Road to Disappearance* (Norman: University of Oklahoma Press, 1941); pp. 3-5; David H. Corkran, *The Creek Frontier, 1540-1783* (Norman: University of Oklahoma Press, 1967), pp. 3-7; and R. S. Cotterill, *The Southern Indians: The Story of the Civilized Tribes before Removal* (Norman: University of Oklahoma Press, 1954), pp. 8-9. These latter two works were most useful in putting matters relating to the Creeks during the colonial period into perspective.

2. Swanton, *The Indians of the Southeastern United States,* p. 664; Debo, pp. 6-7, 8, 12-13.

3. Swanton, *The Indians of the Southeastern United States,* pp. 389-90, 391, 392-93, 682; Debo, pp. 9-10, 11-12.

4. Swanton, *The Indians of the Southeastern United States,* pp. 285-87; Mark Van Doren, ed., *The Travels of William Bartram* (New York: Dover, 1928), pp. 401-02.

5. Verner W. Crane, *The Southern Frontier, 1670-1732* (Ann Arbor: University

of Michigan Press, 1956), pp. 22, 33, 34, 35, 36, 133; Lewis Cecil Gray, *History of Agriculture in the Southern United States to 1860* (Washington, D.C.: Carnegie Institution, 1932; reprint ed., Gloucester, Mass.: Peter Smith, 1958), p. 131.

    6. Crane, pp. 24-25, 9, 36.

    7. Crane, pp. 37, 39-46; Gray, pp. 131-132, 361; Elmer D. Johnson and Kathleen Lewis Sloan, eds., *South Carolina: A Documentary Profile of the Palmetto State* (Columbia: University of South Carolina Press, 1971), pp. 55-56.

    8. Crane, pp. 71, 72, 75-76, 82, 83-85, 95, 107.

    9. Crane, pp. 162, 169, 171; Kenneth Wiggins Porter, *The Negro on the American Frontier* (New York: Arno Press and The New York Times, 1971), pp. 158-59; M. Eugene Sirmans, *Colonial South Carolina: A Political History, 1663-1763* (Chapel Hill: University of North Carolina Press, 1966), pp. 112-14.

    10. Porter, pp. 159-60, 27-28; Crane, pp. 171, 173, 178, 181; Johnson and Sloan, pp. 72-73.

    11. Swanton, *The Indians of the Southeastern United States,* pp. 285-87.

    12. Edward Gaylord Bourne, ed., *Narratives of the Career of Hernando de Soto in the Conquest of Florida as told by a Knight of Elvas and in a relation by Luys Hernandez de Biedma, factor of the Expedition,* 2 vols. (New York: Allerton Book Co., 1922), 2: 114, 123; Swanton, *The Indians of the Southeastern United States,* p. 60; Porter, pp. 97-98; Hodge, p. 52.

    13. Corkran, p. 46.

    14. Crane, pp. 37, 110, 117.

    15. Crane, pp. 22, 113; Gray, pp. 328-29, 361, 1025; Johnson and Sloan, p. 63.

    16. Crane, pp. 184, 215; Gray, p. 1025.

    17. Corkran, pp. 61, 62, 64, 68-69; Sirmans, pp. 134,136, 198.

    18. Corkran, pp. 71, 73.

    19. "Tobias Fitch's Journal to the Creeks," in *Travels in the American Colonies,* ed. Newton D. Mereness (New York: The Macmillan Company, 1916; reprint ed., New York: Antiquarian Press, 1961), pp. 178-181, 185-188, 193-194; Porter, pp. 173-74, 175; Corkran, p. 73.

    20. Porter, pp. 160, 161-62, 171; Chapman J. Milling, *Red Carolinians* (Chapel Hill: University of North Carolina Press, 1940), pp. 152-60; Crane, pp. 239, 241, 244, 247-48; Sirmans, p. 157; "Dispatches of Spanish Officials Bearing on the Free Negro Settlement of Gracia Real de Santa Teresa de Mose, Florida," *The Journal of Negro History* 9 (April 1924), 144-48.

    21. Allen D. Candler, ed., *The Colonial Records of the State of Georgia,* 26 vols. (Atlanta: The Franklin Printing and Publishing Company and The Franklin-Turner Company, 1904-26), 1: 40-41, 50-52, 53, 363; 3: 377, hereafter cited as *Colonial Records of Georgia.*

    22. Kenneth Coleman, *Colonial Georgia: A History* (New York: Charles Scribner's Sons, 1976), pp. 79-80, 83-86; Corkran, pp. 34, 90; Swanton, *Early History of the Creek Indians and Their Neighbors,* pp. 108, 109. For a detailed account of Mary Musgrove, see E. Merton Coulter, "Mary Musgrove, 'Queen of the Creeks', A Chapter of Early Georgia Troubles," *Georgia Historical Quarterly* 11 (March 1927), 1-30; see also "Oglethorpe's Treaty with the Lower Creek Indians," *Georgia Historical Quarterly* 4 (March 1920), 3-16.

    23. Coleman, p. 88.

24. Coleman, pp. 81-82; Crane, pp. 123-24; Sirmans, pp. 187-91, 197; Robert Lee Meriwether, *The Expansion of South Carolina, 1729-1765* (Kingsport, Tenn.: Southern, 1940; reprint ed., Philadelphia: Porcupine Press, 1974), p. 191; Corkran, p. 114.

25. Gray, p. 97; *Colonial Records of Georgia,* I: 352, 427, 495, 506-07, 530, 531-32, 56-62; *Colonial Records of Georgia,* 4 supp. (Atlanta: The Franklin-Turner Company, 1908), p. 272; Corkran, p. 90.

26. Gray, pp. 89, 349; Porter, p. 165.

27. Porter, pp. 165-68, 44, 162-63, 169-70, 171, 189; *Colonial Records of Georgia,* 3: 396; 5: 190-91; 1: 356-57, 532; Johnson and Sloan, pp. 110-11, 114-16; Sirmans, pp. 208-09; Gray, p. 96; Wilbur H. Siebert, "Slavery and White Servitude in East Florida, 1726-1776," *Florida Historical Society Quarterly* 10 (July 1931), 3-5; "Dispatches of Spanish Officials Bearing on the Free Negro Settlement of Garcia Real de Santa Teresa de Mose, Florida," pp. 144-95.

28. Porter, pp. 169, 206, 172-73, 158-59, 178; *Colonial Records of Georgia,* 5: 342; Milling, pp. 63, 123n, 224n; William S. Willis, "Divide and Rule: Red, White, and Black in the Southeast," *The Journal of Negro History* 48 (July 1963), 176.

29. Milling, p. 224; Willis, pp. 175, 162, 163, 169, 170, 173; J. H. Johnston, "Documentary Evidence and the Relations of Negroes and Indians," *The Journal of Negro History* 14 (January 1929), 34.

30. Cited in Willis, p. 165.

31. Meriwether, pp. 73-74.

32. Crane, p. 203; Willis, p. 162.

33. William L. McDowell, Jr., ed., *Colonial Records of South Carolina: Documents Relating to Indian Affairs, May 21, 1750-August 7, 1754* (Columbia: South Carolina Archives Department, 1958), p. 103.

34. McDowell, p. 88.

35. McDowell, pp. 190, 199; Willis, p. 163.

36. McDowell, pp. 272, 319, 350.

37. William L. McDowell, Jr., ed., *Colonial Records of South Carolina: Documents Relating to Indian Affairs, 1754-1765* (Columbia: University of South Carolina Press, 1970), p. 152. All subsequent references to McDowell are from this volume.

38. McDowell, pp. 190, 193, 357, 388; Willis, p. 161.

39. *Colonial Records of Georgia,* 7: 665-67, 705-06; Willis, p. 165.

40. James H. O'Donnell, III, *Southern Indians in the American Revolution* (Knoxville: University of Tennessee Press, 1973), p. 5; Gray, p. 135; Corkran, pp. 211-16. The Creeks had conducted border warfare with the Cherokees for about twenty years. That warfare and the resulting political split among the Creeks caused some bands of Creeks to drift to Florida. Many of these were later to be designated Seminoles, who were to become important in later Creek history. *Colonial Records of Georgia,* 4 supp., pp. 82, 122; Corkran, pp. 149, 211, 212-13.

41. *Colonial Records of Georgia,* 13: 429; 8: 522-24; O'Donnell, p. 7.

42. Coleman, pp. 195, 197; Sirmans, p. 345.

43. Corkran, p. 243.

44. Porter, p. 171; Willis, p. 168.

45. Johnson and Sloan, pp. 144-45.

46. Corkran, p. 254; John R. Alden, *John Stuart and the Southern Colonial Frontier: A Study of Indian Relations, War, Trade, and Land Problems in the Southern Wilderness, 1754-1775* (Ann Arbor: University of Michigan Press, 1944; reprint ed., New York: Gordian Press, 1966), p. 233.

47. Corkran, pp. 260, 263-64, 265; Willis, pp. 163, 170; John Stuart to General Thomas H. Gage, September 26, 1767, and Stuart to Gage, November 27, 1767, Thomas H. Gage Papers, William Clements Library, University of Michigan, Ann Arbor.

48. Stuart to Gage, November 27, 1767, and July 2, 1768, Thomas H. Gage Papers, William Clements Library, University of Michigan, Ann Arbor; Willis, p. 171; Corkran, pp. 265, 266.

49. Corkran, pp. 273-87; Crane, p. 125; *Colonial Records of Georgia,* 12: 407: "Journal of David Taitt's Travels from Pensacola, West Florida, to and through the Country of the Upper and the Lower Creeks, 1772," in Mereness, p. 501, hereafter cited as 'Taitt's Journal."

50. *Colonial Records of Georgia,* 12: 150-53, 316-17; "Taitt's Journal," p. 546.

51. "Taitt's Journal," pp. 547, 551, 554, 555, 558, 541, 552.

52. "Taitt's Journal," pp. 550-51.

53. "Taitt's Journal," p. 543; Debo, p. 35; Coleman, p. 262.

54. "Taitt's Journal," pp. 540-41; Willis, p. 163; Corkran, p. 286.

55. Seymour Feiler, trans. and ed., *Jean-Bernard Bossu's Travels in the Interior of North America, 1751-1762* (Norman: University of Oklahoma Press, 1962), pp. 126-55; Van Doren, pp. 164, 183, 397.

chapter 2

THE BEGINNINGS OF SLAVERY

AT THE OUTBREAK of the Revolutionary War, the Creeks still had extensive land holdings that embraced most of the area in the present states of Georgia and Alabama. Yet the British settlements had begun to encircle the Creeks, the encirclement being nearly completed by the end of the war. The province of West Florida had been created in 1763 from territory ceded by Spain and France, and planters had begun to move into the Pensacola region, the area above Mobile, and the lands in the Natchez region. To the north, beyond the Cherokee lands, were the Cumberland settlements. By 1774 the Mississippi region had an estimated 2,500 whites and 600 blacks. The war brought other settlers, many of them slaveholders, from New England and the Southern colonies and, because of the decline of trade, from the West Indies.[1] Thus encircled, the Creeks found it difficult to remain neutral in the early Revolutionary days. In 1778, several hundred joined the British,[2] and at the close of the war, the Creeks were divided into factions, and the Georgians pressed them for land cessions as war reparations. A complexity was added to postwar Creek-American relations by the fact that the Creeks emerged from the war as slaveholders and were on the verge of adopting a system of African slavery.

After the Revolutionary War, black slaves became a major source of conflict between the Creeks and the Americans because of the exigencies of war and international conflict beyond the Creeks' control. The war had disrupted slave labor in the southern colonies. In the summer of 1782, the loyalists had been allowed to leave Georgia. An estimated 3,100 whites and 3,500 blacks left Savannah. Almost 5,000 went to East Florida, some returning to Georgia when the British left East Florida in 1783-85. There was also confusion concerning titles to slaves because of confiscation of property, court decisions, and abandonment of property. Military activities had allowed slaves to escape. Others followed the two armies, working at various tasks. Many Whigs took their slaves out of the war zones, and during the last two years of the war the Georgia government used slaves as bounty to pay its debts. Still other slaves ran away to the Indians or were stolen by them, and others escaped and set up settlements of their own.[3]

By war's end, the Creeks had become acquisitive regarding slaves. Those in the British service raided South Carolina, taking slaves and other property. After the war, the Creeks refused to sell the blacks because they had been "told by the General before they went into Carolina that whatever plunder they got should be their own property and that they saw the King's Army Seize upon all the Negroes they could get upon which they did the same and intend to carry them to the Nation."[4] After the war, some stolen blacks were among the Eufaulas. While some had apparently been captured by the Indians themselves, others there had been given to them by British agents in payment for their services. These latter blacks were referred to as "King's gifts."[5] Other blacks, like those of Lachlan McGillivray, had come to the Creeks as runaways. McGillivray, a Scottish trader in the Creek country for over three decades, had married the half-French, half-Creek Sehoy Marchand by whom he had daughters Sehoy, Sophia, Jeanette, and Elizabeth and a son Alexander. Besides a trading house at Little Tallassee and warehouses at Augusta and Savannah, McGillivray had maintained plantations on the Savannah River near Augusta on which he had a number of blacks. Because he and his son had worked for the British, McGillivray was forced to return to Scotland, and the Georgians confiscated his lands, livestock, stores, and slaves, except for a few blacks who escaped to Sehoy at Little Tallassee and joined his other blacks there.[6]

Thus, because of the war, slaves were in great demand in Georgia in the 1780s. It had been impossible to hunt runaways during the war, and importation of slaves had ceased. Many of the new immigrants following the war were poor and owned few, if any, slaves and settled for the most part in the uplands where tobacco was becoming an important crop, cotton was farmed for domestic use, and cattle raising was increasing. Yet the state's exports were mainly rice, lumber products, naval stores, and some tobacco and indigo, all requiring large numbers of slaves to work the fields. Where slaves could be found, prices were high, and in the postwar years it became imperative that Georgians recover as many of the blacks lost during the conflict as possible.[7] In January 1783, for instance, some Creeks and Cherokees showed up on the Oconee with a number of blacks, horses, and other property that had been carried off during the war. The Georgia legislature authorized the governor to send a delegation to receive the property and send presents to the Indians.[8]

The problem of runaways to Spanish and Creek lands was not so easily solved. Slaves had escaped to those areas for decades. From 1763 to 1776, Georgians found it easy to pursue fugitive slaves in British-controlled East Florida, but when the territory returned to Spain in 1783, the Spanish governor refused to cooperate with the Georgians on the ground that Madrid had not directed him to do so. He did, however, agree to return stolen slaves. Many Georgians, without the approval of the Georgia governor, entered Florida in armed parties and even as militia units to recover runaways.[9] Before the war the Creeks had been generally cooperative in returning runaways. Georgia now found it more difficult to obtain the return of fugitive slaves because the Creeks had begun to keep slaves. One reason was the rise of a mixed-blood class who made up the greatest number of slaveholders. For the most part, they were the children of traders, adventurers, public officials, and military officials whose activities had brought them to the Creek country during the preceding decades.

Most prominent was Lachlan McGillivray's son, Alexander, who emerged in 1783 as the head of the Creek Confederacy and became known as the "King and Head Warrior of all the Nation." Intensely anti-American and formerly the British assistant commissary to the Creeks, he had begun his rise to power in 1778. He had a plantation and headquarters near the fork of the Coosa and Tallapoosa rivers and maintained other plantations in the Upper Creek country as well. In 1791, traveler John Pope noted, "He has a considerable number of Negroes at his different Plantations, probably more than Fifty, and common Report says, double that Number in the Spanish West-India Islands; as also large stocks of Horses, Hogs, and horned Cattle." Two or three white men oversaw his ranges. Although McGillivray spoke only English and had to address the Creeks through an interpreter, his influence became great, particularly among the Upper Creeks. He solidified his power by building a strong subservient military organization, controlling the traders, and keeping the towns in line by threatening to withdraw their traders. He instituted laws to reduce horse stealing, a growing source of disputes inside the tribe, and centralized the government to a great degree.[10] However, McGillivray had little control over the Seminoles in Spanish Florida.

Deserted by the British at the end of the war and without funds or property, "saving a few negroes," McGillivray turned to Spain, with which he maintained close ties during the next few years, playing Georgia and the United States off against her. The Spanish, in turn, supported McGillivray, as did Panton, Leslie, & Company, a British trading firm that the Spanish had allowed to remain in Florida when they returned in 1784, and with which McGillivray formed close ties. Under McGillivray's direction, the Creeks cooperated with the Spanish in returning runaway slaves. In 1784, in a reply to a request for runaways by Spanish Governor Arturo O'Neill, McGillivray said that the Nation was "pretty well drained" of blacks and that what few were there did not fit O'Neill's description of the runaways. And, in 1786, upon receipt of a list of runaways from O'Neill, McGillivray assured the governor that if the slaves by chance came into the Nation, he would have them returned.[11]

While the Creek traders, with McGillivray's approval, participated in the slave trade, McGillivray was constantly on guard against interlopers. Early in 1784, two whites and some blacks passed through the Lower Creek country on their way from Georgia to Pensacola. McGillivray urged O'Neill to seize the two, whom he called "most noted villains" who had probably killed someone and stolen the slaves. McGillivray himself would have seized them if he had had an opportunity, he said. In 1789, a man named Romain came from the Choctaws with "a great quantity of silverware and a few goods" and developed a scheme to buy blacks in the Nation and take them to New Orleans for sale. Romain left the Nation after he ran afoul of Louis de Milfort, McGillivray's French brother-in-law, who threatened to send Romain to New Orleans in irons.[12]

In that same year, Colonel Moses Kirkland, his son, his nephew, John Linder, and some blacks were passing through the Creek Nation from South Carolina to the white settlements on the Tensaw. Linder, a Swiss engineer and surveyor, had been assisted by McGillivray in settling on the Tensaw during the war. The party stopped at McGillivray's plantation at Little Tallassee, and when they left McGillivray sent one of his black men as a guide. On the road, they met John Catt of Holston but residing at Hilibi, his wife, an Indian woman from Fish Pond town, a Hilibi called the Murderer or Man Slayer (a name he earned for having killed so many men), and a black named Bob, who belonged to Stephen Sullivan of the

Creek Nation. The two groups talked for awhile and then parted, Kirkland's group going on to present-day Murder Creek, which received its name from this incident, where they camped. That night Catt and his cohorts crept upon Kirkland's camp. Bob, the black, took Kirkland's gun, put it to his head while he was sleeping, and shot him. Catt and the Murderer rushed in, armed with a club, a knife, and a hatchet. Catt hit Kirkland's son in the head with a hatchet and cut his throat. He then did the same to Linder. The Murderer killed Kirkland's nephew. The killers spared the blacks, took everything except the clothes on the bodies, and went back to the Creek Nation.

Sullivan's black, Bob, stopped at the residence of Charles Weatherford, McGillivray's brother-in-law, admitted the deed as Catt, too, did later. A posse of four intermarried whites and one black overtook the killers at Stephen Sullivan's house where the Murderer wanted to defend Catt but was prevented from doing so by Sullivan. The posse seized Catt and took him, upon McGillivray's orders, to a point within fifteen miles of Pensacola. They were to turn him over to the Spanish, but they refused him because the murders had not occurred on Spanish territory. McGillivray then sent Louis de Milfort, John Forbes, and Robert Walton to hear Catt's story and, if he was guilty, to execute him. Catt confessed, and they took him ten miles back over the Creek boundary line and hanged him on the path. They left his body hanging for several days, after which it was cut down but left unburied. Both the Murderer and Bob went unpunished, and Kirkland's black remained in the possession of Robert Grierson, an intermarried white man.[13]

During the postwar years, there were numerous slave controversies between the Creeks and whites in the bordering states and territories. A good example was the case of the estate of Peter Randon (also called Randall) of the Tensaw district. Randon had married a Creek woman and upon his death left minor children. Some of his property had been sold under the confiscation acts, although it was later found that the act had not applied to him. Thus, in 1784, John Randon, on behalf of his two brothers David and James, went to the governor of Georgia, who issued an order authorizing him to take the property, which was rightfully his, wherever he could find it. Randon subsequently recovered nine blacks, including Aley, her oldest son Billy, and her increase. In 1785, he set out with his blacks for the Creek country. Two of them, Manuel and

George, escaped from Randon and went to Francis Parris, the son of
Peter Randon's executor. Controversy over the titles to these blacks continued for at least another decade.[14]

McGillivray and his family were also involved in controversies over
blacks. McGillivray's brother-in-law, Benjamin Durant, made a bad bargain
in a slave trade with a man at Mobile, and McGillivray asked Governor
O'Neill to intercede and to help Durant recover his black. McGillivray
also asked the governor to grant Durant the right to sell "a likely young
Negro man" who was of no service to him, who went about stealing
horses "from everyone," and who had "an Indian wench his wife." Durant
owed a great deal of money, and McGillivray urged him to sell the troublesome black to clear up the debts. Sophia Durant, McGillivray's sister, objected, but McGillivray advised it despite her opinion.[15]

McGillivray himself could not escape slave controversies. His plantation at Little Tallassee was replete with dwelling house, orchards, cow
pens, fifty to sixty blacks, and overseers. A lesser plantation, where he
maintained another wife, was on the Little River in the Tensaw district
(present Baldwin County, Alabama) above Mobile. Late in 1788, the
overseer of his blacks at the latter place informed McGillivray that John
Linder had sued the overseer for title to "a Certain Molatto wench who
calls herself Rachel" at the Tensaw plantation. Linder's suit was begun
"at the Instigation of another Molatto wench called Pegy Evans, who pre-
tends to be a relation to the other." According to McGillivray, Peggy
Evans had been brought from Georgia into the Creek country as an inden-
tured slave some years earlier. She was detained by British agent David
Taitt, and when he left the country, he had made out a bill of sale for
her to Stephen Sullivan, who in 1788 had legal title to her. Angered at
the suit, McGillivray gave a warning to Linder, whose family he had helped
settle in the Tensaw district during the war:

I have not looked with a Jealous eye on the extensive & growing encroachments
which the Settlement is daily making on our Lands, which if I had been earnestly
disposed to do, the Nation woud [sic] have soon Convinced You of the Flimzyness
of the rights which You pretend for them, & which You acknowledge to derive
them for trifling presents of Taffia to Vagrant & beggarly alabamons. You are
Short sighted Indeed or You woud Carefully avoid the giving any the least occasion for a discussion, which woud Certainly in the end prove unfavorable to
Your Settlement.

McGillivray, who claimed to have established the Little River plantations to help protect the Tensaw settlement, now he ordered the immediate removal of all of his stock and property back to Little Tallassee.[16]

The Georgians on the Creeks' eastern flank were a constant source of conflict over slaves. Their pressure for more land resulted in treaties at Augusta in 1783, at Galphinton in 1785, and at Shoulderbone on November 3, 1786. The Treaty of Galphinton, a reaffirmation of the Treaty of Augusta, was signed by only a few of the Lower Creek chiefs, who ceded all of the land east of a line running southwest from the junction of the Ocmulgee and Oconee rivers to the headwaters of the St. Mary's. The Creeks also agreed in both treaties to return all blacks, horses, and other property taken since the war. The Treaty of Augusta had been hotly repudiated by most of the Creeks because only a few headmen had signed it, and McGillivray, who had not attended the meeting at Galphinton, had hoped the treaty would be nullified there. Georgians began to occupy the land ceded by these treaties, and in April 1786, the Creeks declared war on Georgia, intending to destroy property and to remove intruders but not to harm those who did not resist them. When the Georgians invited the Creeks to attend the council at Shoulderbone Creek, McGillivray refused to go. The Treaty of Shoulderbone, November 3, 1786, like that at Galphinton, was negotiated with a few Lower Creek headmen under the leadership of Tame King and Fat King. Besides giving up all land east of the Oconee River, the Creek chiefs agreed to return all prisoners, blacks, and other stolen property among them. The Georgia agent to the Creeks was instructed to oversee the release of prisoners, both black and white.[17]

McGillivray and most of the Creeks repudiated this treaty as they had done the earlier ones. In 1784, McGillivray had written to Governor O'Neill of Florida, proposing an Indian alliance with Spain. In 1785, when he refused to meet at Galphinton, he had insisted that the Creeks were a free nation that had made alliances with Spain. Their sovereignty went to the limits of their hunting grounds, and they did not recognize the boundaries set by the Americans and the British. Georgia's seizure of Tame King and Fat King as hostages to ensure Creek compliance with the Treaty of Shoulderbone now resulted in a closer unification of the Creeks.[18]

Georgia had negotiated with the Creeks, ignoring the national government's right to treat under the Articles of Confederation. Thus, it became more apparent to Congress that a consistent Indian policy was necessary. Congress had sent commissioners to Galphinton, but, unlike the Georgians, they had refused to make a treaty because too few of the Creek towns were represented. In 1786, Congress sought to regulate Indian affairs by creating two districts, north and south, each with a superintendent representing the highest authority in the Indian country and regulating trade and travel and enforcing the laws regarding Indian and whites. James White, the first superintendent for the district south of the Ohio River, toured the Creek country in the spring of 1787 and tried unsuccessfully to remove Creek opposition to the Georgia treaties.[19]

The next few years were marked by recriminations, border warfare, and Indian depredations along the frontier. War parties were sent against the Cumberland settlements, and during the winter of 1787-88, the Creeks attacked the Georgia frontier, the raids continuing throughout 1788 and into 1789, most resulting in property theft rather than in deaths. Unlike the raids before the war, which resulted mainly in the theft of livestock and goods, the Creeks now took slaves as well.[20] Blacks had also continued to run away to the Indian country. Between the end of the Revolutionary War and 1790, an estimated sixty or seventy slaves had been stolen by the Creeks or had run away from the citizens of Georgia.[21]

Besides the border difficulties, the Creeks were also beset by other problems. Late in 1787, Spain had begun to weaken in her support of the Creeks, and the following year William Augustus Bowles came among the Lower Creeks with arms and munitions, apparently ambitious to create an independent Indian state with ties to Britain. Although his stay this time was brief, he would, in time, become a rival of McGillivray.[22] To the weakening of Spain's support and the appearance of Bowles was added another threat to McGillivray: the states' cession of western lands to the United States, further completing the encirclement of the Creeks by the Americans. Thus, in 1790, McGillivray accepted the invitation of President George Washington to go to New York and made the journey with his nephews David Tate and Lachland Durant, his two black servants Paro and Jonah, and twenty-four Creek chiefs and warriors. On August 7, 1790, McGillivray and the chiefs signed a treaty which reaffirmed the Treaty of Augusta by ceding land between the Ogeechee and Oconee rivers but not those lands ceded by the Treaties of Galphinton and Shoulderbone. Article three of the treaty said that the Creek Nation would deliver, as soon as practicable, to the commanding officer at Rock Landing on the Oconee all

United States citizens, "white inhabitants or negroes, who are now prisoners in any part of the said nation." If they were not delivered before June 1, 1791, the governor of Georgia was empowered to send three people to the Nation to claim and receive such prisoners and blacks. The treaty as well stipulated that the Creeks and Seminoles were under the protection of the United States and gave McGillivray the rank of brigadier general at a salary of $1,200 per year.[23]

The Treaty of New York did not satisfy the Georgians because it did not reaffirm the Galphinton and Shoulderbone treaties and because they felt that the treaty-making power rested with the states and not the federal government. Too, the treaty had provided that the United States would furnish free domestic animals and tools to help the Creeks adopt the white man's civilization. The Georgians did not like that prospect because it gave a permanency to the Indian title which they were not willing to admit. Thus, the year following the treaty was marked by border clashes, trespasses, intrigue. William Augustus Bowles, claiming to represent England, reappeared in 1791. Son-in-law of Perryman, chief of Osuche (Oswichee) on the Flint, Bowles proclaimed himself general and director of the affairs of the Creek Nation and tried to arouse the Creeks against both the United States and Spain and, renouncing the Treaty of New York, for a time threatened to wrest leadership of the Creeks from McGillivray. The Spanish meanwhile urged the Creeks to violate the treaty obligations and pressed for revision of the Treaty of 1783 to rectify boundaries. Additional excitement was produced by the organization of the Yazoo land company.[24]

Envisioning their scheme as "one of the greatest affairs in the world," the speculators apparently planned a buffer state devoted to agriculture and commerce with America, Europe, and Africa. The latter was to be the source of labor for building the new land. But to succeed the speculators had to have the cooperation of the Creeks, Choctaws, and Chickasaws. They appealed to McGillivray for his influence, holding out the promises of a friendly, independent state with an extensive African trade and of a sizable land grant to McGillivray.[25] These land schemes, however, did not come to fruition. Also, McGillivray's role as leader of the Creeks was near an end. He died on February 17, 1793. William Panton wrote to McGillivray's father in Scotland that McGillivray had died possessed of sixty blacks, three hundred cattle, and a large stock of horses. Had he lived, said Panton, he would "have added considerably to his stock of Negroes."[26]

After McGillivray's death, Mad Dog became the leading chief of the

Creeks. During the next several months, there was peace between the Creeks and the Americans. Although the Creeks remained bound to Spain, to which they had granted exclusive trading rights under McGillivray's direction, United States officials began to consider the establishment of trading houses among the Creeks and concerned themselves with compliance with the Treaty of New York.[27]

Upon his return from New York, McGillivray had told the Creeks that he had promised to give up all of the prisoners and blacks who belonged to the whites but that the Nation was not liable for any that were dead or removed. But instead of complying, the Creeks continued stealing horses and blacks. No apparent effort to return the prisoners or blacks was made until the summer of 1794, when the head men of the Cowetas and Cussetas attempted to do so, fearing reprisals by the Americans since international tensions between them and the English and Spanish had greatly declined. The Cheehaws promised to give up captured horses and blacks among them, and the Cowetas and Cussetas began to collect such property among their people. They sent talks to the Yuchis and others to do the same or have the property taken by force. The Cowetas and Cussetas were convinced that it would do little good to send talks to the Georgians without sending the stolen property; thus they were determined to collect all they could, "both negroes & horses," hoping to bring peace between them and the whites and therefore to allow their people to attend to their hunting. The chiefs sent a talk to the head men of the Tuckabahchees, asking them to send talks to the other Upper Creeks and to direct them to give up stolen property. Refusal to do so, they said, would bring ruin on the Lower Creeks, who were in closer proximity to the Georgians.[28]

By late 1794, the Creeks had not returned either prisoners or blacks as they had promised. James Seagrove, the Creek agent, believed that it was impossible to comply with the treaty and favored compensation to those whites who had legitimate claims. Some of the blacks, however, were given up in 1795, mainly by the Upper towns. That fall, it was learned that a large body of Indians were prepared to set out for the frontiers to take back the blacks they had given up, planning to search first "about the Saw Mills, from thence on the head of the Canoochie & from thence go for the rice Plantations." Georgia Senator James Jackson did not believe that the whole Creek Nation was concerned but that the Indians were "Cheehaws & others of the old Gang."[29]

In 1794, Georgia had appropriated as payment for state troops lands not embraced by the Treaty of New York. President Washington appointed a committee to treat with the Creeks to clear the title to the lands thus appropriated and to address as well the matter of stolen or runaway property and captives. The parties met at Colerain on the St. Mary's. Despite a conflict over authority between the Georgia and federal commissioners, a treaty was signed on June 29, 1796, confirming the Treaty of New York, granting reserves to the United States for military and trading purposes, providing for the erection of two public blacksmith shops, reaffirming the former agreement regarding property, and providing for the return of all prisoners, "white inhabitants and negroes," and property seized since the Treaty of New York. If the property was not delivered by January 1, 1797, the governor of Georgia was authorized to empower three persons to go to the Nation and receive such prisoners, blacks, and property.[30]

In 1796 Benjamin Hawkins was appointed principal temporary agent for Indian affairs south of the Ohio River. His mission was apparently to keep the southern tribes, especially the Creeks, in line by civilizing them according to the white man's standards. Thus, the same year of his appointment, he traveled in the Creek country to learn the condition of the Indians, to introduce them to the benefits of white man's technology, and to persuade them to undertake agricultural production.[31]

Hawkins was pleased to find some agricultural production underway. Little of it, however, was conducted by the natives. In 1791, John Pope had noted that agriculture was "little understood and less Practiced." Only one man—the Bully—seemed industrious to Hawkins, owning sixty-one slaves, over 200 horses, over 400 cattle, and 300 hogs. Most of the agricultural production Hawkins noted was made by white residents. At Hilibi was Robert Grierson, a Scot, who had been many years in the Creek country as a trader. He had learned the language, had married Sinnugee, a Creek, and had had several children. In 1796 Grierson had forty blacks, 300 cattle, and thirty horses. He had a thirty-acre farm on which he raised corn, cotton, rice, peas, beans, squashes, pumpkins, watermelons, colewarts, and peaches. Grierson had a treadle gin on which he and his family ginned their cotton for sale in Tennessee.[32]

Grierson had acquired his slaves from various sources. In 1779 he had bought Eve for sixty pounds sterling from Cornelius Sullivant of West Florida. In 1780, he had bought Tinna (or Tenah) for the same price from John Rogers of the Creek Nation, and for eighty pounds sterling, he had bought a "Mulatto man named Jemmy" from David Taitt. In 1791, he had bought Sharper, his wife Die, and their three children Molly, Jack, and Jim for 275 pounds sterling from George Marbury. In 1795, he had paid the estate of Thomas Scott 550 Spanish millo dollars for Tobie, his daughter Nancy, and Nancy's daughter Belinda. At the same time, William Clark traded Bina and her five children Abigail, Robin, Ameta, Tartar, and Ben for six others belonging to Grierson and gave Grierson Sambo, Mira, and their child Isaac as payment for a debt against the Scott estate, of which Clark was the administrator. Grierson was also in charge of twenty-six blacks who belonged to Scott's estate. In the presence of Creek chiefs Mad Dog and White Lieutenant he turned them over to Clark on October 14, 1795.[33] The blacks that Grierson purchased in the last two decades of the eighteenth century were the founders of several families of blacks who lived with the Creeks throughout the nineteenth century.

Near Atasi (Auttossee) lived Richard Bailey, an Englishman, who by 1796 had lived among the Creeks for forty years. Bailey owned 200 cattle, 120 horses, 150 hogs, and seven slaves. His farm produced fifty bushels of corn per acre.[34]

As Hawkins traveled further into the Upper Creek territory, he found more lands under cultivation and more numerous and better livestock. The Indians seemed willing to cooperate with the government in a program of farming and handicrafts. But positive reception of Hawkins's mission was apparently limited to the mixed bloods and intermarried whites who held high positions in the Nation.[35]

Hawkins found that some of the Lower Creeks were also undertaking farming and husbandry. Timothy Barnard, for instance, was establishing a dairy about a mile from his place. Near the dairy, Barnard's sons Falope and Yuccohpee had begun places of their own. Hawkins found them with their father's blacks at work clearing a field and preparing pine logs for their houses. Three-quarters of a mile farther away, Barnard had another plantation with fine peach trees. Barnard's son Timpooche and his Cusseta wife lived there. They had finished their dwelling house, and Hawkins found them and a "small black boy" clearing land.[36]

These tendencies toward industry and husbandry reflected the great changes taking place among the Creeks. Old Emartle Hutke (White Chief) told Hawkins that he could remember when there were no blankets or hoes and that his father could remember the introduction of the knife and hatchet. The half-bloods told Hawkins that the Creeks had changed in the preceeding twenty years: they had supposedly become a milder, less cruel, and friendlier people.[37] Hence, their receptivity to Hawkins's plans to "civilize" them.

Convinced that the future of the Indians was in cultivation of the soil rather than in hunting, Hawkins spent the next several years in pushing the Indians in that direction. By the time he took office the Creeks in Georgia were being forced to move to new hunting grounds. It was Hawkins' job to convert them from a society with an economy of hunting supplemented by the farming of small patches of land to one with an economy of farming supplemented by domestic manufactures. Hawkins himself was a sterling example of what he wanted the Indians to become. He built his home and agency on the Flint River across from Fort Lawrence. With slaves whom he had brought from North Carolina, he maintained a large plantation on which he farmed diversified crops and maintained herds of horses and cattle. He also manufactured his own tinware, shoes, boots, and saddles.[38] Hawkins introduced the plow to the Indians in 1797. He introduced as well the raising of sheep and the cultivation of flax, wheat, barley, rye, oats, and various varieties of fruit.

With the transformation from a hunting to an agricultural people came the need for labor. Blacks were a logical choice for the Indians. Blacks acquired from the white plantations, either by theft, through purchase, or as runaways, knew farming and husbandry, while the Indians knew little of it. However, the Creeks had not even a loose equivalent of plantation agriculture. Thus they had no need for slave labor equivalent to that on the white plantations, and in most instances those who owned slaves in the late eighteenth century apparently did not use them as the whites did. Evidence of the characteristics of the institution of slavery during the early years is sketchy, but perhaps some insights into slavery among the Creeks proper can be gained from an examination of the institution among the Seminoles.

The Seminoles were Lower and Upper Creeks, as well as remnants of other groups such as the Yuchis, who had left the settled Creek towns and migrated to Florida during the eighteenth century, either voluntarily or as a result of political intrigue, warfare, or civil strive. Their prolonged isolation from the Creeks proper and their slow withdrawal from the Creek Confederation earned them the title of Seminole, meaning wild or runaway.[39]

These Indians had filled a void left by the native population of north-

ern Florida. Early in the eighteenth century, to create a buffer against
the English, the Spanish had persuaded some of the Lower Creeks to
settle at Apalachee, which had been destroyed by the English. The War
of Jenkins' Ear and King George's War drove other Indians south. Cow-
keeper's Oconee band, driven to the lower Chattahoochee by the Yamasee
War of 1715, moved on to the Alachua region where they were well established by 1750. During this same time, other Lower Creeks moved into
the Apalachee region. Some of the Apalachicolas moved south, as did the
Chiahas, who with the Tamathlis were important in establishing the Mikasuki band, first referred to during the British period, 1763-83. These
groups were Hitchiti-speaking. After 1767, Muskogee-speaking people migrated to Florida. In that year, Upper Creeks from Eufaula settled at
Chocachatti, northeast of Tampa Bay. Other Upper Creeks, including the
Tallahassees, settled in West Florida. In 1778, some people of Kolomi,
Fushatchee, and Kan-tcati migrated.[40]

Nearly all of these people, the Yuchis being a notable exception, were
of Muskhogean linguistic stock, speaking Muskogee or Hitchiti, and all
were a part of the confederation. For the most part left to themselves by
both the Spanish and the British, these Indians had firmly established
themselves on Florida soil and, though generally British in sentiment,
had managed to stay out of the American Revolution.[41] Loosely affiliated
with the Creeks, they were never under McGillivray's control as were the
Creeks proper and after the Revolutionary War began to emerge as a
separate tribe.

Shortly after the Revolutionary War, the Seminoles, like the Creeks,
began to acquire people of African descent as slaves. Several families,
acquired through purchase, theft, or escape from nearby plantations,
lived among the Indians as slaves or free blacks and were part of an alliance of blacks and Seminoles that had begun about the time the Seminoles were first being recognized as a tribe separate from the Creeks.
The exact date that the alliance began is uncertain. Although Spain had
granted asylum to runaway slaves since the late seventeenth century
and large numbers of blacks had sought refuge in Florida after the
Seminoles arrived there, as late as 1774, blacks were apparently not
living among the Seminoles. As slaves continued to escape from the
American colonies, settlements of blacks sprang up in Florida, but their
relations with the Indians were not always good.[42]

Once the Seminoles began keeping blacks, those blacks and the enclaves of free blacks, mainly runaways from the American states, brought the Indians into conflict with not only whites but the Creeks as well. Escape of blacks to Indian country irritated the whites, and there were accusations of slave stealing from all sides. However, the greatest source of irritation between Seminoles and Creeks came from the Creeks' insistence on authority over matters relating to slaves among the former, whom they considered a part of the Creek confederacy. When in the Treaty of New York and the Treaty of Colerain the Creeks agreed to return all runaways in their country, they meant those among the Florida Indians as well.[43]

Although there is an absence of descriptions of the institution of slavery among the Seminoles during the early years, one can speculate with some assurance about its characteristics. One scholar has postulated that the Seminoles were at first simply impressed enough with the prestige attached to ownership of Africans to exchange livestock for them but, not subscribing to the whites' system of economics, were at a loss as to what to do with them. The Indians therefore gave them tools with which to build houses of their own and set them to work cultivating crops and raising livestock of their own, a small portion of which the master took as tribute. This assessment appears to have been based on descriptions of slavery written a generation after it began among the Seminoles.[44] However, because the Seminoles were in Spanish territory until 1821, they remained more isolated from the whites than did the Creeks. Nevertheless, evidence indicates that slavery among the Creeks during the late eighteenth century was very similar to that among the Seminoles at the time of the Spanish cession.

By the time of the "change of flags," as the Indians called it, slavery among the Seminoles had assumed characteristics which alarmed white planters in the region. Travelers among the Seminoles in the early 1820s noted a kind, even indulgent treatment of slaves by Seminole masters who required little labor from the blacks. According to one writer, "Though hunger and want be stronger than even the *sacra fumes auri*, the greatest pressure of these evils, never occasions them to impose onerous labours on the Negroes, or to dispose of them, though tempted by high offers, if the latter are unwilling to be sold."[45] The blacks lived in separate towns from the Indians and, like the Indians, planted and cultivated fields in common, apart from the Indian fields. They also owned large herds of livestock. The masters took only an annual share

or tribute of the produce and livestock. As a result, the slaves never produced a surplus for trade for their masters and apparently barely supported them.[46]

For the most part, the Seminole blacks lived as their masters and allies
did. They dressed in Seminole fashion and lived in houses built of timbers
and shingles lashed to posts and rafters with strips of oak. The men owned
guns and supplemented their diet with game. Described as "stout, and
even gigantic" in comparison to the Indians, these blacks were apparently
more clever than their masters. Most spoke Spanish and English as well
as the Indian languages. As a result, they were called upon more and
more frequently as interpreters and go-betweens when the Indians dealt
with the whites. By 1822, for instance, Whan (or Juan), a former slave of
King Payne's, had already emerged as a principal interpreter, the Seminoles
placing "the utmost confidence in him, when making use of his services,
in their dealings with the whites."[47]

How many of these blacks belonged to the Indians by legitimate purchase is uncertain; many were fugitives. The lax system of slavery and the
Indians' kind treatment of the fugitive blacks among them were not com-
patible with the interests of Florida planters, who viewed the system with
alarm. Both Indians and blacks, who had been taught by the Spanish to
distrust the Americans, began to fear the loss of their land and their freedom.[48]

As contact with the whites increased, the Seminoles grew more dependent on the blacks. Their common distrust of the Americans, the blacks'
greater agricultural skill and the resulting economic advantage, and their
ability to speak English contributed to the dependency as well as to a
tendency by the Seminoles to view the blacks in many instances as allies,
if not as equals.[49] This peculiar relationship, which later became significant during the Second Seminole War, was no doubt fostered by the
blacks, for the life they pursued among the Seminoles must have looked
easy indeed in comparison to the slave's life on the white plantations. In
1823, Horatio L. Dexter wrote of the Seminole blacks:

The Negros possessed by the Indians live apart from them & they give the master
half of what the lands produce. He provides them nothing & they are at liberty
to employ themselves as they please. The Indian Negros are a fine formed athletic
race, speak English as well as Indian & feel satisfied with their situation. They have

the easy unconstrained manner of the Indian, but more vivacity & from their understanding both languages possess considerable influence with their masters.[50]

In 1827, Seminole Agent Gad Humphreys wrote:

The negroes of the Seminole Indians, are wholly independent, or at least regardless of the authority of their masters; and are slaves but in name; they work only when it suits their inclination and are their own Judges, as to what portion, of the products of the labour, shall go to their owners; their habits are, with few exceptions, indolent in the extreme, on which account, their example is calculated to have a baneful influence upon the Indians, whom it is desirable and necessary to withdraw as fast as practicable from their erratic and idle habits, to the pursuits and practice of industry, without which, they will not, as game is rapidly diminishing, be able much longer to exist in Florida.

Still more important to Humphreys was the great influence the blacks had over their masters. They suggested to the Indians that the whites were "hostile to all who differ from them in complection" and reminded the Seminoles of injuries they had suffered at the hands of the whites. The Seminoles looked upon the blacks "rather as fellow sufferers and companions in misery than as inferiors."[51]

At first, blacks among the Creeks proper, like those among the Seminoles, apparently were not forced to work the fields any more than the Creek women were. In 1791, for instance, Caleb Swan noted that "The women perform all the labor, both in the house and field, and are, in fact, but slaves to the men, being subject to their commands without any will of their own, except in the management of the children. They are universally called *wenches*; and the only distinction between them and the negro women is, that they have Indian children."[52]

In 1796, Hawkins visited Mrs. Sophia Durant, the oldest sister of Alexander McGillivray, at her home a little below the juncture of the Coosa and Tallapoosa rivers. Her husband Benjamin Durant, of Huguenot descent, was described by Hawkins as "a man of good figure, dull and stupid, a little mixed with African blood." The Durants had a large family, and eight of their children lived with them in a small hut, "less clean and comfortable" than any Hawkins had seen belonging to an Indian, however poor. Mrs. Durant had eighty slaves, forty of whom were capable of working. Yet, because of what Hawkins called "bad management" they were all idle. According to Mrs. Durant, their idle-

ness was due to a lack of tools and to a misunderstanding between her
and William Panton, the Pensacola trader, who had refused to supply
her with anything. Hawkins noted the same kind of "bad management"
in McGillivray's other sister, Mrs. Charles Weatherford, who Hawkins said
lived "well in some taste, but expensively. Her negros do but little, and
consume everything in common with their mistress, who is a stranger to
economy." Mrs. Weatherford, too, was out of credit with Panton.[53]

In 1799 Hawkins revisited some of the people he had visited in 1796.
At Hilibi, Robert Grierson still maintained his large herds, and since 1796
had set up the manufacture of cotton cloth, hiring Rachel Spillard of
Georgia to superintend the weaving and employing eleven hands—red,
white, and black—in spinning and weaving and the rest of his household
in raising and preparing cotton. Grierson had also increased his slave
holdings. Hawkins found that since 1796 Mrs. Durant had greatly reduced
the number of her slaves. She had fourteen working blacks, but she seldom
made enough bread, and they lived poorly. Her sister Mrs. Weatherford
had about thirty blacks. Hawkins described her as "extravagant and heed-
less," neither spinning nor weaving and having "no government" of her
family. Her son David Tate had been educated in Philadelphia and Scotland and promised to do "better." At Tallassee, head warrior Peter
McQueen, a half-blood who was a "snug trader" and who had "a valuable
property in negroes and stock," had begun "to known their value." Alexander Cornell at Tuckabahchee had nine blacks "under good government,"
and some of his family had good farms. At Thlotlogulgau (an Okchai settlement known as Fish Ponds) lived Hannah Hale, a white woman who had
been captured by the Creeks on the Ogeechee River near Rogers Fort
when she was eleven or twelve years old. The wife of Far Off, the head
warrior of the town, she had sixty head of cattle, some hogs, and one black.
Whereas in 1796 Hawkins thought the blacks an economic detriment to
the Creeks, in 1799 he stated that where the blacks were in the Nation,
there were "more industry and better farms."[54] Hawkins used most of the
slave owners as examples of the progress of civilization among the Creeks.

Benjamin Hawkins' observations about slavery among the Creeks in
1796 suggest that the lack of productivity in the slaves resulted less from
the mismanagement of individuals than from the characteristics of the institution of slavery in the Creek Nation. Robert Grierson, for instance, had
forty blacks on a thirty-acre farm. Yet, Hawkins says, Grierson found "no
difficulty in hiring Indian women to pick cotton." Of course, great herds

such as his, which ran in the woods, would have required a number of herdsmen. Mrs. Richard Bailey, on the other hand, was exceptional in the governance of her slaves. While visiting the Bailey home, Hawkins wrote, "The black people here are an expense to their owners except in the house where I am. They do nothing the whole winter but get a little wood, and in the summer they cultivate a scanty crop of corn barely sufficient for bread."[55]

Such comments suggest that the blacks were no more obligated to support their masters than to support themselves. If one considers the system of slavery that developed among the Seminoles—that is, the slaves' living separately, farming their own crops, and paying tribute to the master— and that which later developed among the Creeks—that is, the slaves' farming the master's field as well as their own—he might conclude that both systems had their roots in the Creek concept of communal farms. Under that system, as Bartram described it in the 1770s, each person enjoyed the fruits of his own labor, but each person deposited a quantity of corn, after his will, in a large crib. The corn so given seemed to be "a tribute or revenue to the mico [leader of the town]," but it was, in reality, a donation to the public treasury.[56] There is little doubt that agriculture based on slave labor among the Creeks in the early years was more nearly like the Creeks' than the white man's system of agriculture.

Hawkins' records reveal as well that blacks were employed at tasks other than tending herds or cultivating crops. In late 1797 Hawkins directed Alexander Cornell, his assistant agent and interpreter, to have a public blacksmith shop erected near Cornell's home at Tuckabahchee. Hawkins had engaged a smith named Tuns, and he instructed Cornell to have Tuns oversee Cornell's blacks and those of the Mad Dog in making fences and clearing the land. The following spring, Hawkins wrote Cornell that he had sent "by Michael's Black man" an anvil, which completed the works at the Tuckabahchee shop. In May 1797, Timothy Barnard reported from Flint River that his black Joe had just returned from Fort Fidins where he had delivered to the commanding officer six horses that had been delivered by the Lower Creeks to be restored to their white owners.[57]

Some blacks were also used as interpreters. Because historical circumstances differed, the Creeks did not find it necessary to depend on black interpreters to the extent that the Seminoles did. In 1858 Thomas S. Woodward wrote of the blacks among the Indians:

Indian negroes generally have a double advantage in the recollection of things, if not names, over those raised among the whites. They are raised to man or womanhood with their owners; and in many instances they are better raised— always on an equality, and not one in fifty but speaks the English as well as the Indian language. Nearly all of them, at some time or other, are used as inter- preters, which affords them an opportunity to gather information that many of their owners never have, as they speak but one language.

However, blacks were not generally taken into the Creek chiefs' con- fidence concerning matters of national import and were not used to any great extent as interpreters in official concerns. There were, how- ever, black interpreters among the Creeks. Ketch, for instance, who had tended George Galphin's cowpens near present-day Louisville, Georgia, was also Galphin's interpreter during colonial days. When Hawkins was on his tour in late 1796, he stopped at New Yorker Town at the trading house of James Sullivan, where a few Indians visited and talked with him. But, he said, the conversation was "not very interesting, as my interpreter, a black woman, was not very intelligent." And Big Warrior, whose wife owned fifty to sixty slaves, had a black interpreter at Tuckabahchee in 1811. One well-known black interpreter was Joseph Bruner, who was General Jackson's interpreter during the Red Stick War and was later called on as interpreter by Opothleyohola. For his services as interpreter, Bruner received a grant of one half-section of land under the seventh article of the Treaty of 1832.[58] Bruner, however, was an exception. Blacks usually were not privy to the negotiations between the Creeks and the Americans and did not occupy the powerful position of being necessary to give "a sense" of the white man's meaning as the black interpreters did in the Seminole country.

Blacks in the Creek country also had freedom of movement. They were often sent long distances on various missions, either for public officials or private citizens. While Hawkins was at Bailey's in 1796, blacks from the towns above stopped on their way to Mrs. Durant's for Christmas. They told Hawkins that at Christmas "they made a gathering together at Mrs. Durant's or her sister's, where there lived more of the black people than in any other part of the nation. And there they had a proper frolic of rum drinking and dancing. That the white people and Indians met generally at the same place with them and had the same amusement."[59]

Although the blacks had freedom of movement, they did not live in separate villages as did the Seminole blacks. They lived in separate dwellings called "negroe houses" on the premises of their masters. And, like their masters, many of them practiced polygamy.[60]

The slaves were allowed to accumulate personal property. In the absence of contemporary evidence we must rely on that of a generation after slavery began. In the 1820s slaves owned their own household goods—beds, tables, chairs, quilts and other bedding, utensils, including both tinware and earthen pots, bowls, and pans. They owned musical instruments, such as fiddles, weaving equipment, spinning wheels, axes, carpentry tools, and farming equipment. Slaves were expected to support themselves. Therefore, they raised domesticated fowls and farmed small patches of corn, which supplied their staple dish sofky, rice, and cotton. They stored their grain for future use, and some apparently spun and wove the cotton. There is no evidence, however, that the slaves were allowed to keep livestock as the Seminole blacks were allowed to do.[61]

The absence of specific descriptions of the blacks' mode of dress leaves much to speculation. If the blacks among the Seminoles dressed in Seminole fashion, it is probably safe to assume that those among the Creeks proper dressed much like the Creeks. But some details of dress are certain. Spinning and weaving equipment suggests homespun, but by the time the Creeks began to keep slaves they were dependent on trade goods, including cloth, from which were made colorful hunting shirts and dresses. Some blacks wore moccasins, and some of the men adopted the turban, popular among the Yuchis, Creeks, and Seminoles, an article of dress that persisted among some Creek blacks until the late nineteenth century.[62]

The slaves also adorned themselves with rings, beads, and brooches. The men owned tomahawks and club axes, but whether they habitually carried these weapons is uncertain. It might be assumed that they did, for as one observer later noted, the blacks were like the Creeks in everything but color.[63]

In the early days of slavery, the Creeks apparently adopted the concept of individual ownership of slave property. How much their concept of the relationship between master and slave was based on earlier tribal practices is uncertain. It is generally held by ethnologists that true slavery did not exist except among the Northwestern coastal tribes and that in-

stances reported as slavery in early histories of the Southeastern tribes
were in reality instances of adoption. Captives, especially women and
children, were war prizes, and the majority of them were adopted to replace tribal members lost in warfare. Some adopted members were no
doubt treated harshly, thereby causing European observers to presume
that they were slaves. The Creeks had observed the English capture of
Indians to be sold as slaves. They had even assisted in slaving raids and
had received captives as war prizes following their raids with the English
in northern Florida in the first decade of the eighteenth century.[64]

Bartram observed some Yamasee captives among the Seminoles in
the early 1770s. He called them "slaves," who waited upon the chief and
apparently feared him. But Bartram noticed that they dressed better
than the chief did and that the "slave" men and women were allowed
to marry among the Indians. Their children were "free, and considered
in every respect equal" to the Indians. Elsewhere, Bartram wrote of the
Upper and Lower Creeks: "I saw in every town in the Nation and Simi-
noles [sic] that I visited, more or less male captives, some extremely
aged, who were free and in as good circumstances as their masters; and
all slaves have their freedom when they marry, which is permitted and
encouraged, when they and their offspring are every way upon an equality
with their conquerers."[65] There is no evidence to show that the "introduction of black slaves among the Muskhogean tribes and others materially
changed the status of the Indian prisoner of war."[66] The greatest influence of aboriginal adoption practices upon the institution of slavery
apparently had less to do with the concept of the state of servitude than
with the attitude toward amalgamation, which was common among blacks
and Creeks in the first three decades of the nineteenth century.

To whatever native practices the Creeks had regarding slaves were
added European practices quickly adopted by individual Creeks. An
example is the treatment of the slave as individual property to which one
had legal title. The first slaveholders among the Creeks were Europeans,
who maintained legal titles attested to by bills of sales. That practice was
followed by their mixed-blood offspring. In the fall of 1797, Simothly,
a Hitchiti Indian, called at St. Mary's to complete a sale of two blacks
to Captain John Girideaux. Simothly and Mad Warrior had sold them to
Girideaux for $400 and had gone to the United States factory (trading
house) and bought $100 worth of goods each on credit on the basis of
the bargain. Simothly wanted his debt extinguished and the rest of his

money in cash, while Mad Warrior was willing to consider the bargain closed if Girideaux would simply extinguish his debt. Creek Agent James Seagrove advised Girideaux to settle with Simothly since he belonged "to a gang who might be very troublesome on our frontiers if sent away displeased."[67]

In November 1797, Robert Walton, the resident trader at Tuskegee, complained that John Galphin had sold a black claimed by Walton to William Kennard (Kinnard) of Cowpen in the Seminole country. Walton claimed that about three years earlier he had put the black out on loan. After that, Galphin wanted to buy the black but was refused. Galphin claimed that Noah Harrod had taken the black to Kennard to exchange for one whom Mrs. Sophia Durant had sold to Kennard, while Harrod claimed that it was Galphin who sold the black to Kennard. Mrs. Durant claimed that the black had belonged to her father and had been in the Nation twelve or thirteen years. At the time of the controversy, the black was allegedly in the possession of some Indians in a village called Mc-Cullee.[68]

A Creek named Stomolutkee had an old black called Tom whom he had traded to Noah Harrod for another black. In the spring of 1798 Stomolutkee wanted to sell Tom to Christian Russel, a Silisian trader at Coweta, who knew where the black was and was willing to go after him for "200 chalks" and a rifle. Stomolutkee wanted Hawkins to make out the papers so that Russel could get title to Tom and go take him.[69]

Late in 1797, Joseph Thompson of Tensaw complained to Hawkins that Zachariah McGirth of Tuckabahchee had prevailed upon two blacks, Nawne Londy (called Mundy) and Nancy, during the preceding summer to run away from Thompson's plantation to the Creek Nation. In 1793, McGirth had sued for the blacks before the commandant at Tensaw and failed to get them because Thompson had produced bills of sale dated 1782 and 1787. When Thompson missed the blacks, he and his neighbors pursued and overtook McGirth and George Cornell near Richard Bailey's. McGirth admitted having the blacks, and Hawkins ordered him to appear before him to answer Thompson's complaint. According to McGirth the blacks had been sold to his wife Louisa by James McGirth, Zachariah's father. By deposition, the elder McGirth of Cowpens County, Georgia, said that in about 1780 he had purchased Mundy in Georgia and had bought Nancy at the time the British were evacuating East Florida. The blacks were stolen and about four years later were found in the possession of Samuel Moore, Thompson's father-in-law, in West Florida. Zachariah McGirth claimed that Thompson had the blacks.[70]

In April 1798, Joseph Hardridge called on Hawkins to complain that he had bought a black named Summer from Noah Harrod for $300 and had paid him but was later informed by Harrod that Summer was mortgaged to Edward Price, the United States factor at Fort Wilkinson. That summer, Price received title to Summer, who was sent to him by Timothy Barnard. However, Summer never arrived at the factory, and Price assumed he had run away and asked the military officials to seize him if he came their way.[71]

In November 1799, John Headham had in his possession a black named Sandy, about forty-five or fifty years old, whom he had bought from Faukolusta of Osuche for fifteen head of cattle. Then he found out that Sandy was claimed by Israel Bird of Bryant County, Georgia. In November, Jesse McCall and James Bird demanded the black.[72]

Such instances as these suggest a clear understanding of the concept of legal title to slave property. Further evidence of this understanding is the Creeks' return of slaves to their rightful owners in Georgia as well as their recording bills of sale and wills transferring slave property in the courts of Alabama and Georgia in the early nineteenth century. Further evidence that title was clearly related to the state of servitude is the distinction made between slaves and free blacks. When free blacks were first permitted in the Creek country and how many of them there were in the late eighteenth century is uncertain, but they were there as early as 1797 when Richard Thomas, Hawkins' clerk, sent free black John Thompson to W. T. Marshall, a trader at Coweta, who was "very well off in negroes, cattle, etc.," and requested that Marshall let Thompson have twenty dollars on Thomas' account.[73]

The Creeks made distinctions between slaves and free blacks in the matter of property ownership. Free blacks were allowed wider latitudes. Like the Seminole slaves and free blacks, they owned livestock—hogs, cattle, horses—which was denied the slaves. Also like the Seminole blacks, they could own weapons—rifles and muskets—which were also apparently denied the slaves. They owned, as well, greater numbers of tools, such as saws, axes, hatchets, hammers, augers, and chisels.[74]

The institution of slavery as it developed among the Creeks was no doubt shaped in part by the government's policy of "civilizing" the Indians. By 1801, Benjamin Hawkins' efforts among the Creeks had had visible

results. In 1801, President Jefferson reported that the Creeks were raising
horses, cattle, sheep, and goats. They were settled in villages in new ground
and were fencing their fields. There were fifty to seventy plows among the
Creeks. There was a well-established peach tree nursery in the Lower
Creek country, and one had recently been established among the Upper
Creeks. Some small quantities of short staple cotton were being sold,
the Indians were experimenting with sea island cotton under Hawkins'
supervision, and there were sound beginnings in the household arts and
domestic manufactures. A conversion to agriculture would mean that less
land would be needed to support the tribe as hunting became less important and would thus make way for more land cessions. In 1803, Hawkins
was made agent to the Creeks alone, and he was able to concentrate his
efforts on them. By 1807, Jefferson could report that the tribes of the
Southwest were well in advance of others in agriculture and the useful arts.
In 1809 Hawkins wrote to the governor of Georgia: "The agency is crowded
with applicants for implements of husbandry and domestic manufactures
and with Indians learning to weave." At first the Georgians were not pleased
with Hawkins' attempts to domesticate the Creeks, for it gave a sense of
permanency to the Indians' residency in the region. They began to realize,
however, that changing the Indians' habits from hunting to farming reduced their need for hunting lands, and in 1805, Jefferson pointed out
that with agriculture the Indians could control their food supply and
would in time find it in their interest to divest themselves of surplus
lands. Early the following year, the *Georgia Republican* praised Hawkins'
success during the preceding decade as being "without parallel in the
history of savage nations."[75]

The institution of slavery as it was established in post-Revolutionary
days was also no doubt shaped in part by other changes taking place in the
Creek country at the time. The governmental system was changing. Mc-
Gillivray had centralized the government to some degree. Under Hawkins'
direction, in September 1799, the Creek chiefs assembled and adopted a
plan to carry out the laws of the Nation and appointed warriors to see that
the law was executed. In 1801, President Thomas Jefferson reported that
the National Council met at Tuckabahchee once a year, each town sending
deputies to do national business. The towns retained a good deal of auto-
nomy with their own government and presiding chief (micco).[76] Also, by
the 1740s they had become an acquisitive people and were now dependent
on trade goods to supply their needs.[77] Their hunting lands had shrunk,
and the game was disappearing, forcing a change in their life style. They

had turned to livestock raising to supplement their subsistence farming and hunting. There was also an increase in the mixed-blood population, who were particularly susceptible to imitating their white forebears and who led the way in adopting African slavery as a way of supplementing the labor force necessary for agricultural production. Along with these changes came a growing sense of individual ownership of property, and, as more and more land became necessary to support individual households and herds, the town structure began to weaken, especially among the Lower Creeks. Individuals moved out on their own and established homes which the whites called "plantations."

To assume, however, that slavery among the Creeks was even a loose equivalent of the plantation slavery of Georgia or the Carolinas would be a mistake. Despite social changes, the Creeks were still a society with strong aboriginal ties. Though they tended toward agriculture, they were not agricultural in the sense that the whites were. They still hunted and maintained vast herds of cattle. Field work consisted of farming small patches of vegetables, corn, and rice. But labor was shared. Indian women still worked the fields. In his first sojourn among the Creeks, Benjamin Hawkins found the men laboring beside their slaves in clearing land and building houses. Freedom of movement and accumulation of personal property were not typical in the states. But in the second decade of the nineteenth century, the institution of slavery among the Creeks was destined to undergo changes in the wake of the War of 1812 and the devastating effects of the Red Stick War of 1813-14.

NOTES

1. David H. Corkran, *The Creek Frontier, 1540-1783* (Norman: University of Oklahoma Press, 1967), p. 252; Cecil Johnson, "Expansion in West Florida," *Mississippi Valley Historical Review* 20 (March 1934), 481-96.

2. For a detailed treatment, see Corkran, pp. 288-315; and James H. O'Donnell, III, *Southern Indians in the American Revolution* (Knoxville: University of Tennessee Press, 1973), pp. 80-82, 87, 121-23; see also R. S. Cotterill, *The Southern Indians: The Story of the Civilized Tribes before Removal* (Norman: University of Oklahoma Press, 1954), pp. 37-38, 40-42, 46.

3. Kenneth Coleman, *The American Revolution in Georgia, 1763-1789* (Athens: University of Georgia Press, 1958), pp. 145, 146, 170-71.

4. Quoted from O'Donnell, p. 82; see also Corkran, p. 320.

5. Benjamin Hawkins, *A Sketch of the Creek Country in the Years 1798 and 1799,* Collections of the Georgia Historical Society, vol. 3, pt. 1 (New York: Wil-

liam Van Norden Printer, 1848), p. 66.

6. Angie Debo, *The Road to Disappearance* (Norman: University of Oklahoma Press, 1941), p. 39; Corkran, pp. 116, 165; Peter A. Brannon, "The Pensacola Indian Trade," *Florida Historical Society Quarterly* 31 (July 1952), 1, Marion Elisha Tarvin, "The Muscogees or Creek Indians 1519 to 1893," *The Alabama Historical Quarterly* 17 (Fall 1955), 128, 132. A good survey of Lachlan McGillivray's trading activities appears in Mary Ann Oglesby Neeley, "Lachlan McGillivray: A Scot on the Alabama Frontier," *The Alabama Historical Quarterly* 36 (Spring 1974), 5-14.

7. Coleman, pp. 211-12, 214-15, 216.

8. Allen D. Candler, ed., *The Revolutionary Records of the State of Georgia,* vol. 2 (Atlanta: The Franklin-Turner Company, 1908), p. 412.

9. Coleman, pp. 265, 266.

10. O'Donnell, p. 135; Cotterill, pp. 50, 41, 46; Coleman, p. 239; Debo, p. 39; John Pope, *A Tour Through the Southern and Western Territories of the United States of North-America; the Spanish Dominions on the Mississippi, and the Floridas; the Countries of the Creek Nations; and Many Uninhabited Parts* (Richmond, Va.: John Dickson, 1792; reprint ed., New York: Charles L. Woodward, 1888), p. 49. The most extensive study of McGillivray is John Walton Caughey, *McGillivray of the Creeks* (Norman: University of Oklahoma Press, 1938). Good studies of McGillivray's rise to power are James H. O'Donnell, III, "Alexander McGillivray: Training for Leadership, 1777-1783," *Georgia Historical Quarterly* 49 (June 1965), 172-86; and Lawrence Kinnaird, "International Rivalry in the Creek Country: Part I, The Ascendancy of Alexander McGillivray, 1783-1789," *Florida Historical Society Quarterly* 10 (October 1931), 59-85.

11. Cotterill, pp. 61, 62; Coleman, pp. 239, 240, 241; Brannon, p. 1; Marie Taylor Greenslade, "William Panton," *Florida Historical Society Quarterly* 14 (October 1935), 115; Alexander McGillivray to Arturo O'Neill, January 3, 1784, and February 10, 1786, in Caughey, pp. 67, 103.

12. McGillivray to O'Neill, March 10, 1783, and February 5, 1784, and McGillivray to William Panton, August 10, 1789, in Caughey, pp. 61, 69, 249. Louis de Milfort was a Frenchman who married McGillivray's sister and became commander-in-chief of the Creek warriors.

13. Benjamin Hawkins, *Letters of Benjamin Hawkins, 1796-1806,* Collections of the Georgia Historical Society, vol. 9 (Savannah: The Morning News, 1916), pp. 79-81; Brannon, pp. 7-8; "First Anglo-American Settlements," *Notes,* A. B. Meek Papers, and "Place Names in Choctaw and Creek," *File 60,* H. S. Halbert Papers, Manuscripts Division, Alabama Department of Archives and History, Montgomery. Forbes was a British trader associated with the Panton company. John Forbes and Company succeeded the Panton trading firm in Pensacola.

14. Hawkins, *Letters,* pp. 203, 263-64.

15. McGillivray to O'Neill, July 12, 1787, in Caughey, p. 159.

16. Caughey, p. 61n; McGillivray to John Linder, December 28, 1788, in Caughey, pp. 212-13; Tarvin, p. 133; H. S. Halbert and T. H. Ball, *The Creek War of 1813 and 1814* (Chicago: Donohue & Henneberry, 1895; reprint ed., Frank L. Owsley, Jr., ed., University; University of Alabama Press, 1969), p. 28.

17. Merritt B. Pound, *Benjamin Hawkins—Indian Agent* (Athens: University of Georgia Press, 1951), pp. 45, 54; Cotterill, pp. 70, 65-66, 72; *House Executive Document 91*, 20 Cong., 2 sess., p. 9 (hereafter cited as *Document 91*); Coleman, p. 245.

18. Pound, pp. 37, 38-39, 42, 54; Debo, pp. 40-41; Cotterill, p. 73.

19. Pound, pp. 35, 53, 55; Coleman, p. 247; Cotterill, p. 73.

20. Pound, p. 56; Coleman, pp. 249, 250; Cotterill, p. 74; Debo, p. 44. In a raid near Nashville, they killed two men and stole four horses and Sam, a slave of James Bosley. At about the same time, the Creeks took from Toogaloo a slave of Samuel Isaacs of Pendleton County, South Carolina. On April 15, 1790, the Creeks stole Ned, a seventeen-year-old black belonging to Edmund Gamble, who lived near Nashville. Hawkins, *Letters,* pp. 174, 175.

21. Hawkins, *Letters,* pp. 204, 228, 233; Kenneth Wiggins Porter, *The Negro on the American Frontier* (New York: Arno Press and The New York Times, 1971), p. 49. In 1787, Lucy, a twelve-year-old, ran away from the plantation of John Lang near Oconee, and in 1790 a black ran away from the plantation of William Fitzpatrick in the same area. In the latter year, two slaves escaped to the Creek Nation from the plantation of Henry Carleton of Green County, Georgia. Hawkins, *Letters,* p. 175.

22. Cotterill, pp. 76-77, 78. The authoritative treatment of Bowles's career is J. Leitch Wright, Jr., *William Augustus Bowles; Director General of the Creek Nation* (Athens: University of Georgia Press, 1967).

23. Cotterill, pp. 83-84; Coleman, pp. 251, 252; Pound, p. 58; Tarvin, pp. 130, 131-32; Charles J. Kappler, comp. and ed., *Indian Affairs: Laws and Treaties,* 2nd ed., vol. 2 (Washington, D.C.: Government Printing Office, 1904), pp. 25-29.

McGillivray's slave Jonah lived past the Civil War and died at the home of Mrs. Josephine Driesbach in Baldwin County, Alabama. Tarvin, pp. 142-43.

The following story has been told about Paro. In 1773, Thadeus Lyman and Matthew Phelps led a colony of "most intelligent and reputable" people and their slaves from Connecticut to a 20,000-acre tract of land on Bayou Pierre near present Port Gibson, Mississippi. During the Revolutionary War, they fled from the Spanish and traveled cross-country to the English settlements on the Tensaw. After a harrowing trek, they reached the Coosa above Wetumpka and made their way to McGillivray's place at Hickory Ground. McGillivray was gone, and his Indian followers wanted to kill the whites because they thought them to be Georgians or Virginians. But Paro said that if they were who they claimed to be, they would have papers to prove it and could "make the paper talk." Among the group was Jonathan Dwight, brother of the president of Yale College. Dwight brought forth a long letter and pretended to read an account of their wanderings and sufferings while Paro translated to the Indians, and the Indians were moved from hostility to pity and admiration. "First Anglo-American Settlements," *Notes,* A. B. Meek Papers, Alabama Department of Archives and History, Montgomery.

24. Pound, pp. 59, 81, 82; Cotterill, pp. 90-93. See Wright, especially page 149, for a concise statement of Bowles' ambitions. See also, Lawrence Kinnaird, "The Significance of William Augustus Bowles' Seizure of Panton's Apalachee

Store in 1792," *Florida Historical Society Quarterly* 9 (January 1931), 156-92.

25. Alexander Moultrie to Benjamin Farrar, January 24, 1790, and Moultrie to McGillivray, February 19, 1790, in Arthur Preston Whitaker, "The South Carolina Yazoo Company," *Mississippi Valley Historical Review* 16 (December 1929), 383-94.

26. Greenslade, p. 115.

27. Cotterill, pp. 99, 102, 106, 111-12.

28. *Document 91,* p. 7; D. C. Corbitt, ed., "Papers Relating to the Georgia-Florida Frontier, 1784-1800," *Georgia Historical Quarterly* 24 (June 1940); 154-56.

29. *American State Papers: Documents, Legislative and Executive of the Congress of the United States, from the First to the Third Session of the Thirteenth Congress, Inclusive, Commencing March 3, 1789, and Ending March 3, 1815,* Indian Affairs, vol. 1 (Washington, D.C. Gales and Seaton, 1832), p. 546; *Document 91,* p. 7; Lilla M. Hawes, ed., *The Papers of James Jackson, 1781-1798,* Collections of the Georgia Historical Society, vol. 11 (Savannah: The Georgia Historical Society, 1955), p. 88.

30. Pound, pp. 82, 84, 88-89, 92; Kappler, vol. 2, pp. 46-50.

31. Pound, pp. 99-100, 103. Hawkins was born in North Carolina in 1754; in 1781 he was elected to the Continental Congress and served five terms. Pound, pp. 4, 13.

32. Pope, p. 64; Hawkins, *Letters,* pp. 29-31.

33. Bills of sale, May 23, 1779, March 21, 1780, April 17, 1780, February 12, 1791, October 14, 1795, and Affidavits and receipts, October 13, 1779, October 14, 1795, and October 17, 1795, "Interesting Notes Upon the History of Alabama," section 8, Albert J. Pickett Papers, Alabama Department of Archives and History, Montgomery.

34. Hawkins, *Letters,* pp. 40-41.

35. Pound, p. 110.

36. Hawkins, *Letters,* p. 86; in 1797, Timothy Barnard was appointed assistant principal temporary agent for Indian affairs south of Ohio.

37. Pound, pp. 113, 109.

38. *American State Papers,* Indian Affairs, 1: 647; Pound, pp. 103, 140, 141-42, 147; Arthur Preston Whitaker, *The Mississippi Question, 1795-1803: A Study in Trade, Politics, and Diplomacy* (New York: The American Historical Association, 1934; reprint ed., Gloucester, Mass.: Peter Smith, 1962), p. 77.

39. Frederick Webb Hodge, ed., *Handbook of American Indians North of Mexico,* 2 pts. (Washington, D.C.: Government Printing Office, 1910), 2: 500; John K. Mahon, *History of the Second Seminole War, 1835-1842* (Gainesville: University of Florida Press, 1967), p. 7; R. M. Loughridge, comp., *English and Muskokee Dictionary* (St. Louis: J. T. Smith, 1890; reprint, Okmulgee, Okla.: B. Frank Belvin, 1964), p. 183.

40. Mahon, pp. 2-7; John R. Swanton, *The Indians of the Southeastern United States,* Bureau of American Ethnology Bulletin, no. 137 (Washington, D.C.: Government Printing Office, 1946), p. 181; William C. Sturdevant, "Creek into Seminole," in *North American Indians in Historical Perspective,* eds. Eleanor Burke Leacock and Nancy Oesterich Lurie (New York: Random House, 1971), pp. 101-03; Swanton,

Early History of the Creek Indians and Their Neighbors, Bureau of American Ethnology Bulletin, no. 73 (Washington, D.C.: Government Printing Office, 1922), pp. 398-405.

41. Mahon, pp. 7, 18-19; Sturdevant, p. 93.

42. For an authoritative account of blacks in Florida, 1670-1763, see Porter pp. 155-81; see also, Mahon, pp. 19, 20.

43. Mahon, p. 20; Hawkins, *A Sketch,* Appendix.

44. Porter, pp. 186-87.

45. [William Hayne Simmons], *Notices of East Florida* (Charleston, 1822; reprint ed., Gainesville: University of Florida Press, 1973), pp. 42, 50.

46. [Simmons], p. 76; Porter, pp. 46, 187, 189-90; Coe, pp. 14-15.

47. [Simmons], pp. 45, 76-77; Porter, p. 47.

48. [Simmons], pp. 75, 42, 44.

49. Porter, p. 47.

50. List of Seminole Towns and Report of Horatio L. Dexter, National Archives Microfilm Publications, *Microcopy M271* (Letters Received by the Secretary of War Relating to Indian Affairs, 1800-1823) 4: frames 507, 513.

51. Gad Humphreys to Acting Governor William M. McCarty, September 6, 1827, in Clarence Edwin Carter, comp. and ed., *The Territorial Papers of the United States,* 26 vols. (Washington, D.C.: Government Printing Office, 1934-1956; National Archives, 1958-1962), 23: 911.

52. Caleb Swan, "Position and State of Manners and Arts in the Creek, or Muscogee Nation in 1791," in *Information Respecting the History, Condition and Prospects of the Indian Tribes of the United States,* by Henry Rowe Schoolcraft, 6 vols., (Philadelphia: J. B. Lippincott & Company, 1855; reprint ed., New York: Paladin Press, 1969), 5: 272.

53. Hawkins, *Letters,* p. 43.

54. Hawkins, *A Sketch,* pp. 26, 29, 31, 39, 44, 49, 50, 66; Bill of Sale, December 4, 1798, "Interesting Notes Upon the History of Alabama," section 8, Albert J. Pickett Papers, Manuscripts Division, Alabama Department of Archives and History, Montgomery.

55. Hawkins, *Letters,* pp. 30, 47, 49.

56. Mark van Doren, ed., *The Travels of William Bartram* (New York: Dover, 1928), p. 401.

57. Hawkins, *Letters,* pp. 29, 268, 298, 463.

58. Thomas S. Woodward, *Woodward's Reminiscences of the Creek, or Muskogee Indians, Contained in Letters to Friends in Georgia and Alabama* (Montgomery: Barrett & Wimbash, 1859; reprint ed., Mobile: Southern University Press for Graphics, Inc., 1965), pp. 94, 92; H. S. Halbert and T. H. Ball, p. 66; Notes by Rev. Lee Compere, section 24, "Interesting Notes Upon the History of Alabama," Albert J. Pickett Papers, Manuscripts Division, Alabama Department of Archives and History, Montgomery; D. S. Mitchell to T. Hartley Crawford, June 1, 1842, National Archives Microfilm Publications, *Microcopy M234* (Office of Indian Affairs, Letters Received) 226: W1883-42, hereafter cited as *M234,* followed by the roll number; Kappler, 2: 342.

59. Hawkins, *Letters,* pp. 268, 298, 463, 48-49; Andrew Ellicott, *The Journal of Andrew Ellicott* (Philadelphia: Budd & Bartram, 1803; reprint ed., Chicago: Quadrangle Books, 1962), p. 219.

60. National Archives Microfilm Publications, *Microcopy 574* (Special Files of the Office of Indian Affairs, 1807-1904) 27: frame 958, hereafter cited as *M574,* followed by the roll number. For evidence of polygamy see John Casey to Isaac Clark, July 11, 1838, *House Document 225,* 25 Cong., 3 sess., pp. 119-20, and List of Slaves Owned by Miccopotokee or Copiah Yahola, April 29, 1835, in *M234-*802: D153-56.

61. *M574-*27: frames 775, 991, 1121, 1122, 1140.

62. For evidence of the turban as an article of dress, see the photograph of Paro Bruner on p. 152 of this volume.

63. *M574-*27: frames 994, 1121; B. S. Parsons and Thomas J. Abbott to Lewis Cass, September 7, 1832, *M234-*223: frame 306; Parsons to Cass, October 16, 1832, in J. H. Johnston, "Documentary Evidence and the Relations of Negroes and Indians," *The Journal of Negro History* 14 (January 1929), 37.

64. Hodge, 2: 599-600.

65. Van Doren, pp. 164, 183.

66. Hodge, 2: 600.

67. Hawkins, *Letters,* p. 200; Edward Price to Captain John Girideaux, October 13, 1797, National Archives Microfilm Publications, *Microcopy M4* (Records of the Creek Trading House, 1795-1816) 1: 92-93, hereafter cited as *M4,* followed by the roll number. The United States established its first factory, or trading post, for the Creeks in 1796 at Colerain, in an attempt to regulate trade with the Indians and to create friendly relations with them by keeping prices low. The factory was moved subsequently to Fort Wilkinson, Ocmulgee Old Fields, Fort Hawkins, and Fort Gaines. *M4-1;* introduction.

68. Hawkins, *Letters,* p. 245.

69. *Ibid.,* p. 304.

70. *Ibid.,* pp. 219, 220, 259; Pound, p. 130.

71. Hawkins, *Letters,* p. 483; Price to Ens. Sam Allinson, August 7, 1798, *M4-*1: 155.

72. Hawkins, *Letters,* p. 339.

73. Ibid., pp. 464, 467.

74. *M574-*27: frames 975, 1122, 1140.

75. Pound, pp. 143, 144, 145, 146, 147, 160, 164; Whitaker, *The Mississippi Question,* p. 77.

76. Pound, pp. 162, 163.

77. Corkran, p. 53.

chapter 3

RED STICKS
AND SEMINOLES

DURING THE FIFTEEN years preceding the War of 1812, Creek relations with Georgia had been fragile. After the Treaty of Colrain, the increasing number of runaway blacks in the Creek Nation became a source of constant trouble. It was Benjamin Hawkins' job as agent to see that they were returned.[1] In late 1797, he reported to the governor of Georgia that the Creeks had improved "a little in their efforts to maintain a friendly intercourse with their neighbors." He offered rewards to induce them to return slaves and other property, and at a meeting of Upper and Lower Creeks and Seminoles at Tuckabahchee in 1798 he asked the chiefs to give attention to the problems of horse stealing and encouraging blacks to leave their masters and go to the Creek country. Cusseta Tustenuggee, speaking for the Lower towns, and Yohola Micco of the Upper towns said that they would do what they could.[2] The Georgians tied the return of property to demands for land cessions. In 1802 Georgia made what was known as the Compact of 1802, in which she agreed to sell her western land claims to the United States, and the United States promised that the Indian title to lands within the state would be removed as soon as possible. Georgians set about obtaining their goal in their own way. In the fall of 1801 they planned a meeting at Oconee to demand all property taken since the Treaty of New York (1790) and, if it could not be restored, to demand Creek lands as far west as the Ocmulgee. On June 16, 1802, the government negotiated the Treaty of Fort Wilkinson in which the Creeks gave up Indian claims to a strip of land on the west bank of the Oconee River from Rock Landing up to the High Shoals of the Apalachee and a narrow strip between the Altamaha and St. Mary's rivers. And, in the fall of 1805, Hawkins and six chiefs went to Washington and concluded a treaty which ceded all Creek lands between the Oconee and Ocmulgee as far north as the High Shoals of the Apalachee. In 1804 Georgia appointed agents to secure property they claimed was being held by the Indians. On July 2, 1805, the commissioners addressed the Creek chiefs at Coweta, asked them to honor their treaties, and demanded that all blacks, prisoners, horses, cattle, and other property be returned to Georgia citizens.[3]

Between 1806 and 1810, there was relative peace between the Creeks and whites, despite the ever present thefts, illegal trading, and mutual trespass. Hawkins continued to return runaway slaves when possible. Hawkins' efforts, however, could not satisfy the Georgians. In October 1810, Georgia Governor David B. Mitchell appointed Daniel Stewart to go to the agency and demand the return of all Georgia property. He had a detailed list of all claims, many of which went back to 1775. Hawkins thought them neither just, accurate, nor valid under the treaties.[4] Georgia's demands for the return of property and for land cessions were interrupted, but only momentarily, by the outbreak of the War of 1812.

Meanwhile, the Creeks were beset by a number of internal problems. First, since McGillivray's death, the Creeks had been factionalized to a much greater degree than they had been under his leadership. Second, the purchase of Louisiana had necessitated the building of roads across the Creek country. A horse path, opened in 1805, was followed in late 1811 by a road from Athens, Georgia, to Fort Stoddard (north of Mobile), permission for which the Creeks granted in return for a thousand spinning wheels and a like number of pairs of cotton cards. The Upper Creeks opposed the roads, which they said would bring trouble to the Creeks, for "the great god made us and the lands for us to walk on." Third, at about the time the road was completed, Tecumseh, the great Shawnee, arrived at Tuckabahchee, urging the Creeks to join the other tribes in throwing off the white man. His words inflamed the Creeks, especially the young warriors. Early historians tended to cite Tecumseh's visit as a major cause of the Creek War of 1813-14, but scholars have recently tended to treat its beginning phases as a civil war, brought on by a Creek faction that had long been dissatisfied with the acculturation foisted upon the Creeks by Benjamin Hawkins and fostered by the tribal government.[5] The war had such devastating consequences for the Creeks that it deserves treatment here. While events often overshadow the participants in historical documents, some insights into the participants can be gained. Blacks, for instance, were present in all stages of the Red Stick War, and during the years of violence leading to the First Seminole war in 1817, they played an increasingly important role in the hostilities.

The specific events that sparked the civil war were reprisals for the execution of Creek murderers. In the spring of 1812 several whites were murdered, including a family on Duck River, Tennessee. The Creeks hunted down and killed the murderers who were members of the dissatisfied faction. Early in 1813 seven white families were killed on the Ohio River by Creeks on their way back to the Creek country after a visit to the Shawnees. The death penalty was assessed against the murderers, and in April eight of them were killed. In the wake of Tecumseh's visit, the phophetic movement had begun among the Creeks in the Alabama towns, and the prophets now stirred the dissatisfied faction to action. They set out to conduct a war of revenge, to execute the Creek leaders, to kill Benjamin Hawkins, and to destroy the vestiges of the white man's civilization. Led by Menauway of Okfuskee, Peter McQueen, Hossa Yahola, and the Tame King of Tallassee, Josiah Francis or the Prophet, and Seekabo, a Shawnee prophet who had been among them since Tecumseh's visit, the hostile Creeks, or Red Sticks as they were called, went to war in the summer of 1813. In July they killed nine of their friends' executioners, burned several villages under the influence of Hawkins, slaughtered livestock, and laid seige to Tuckabahchee, which was subsequently rescued by the Lower Creeks, its inhabitants going to Coweta. From there the Creeks launched raiding parties against the Red Sticks, killing and capturing them and taking their blacks.[6]

Knowing that they would need arms and munitions to conduct their war, the Red Sticks sent a force of Tallassees under Peter McQueen, Atasis (Auttosees) under Jim Boy (or High Head Jim), and Alabamas under Josiah Francis to Pensacola to secure the supplies. On their way, at Burnt Corn Spring, they plundered and burned the home of the half-blood James Cornell, severely beat one of Cornell's blacks and a white man, and stole Cornell's wife to be sold as a slave in Pensacola. There, the Red Sticks demanded arms from John Forbes & Company, under which name the Panton company had been reorganized, telling John Innerarity that the Forbes company had gotten rich in the Creek country and therefore owed something to the Creeks. The Indians also demanded arms from the Spanish government. The militia was called out, and the Creeks left, but not before the governor had relented and given them a present of about a thousand pounds of powder and "a proportion of Ball &c."[7]

A boast of the Red Sticks that they would take Mobile caused some concern to Innerarity, whose brother James ran the Forbes store there. Planters in that area began to desert their plantations, which act, thought Innerarity, invited the Indians to destroy the property. Innerarity suggested that, since his brother was situated on the water's edge, he keep a barge or canoe ready to remove his blacks or to arm the blacks if necessary. He felt that their situation was not perilous as long as the trouble was confined to the Creeks; should the Seminoles enter the fighting, however, it would be a different matter.[8]

The Red Sticks had openly declared that they intended to attack the growing settlements on the Tombigbee and the Alabama rivers. These settlements had begun, with McGillivray's help, during the Revolutionary War and had grown steadily since them. Fort Stoddard had been established in 1799 a few miles below the juncture of the Alabama and the Tombigbee. By 1801 the population in the river settlements was estimated at 750, of whom 500 were white, and by 1812 there were about 2,000 whites and about as many blacks. In 1813, these people learned that Mc-Queen's party planned to go north from Pensacola to Whetstone Hill, about eighty miles east of the Tombigbee, where they would be met by a party from the Creek Nation, divide up the military stores obtained from the Spanish, and then attack the frontier. When the whites learned that McQueen had procured arms, they mobilized and, with a number of mixed-blood Creeks led by Dixon Bailey, David Tate, and James Cornell, met McQueen's and Jim Boy's warriors on July 27, 1813, at Burnt Corn Creek.[9]

Their force of 180 surprised the Red Sticks and overran their camp, which many of the troops began to plunder. The Creeks rallied and routed the whites and mixed bloods. Among the six Red Stick casualties was a black man who had been killed early in the fighting. He was a cook at work in the camp when the attack began. He had had time to escape but apparently believed that since he was a slave and not armed he had nothing to fear from the whites. Whether there were other blacks present in the fighting is uncertain. Jim Boy (or Tustenuggee Emathla), according to his contemporaries, was part African and part white. A powerful man, over six feet tall, Jim Boy was usually praised as a fine specimen, but in 1838, one military official called him a scoundrel who combines "all the vices of white, Indian, and negro, without the virtues of any." A few years later, he was referred to by another officer as "a colored mixed."[10]

In the wake of the Burnt Corn fiasco, settlers on the Tombigbee and the Alabama were alarmed and confused. Many left their farms, crops, and livestock to the Red Sticks and fled to the west side of the Tombigbee. Five hundred fifty-three whites, mixed bloods, and their slaves fortified themselves in Fort Mims, a stockade built in July 1813 by farmer Joseph Mims on Lake Tensaw, near the juncture of the Tombigbee and Alabama.[11]

Bent on revenge for Burnt Corn, the Red Sticks planned to attack Fort Mims. The Red Stick force, comprised of warriors from thirteen of the Upper towns, stopped at a plantation a few miles from the fort and captured some blacks, but they were permitted to escape by William Weatherford, one of the Red Stick leaders. On August 29, two blacks owned by John Randon were out tending cattle, saw Indians in war paint, and reported it to the people at Fort Mims. Major Daniel Beasley, the overconfident commandant at the stockade, investigated but put little faith in the report because some of Randon's blacks had been sent earlier to his plantation for corn and had reported that Indians were looting the farm. The latest report seemed to be simply another report, and one of Randon's slaves was whipped for unnecessarily alarming the garrison.[12] Had the inhabitants of Fort Mims heeded these blacks' warnings they might have been spared the disaster that followed.

The Red Sticks got within thirty yards of the stockade gates before they were detected. At noon on August 30, they attacked. In the fighting that ensued, blacks were involved on both sides. There were contemporary charges that a black named Joe had "conducted the Indians to the massacre at Fort Mims." According to Benjamin Hawkins, Joe and two other blacks belonging to Zachariah McGirth had been sent to McGirth's plantation after corn and had been taken by the Indians. Hawkins assumed that the blacks had given the Red Sticks information about the situation at the fort. Joe was captured late in 1814 about nine miles from Pensacola, where he had fled with the Red Sticks. According to a black who escaped the battle, a black named Siras cut down the pickets to let the Indians in, and Seekabo the Shawnee prophet and "some of the McGillivray negroes" set fire to the buildings by shooting fire arrows into them. On the other hand, one "large and powerful" black fought the Indians with an axe, striking them down as they came through a break in the wall, but he was finally killed by knives and clubs. One account of the battle says that a black tried to carry a child of mixed-blood Dixon Bailey to safety but became confused and ran to the lines of the Indians and was killed. However, according to Dr. Thomas G. Holmes, who also escaped from the battle, Bailey ordered Tom to take his ill fourteen-year-old son Ralph to safety, and the pair escaped unhurt. But Tom returned to the fort because he apparently assumed that the Indians would not kill the child. They nevertheless dispatched the child with a war club.[13]

Historians disagree on the exact number killed at Fort Mims. It has been generally held that about 500 whites, mixed-blood Creeks, and blacks died. However, a more recent, conservative estimate indicates that between 247 (the number of bodies later buried) and 260 whites and mixed bloods were killed and that an estimated 100 blacks as well as some white and mixed-blood women and children were carried off. Captain J. L. Kennedy of the burial party counted the bodies of the nine blacks. Others, including blacks, escaped. Some who had been outside the pickets when the attack occurred went down river to Fort Stoddard. Zachariah McGirth had taken two of his blacks up Tensaw Lake the previous day to gather corn and pumpkins at his farm and was there when the firing began. Other blacks who escaped included Hester, a woman, and Lizzie, a girl who was saved by Susan Stiggins, a kinswoman of William Weatherford, and Tom, who belonged to the McGillivray family. Hester, who belonged to Benjamin Stidham, allegedly swam the Alabama River, kept the road to the Tombigbee, swam that, and the next morning was the first to tell the news of the disaster to General F. L. Claiborne at Mount Vernon near Fort Stoddard. Another black who escaped informed the friendly Creeks that he was hiding in the corner of a house when a Red Stick saw him and told him to come out, that the "Master of Breath" had told them to kill no one but whites and "half breeds."[14]

Most of the survivors of the Fort Mims disaster were blacks, for from the beginning of hostilities it was the practice of the Red Sticks to take blacks as slaves instead of killing them or, as indicated above, promise them their freedom, apparently in a bid to prevent their fighting for their masters. Blacks may have willingly joined the Red Sticks because of American war policy. When Governor William C. C. Claiborne learned of Fort Mims, he told the colonels of the Mississippi militia that it was rumored that "many slaves" had left their masters and joined the Red Sticks. Claiborne ordered the colonels to conduct regular military patrols and to recommend to the citizens of their districts that they "maintain a proper discipline among their slaves." In his letter ordering F. L. Claiborne to take command of the Mississippi Territory Volunteers and Militia, Brigadier General Thomas Flournoy, commanding the Seventh Military District, ordered Claiborne to go to the Indian towns and literally to burn, kill, and destroy, emphasizing that "all negroes, horses, cattle, corn and other property that cannot be conveniently brought in, must be destroyed." In subsequent years, Claiborne's son asked that the order not be judged too harshly, that the reader "remember the atrocities the savages were then perpetrating on the frontier, the fall of Ft. Mims and the fact that negroes were in all the war parties and more savage and inexorable than the Indians themselves."[15] However, evidence has not to date borne out either of the last two accusations.

The taking of blacks as slaves does not appear to be a policy the Red Sticks arrived at after the fighting began but one followed from the beginning of the civil conflict. In March 1812, Thomas Meredith, Sr., was murdered on the mail road near a house of entertainment run by Samuel Moniac, a mixed blood. In fear of the consequences of the murder, Moniac left his house on the mail road and went to his plantation on the Alabama where he stayed for a time before taking some steers to market at Pensacola. While he was gone, his brothers and sisters, who were members of the disaffected party, came to his plantation and took a number of horses and thirty-six of his blacks.[16]

The taking of slaves raises questions about the theories of some who treat the War of 1813-14 strictly as a nativistic movement among the Creeks.[17] If, as they stress, it was an attempt to overthrow the process of acculturation begun by Hawkins, why were the Red Sticks so intent on amassing slaves—perhaps the most outstanding symbol of the agricultural system espoused by Hawkins and his superiors? If the taking of slaves can be explained as war policy, why did the Red Sticks not, when they escaped with their slaves to Florida, rid themselves of that final vestige of civilization in a land where they could more nearly have done it than in the Creek Nation proper? It may be that they intended to trade them to the Spanish for munitions or that they hoped to divest the mixed bloods of their work force. The blacks were highly mobile war prizes, who, in many instances, were probably willing to travel with their captors and serve them as retainers, herdsmen, messengers, and spies. As subsequent events would demonstrate, practical matters of survival in warfare became more important then any ideological considerations as blacks played an increasingly significant roll in warfare that plagued the Creek-Seminole frontiers during the next several years.

After the fight at Fort Mims, the Indians camped about a mile from the fort and, until about noon the following day, busied themselves with scouring the countryside for blacks and livestock, which they carried off with them. During the weeks subsequent to the battle, the Indians roamed the Tensaw region, killing and plundering the inhabitants, and taking their blacks. They captured Ransom Kimbrell's blacks, who were later recovered. Inhabitants holed up at Fort Madison included Moses Savel, a mill owner. During the last of September 1813, he and some men went to his mill on Bassett's Creek to do some grinding. After they finished their work, they left Phil Creagh, a black, to close up, and he was captured. Phil stayed with the Red Sticks for four days, during which he showed no apparent desire to escape, so the men left him with their families while they went hunting. Phil watched for his chance and escaped. During those subsequent weeks, other blacks who had been with the Indians escaped or were captured and gave intelligence to the friendly Indians and Americans. In assessing the attack on Fort Mims, Hawkins wrote the secretary of war: "Yet, how such a party should get there, when there were a great many half-breeds, and negroes, who speak the Indian language, and have commissions in the hostile towns, and the party to go to the lowest settlement, and return as they did, undiscovered, and unmolested, is to me a very extraordinary thing."[18]

In order to keep informed on the movements of the Indians, the volunteers in the Tensaw region sent out spy parties. One, composed of Taney Walker, another white man named Foster, and a free black named Evans, went out in October. They left Montgomery Hill, crossed the Alabama, and traveled east to Burnt Corn, where they discovered many Indian signs. On their way back, they camped near the river. At dawn the next day, a black approached their camp and asked if they were Indians or whites. Evans replied that they were Indians, but Walker uncovered himself about that time. The black, seeing that he was white, announced that fact and several guns were fired at Walker and Evans. Evans was killed, but Foster, who was some distance from the camp, and Walker escaped.[19]

Shortly thereafter, in November, a detachment of Mississippi volunteers went out from Fort Madison to drive the Red Sticks, who had been raiding in small parties, to the east side of the Alabama. During their expedition, Captain Samuel Dale, James Smith, and Jeremiah Austill, using a small canoe, attacked nine Indians in a large, flat-bottomed canoe. The small craft was paddled by Caesar, a free black "who lived with the friendly Indians." When the three men tried to fire their guns, only one discharged, the priming in the others having got wet. Caesar paddled alongside the Indians' canoe and held the two crafts together while the whites and Indians fought a hand-to-hand battle, and when it was over, all of the Indians were dead. According to Austill, in the scuffle with the last Indian, Caesar handed a musket to Dale, who stuck the Indian with the bayonet. Caesar, who played an important role in the fight, was the son of Sullivan's Bob, who had been involved in the Kirkland murders in 1789, and Tabby, who had been stolen from a Georgian named Cook.[20]

The battle at Fort Mims transformed the Creek civil war into a war with the United States. In July 1813, Congress had authorized the governors of Georgia and Tennessee to raise troops to go against the Creeks if it became necessary. This act was prompted by the urgings of those governors and the governor of Mississippi Territory, who apparently knew that a war with the Creeks would result in land cessions by the Indians. General Floyd, at the head of the Georgia militia, invaded the Creek country in October 1813, built Fort Mitchell, and made forays against the Creeks. In December, General Claiborne of Mississippi, assisted by a number of Choctaws under Pushmataha, also invaded the Creek country.[21]

Claiborne's objective was Holy Ground, on the south bank of the Alabama River between Pintlala Creek and Big Swamp Creek in present-day Lowndes County, Alabama. At Holy Ground Town, about two miles north of present-day Whithall, was the Alabama council house, the meeting place of the prophets. It was to that place that Weatherford, Hossa Yohola, Josiah Francis, and other leaders retired after Fort Mims and made their headquarters. On December 23, 1813, Claiborne's forces overran the town and burned it. As the cabins burned, the door of one suddenly flew open and "a large mulatto negro" sprang out and was shot down instantly by the troops. He was apparently a runaway slave who had thought to escape capture by hiding in the cabin. In the Battle of Holy Ground, the Creeks used blacks as warriors. When the fighting was over, there were twenty-one Creek and twelve black bodies. The Choctaws scalped the Creeks and the blacks, keeping the Indian scalps as trophies but throwing the blacks' scalps away.[22]

On January 27, 1814, General Floyd's troops defeated the Red Sticks at

Camp Defiance. By that time, General Andrew Jackson had begun his second campaign. In his first, during the fall of 1813, he had killed several hundred Red Sticks at Tallasseehatchee and Talladega. At Tohopeka, or Horseshoe Bend, on March 27, 1814, his troops engaged an estimated 1,000 Creeks, killing nearly 800.[23] This battle effectively broke the Red Stick resistance.

Some of the whites, assuming that the war was over, returned home. A case in point was Gerald Byrne, who had taken his family to Mobile after the fall of Fort Mims. In April 1814 Byrne took some of his blacks to his plantation to put in a crop. The Creeks attacked Byrne's house, killing him and two men who had stopped to see him. One of his blacks was also killed in the fighting, and others were taken prisoner.[24]

It was not until August 9, 1814, that Jackson negotiated a peace at Fort Jackson, the site of old Fort Toulouse. The treaty, which ended the Creek War, punished the friendly Creeks as much as it did the Red Sticks. The Creeks ceded over twenty million acres of land west of the Coosa and north to the Cherokee boundary, south to Florida, and east from the Tombigbee to the Chattahoochee, as well as a wide strip of Lower Creek lands along the Florida border from the Flint to the western boundary of the cession of 1802.[25]

Most of the hostile chiefs did not attend the treaty negotiations and considered themselves still at war. Only one signed the treaty. Eight of the Tallapoosa and Alabama towns led by McQueen, Hossa Yohola, Savannah Jack, Josiah Francis, the Durants, and others, numbering more than 1,000, escaped to Florida. Menauway was in hiding, and others were dead. Signers of the treaty included Big Warrior for the Upper Creeks, Tustenuggee Hopoie for the Lower Creeks, Timpooche Barnard for the Yuchis, William McIntosh for the Cussetas, Noble Kinnard for the Hitchiti, John O'Kelly for the Coosas, John Carr for the Tuskegees, and Alexander Grayson for the Hilibis.[26]

The Red Sticks who were forced to flee the Creek Nation lost most of their property through confiscation. Many were slaveholders who owned large numbers of slaves. Peter McQueen himself owned about thirty grown blacks, who were confiscated by a half-blood named Barney and by James Cornell. It had been Jackson's policy to capture the slaves of the Red Sticks when possible and to hold them for exchange or ransom. In the fall of 1813, he had captured a Choctaw woman, a slave of Cotalla, who had given her "to his negro fellow for a wife." The woman and her three children were held by the army not for exchange or ransom, but to be returned to the Choctaws as soon as the woman's family could be discovered. Other blacks were taken from Kelly's town on the Coosa River below Fort Strother. In violation of Jackson's orders, some of the prisoners were carried off by soldiers and the friendly Choctaws and Cherokees. In April 1814, Fushatchee Micco and William Weatherford surrendered to Jackson at his camp at the junction of the Coosa and Tallapoosa, bringing with them eighteen of the blacks captured at Fort Mims and promising to bring in others and any other prisoners they could. Two months later, troops under Lieutenant Colonel Thomas H. Benton descended the Alabama River from Fort Jackson to Fort Claiborne, capturing more Indians and blacks on the way.[27]

Some Red Sticks neither lost their property nor were exiled. William Weatherford, for example, gave Jackson the uncorroborated story that when he saw that the Indians would not be controlled at Fort Mims, he left the fighting before the butchery began and went ten miles away to the plantation of his half brother David Tate, where he hid Tate's blacks in the cane brakes to prevent the Red Sticks from carrying them off. Weatherford threw himself on Jackson's mercy, maintaining that he had actually tried to prevent hostilities, and Jackson released him. After the war Weatherford settled on the east side of the Alabama near Little River in lower Monroe County, Alabama, where he had a good farm and worked about forty slaves.[28]

Jackson's policy of capturing the Red Sticks' blacks was probably aimed more at reducing the laboring class among the Indians and at removing a source of ready cash that could be converted into Spanish munitions than at preventing the blacks from joining the Red Stick fighting force. Despite some later charges, the Battle of Holy Ground was apparently the only battle in which Creeks had used blacks as warriors. Kinnie Hadjo, a Creek warrior who had been in the battle, years later criticized the Red Sticks for having done so, saying that the Indians had compromised the Nation's dignity by using "such a servile and degraded race" in the fighting. The act, he said, exasperated the whites and increased "the bitterness of their prejudices against the Creeks."[29] However, the Red Sticks who sought refuge in Florida and carried on their warfare against the Americans would find themselves in subsequent years with blacks as comrades in arms.

By the time of the Red Stick War, a close military relationship between the Seminoles and blacks had already developed. As the work of Kenneth Wiggins Porter has shown, slavery among the Seminoles had taken a different direction from that among the Creeks, in part because of the exigencies of political intrigue and war on the Florida frontier during the decades following the Revolutionary War. However, in a recent study which attempts to synthesize the evidence on African slavery among the Indians, William G. McLoughlin finds that explanation incomplete regarding the freedom allowed the Seminole blacks. The blacks among the Indians were, after all, still slaves and not equals, he says. McLoughlin theorizes that the Indians insisted on distinctions between themselves and blacks on the basis of "racial prejudice or racism" acquired during the Indians' struggle to maintain their identities, through adaptation in agricultural practices, and through the influence of slaveholding missionaries.[30] However, McLoughlin presents little evidence relating to the Seminoles and turns his attention to other tribes, particularly the Cherokees.

While McLoughlin's theory may be somewhat applicable to the Seminoles of the mid-nineteenth century, there is little evidence that it applies before their removal to the West. During that time, rather, the relationship between Seminoles and blacks seems to have been based in great measure, as Porter says, on political and military expediency. Established among the Seminoles at the time they were emerging as a separate tribal entity, the institution of slavery was shaped by the same international pressures that William Sturdevant says established the tribe.[31] Encouraged in their distrust of the Americans by both the British and the Spanish, the Florida Indians and their blacks found themselves taking the warpath together against a common enemy during the second decade of the nineteenth century. The role of comrades in arms with their Indian masters, in turn, shaped the institution of slavery as it was practiced among the Seminoles, and it had a direct bearing upon the future of the Red Sticks who escaped to the Seminoles.

The first significant military alliance of Seminoles and blacks occurred during the so-called Patriot War of 1812, when American settlers in Spanish East Florida revolted and attempted to annex the territory to the United States. Participation of Seminoles and their blacks in the resulting battles and skirmishes has been well documented.[32] The war made two points clear: the blacks were formidable warriors, and by 1812 there was a close alliance between some Seminole bands and number of blacks who lived near them in separate towns and fought when the Indians called them into service. It also became apparent to southern slaveholders that the black settlements in the Seminole country and elsewhere in Florida represented a threat to slavery in the nearby states. American forces assisting the Patriots had penetrated the Alachua country early in 1813, destroying the settlements, including one black town. Thus, when the Red Sticks arrived in Florida, they found a military alliance between the Seminoles and blacks, an alliance which they would soon join.

Not considering themselves a part of the Creek confederacy, most of the Seminoles had remained neutral during the Red Stick War. In 1813 the Mikasuki had tried to join the Red Sticks but were prevented from doing so by the Lower Creeks. While for the most part the war had not affected them, the peace did. The Treaty of Fort Jackson ceded lands on the Chattahoochee and Flint rivers "near the heart of the Seminole Nation."[33] Seminole distrust of the Americans was encouraged by the British who had begun operating actively in Florida shortly after the Battle of Horseshoe Bend. They began immediately to develop a coalition force of Seminoles, blacks, and refugee Red Sticks to carry on their war against the Americans.

Early in the War of 1812, British military officials felt that it would be necessary to undertake diversionary tactics in the south to take pressure from the British in the north. In September 1813, a British ship arrived at Pensacola, and the captain met with a delegation of Creeks and Seminoles who asked for British arms and personnel to train them for war against the Americans. In April 1814, Captain Hugh Pigot was sent to Florida. Near Pensacola he found about nine hundred starving and unarmed Red Sticks, who had fled to the area after the Battle of Horseshoe Bend. Pigot also found the Indians at Apalachicola short of supplies and realized that supplying the Indians with provisions was necessary if they were to be useful as an ally. Before leaving Florida, Pigot appointed George Woodbine as agent to the Creeks. Woodbine made the Apalachicola River the center of his activities, an act which Americans viewed as an attempt to revive the Red Stick War by arming the Indians and blacks.[34]

The friendly Creeks, too, were suspicious of British motives. Big Warrior claimed that the British had three hundred of the Creek Nation's blacks under arms on the Apalachicola and that more were running away. In August 1814 he reported that a black named March and one from the Stidham plantation had run away to Florida and then returned to the

Nation, stealing two black women from the Hardridge farm and fourteen blacks from the Stidham farm and carrying them to the British. Big
Warrior believed that the British had not come to be the Indians' friend
but had come instead for the blacks. Lower Creek head man William
McIntosh suggested that he head a party to go to Florida to find what the
British meant by arming the blacks. Although the Creeks were not at war
with the British, he said, they were prepared to return fire if fired upon.[35]

In the summer of 1814, the Seminoles sent a nephew of the Black
Factor, a Creek, as messenger to the Red Sticks near Pensacola, inviting
them to come to the Apalachicola. Black Factor told them to lie still
and do nothing until everything was ready and the order was given to
strike. He told them that the British had brought "plenty of guns," had
landed some soldiers, and had gone after black troops from the Islands.
Upon their return, all would be ready. Woodbine had been authorized
to feed the Red Sticks, and under his direction they were drilled and
trained in the use of the bayonet. However, despite the promises, he was
limited by a lack of weapons to put in their hands.[36]

On the Apalachicola, Woodbine found support in Thomas Perryman,
whose village was on the Chattahoochee. Woodbine and Perryman worked
to persuade Kinhijah (Kinhache), also known as Capichee Micco, of the
Mikasuki no longer to restrain his young men and to make war on the
Americans. Woodbine allegedly offered him $100 for every trader, cow-
keeper, or other American and for every black they captured. Woodbine
obtained an agreement, marked by Perryman for the Seminoles and Capichee Micco for the Mikasuki, in which they agreed to turn over all prisoners to him. Agent Benjamin Hawkins, who charged that the headquarters
of "the encouragers of Mischief" was at Perryman's, reported in November 1814 that ten blacks had arrived there from Pensacola and a hundred
more were expected to join Woodbine. Hawkins believed that Perryman's
town was inside the limits of the United States and urged that something
be done about him.[37]

Later that same month, Hawkins reported that although Capichee Micco
was not unfriendly, he could not govern his young men who were ready
to join the war parties of either the British or the Indians in predatory warfare and who gave "encouragement to the Negroes to run to them." The
Hitchiti towns called Fowl Town and Oketeyoconne, both breakaways
from the Lower Creek towns, were hostile. The inhabitants of Fowl Town
urged the Red Sticks to wage war against the Americans, and, Hawkins

charged, the British offered them bounties for scalps, provided them clothes and munitions, and encouraged them to plunder horses and blacks from the Americans and friendly Indians. Using Perryman's as headquarters, raiding parties had been sent out three times. The first had plundered slaves from the mixed bloods; the second had plundered the plantations of two Georgians and that of Timothy Barnard in the Creek Nation and also took five slaves from Hawkins himself. The third party had been captured near the Creek Agency but had escaped.[38]

In laying plans for their massive attack in the Gulf Coast region, the British had sent Major Edward Nicholls to command their activities in West Florida, where, with Woodbine, he was to raise a force of Indians and runaway blacks to raid the settlements, create panic among the Americans, and lay plans for an attack on New Orleans. Upon his arrival in August 1814, he had taken command of Spanish Pensacola, recruited all of the local blacks, and drilled them and the Indians. By the end of the year, Nicholls had allegedly trained about 3,000 Red Sticks and Seminoles and enlisted four hundred blacks. To the Red Sticks was held out the possibility of returning to the boundaries that existed before 1811 and of ridding their nation of the agent's civilization policy. To the blacks was held out the possibility of free status and of land in Florida or in the British West Indies. And to the Seminoles was held out the prospect of British trade and protection from American encroachment.[39]

The British had mistakenly counted on an alliance with the Creeks in general and had apparently been unaware of the antagonism between the Red Sticks and the Lower Creeks which had created a permanent rupture between them. British support, therefore, rested with the Mikasukis, Alachuas, and refugee Red Sticks, all known generally as the Seminoles, as well as with the blacks.[40]

Convinced that the Americans wanted to annex all of Florida, the Spanish had not resisted the arrival of the British. But now they began to have second thoughts. The British had treated badly the citizens and officials. Nicholls had accused officials of the John Forbes Company of treason, had tried to abduct their slaves, and had moved the Spanish garrison to Apalachicola where some of the men, mostly black troops from Cuba, were used as a labor force.[41] Andrew Jackson gave the Spanish some relief when he captured Pensacola late in 1814.

At Prospect Bluff on the Apalachicola, the British had built a fortification and organized Indian and black troops for forays against the Americans. After the fall of Pensacola and the British failure at New Orleans, Red Stick chiefs McQueen and Francis, Mikasuki chief Capichee Micco, and the head men of the blacks began to doubt the British ability to protect them. But the British convinced these chiefs and others such as Perryman that through negotiation they could regain for the Indians the boundary lines that had existed before 1811. However, the British failed on that count, too, and withdrew, leaving the Apalachicola fort with four heavy pieces of ordnance and ten thousand weight of powder. Their idea was to keep the Indians loyal to England, using the fort as a trading center. Instead of Indians, it was blacks who took command of the fort, which became known as Negro Fort. About four hundred blacks had been trained by the British. At the end of the War of 1812 some sailed away on British ships, having been sent by Nicholls to "the British colonies," where they were to be free settlers and have land given to them. The rest of the blacks remained near the post.[42]

Josiah Francis accompanied Major Nicholls to England in 1815. With three other Red Sticks, he carried a message to the King from thirty Creek chiefs, asking for assistance in preventing starvation. However, the Prophet failed to get the response he wanted from the high officials, who refused to continue any official involvement with the Indians living in the United States, in accordance with the negotiations at Ghent, and Francis soon returned to the United States.[43]

Early in 1816, Indians made a raid near Fort Claiborne, killing two men and stealing several horses and blacks. General Edmund P. Gaines, commanding the United States forces on the border, saw this act as "evidences of unfriendly temper" among the Creeks, who he said would doubtless deny any part in it since it was probably committed by a remnant of the Red Sticks below the Florida line. By this time, the few Indians as well as a few blacks who had been left at Negro Fort had moved eastward, leaving the post to the blacks. About a thousand runaways from the Florida plantations and from Alabama and Georgia sought its protection and settled in the surrounding region while at the Fort from 250 to three hundred blacks were under the command of the black leader Garçon.

Using the fort as a base, blacks and hostile Creeks continued, through alleged "secret practices," to encourage blacks to run away from Georgia and the Cherokee and Creek Nations.[44]

Creek Agent Benjamin Hawkins was convinced that something must be done soon or Georgia would "be dispoiled of all their negros on their frontiers." He called a meeting of the Upper and Lower Creeks on March 29, 1816, and suggested that the Creeks apprehend and deliver the run-away slaves in the Floridas, insisting that the Muscogees were the rightful owners of the lands there and could and should catch the slaves. Urged by Hawkins' offer of a fifty-dollar reward for each one delivered, they were willing to go, and Little Prince went to the Seminoles and asked their cooperation. The Creeks were concerned about the build-up of American troops on the frontier and about the public agitation for them to cross the line into Florida. Hawkins argued that the Creeks had stood by while an enemy foreign power (the British) had built the fort and gar-risoned it with blacks belonging to the people of the United States. If the fort had been made without Creek consent, then why was it permitted to remain? Hawkins asked, If the Creeks' enemies took possession of Florida for hostile purposes, could the Creeks blame their friends for taking possession of it for friendly purposes?[45]

General Jackson believed that if the people at the fort harbored blacks belonging to United States citizens or to friendly Indians or encouraged slaves to desert their masters, the fort must be destroyed. He ordered General Gaines to investigate: "I have very little doubt of the fact that this fort has been established by some villains for the purpose of mur-der rapine and plunder and that it ought to be blown up regardless of the ground it stands on and. . . if your mind should have formed the same conclusion, destroy it and restore the stolen negroes and property to their rightful owners."[46] Jackson asked the Spanish commandant at Pensacola to have the Negro Fort destroyed and to return to the Ameri-cans and friendly Indians the blacks harbored there.[47]

By summer of 1816, the blacks at Negro Fort had extensive fields under cultivation and were allegedly committing depredations in the surrounding area. There was another large settlement of blacks at the mouth of the Suwannee. American slave owners demanded the destruc-tion of the post, and military officials were apparently looking for an excuse to carry out their wishes because supplies for American forts were transported up the Apalachicola. In mid-July 1816, an American boat's crew was ambushed by Indians and blacks, and on July 27, Ameri-can forces and a group of Lower Creeks under William McIntosh leveled the fort, killed 270, captured 64 of its inhabitants, and executed Garçon. Survivors fled eastward and joined the blacks and Seminoles on the Suwannee, where the latter had fled after the Alachua towns had been destroyed in 1813. In their villages on the Suwannee and along the coast south to Tampa Bay, the blacks prepared to retaliate for destruction of Negro Fort.[48]

When the Creeks invaded Florida to destroy the Fort, Peter McQueen and his Red Stick followers raised arms to go against them, but when they found that the fort had been destroyed, they scattered. McIntosh and the Creeks brought the captured blacks up to Fort Mitchell and sold some of them as war prizes to various people. Others, the property of Creeks, were apparently appropriated by McIntosh himself and not returned to the owners. These captives were the source of several slave claims in the Creek Nation during the following decade.[49]

Indian and black hostilities were to prove useful to British adventurers. The belief by some that Britain might possibly acquire Florida fostered land schemes in the minds of Nicholls and others and protracted British presence in Florida. Woodbine, for instance, with his cohort Robert Ambrister, developed a scheme for using the Florida Indians and blacks to establish an independent Florida. Bahamian trader Alexander Arbuthnot combined land schemes with one to monopolize trade with the Red Sticks, Seminoles, and blacks. He arrived at Suwannee early in 1817 with a shipload of munitions and supplies, and Woodbine arrived in the Apalachicola area. In February, Woodbine's arrival was duly noted by the Americans, who learned that he had left his agent among the Indians and blacks to stir them up "to acts of hostility" against the country while he returned to the West Indies for supplies. A recent raid by the Indians into Wayne County, Georgia had convinced the governor of that state of what the Indians and blacks would do when they received supplies.[50]

Later that month reports came from Fowl Town, east of Fort Scott near the Florida boundary, that there were many stolen horses, cattle, and hogs from Georgia in the village. Its inhabitants, informants said, "speak in the most contemptuous manner of the Americans, and threaten to have satisfaction for what has been done—meaning the destruction of the negro fort." Another informant from the Suwannee towns alleged to have seen six hundred armed blacks on parade there. They had chosen officers and were going through military drills. There were supposedly a like number of Indians. Their numbers swelled daily, it was reported, and they were eager for an engagement with either the Americans or with McIntosh's Lower Creeks, whom they pledged to give something more than they had received

at Negro Fort. Peter McQueen was reported as one of the heads of the
"hostiles," who were anxious for war. Bowlegs was recognized as chief,
except for one or two renegade chiefs, one of whom was Capichee Micco,
and the blacks had chosen Nero, Bowlegs' slave, as their commander.[51]

While Woodbine was sometimes out of the territory, Robert C. Ambrister, his agent, remained among the blacks, supporting them and urging them to stand their ground before the Americans or "be driven into
the sea." He assumed Nero's task of drilling the black warriors and replaced Arbuthnot as an adviser to Bowlegs.[52]

Fowl Town was the site of the first clash between American troops and
the Florida Indians. Hostile since the war, Fowl Town was apparently a
receiving point for property stolen in Georgia. In the fall of 1817, head
man Neamathla, a Red Stick, warned the Americans not to cross to the
east side of the Flint, claiming the land was his. General Gaines sent 250
troops under Major David Twiggs to bring the chief and warriors to Fort
Scott. A fight ensued, several Indians were killed, many were wounded,
and the town was burned. The attack was approved of by Secretary of
War John C. Calhoun and by the president, who hoped the show of force
would dissuade the Indians from further depredations. However, Calhoun gave General Gaines discretionary authority to cross the line into
Florida if the Indians persisted in hostilities, unless they took shelter
under a Spanish fort.[53]

In retaliation for the Fowl Town fight, on November 30, the Indians
ambushed an American boat on the Apalachicola, killing thirty-five of its
occupants, and Indians and blacks laid seige to five other boats which
were finally rescued. On December 13, Indians from Fowl Town captured
two agents of Forbes & Company and took them to the black towns on
the Suwannee where they were charged with complicity in the destruction of Negro Fort. They were tried, but before punishment could be
meted out Nero intervened on their behalf. The border war continued as
the Indians raided plantations, killed settlers, and stole livestock and
blacks.[54]

General Gaines was replaced by Andrew Jackson. Once more the Red
Sticks faced their old enemy. The size of Jackson's enemy varied according to the observer. Friendly Indians estimated the number of
Seminole and Red Stick warriors at more than two thousand and the
blacks at nearly four hundred, their numbers increasing daily. Another
estimate set the number of blacks and Indians at eight hundred to twelve

hundred. Jackson arrived in Florida in March 1818 with a force of 3,300 of whom 1,500 were friendly Creeks. While his Tennessee volunteers and Creeks under McIntosh were destroying Mikasuki, where they killed Capichee Micco, Jackson captured St. Marks where he had heard were Red Sticks Peter McQueen and Josiah Francis as well as Woodbine and Arbuthnot, whom he later tried and executed. Jackson's next objective was Bowlegs's town and the black settlements on the Suwannee. Warned by Arbuthnot, the Indians withdrew, leaving the major part of the fighting to the blacks under Nero. Some two or three hundred held off Jackson's force at the black settlements on the west side of the Suwannee while the rest made their escape. The Indian and black towns were burned, and Ambrister was captured and later executed. Jackson then returned to Pensacola, captured it, and, leaving it occupied, returned home.[55] Thus ended the First Seminole War.

Jackson's invasion had not only effectively pushed the Indians and enclaves of blacks farther from the borders of the United States, but it also led to the annexation of Florida. Jackson had marched across Spanish territory and waged war on it without opposition from Spain. A cession treaty was signed with Spain in 1819, and the transfer took place in 1821. Once inside the confines of the United States, the Seminoles, Red Sticks, and blacks, whose destinies were inalterably intertwined, faced an uncertain future. Demoralized by Jackson's invasion, impoverished by the loss of stores, crops, and property, and faced with reestablishing their settlements, they watched helplessly as the Americans entered Florida, opening plantations and restricting the bounds of Seminole lands.

After the Florida cession, the Americans at once began to ponder the disposition of the Seminoles. There was some agitation to remove them. The obvious solution was to send them back to the Creeks, although, of course, the Seminoles would resist. They had broken completely with the Creeks, whom they distrusted and whom the Red Sticks particularly hated. The alternative was to confine them to a smaller area. A treaty council at Moultrie Creek in September 1823 resulted in a treaty that provided for removal of the Seminoles to a reservation in the central part of the Florida peninsula.[56]

The treaty was significant in Seminole affairs because it was the first treaty the United States had negotiated with the Seminoles as a separate tribe. Georgia negotiators had always insisted that the Seminoles were part of the Creek Nation. American negotiators were doing likewise, even during the negotiations of the Moultrie Creek treaty.[57] The Treaty of Moultrie Creek effectively recognized a distinction between the Creeks and Seminoles. In subsequent years, American officials would try to negotiate a reunion of the two tribes, but they would not succeed for over three decades, and then the old hostilities would prevent the union from succeeding.

The destiny of the Red Sticks now lay with the Seminoles. In 1818 Jackson had ordered many of the Red Sticks back to the Creek country. He insisted that they had no claim to Florida lands and could live peaceably among the Creeks. But their hatred for the Creeks was now too great. They had lost their civil war and had been forced to flee their homes and live in destitution. Early in 1817, for instance, Arbuthnot had written to the commanding officer at Fort Gaines on the behalf of Peter McQueen, asking for the return of McQueen's slaves. One of his blacks, Joe, had been taken away from him after the Red Stick War and was supposedly at Fort Gaines. Ten of his grown blacks had been seized by Barney, a half-blood, who sold nine and kept one girl. James Cornell had taken twenty of McQueen's "able negroes." If they could be persuaded to give up the blacks, McQueen wanted them put in the care of a "faithful" black named Charles, who would taken them to McQueen on the Oklochnee River. Antagonism had been increased when the Red Sticks raided the Creeks and the Creeks sent slaving expeditions among them, and they could not forget that the Lower Creeks had waged war upon them. In 1818, McIntosh's Creeks under Jackson's command had fought two hundred Red Sticks under Peter McQueen at Econfina, killing thirty-seven, and capturing nearly a hundred women and children. McIntosh's warriors had also captured blacks during this campaign. Secretary Calhoun wanted them held at Fort Gadsden to avoid the speculation that might arise if they were taken to the Creek country. Some were delivered to their owners, but others were retained by the Creeks.[58]

Because of the exigencies of their condition since 1813, the Red Sticks had often found themselves in military alliance with blacks. As a result of the close relationship, they developed, like the Seminoles, a much laxer system of African slavery than the Creeks proper would allow. Thus, the political and social odds were too great for peaceful reunification with the Creeks, a reunion which the Red Sticks opposed during the next several decades.

The Creeks made their attitude toward the Florida Indians clear in early 1819. They blamed the First Seminole War on the Red Sticks and the British. The Seminoles, whom the Creeks considered only the inhabitants of Bowlegs' town, were blameless and, according to the Creeks, "never fired a gun at us all the war." The real enemies of the United States were McQueen, Francis, and others who had fled to Florida during the Creek War. The Creeks blamed the British for having left arms, ammunition, and fortifications for the Red Sticks and runaway blacks and accused Arbuthnot of raising them "to do mischief." The Creeks rejected the government's idea of returning the Red Sticks to the Creek Nation on an equal basis: "You are going to take all our land in Florida & going to throw all these people back in our nation, we think that is hard that you should take all our land, the old enemy take all our negroes and now you want to send them back all in to our nation. We think this will be imposing upon us very much."[59]

As a result of the First Seminole War, the Red Sticks migrated to the Tampa Bay region. At the negotiations at Moultrie Creek the Red Stick chief Neamathla insisted that the Seminoles considered the Red Sticks as part of their tribe. When the Second Seminole War broke out in 1835, some of the leading war spirits were Red Sticks, among the most notable of whom were Jumper (Ote Emathla) and Osceola, a great-grandson of James McQueen, the Creek trader.[60] By that time there was no doubt about their amalgamation into the Seminoles. That amalgamation was the source of conflict between the Seminoles and the Creeks, especially regarding slave claims and slave issues, during the post-removal decades of the 1840s and 1850s.

NOTES

1. For typical claims see Benjamin Hawkins, *Letters of Benjamin Hawkins, 1796-1806,* Collections of the Georgia Historical Society, vol. 9 (Savannah: The Morning News, 1916), pp. 174, 175, 194, 200, 203, 204, 215, 216, 228, 233, 242, 260, 263-64, 267, 270; hereafter cited as *Letters.*

2. Merritt B. Pound, *Benjamin Hawkins—Indian Agent* (Athens: University of Georgia Press, 1951), pp. 174-75; Hawkins, *Letters,* pp. 242, 314, 315, 320, 325, 327, 331, 332, 333, 334, 335.

3. Cusetuh King et al. to Mad Dog and Other Chiefs, September 26, 1801, National Archives Microfilm Publications, *Microcopy M271* (Letters Received Relating to Indian Affairs, 1800-1823) 1: frame 46 (hereafter cited as *M271,* followed by the roll number); Charles J. Kappler, comp. and ed., *Indian Affairs:*

Laws and Treaties, 2nd ed., 4 vols. (Washington, D.C.: Government Printing Office, 1904), 2:58-59; Pound, pp. 174, 183, 186-87; Hawkins, *Letters,* p. 439.

4. Pound, pp. 175, 187, 188.

5. Indian Talk, May 15, 1811, and Benjamin Hawkins to William Armstrong, April 26, 1813, *M271-2*: frames 753, 765; Pound, pp. 208-10; Arthur H. Hall, "The Red Stick War: Creek Indian Affairs during the War of 1812," *The Chronicles of Oklahoma* 12 (September 1934), 266, 270, 272-74; R. S. Cotterill, *The Southern Indians: The Story of the Civilized Tribes before Removal* (Norman:University of Oklahoma Press, 1954), p. 177; Secretary of War to Hawkins, July 20, 1811, National Archives Microfilm Publications, *Microcopy M15* (Letters Sent Relating to Indian Affairs, 1800-1824) 3: 90, hereafter cited as *M15,* followed by the roll number.

6. Secretary of War to Hawkins, June 22, 1812, *M15-3*: 137; Cotterill, pp. 176-77, 178-80; Pound, pp. 223-25, 227; H. S. Halbert and T. H. Ball, *The Creek War of 1813 and 1814* (Chicago: Donohue & Henneberry, 1895; reprint ed., Frank L. Owsley, Jr., ed. University; University of Alabama Press, 1969), p. 93; Hall, pp. 274, 277-78; Hawkins to Armstrong, July 26, 1813, and Hawkins to Secretary of War, August 23, 1813, *American State Papers: Documents, Legislative and Executive of the Congress of the United States, from the First Session of the First to the Third Session of the Thirteenth Congress, Inclusive, Commencing March 3, 1789, and Ending March 3, 1815,* 38 vols. (Washington, D.C.: Gales and Seaton, 1832), Indian Affairs I: 849, 852.

7. Big Warrior to Hawkins, August 14, 1813, and Hawkins to Armstrong, July 20, 1813, *American State Papers,* Indian Affairs 1: 851, 849; Halbert and Ball, pp. 125-26; Cotterill, p. 180; Elizabeth Howard West, "A Prelude to the Creek War of 1813-1814 in a Letter of John Innerarity to James Innerarity," *Florida Historical Quarterly* 18 (April 1940), 247-57.

8. West, pp. 257-58.

9. Halbert and Ball, pp. 28-32, 131; West, pp. 263-64; Pound, p. 228; Cotterill, p. 180; "Burnt Corn Engagement," Battles of the Creek War, file 59, H.S. Halbert Papers, Manuscript Division, Alabama Department of Archives and History, Montgomery.

10. Big Warrior to Hawkins, August 4, 1813, *American State Papers,* Indian Affairs, 1: 851; Kenneth Wiggins Porter, *The Negro on the American Frontier* (New York: Arno Press and The New York Times, 1971), pp. 49, 108; Halbert and Ball, pp. 135-36; John C. Casey to Issac Clarke, July 11, 1838, *House Executive Document 225,* 25th Cong., 3 sess., p. 119; Carolyn Thomas Foreman, "The Brave Major Moniac and the Creek Volunteers," *The Chronicles of Oklahoma* 23 (Summer 1945), 101; Ethan Allen Hitchcock, *A Traveler in Indian Territory: The Journal of Ethan Allen Hitchcock, Late Mjaor-General in the United States Army,* ed. Grant Foreman, (Cedar Rapids, Iowa: The Torch Press, 1930), pp. 151-52.

11. West, p. 263; Halbert and Ball, p. 148; James W. Holland, "Andrew Jackson and the Creek War: Victory at the Horseshoe," *The Alabama Review* 21 (October 1968), 247.

12. Hawkins to General Floyd, September 30, 1813, *American State Papers,*

Indian Affairs 1: 854; Cotterill, p. 180; Halbert and Ball, p. 150; Major Daniel
Beasley to General F. L. Claiborne, August 30, 1813, in James F. Doster, "Let-
ters Relating to the Tragedy at Fort Mims: August-September, 1813," *The Alabama
Review* 14 (October 1961), 282.

Weatherford, the son of Charles Weatherford and Sehoy McGillivray and known
as Red Eagle, died in 1826. Halbert and Ball, p. 173.

13. Hawkins to Secretary of War, Chiefs at Coweta to Hawkins, September 16,
1813, *American State Papers,* Indian Affairs 1: 853; Brig. Gen. James Winchester
to Maj. Gen. Andrew Jackson, December 24, 1814, War of 1813-1814—Winchester
Correspondence, Military Division, Alabama Department of Archives and History,
Montgomery; Porter, pp. 50, 108; Halbert and Ball, pp. 155-56, 158, 161-62; A. B.
Clanton, "Massacre at Fort Mims," *The Meridian Daily News,* September 4, 1890,
in "Reminiscences of Fort Mims and of Caleebe," A. B. Clanton Papers, and Notes
of Dr. Thomas G. Holmes, section 25, "Interesting Notes Upon the History of
Alabama," Albert J. Pickett Papers, Manuscripts Division, Alabama Department of
Archives and History, Montgomery.

14. Halbert and Ball, pp. 157, 160, 174; Porter, p. 50; Cotterill, p. 181; Holland, p. 248; "Fort Mims Massacre," Battles of the Creek War, file 59, H. S. Halbert Papers; Frank L. Owsley, Jr., "The Fort Mimms Massacre," *The Alabama
Review,* 24 (July 1971), 201-02; Capt. J. L. Kennedy to Claiborne, September 9,
1813, section 7, notes of Col. Robert James, section 12, and Notes of Dr. Thomas
G. Holmes, section 25, "Interesting Notes Upon the History of Alabama," Albert
J. Pickett Papers; Doster, p. 283; Chiefs of Coweta to Hawkins, September 16,
1813, and Hawkins to Secretary of War, September 16, 1813, *American State
Papers,* Indian Affairs 1: 853; Marion Elisha Tarvin, "The Muscogees or Creek
Indians, 1519 to 1893," *The Alabama Historical Quarterly* 17 (Fall 1955), 142.

15. Brig. Gen. Thomas Flournoy to Claiborne, October 12, 1813, section 7,
and Notes of John F. H. Claiborne, section 5, "Interesting Notes Upon the History
of Alabama," Albert J. Pickett Papers; William C. C. Claiborne to Colonels of the
Militia, September 8, 1813, in W. C. C. Claiborne, *Official Letter Books of W. C. C.
Claiborne, 1801-1816,* ed. Dunbar Rowland (Jackson: Mississippi State Department of Archives and History, 1917) 6: 265.

16. Deposition of Samuel Moniac, August 2, 1813, section 7, "Interesting
Notes Upon the History of Alabama," Albert J. Pickett Papers; Halbert and Ball,
p. 91.

Samuel Moniac was the son of William Moniac, who had come to the Creek
Nation with a remnant of the Natchez in 1756, and Polly Colbert, a Tuskeegee
woman. Samuel married William Weatherford's sister. J. D. Driesbach, "July 28,
1883—A Short Addenda [sic] to the Paper Furnished by the Writer on June the
28th, 1877," J. D. Driesbach Papers, Alabama Department of Archives and History,
Montgomery.

17. Thereon A. Nunez, Jr., "Creek Nativism and the Creek War of 1813-1814,"
Ethnohistory 5 (Winter 1958-Summer 1959), 1-17.

18. Chiefs at Coweta to Hawkins, September 16, 1813, Hawkins to Secretary
of War, September 16 and 21, 1813, and Hawkins to General Floyd, September 30,

1813, *American State Papers,* Indian Affairs 1: 853, 854; Halbert and Ball, pp. 207-09, 197, xxvn.

19. Notes Furnished by Col. Jeremiah Austill, section 1, "Interesting Notes Upon the History of Alabama," Albert J. Pickett Papers.

20. *Ibid.,* "Jeremiah Austill," *The Alabama Historical Quarterly* 6 (Spring 1944), 83-86; Halbert and Ball, pp. 230-34; Thomas S. Woodward, *Woodward's Reminiscences of the Creek, or Muskogee Indians, Contained in Letters to Friends in Georgia and Alabama* (Montgomery: Barrett & Wimbash, 1859; reprint ed., Mobile: Southern University Press for Graphics, Inc., 1965), p. 95.

21. Secretary of War to Hawkins, July 22, 1813, *M15*-3; 161; Cotterill, pp. 181, 184-85.

22. Halbert and Ball, pp. 244, 246-74, 257, 258; Cotterill, p. 185; Porter, pp. 108-09.

23. Pound, pp. 233, 235; Cotterill, p. 187; John K. Mahon, "British Strategy and Southern Indians: War of 1812," *Florida Historical Quarterly* 44 (April 1966), 287.

24. Mr. Byrne's Account of His Father's Death, section 20, "Interesting Notes Upon the History of Alabama," Albert J. Pickett Papers.

25. Kappler, 2: 107-10.

26. Cotterill, p. 188; Kappler, 2: 109-10.

27. Robert Arbuthnot to Officer Commanding Fort Gaines, March 3, 1817, *American State Papers,* Indian Affairs, 2: 156; Andrew Jackson to Leroy Pope, Ocrober 31, 1813, David Smith to Jackson, April 4, 1814, Jackson to Willie Blount, April 18, 1814, and Jackson to David Holmes, April 18, 1814, in *Correspondence of Andrew Jackson,* 7 vols., ed. John Spencer Basset (Washington, D.C.: Carnegie Institute, 1926; reprint ed., New York: Krause Reprint Co., 1969), 1: 339, 472n, 495, 503, 504-05, and Holmes to Jackson, June 19, 1814, *Correspondence of Andrew Jackson* 2: 8; Notes of Thomas G. Holmes, section 25, "Interesting Notes Upon the History of Alabama," Albert J. Pickett Papers.

28. Halbert and Ball, pp. 284-85; Dreisback, "Papers Presented to Alabama Historical Society—Subject, Indians, 1877-1883," J. D. Driesbach Papers; Notes of Robert James, section 12, "Interesting Notes Upon the History of Alabama," Albert J. Pickett Papers.

29. Halbert and Ball, pp. 258-59.

30. William G. McLoughlin, "Red Indians, Black Slavery and White Racism: America's Slaveholding Indians," *American Quarterly* 24 (October 1974), 370-79.

31. William C. Sturdevant, "Creek into Seminole," in *North American Indians in Historical Perspective,* eds. Eleanor Burke Leacock and Nancy Oesterich Lurie (New York: Random House, 1971), pp. 93-105.

32. Authoritative treatment of the war appears in Porter, pp. 183-203; see also Charles H. Coe, *Red Patriots: The Story of the Seminoles* (Cincinnati: Editor Publishing Company, 1898; reprint ed., Gainesville: University Presses of Florida, 1974), pp. 11-13, and Robert L. Anderson, "The End of an Idyll," *Florida Historical Quarterly* 42 (July 1963), 37-39.

33. J. Leitch Wright, Jr., "A Note on the First Seminole War as Seen by the

Indians, Negroes, and Their British Advisers," *Journal of Southern History* 34 (November 1968), 567, 569; Cotterill, p. 184.

34. Mahon, pp. 285, 287-88; Frank L. Owsley, Jr., "British and Indian Activities in Spanish West Florida During the War of 1812," *Florida Historical Quarterly* 46 (October 1967), 114-15; Flournoy to Hawkins, June 19, 1814, *American State Papers,* Indian Affairs 1: 859; Holmes to Jackson, June 19, 1814, *Correspondence of Andrew Jackson,* 2: 8.

35. Big Warrior to Hawkins, August 15, 1814, *Correspondence of Andrew Jackson,* 2: 36n.

36. Statement of John Tarvin, July 5, 1814, "War of 1813-14—Benton and Fort Montgomery," Military Division, Alabama Department of Archives and History, Montgomery; Mahon, pp. 288, 291.

37. Mahon, p. 289; Hawkins to Jackson, November 11, 1814, "War of 1813-1814—Hawkins and Lower Creeks," Military Division, Alabama Department of Archives and History, Montgomery.

38. Hawkins to Major General McIntosh, November 26, 1814, "War of 1813-1814—Hawkins and Lower Creeks."

39. Oswley, "British and Indian Activities in Spanish West Florida," pp. 117, 118; Wright, "A Note on the First Seminole War," pp. 566-67; Hall, p. 289.

40. Mahon, p. 292.

41. Owsley, "British and Indian Activities in Spanish West Florida," pp. 113, 118-19.

42. Wright, "A Note on the First Seminole War," pp. 567-68, 569; Capt. Ferdinand Amelung to Jackson, June 4, 1816, and Lieut. Col. Edward Nicholls to Hawkins, April 2, 1815, *Correspondence of Andrew Jackson,* 2: 242, 208n.

43. Mahon, p. 301; Wright, "A Note on the First Seminole War," pp. 571, 572.

44. Edmond P. Gaines to John Coffee, February 10, 1816, *M271*-1; Porter, pp. 216-17; Amelung to Jackson, June 4, 1816, and William Crawford to Jackson, March 15, 1816, *Correspondence of Andrew Jackson,* 2: 242, 236.

45. Hawkins to Crawford, April 2, 1816, *M271*-1: frame 1125; Anderson, 45-46.

46. Jackson to Gaines, April 8, 1816, *Correspondence of Andrew Jackson,* 2: 238-39.

47. Jackson to Commandant at Pensacola, April 23, 1816, *Correspondence of Andrew Jackson,* 2: 241-42.

48. Authoritative treatment of Negro Fort appears in Porter, pp. 51-52, 215-20; see also, Anderson, pp. 40-47.

49. William McIntosh et al. to Secretary of War, March 9, 1819, *M271*-2: frame 1242; James A. Everett to John H. Eaton, May 25, 1829, National Archives Microfilm Publications, *Microcopy M234* (Office of Indian Affairs, Letters Received) 222: frames 147, 220, 774.

50. Wright, "A Note on the First Seminole War," pp. 570-73; Porter, p. 222; Governor of Georgia to Gaines, February 5, 1817, *American State Papers,* Indian Affairs 2: 155.

51. Lieut. Richard M. Sands to Col. William King, March 15, 1817, and George Perryman to Sands, February 24, 1817, *American State Papers,* Indian Affairs 2:

155; Porter, p. 222. For an authoritative treatment of the First Seminole War, see Porter, pp. 221-36, and Mahon, *History of the Second Seminole War, 1835-1842* (Gainesville: University of Florida Press, 1967), pp. 18-28.

52. Porter, p. 223.

53. Gaines to Jackson, November 21, 1817, *American State Papers,* Indian Affairs 2: 160; John C. Calhoun to Gaines, December 9, 1817, and December 16, 1817, *M15*-4:105, 108.

54. Porter, p. 225.

55. Porter, pp. 224-25; Gaines to Jackson, November 21, 1817, *American State Papers,* Indian Affairs 2: 160.

56. *American State Papers,* Indian Affairs 2: 429-31; Secretary of War to John R. Bell, September 28, 1821, in Clarence Edwin Carter, comp. and ed., *The Territorial Papers of the United States*, 26 vols. (Washington, D.C.: Government Printing Office, 1934-56), 22: 220. An authoritative account of the Moultrie negotiations and events leading to them appears in Mahon, *History of the Second Seminole War,* pp. 29-50.

57. *House Executive Document 91,* 20 Cong., 2 sess., p. 9; Talk of Col. Gadsden, August 6, 1823, *American State Papers,* Indian Affairs 2: 437-38.

58. Mahon, *History of the Second Seminole War,* p. 31; Arbuthnot to Officer Commanding Fort Gaines, March 3, 1817, *American State Papers,* Indian Affairs 2: 156, and *M271*-2; frame 84; Gaines to Jackson, July 10, 1817, *Correspondence of Andrew Jackson,* 2: 305-06; Porter, pp. 228-29; Calhoun to D. B. Mitchell, October 8, 1818, and October 26, 1818, *M15*-4: 220, 222; *House Executive Document 91,* 20 Cong., 2 sess., p. 8.

59. McIntosh et al. to Secretary of War, March 9, 1819, *M271*-2: frame 1242.

60. Porter, p. 233; Mahon, *History of the Second Seminole War,* pp. 28, 45, 127, 91.

chapter **4**

SLAVERY AND
SLAVE CLAIMS

THE TWO DECADES following the Red Stick War were two of the most significant in the history of the Creek Nation. It was a time of great change among the Creeks, marked by factional strife, the cession of Creek lands in exchange for lands west of the Mississippi, harassment of Indians by whites, removal of many Creeks to the Western lands, and frequent slave controversies. It was also a time during which the institution of slavery among the Creeks underwent changes that were to become a source of conflict between them and the Seminoles in the trans-Mississippi West.

Despite attempts by the government to "civilize" the Creeks, they had no written laws until 1818, when William McIntosh and other Lower Creek chiefs wrote down a code of eleven laws. Included was one relating to blacks: "This agreed, that if a Negro kill an Indian, the Negro shall suffer death. And if an Indian Kill a Negro he shall pay the owner to [sic] the value."[1]

This code suggests that Lower Creeks were changing rapidly regarding slavery. Less than a decade later, they had a slave code much more restrictive than any code the neighboring Seminoles ever adopted. In early 1825, at the request of Governor George M. Troup of Georgia, Chilly McIntosh, son of William McIntosh and cousin to the governor, wrote down the laws of the Creek Nation. According to the McIntosh manuscript, the 1818 law was repeated: a black suffered death for killing an Indian or another slave. If an Indian killed a black, he must pay the owner his value or suffer death. The law provided for the emancipation of blacks by their owners, the freed black to be "considered a freeman by the Nation," and relieved owners of any obligation "for any trade or bargain" made by their slaves. The law also provided for a reward of fifteen dollars for capturing runaway slaves and carrying them to the persons appointed by the Nation to receive them.[2]

Amalgamation of the races, which had existed from the beginning, was now discouraged. In 1787, Alexander McGillivray encouraged his brother-in-law Benjamin Durant to sell "a likely young Negro man," who had "an Indian wench his wife." Durant himself was described by Benjamin Hawkins as "a little mixed with African blood." Jim Boy, the warrior and chief of Burnt Corn fame, was supposedly part African. How much the Creeks disliked amalgamation during the early decades of slavery is uncertain, but by the time Chilly McIntosh recorded the Creek laws in 1825, there was evidence of growing racial prejudice, at least among the Lower Creeks. Law 20 reads, "If any of our people have children and Negroes and either of the children should take a Negro as a husband or wife—and should said child have a property given to it by his parent the property shall be taken from them and divided among the rest of the children as it is a disgrace to our Nation for our people to marry a Negro."[3]

An interesting case of amalgamation was that of Mary Ann Battis, born in the Creek Nation about 1810. Her mother was the offspring of a black woman and a half-white, half-Indian man. Mary Ann's father was white. She was very fair, yet her family was "extremely dark," her mother having had other children by blacks. Mary Ann began attending Asbury Mission school shortly after it opened, and she became educated. In 1827, her family wanted her to leave the mission and go home with them, but she persuaded them to allow her to go to Milledgeville, Georgia, with the missionaries. Upon her return to the Nation a year later, her family took her home with them. When the Creeks began to emigrate to the West, her family planned to go, and Mary Ann returned to the mission to seek asylum so she would not have to accompany her family. It is apparent from the account of the incident by Mrs. Jane E. Hill of the mission family that at least in her opinion the contrast in complexion between Mary Ann and her family was too great and that color consciousness was basic to her rejection of her family. David Brearley, agent to the McIntosh faction of Creeks, saw the incident in a different light. He believed that Mary Ann resisted her family's overtures because the Hills were anxious about her possible removal and that out of their company she would even favor removal to the West. He charged the Hills with

trying to thwart his efforts to remove the Indians to the West, for if
they could conquer the mother's desire to emigrate, they would prevent
a number of families from going.[4] It may be, if Brearley was right, that
Mary Ann was not concerned about color but that stressing color consciousness was a way of the Hills to keep the family separated.

Whereas blacks were at first apparently allowed to accumulate property as were those among the Seminoles, and Creeks now began to put
restrictions on such property. Chilly McIntosh's Law 21 reads: "Slave
shall not raise property of any kind. If the master does not take it from
them the law makers shall and they may do as they please with the
property." However, some slaves apparently continued to accumulate
property, for in 1825, the Creeks confiscated property of blacks belonging to General William McIntosh, Samuel Hawkins, Sally Hawkins, Louisa
McIntosh, and Elizabeth Grierson. Those blacks were later reimbursed
for their losses.[5]

There was also a growing dislike for preaching Christianity to the blacks
and for their assembling, although there was no law against it. In the
spring of 1828, for instance, it was rumored that Tuskeneehau objected
to slaves' meeting, as had become the occasional practice, for religious
services with Lee Compere, a Baptist missionary, on the road at With-
ington Station near Tuckabahchee. It was also rumored that Tuskeneehau
had ordered the blacks' meetings broken up, but upon being asked about
it the chief denied the rumor. In May, upon the orders of Opothleyohola,
the recognized leader of the Upper Creeks, twenty-five to thirty Indians
broke into Compere's home while he was away and interrupted his family
and several blacks in Sabbath services. They searched every room, tossed
the beds about, and overturned the furniture. They seized the blacks,
tied them, led them into the yard one by one, tied them to a post, and
whipped them. One was a twelve-year-old girl whom they tied, compelled to watch the whippings, and then, in Compere's words, "led her
like the rest to the fatal post deliberately turned up her clothes, tied
them fast around her neck & in addition to the beating she had to undergo from such merciless hands was compelled to bear the licentious exam-
inations of that band of ruffins [sic]."[6]

Angered, Compere confronted the Creeks. Opothleyohola assured him
that as an individual he had no objections to the blacks' meetings at
Compere's. Neither did Yargee, who owned most of them, but Yargee

claimed that Tuskeneehau had objections. Compere went to the Tuck-abahchee square and demanded to know on whose authority the Indians had acted, vowing to seek redress through the Indian Department. He was so concerned about Creek opposition to religious instruction that he considered giving up his mission and going west to serve the parties of Creeks who had emigrated.[7]

The Upper Creek chiefs did not give Compere a reason for forbidding the preaching of Christianity, probably because they believed that they owed no explanation. Whatever the reason, their dislike for preaching was maintained after they removed to the West. Events there indicate that the dislike was not based in fear of abolitionism, although that was the apparently baseless charge, but rather in jealousy of power. Tribal power had been severely weakened by the Red Stick War, and efforts to remove the Creeks threatened it even more. Both before and after removal it was characteristic of the Upper Creek chiefs to resist any inroad upon their control over the people. That resistance, perhaps, explains their concerns about preaching.

Although laws and social practices regarding blacks had grown severer in some parts of the Creek Nation following the Red Stick War, vestiges of the old Creek life still existed. In 1820, Adam Hodgson noted several neat and flourishing Creek farms. But, he wrote, "my pleasure was alloyed by observing, that the labour generally devolved on either the African negro, or the Indian wife. As few of the Creeks are rich enough to purchase many negroes, all drudgery is performed by the women." A decade later, James Stuart observed, "But Europeans would be surprised to hear that many of these people have large property in slaves and cattle; some of them to the extent of thirty slaves, and great herds of cattle. Still, however, most of the Creeks are fonder of hunting, and amusements of that kind, than of a civilized life."[8] It should be noted, however, that the old ways persisted more intact among the Upper Creeks than among the Lower Creeks.

There were other differences between the groups that emerged as well. The glimpses of slavery presented above indicate that the Lower Creeks wrote down the laws, including the slave code. The Upper Creeks did not write their laws until after removal. The chiefs apparently maintained more personal control of local matters than did the Lower Creek chiefs. In the matter of slave titles, for instance, some of the cases presented below indicate that the Upper chiefs more often intervened in slave controversies than did the Lower chiefs, but like the Seminole chiefs, both the Lower and Upper chiefs sanctioned sales of blacks. Amalgamation appears to have been more common among the Upper than the Lower Creeks, and the breakdown of town structure and the rise of individual farms were more rapid among the Lower Creeks.

Because of geographic location, the Lower Creeks bore the brunt of pressure from the whites. During the preceding forty years, land cessions had greatly reduced their territory, thereby reducing their ability to hunt and forcing changes in their life styles. They strongly felt the need to change in order to get along with the whites, as witnessed by the writing of their laws in 1818. Signed at Broken Arrow by McIntosh, George Lovett, Noble Kinnard, Samuel Hawkins, and Cohause Emauthlau, the endorsement of the laws read: "These are the Laws I have made for my Nation, and have given up our old Laws that our old people had in their old ways. I hope they will raise our Nation and make all our poor people love one another, and love our white Brothers."[9] When it became apparent that the whites would not be placated, the Lower Creeks were the first to cede their lands and agree to remove.

However, the Lower Creeks were under other kinds of pressure that apparently had great influence on their writing a severer slave code than did the Upper Creeks. The most important of these pressures was the large number of blacks with the Indians in Florida. In 1823, there were an estimated 430 blacks among the Indians in Florida, many of them affiliated with former Red Sticks. Of the 105 inhabitants of the village headed by Oponey, formerly of Okmulgee, 40 were black.[10]

The number and militant posture of the Florida blacks were disturbing to white plantation owners in Georgia and Florida. Whites had been disturbed when blacks took the field with the Seminoles in the Patriot War of 1812, and it was largely at the whites' insistence that American forces invaded Florida in 1816, when Jackson destroyed the Seminole and black camps on the Suwannee. Lower Creek warriors were involved in both of these invasions, and it was the lower Creeks who yielded to white pressure to make slaving raids into Florida during the years following the First Seminole War.

The laxity of the slave system and the militancy of the blacks among the Seminoles was in some ways as dangerous to the Lower Creeks as it was to the whites. In September 1827, Seminole Agent Gad Humphreys reported to Acting Governor William M. McCarty of Florida that citizens had applied to him for permission to buy blacks from the Seminoles, but Humphreys was unsure of his authority to grant it. In many cases he felt it an advantage to the Indian to sell because the blacks were too in-dependent of their owners' authority. They were slaves in name only, deciding for themselves when to work and what portion of their produce to give to the master.[11] Humphreys, of course, applied white standards to the Seminoles and ignored the fact that the Indians had allowed the system to develop as it did.

At the time Humphreys was writing, there were several Creek slave owners who had resided for some years in Florida but wanted to return to the Creek Nation. However, they could not prevail upon their slaves to accompany them. The Creeks had repeatedly asked Humphreys to give them liberty to sell the blacks. The Indians claimed the right to sell but could not find buyers because the whites could not obtain permission to buy.[12]

Creeks in the Creek Nation proper, particularly the Lower Creeks, no doubt had difficulty enforcing their slave code because of constant inter-course between the Creeks and the Seminoles. In July 1824, Governor William DuVal of Florida informed the secretary of war that many of the Indians in the St. Marks region were Creeks who had gone to Florida during the preceeding three or four years, and DuVal promised to en-courage as many as he could to return to their own country. Another party of Creeks left the Nation several years earlier and had lived occasional-ly in the settlements in Georgia and Florida. They left the Creek country for Florida in the summer of 1826. During the following December these Creeks committed a murder on the west side of the Oscilla River in Florida, killing a white man, four children, and one black. Governor DuVal called out the militia because he believed discontented Creeks and Indians for-merly of Mikasuki had been "communicating freely" and that they threat-ened to "lay waste the Country." He concluded, "This Outrage is the fore-runner of some Desperate Movement of these restless beings of both Na-tions."[13]

Intercourse between the Creeks and Seminoles resulted in controversies over slaves, but there were other sources of such conflicts as well. Some grew out of the claims of friendly Creeks against the hostiles during the Red Stick War. The terms of peace offered to the Creeks by Major General Pinckney on April 23, 1814, and the preliminary treaty at Fort Jackson the following August had provided for indemnification for losses sustained by the friendly Creeks during the Red Stick War. Claims were taken in 1815 by Benjamin Hawkins' assistant agent, Christian Limbaugh. Some blacks claimed losses. At Cusseta were Harry, Primus, and Jupiter, who belonged to David Carr; at Tuckabahchee was Andrew, who belonged to Big Warrior. At Thlocotchcau were Moses and Tom, apparently free blacks. However, since repayment of blacks was not expressly provided for in the terms of peace, their claims were rejected. In 1817, Congress appropriated $85,000 to pay the friendly Creek claims. Some were liquidated that summer and the following January.[14] However, some cases were not simply settled and dragged on for years, especially those regarding the loss of slaves.

The friendly Creeks had lost many slaves to the Red Sticks who had taken them into Florida. After the destruction of Negro Fort, some were taken to Amelia Island and from there sent to Charleston. In 1817, the heirs of Benjamin Hawkins, who had died the year before, recovered two of Hawkins' blacks there, and the Creeks asked the secretary of war for a letter to assist them in recovering any of theirs that might be in Charleston.[15]

Other cases grew out of the flight of the friendly Creeks from the Nation during the war. Mrs. Hawkins, grandmother of Creek interpreter Sam Hawkins, fled with several of her slaves into the Cherokee Nation, where John Sawry and John Walker, both half-blood Cherokees, took the slaves. After the peace, Andrew Jackson issued an order for their delivery, to which Sawry complied but Walker did not. He sold thirteen, and when the Creeks appealed to Jackson, he referred the case to the War Department; by 1818, when the Creeks raised the issue again, nothing had been done.[16]

Another well-known case was that of Robert Grierson, the Scot who had married into the tribe. In late 1812 or early 1813, to escape the civil strife in the Nation, he moved into Jasper County, Georgia, with from seventy to one hundred slaves. He resided with Henry Walker until after the Treaty of Fort Jackson. Walker asked for payment for the support of Grierson and his blacks, but Grierson considered the services of his slaves to Walker as sufficient pay. Walker sued Grierson in the Superior Court of Jasper County and, in August 1817, won a sizable judgment, but before the case was settled, Grierson had taken the blacks back to the Creek Nation. Walker went before the council and demanded a seizure of enough of Grierson's property to satisfy the judgment, but the chiefs refused. Meanwhile, chief William McIntosh had purchased Walker's right to the judgment, had Grierson's blacks assessed, and seized the following: James, Jenny, and their children Campbell, Rose, and Molly; Robert, Rose, and their child Brister; Ben, Grace, and their child Celia; Tartar, Malinda, and their children Biner, Cloe, and Nancy; Amiter, Abegail; Dicy; Cato. On May 22, 1820, the chiefs approved a bill of sale for these blacks, whom McIntosh willed to his Cherokee wife Susannah and her children.[17]

Before the blacks were seized, however, Grierson complicated the matter by willing some of the contested blacks to his children. In 1817, he willed the following blacks to his daughter Elizabeth: Dy, Molly, Grace, and her child, Rina, Ben, Deana, Luamina, Hope, Nelly, Isaac, Lucy, Daniel, Amitto, Amitto Sr., and Rena, and her children Polly, Lidia, Nero, Dick, and Dan. To his daughter Catharine, Grierson willed James and his wife Venus with their children Sam and Robin; Amanda; Will; Hector; Mary Ann; Abegail, and her children Judy, Kit, and John; Will (second); Dy; and Dan. In 1818, Elizabeth Grierson made a will in which she granted Dick his freedom upon her death. The matter was complicated even further upon Grierson's death when William McIntosh, as commissioner on the part of the Creek Nation and the executor of Grierson's estate, divided Grierson's slaves as follows: To Sandy Grierson went Jim, Eames, Kenty, Die, Sharper, Teener (daughter of Betty), and Hector; to Sally Hawkins went Amato, Hannah, Isaac, and Ben; to Catherine Grierson went Quabner and his wife Mandy; to Thomas Grierson went Quash, Betty his wife, Aaron, and Ireland; to David Grierson's children went Mary Ann and Scott; to Samuel Hawkins went Will; and to McIntosh went Samuel. In 1819, apparently after McIntosh seized his share of Grierson's blacks and had made this division of property, Elizabeth Grierson appointed a white attorney James Bates to recover Dy, Molly, Grace, and her child Rina, Ben, Deana, Luamina, Hope, Nelly, Isaac, Daniel, Amitto, Amitto Sr., Rina, and her children Polly, Lydia, Rose, and Dick, Jr., who had been "taken illegally" from her in the Creek Nation. As will be shown later, the contention regarding the Grierson slaves laid the groundwork for several slave controversies for several years to come. Some of these were among those Elizabeth Grierson claimed as lost in 1825, when the Upper Creeks confiscated the property of the McIntosh faction of Creeks.[18]

One of the most celebrated slave controversies of this period involved Creek agent David B. Mitchell, who was appointed agent on October 3,

1816, following Benjamin Hawkins' death. In late 1817 and early 1818, two groups of blacks directly from Africa were brought to the agency, where they remained for some time. It was generally believed that they had been smuggled into the Creek country from Amelia Island for sale in violation of the federal and Georgia statutes forbidding the importation of slaves for sale. There is evidence to support the belief that Mitchell was somehow involved.

The first to accuse Mitchell was United States Factor Daniel Hughes, who wrote confidentially to Thomas L. McKenney, the head of the Indian Office, that there was "something strangely mysterious" about the agent and his assistants who sometimes numbered four or five. Their object, Hughes thought, was to divert Indian trade from the United States factory and to create a monopoly for themselves. He accused the agent of seizing "a numerous drove of African Negroes" smuggled into the Nation by William Bowen and others and then keeping the blacks at the agency for many weeks while Bowen went to Amelia Island for sixty more. The implication was that the agent and Bowen were in collusion.[19]

General Edmund P. Gaines became concerned that the traffic in such slaves might somehow interfere with the military activities against the Seminoles then in progress along the Florida border. Both he and General Andrew Jackson asked that Mitchell be required to explain the matter. Mitchell, of course, denied that the slaves had anything to do with national policy on the Spanish frontier or that the slaves were for sale and did not violate the federal or state laws.[20]

The blacks had been smuggled into the country by William Bowen, a former employee of Benjamin Hawkins and currently employed by a trading firm in Savannah. Bowen had bought a cargo of African slaves at Amelia Island in the fall of 1817, landed about fifty of them in East Florida, and then sent them overland to the Creek agency. They were put on Mitchell's plantation where houses were built for them and they were put to work. During the next four weeks they were looked after by Bowen and Mitchell. John Oliphant was hired to dole out provisions to them. Then Bowen, Oliphant, and a Creek named Tobler went to Amelia Island where they received about forty more slaves whom they took to East Florida and then up the St. Mary's to Camden County, Georgia. Apparently afraid that he was on the verge of detection, Bowen had a bill of sale executed for forty-two of the slaves in the name of William Love to Tobler. These were then taken to the agency and lodged with the others.[21]

In late January 1818, Mitchell decided to let forty-seven of the blacks go. Besides being convinced that the slaves were not for sale, he said, there was a scarcity of provisions, and their presence became inconvenient. Bowen produced a bill of sale for them and established bond with Jared E. Gross as security. Gross, who was a member of the house of A. Irvin, Gross & Company of Georgia, took the blacks and started through the Creek Nation.[22]

Meanwhile, McQueen McIntosh, Surveyor of Customs for the District of Brunswick, Georgia, had heard about the blacks, decided they had been smuggled into the country, and wanted to seize them. He received assurances from General Gaines that the army would offer him any assistance necessary. When he found that Gross had left the agency with the forty-seven blacks, he pursued them and on February 4 seized the blacks and arrested Gross. One of the men whom McIntosh had engaged to help him went to the agency to warn Mitchell that McIntosh was on his way to seize the others. But Mitchell was en route to Milledgeville, and the agency was in charge of his son William, who sent a desperate letter after his father, informing him of events. By runner, Mitchell sent a letter denying any interest in the blacks and told his son to give them up if they were demanded. McIntosh camped near the agency that night and went to Mitchell's slave houses where he found fifteen Africans. The blacks informed McIntosh and Captain G. W. Melven that on the previous night Mitchell's overseer had supplied a number of blacks with provisions and had taken them out into the woods. McIntosh followed their trail and found fifteen more slaves. They tried to escape but were captured, and the thirty captured in all were taken to the agency where the other forty-seven had been brought by that time. Then William Mitchell told them that there were "a number of small African Negroes" in the slave huts in his father's yard and rounded up eleven more. That brought to eighty-eight the number seized by McIntosh. After McIntosh left the agency, Mitchell came after him saying that three Africans remained at the agency, but McIntosh refused to go back. He returned to Darien and turned the slaves over to his brother W. J. McIntosh, collector for the District of Brunswick, and reported to the secretary of the treasury on March 8, 1818.[23]

The secretary of the treasury found no fault with Agent Mitchell, the attorney general refused to deliver an opinion regarding the blacks, and the State of Georgia seized them. An agent of the governor took them, much to Collector McIntosh's consternation, and the secretary began to suspect that avarice had entered the motives for the seizure. Mitchell, of course, accused both McIntosh and Captain Melven of having expected a portion of the blacks for their efforts. The blacks were apparently distributed to various Georgia citizens who gave bond for their forthcoming. As was general practice, the bond was only a fraction of the value and was given with the idea of forfeiture, a practice which the Georgia legislature sought to stop in late 1818.[24]

In the summer of 1819, the case was revived when William Moore, a long-time white resident of the Creek Nation, charged Mitchell with being "an imposter" guilty of "unlawful and knavish conduct." Governor John Clark of Georgia began collecting evidence to incriminate Mitchell in the slave smuggling case. John Loving of Jackson County testified that in 1817 he had considered purchasing Africans at Amelia Island. He asked Mitchell if he would sanction their being taken through the Indian country. Mitchell allegedly told him that he would, that he had been thinking of doing the same thing himself. However, Loving became convinced that to bring the slaves into Georgia would violate the law and dropped the idea.[25]

Thomas S. Woodward testified that in 1817 he had been asked to go to Amelia Island to buy African slaves but had neither the desire nor the finances to do so and was informed that Mitchell would furnish him the money in return for a percentage of the profits. William Moore also gave testimony in which he confessed to having read Mitchell's private mail and produced a letter from Bowen to Mitchell, incriminating Mitchell in the slave smuggling. When Governor Clark confronted Bowen with the letter, he admitted having written it but denied that Mitchell was ever to have received it. The letter was published in the *Georgia Journal* on November 2, 1819.[26]

In the spring of 1820, additional evidence was taken on both sides amid charges of illegal proceedings. When the case was given to judges of the Sixth Circuit Court at Milledgeville for hearing, they decided that there was no law under which to prosecute. Mitchell took his case to the secretary of war that summer. Attorney General William Wirt refused to render an opinion because he said that the evidence has been irregularly taken and asked that it be taken again, but both sides were reluctant to do so. The president then took the matter in hand, and on February 16, 1821, Secretary of War Calhoun informed Mitchell that the president believed "the charges are substantially established" and dismissed Mitchell from service.[27] Mitchell was replaced by John Crowell.

Other slave controversies of this period grew out of the Georgians' claims for lost property, which had been an issue at one with Georgian demands for land cessions since the early years of the century. Now they asked for more. For several years following the treaty of Fort Jackson, they had left the Creeks alone, apparently satisfied that the United States would carry out its agreement in the Compact of 1802 and remove all Indians from their borders. The Red Sticks, who had constituted the hunting class among the Creeks, were gone, and they no longer foraged along the frontier, thus reducing border antagonism. In late 1818, however, the Georgians revived an old issue when the state legislature passed a resolution giving the governor the authority to appoint a commission of three to go the Creek Nation to demand the return of blacks, horses, cattle, and other property allegedly still held in violation of the treaties of New York and Colerain. A similar commission appointed in 1810 had failed. This time, Governor William Rabun took the issue to Secretary of State John Quincy Adams. By 1820, the Georgians were openly insisting on more land and a fulfillment of the Compact of 1802.[28]

In January of 1820, several Georgians filed claims for the loss of slaves to the Creeks. John Whitehead claimed five blacks—Hector, Dido, Rose, Daphne, and Chloe—taken from his Liberty County plantation in 1789, at which time the Indians killed another slave, Will. Hector and Dido had lived together as man and wife, and in 1820 Whitehead was informed that they had eight children and grandchildren and that they had been taken to Florida at the end of the Red Stick War. Daphne had two daughters with three children each, and they were all at Kinnard's in 1820. Rose had been sold several years earlier to Panton, Leslie & Company. Chloe had two sons, but Whitehead had been unable to learn where they were. He claimed to have tried every means to retrieve them.[29]

William Ball claimed twenty blacks and "several others" he could point out but could not find. Some had been traded into Florida and were at St. Augustine. These blacks descended from ten who had been stolen from Ball's Liberty County plantation in 1788 or 1789, at which time three others had been killed. Through the years he had tried repeatedly to regain them. In 1805, two of them were sent by Benjamin Hawkins to Fort Hawkins, but before Ball could get there, one had escaped back to the Creeks. However, Ball had subsequently been paid for him. His efforts to regain the others had proved fruitless despite Hawkins' frequent promises that they would be returned. In 1818 Ball had learned where fifteen of them were, but Mitchell refused to have them seized, saying that it was up to the government to have them seized or to pay for them. A few months later Ball learned where twenty of the blacks were but had been unable to get them. He urged Governor Clark to push the matter forward, for only two of the old blacks remained alive, and he needed them to identify some of the younger ones.[30]

Finally, William Cabniss applied for help in retrieving his black, Jerry, who had run away to the Creek Nation in 1817. When Cabniss's agent went to Billy McGirt, the Creek who had Jerry, McGirt refused to give him up unless $400 was paid. Cabniss then got a letter from Mitchell saying that the black would be given up for $100, but when Cabniss's agent went for the slave, the Creeks refused to give him up.[31]

It was in response to pressure to settle such claims that in August of 1820, the president appointed a commission to treat with the Creeks. In his instructions to the United States commissioners, Secretary John C. Calhoun informed them that commissioners had been appointed by the State of Georgia to present claims for property of Georgia's citizens under the provisions of the Treaties of New York and Colerain. Calhoun instructed the United States commissioners to give them every aid possible. Disagreement erupted between the two sets of commissioners, and the secretary ordered the United States commissioners to cooperate with the Georgians since the negotiations were being conducted at Georgia's request and for her benefit. The commissioners quit and were replaced by David Meriwether and Daniel M. Forney.[32]

At Indian Springs, Meriwether and Forney addressed the Lower Creeks, the only ones attending, asking them to listen to the Georgia commissioners' complaint. The latter commissioners reminded the Creeks that at Augusta, Galphinton, Shoulderbone, New York, and Colerain, the Creeks had promised to restore all property which had been taken from the Georgians. On December 28, 1820, they laid before the chiefs a statement of the claims of Georgians to property not returned under those treaties.[33]

The Georgia commissioners were answered by General William McIntosh. Unaware that they had been called together to hear such claims against them, the Creeks were taken by surprise. McIntosh had looked over the statement of claims, but "many items" in the account he knew nothing about. He maintained that when McGillivray had returned from New York, he had told the Creeks they were to deliver all prisoners and blacks belonging to whites but that they were not liable for any that were dead or removed. Before the Treaty of Colerain, some of the white and black prisoners were collected, principally from the Upper towns, and delivered to James Seagove, the agent. At Colerain, claims similar to the current one were presented, but the chiefs had refused to acknowledge them except for those items embraced within the Treaty of New York. At the Treaty of Colerain, the chiefs agreed to restore stolen property, and they collected and delivered to Benjamin Hawkins a number of blacks. Never did Hawkins say anything to the chiefs about claims that predated the Treaty of New York as the Georgians were now doing. McIntosh maintained that he had returned and delivered some blacks since he became chief. During the War of 1812, the British had carried off a number of slaves from the Nation and had left some at Negro Fort. When McIntosh and his warriors had helped take the fort, the black prisoners were taken by Colonel D. L. Clinch for return to their owners. There were other blacks with the Seminoles, and McIntosh had joined Jackson's forces and had taken some of the blacks, "which were reported to the United States' agent, and some of them delivered." Some were still with the Seminoles. If the president would admit that the Seminole country belonged to the Creeks, McIntosh said that he would take his warriors down there and bring back and deliver all he could get. McIntosh maintained that the Creeks had complied with the Treaties of New York and Colerain but promised that if any of the blacks still remained in the Nation, he would hunt them out and deliver them or pay for them. He was willing to pay what was just, but, he said, "If two friends, one owe to the other, even individuals, they should not be too hasty in calling for pay, when the debtor is unable to pay."[34]

The Georgia commissioners were disappointed that the Creeks were not disposed to restore the property and blacks allegedly taken or destroyed by the Creeks before the Treaty of New York. They insisted that they knew of or had heard of very few blacks having been returned or paid for, except runaways, while a number had been stolen or otherwise had got into the Nation and had not been accounted for. The Georgians held the Creeks responsible for blacks carried away by the British or killed during the War of 1812. Had the blacks remained in Georgia, they would have been safe, argued the Georgians. It was the Creeks' act which carried the blacks to the scene of war. They insisted on payment not only for the blacks allegedly taken but for their increase and for their use. As for the blacks among the Seminoles, the Georgians considered the Seminoles a part of the Creek Nation and looked to the Creeks for justice. Nevertheless, the Georgians agreed with the Creek request to submit the claims to the president for decision.[35]

In the treaty negotiated at Indian Springs on January 8, 1821, a sum of $250,000 was set aside out of the amount due the Creeks for the land cession to pay in full the claims of Georgians against the Creeks. Forney and Meriwether believed the actual debt would be considerably less. A special commission appointed by President James Monroe audited the claims. They admitted claims under the treaties predating the Treaty of New York and held hearings so distant from the Creeks that the Indians could not appear and make counterclaims. Yet "a considerable balance" of the $250,000 remained after all of the claims were paid. Still the Georgians were not satisfied. They claimed that the Treaty of Indian Springs had been so construed as to exclude some claims against the Creeks, and in 1823 the legislature petitioned the president to admit all claims arising before the Act of 1802. The treaty excluded all claims previous to the Treaty of New York except for slaves and all claims after it and before the Treaty of Colerain except for the property expressly provided to be given up by the latter. The treaty also stipulated that the commissioners of Georgia relinquished all claims "for property taken or destroyed" before the Act of 1802. The Georgia legislature and Governor George M. Troup objected to that construction. As late as 1825 Georgians were still maintaining that the claims were open to settlement.[36]

In response to the Georgia commissioners' demands for the blacks among the Seminoles, in the early summer of 1821 the Lower Creek chiefs authorized a slave-hunting expedition under Captain William Miller to go to the Seminole country and look for runaways. Miller was directed not to plunder the Seminoles or whites, and he later claimed that he did not take from the possession of any white or Indian a single black except one that he took from a British vessel belonging to the celebrated Major Nicholls lying at anchor at Tampa Bay. The blacks he took were acknowledged by the inhabitants of the country to be runaways. In all, the Creeks captured ninety-three blacks.[37]

The Creeks in the expeditionary force knew that some of the blacks belonged to John Innerarity of Forbes and Company at Pensacola and

called at the home of William Hambly in Florida and left them to be giv-
en to Innerarity. But before Hambly could act, half-blood Creek Joseph
Marshall informed the Creek council that Innerarity, as administrator of
the estate of Marshall's father, was deeply indebted to the estate and
that Marshall had no means of forcing a settlement. The council therefore ordered Marshall to take the twelve blacks and hold them until the
estate was settled, and the action was later sanctioned by the secretary
of war. Creek Agent John Crowell informed Innerarity of the secretary's
action and asked him to settle the matter of the estate. Besides these
twelve blacks, nine were delivered to Concharta Micco, one each to white
men Anthony McCulloch and William Hambly, one to Daniel Perryman,
two to John Stedham, and seven to William Kinnard, all Indians. John,
a free black, was set free. The remaining fifty-nine were taken to the
Creek agency, where Crowell suggested that they be held until he could
advertise them to find the owners.[38]

Secretary Calhoun was angry that the chiefs "should seize upon the
very moment" when Florida was about to pass from Spain to the United
States "and when everything was in confusion, to use the superior force
of the Creek Nation over the weakness of the Seminoles, to impose on
and plunder them." Had the Creeks waited, the United States would have
obtained the blacks for them, he said. Crowell was directed to advertise
the blacks and find their owners. After notices in the Georgia and Florida
gazettes, Crowell delivered twenty-nine to agents of Florida residents.
Crowell was then directed to return all of those not claimed to the Creeks
with the understanding that they would be restored to their owners should
they subsequently appear. In the summer of 1823, Crowell reported that
nine blacks had escaped, five more had been delivered to owners, two had
died, four had been set at liberty as free men, and nine remained on hand
in the possession of Indians.[39]

As late as the spring of 1824 a few of the blacks were still unclaimed
by their owners. The blacks acknowledged that they belonged to whites,
and their owners had been notified through advertisements in the papers.
Agent Crowell recommended that the blacks be sold and that the Nation
be held accountable to the owners for the net proceeds. As late as 1826,
the claim of John Innerarity regarding the slaves in Marshall's possession
was still unsettled.[40]

Some slave controversies grew out of the internal strife in the Creek
Nation. William McIntosh of the Lower Creeks cooperated with the

government officials in securing land cessions and laying the groundwork for removal of the Creeks. At his suggestion, in July 1824, the president appointed commissioners to treat with the Creeks for the remaining Creek lands in Georgia. Two months earlier the Creek council at Tuckabahchee, over the dissenting voice of McIntosh alone, had passed a resolution condemning to death any chief who signed away Creek lands. Nevertheless, at Indian Springs on February 12, 1825, the commissioners treated with the Lower Creek head men of eight of the fifty-six Creek towns, who ceded all the Georgia lands and nearly all Upper Creek lands in Alabama in return for an equal number of acres between the Arkansas and Canadian Rivers west of Arkansas. For his assistance, McIntosh was to receive $25,000 for his property upon his emigration to the West. The Senate ratified the treaty, and the Creek council sent out a squad of warriors who killed McIntosh and one of his followers at his residence, burned his home, killed one of his sons-in-law, tried to kill another, and confiscated McIntosh's property and that of his followers. Upon investigation, the president refused to execute the treaty, and a Creek delegation went to Washington where in January 1826 they got the former treaty set aside but in a new treaty ceded nearly all of the Creek lands in Georgia. The tenth article of the treaty provided for investigating and payment of damages sustained by the McIntosh party.[41]

On June 29, 1825, the Creek chiefs had pardoned the McIntosh party and decreed that the property they had with them when they fled the Nation was theirs. The chiefs also decreed that property lost or destroyed contrary to the known laws of the Nation would be restored or paid for by the Nation. The property lost was considerable. McIntosh himself had two plantations. At his principal residence on the Chattahoochee, where he was killed, lived his two wives Susannah and Peggy. At his plantation on the western branch of the Tallapoosa lived his wife Eliza, the daughter of Stephen Hawkins. One of Hawkins' wives was Jenny, McIntosh's daughter. Hawkins had a plantation on the eastern branch of the Tallapoosa and another plantation where another of his wives lived.[42]

Besides a grist mill, a cotton gin, standing crops, household goods, personal property, and large herds of cattle (McIntosh alone had nearly 800 head), hogs, horses, and sheep, the McIntosh party entered claims for the loss of a large number of slaves. Seventy-four belonging to McIntosh alone were confiscated and later claimed by his son Chilly. Samuel Hawkins, McIntosh's brother-in-law who was killed, lost slaves Sam, Renty,

Toney, Robbin, Cate, John, Fanny, Phillis, Polly, Penney, Peggy, Abigail, Peter, Dicey, and Eliza. Louisa McIntosh lost Jehry, Lewis, George, Lucy, Molly, Pagey, Tilday, and Jyanah, a child. Sally Hawkins lost David, Molly, and Billy. Chilly McIntosh was away at his father's plantation when the Creeks collected his blacks and took them to the agent's house. Chilly's wife and sister went to the agent and explained the situation of their crops, and the Creeks released two men and a woman cook to go back home and sent some of the women and children to Osuche town.[43]

Blacks in the McIntosh party also suffered losses. Samuel Hawkins' blacks—John, Phillis, Cato, and Sam—presented claims for losses as did Sally Hawkins' Billy, Louisa McIntosh's Mary, James, Pompey, Toney, Molley, Pajus, and Jeffrey, and Elizabeth Grierson's Venus, Dick, Ben, Quabner, Issac, Nelly, Juda, Abram, and Amritta. A free black named Pompey lost six head of cattle, six hogs, blankets, rifle, musket, tools of various kinds, household goods, farming equipment, saddles, fifty chickens, and other items. Finally, a free black named Dick lost, among other things, a mare, a rifle, twenty cattle, and thirty hogs. The claims for most of the slaves were for personal effects, household items, grain, vegetables, and farming and carpentry tools. However, Samuel Hawkins' John lost a fiddle, and his Cato lost a rifle, a musket, a shot gun, five silver rings, and four silver brooches. Elizabeth Grierson's Juda included in her losses weaving equipment and a large number of poultry; Abram listed poultry and clothing for five children; Amritta claimed two bottles of rum, poultry, ten bushels of rice, beads, eight rings, and ten silver brooches; Venus claimed a spinning wheel, corn, rice, and seed cotton; and Ben listed a "Tommy hawk," a saddle, and clothing for four children.[44]

William McIntosh's blacks were claimed by his son Chilly, who argued that he had the best claim for them. Fifty-four slaves were returned to Benjamin Hawkins and Chilly McIntosh. McIntosh regained all of his own slaves except Amy, who had been "raised in the family from a child, young likely & valuable wench"; Rose, "a large & likely wench"; and Sarah, Rose's daughter, thirteen or fourteen years old. When Samuel Hawkins's slaves were confiscated, the Creeks also took forty head of cattle to feed them with, and two months later, the blacks and half of the cattle were returned to his family. On October 8, 1825, Stephen Hawkins bound himself to the chiefs to keep Sam, Renty, Phillis, Peter, Abagail, Peggy, and John for the benefit of the children of Samuel Hawkins until the children became of age. Liza, who had not been paid for by Samuel, was returned on the condition that Stephen sell her or pay for her out of Samuel's property for the benefit of the children. Hawkins agreed to keep the slaves within the bounds of the Creek Nation until the children could take possession. The others apparently had their slaves returned, for Charles P. Tutt, sent by the government to investigate the claims, did not recommend that they be paid for.[45]

Although the blacks were returned to the McIntosh party by the chiefs, the Nation had accounts against the McIntosh Creeks. One was a note by Benjamin Hawkins promising to make good a purchase of "a parcel of Negroes" from David Bruner. Others were against William McIntosh for property in the amount of $1,500 taken from blacks and appropriated to private use, for blacks taken at Negro Fort, the property of an Indian named Holmes and not accounted for in the amount of $2,400, and for thirty-one blacks brought from Florida and purchased by Daily and Schenche for $1,500.[46]

Charles P. Tutt completed his investigation of the McIntosh party claims in October 1826, and filed the claims with the recommendation that the Creek Nation return or pay for all property lost or destroyed. He also recommended that the Creeks be required to return to Chilly McIntosh the slaves Amy, Rose, and Sarah, if they were still alive, by the first of April, 1827, or to pay him $1,000. Tutt's report was approved by the secretary, and the claims were paid out of the Creek annuity.[47]

In the succeeding months, claims were filed for slaves which McIntosh had allegedly not paid for during his lifetime, and in 1828, one of McIntosh's widows presented Agent John Crowell a claim for "a parcel of Negroes," whom she alleged were taken by the party who executed her husband and had not been returned or paid for. The Nation refused to pay the claim, maintaining that all property taken or destroyed had been returned or paid for out of the Creek annuity, which they considered a final settlement of the McIntosh claims. William McIntosh had acquired title to some of his blacks by virtue of having bought the right of Henry Walker to a judgment in a suit against Robert Grierson. After McIntosh's death Thomas Grayson (Grierson) got possession of the blacks, carried them to Alabama, and instituted suit for title. The court of Montgomery County decreed the blacks the property of Robert Grierson's heirs. The heirs sold them to John G. Ross of the Cherokee Nation, who took them to the Creek Nation west of the Mississippi.[48]

Other slave claims arising in the late 1820s grew out of the First Seminole War nearly a decade earlier. McIntosh's Creek warriors had captured "a considerable number" of blacks belonging to the Seminoles and Red Sticks and had brought them up to Fort Mitchell in the Creek Nation and sold them as war prizes. Among the purchasers was James A. Everett of Fort Valley, Georgia, who kept the blacks only a short time, when they ran off and rejoined the Florida Indians. In 1827, Everett hired an agent to go to Florida to recover the slaves through the Seminole agent. He seemed about to succeed when word came from the governor that titles based on capture would not be recognized. In early 1829, Everett took his claim to the secretary of war. The decision that had stymied Everett's attempts had grown out of a claim by Z. Kingsley for a black woman in the possession of the Seminole Philip, whom the secretary ordered to give up the slave. A related case was the claim in 1828 of John Buck for blacks captured among the Florida Indians but belonging to Benjamin Chaires. Buck was refused title. Thus, when Everett took his claim to Washington in 1829, Commissioner Thomas McKenney asked Secretary P. B. Porter for a decision to deny title by sale to blacks captured specifically in the Seminole war, "and leave the parties to seek their redress in their own descretion through the legal channels."[49]

In 1829, former agent David R. Mitchell presented a claim against Opothleyohola and James Moore, the latter of whom had lived near Fort Mitchell before he removed to the Creek lands west of Arkansas. Moore had bought seven blacks from Mitchell's brother on a note for $1,186.50 on February 22, 1820. Moore did not pay. In 1826 Moore acknowledged his debt to Mitchell and promised to pay, and when he did not Mitchell threatened to have him seized by white authorities. However, Opothleyohola intervened, promising to stand for Moore's debt if he failed to pay. In November 1826, Mitchell appeared at the council at Tuckabahchee, at which time Moore promised to sell eight to nine hundred dollars' worth of cattle, but Opothleyohola this time directed him not to pay. Neither would he give up the blacks. He even called them before Mitchell and told him that there they were, but to touch them would be to risk his life. About the middle of April 1827, Mitchell got a writ from the Alabama circuit court for Moore's appearance, but before the case could be heard, Moore left the Nation. Opothleyohola took the blacks and refused to give them up. In the summer of 1828, Mitchell found that William Walker, who was assisting David Brearley in emigration of the Creeks, had sent Sanco, his wife, and family to a camp near Fort Williams. While they were there Opothleyohola informed Mitchell that he had all bills of sale for the blacks and that Mitchell must come to be paid. However, the blacks were taken by Walker to a place near Gunter's Landing in the Cherokee Nation where Moore was then hiding. In September 1828, Moore paid Richard Fields, a Cherokee, $200 to take the blacks to Arkansas. In February 1829, Walker returned, but at a council Opothleyohola refused to have anything to do with the debt, got angry with Mitchell, and ordered him out of the square. Mitchell then had a writ sworn out for Opothleyohola in Montgomery County, but the chief refused to give security or to be taken out of the Nation and surrounded himself with seventy warriors, saying that he could raise two hundred in a few minutes. Thus Mitchell took his case to Secretary John H. Eaton, asking him to order the agent to force a settlement. Later that year, he took the case to Andrew Jackson.[50] This action got no results. Although Mitchell pursued his claim for several years in the West, he never received satisfaction from Opothleyohola.

In 1832, Moore himself (an intermarried white for thirty years) had slave troubles. About 1829, he had purchased four blacks from Elizabeth Grayson (Grierson) for $1,200, and by natural increase the slaves numbered six. In 1832 a suit for recovery of the blacks was instituted against Moore in the Shelby County, Alabama, circuit court by Benjamin Hawkins. Suits were also instituted by other members of the Hawkins family against others who had purchased blacks formerly belonging to the same estate.[51] This slave controversy was like so many others that followed the Creeks to the West, where they dragged on for years.

The years between the Red Stick War and Creek removal to the West were important in the development of African slavery among the Creeks. It was the time during which they developed their first slave code, which formed the basis for the Creek slave laws until the Civil War. The code was predominantly that of the Lower Creeks who, because they removed early, held dominance in the West over the Upper Creeks, who were greatly weakened by their resistance to removal. During the decades before removal, the Creeks also began to look upon the blacks as property more than ever before. As a result, they became embroiled in slave controversies among themselves and with whites in the neighboring states.

As the pressure for removal increased, slave controversies became more common, and many claims not settled during this period and revived in the West after removal proved a source of difficulty between the Creeks and citizens of the United States. More important, however, were the widening differences between slavery as it was practiced by the Creeks and Seminoles. Those differences became the basis of years of controversy over slavery between the two tribes in the West.

NOTES

1. Code of Laws of the Creek Indians, June 12, 1818, National Archives Microfilm Publications, *Microcopy M271* (Letters Received Relating to Indian Affairs, 1800-1823) 2: frame 771, hereafter cited as *M271*, followed by the roll number.

2. Antonio J. Waring, ed., *Laws of the Creek Nation,* University of Georgia Libraries Miscellaneous Publications, no. 1 (Athens: University of Georgia Press, 1960), pp. 19, 21, 23.

3. Alexander McGillivray to Arturo O'Neill, July 12, 1787, in John Walton Caughey, *McGillivray of the Creeks* (Norman: University of Oklahoma Press, 1938), p. 159; Benjamin Hawkins, *Letters of Benjamin Hawkins, 1796-1806*, Collections of the Georgia Historical Society, Vol. 9 (Savannah: The Morning News, 1916), p. 43; Waring, pp. 20-21.

4. Jane E. Hill to Thomas L. McKenney, May 29, 1828, and Andrew Hamill to Peter B. Porter, September 12, 1828, National Archives Microfilm Publications, *Microcopy M234* (Office of Indian Affairs, Letters Received) 221: frames 84 and 815 (hereafter cited as *M234*, followed by the roll number); David Brearley to Porter, June 27, 1828, *M234*-236: frame 25.

5. Waring, p. 21; Claims of the McIntosh Party, *M234*-220: frames 774-76.

6. Lee Compere to McKenney, May 20, 1828, *M234*-221: frame 703. Compere, a native of Market Harbor, England, was born in 1790. He had been a missionary to the blacks in Jamaica before coming to the Creek country. He died in Texas in 1871. See Carolyn Thomas Foreman, "Lee Compere and the Creek Indians," *The Chronicles of Oklahoma* 42 (Autumn 1964), 291-99.

7. Compere to McKenney, May 20, 1828, and August 15, 1828, *M234*-221: frames 730, 703.

8. Adam Hodgson, *Remarks During a Journey Through North America in the Years 1819, 1820, and 1821 in a Series of Letters* (New York: Samuel Whiting, 1823), p. 269; James Stuart, *Three Years in North America* (Edinburgh: Robert Cadell, 1833), p. 176.

9. Code of Laws of the Creek Indians, June 12, 1818, *M271*-2: frame 771.

10. List of Seminole Towns, Report of Horatio L. Dexter, *M271*-4: frames 507, 513.

11. Gad Humphreys to Acting Governor William McCarty, September 6, 1827, in *The Territorial Papers of the United States,* comp. and ed. Clarence

Edwin Carter, 26 vols. (Washington, D.C.: Government Printing Office, 1934-1956; National Archives, 1958-1962), 23: 911, hereafter cited as *Territorial Papers.*

12. Humphreys to McCarty, September 6, 1827, *Territorial Papers,* 23: 911-12.

13. William DuVal to Secretary of War, July 12, 1824, and December 8, 1826, *Territorial Papers,* 23: 13, 685-86; John Crowell to George M. Troup, December 17, 1826, and DuVal to Troup, December 8, 1826, *M234*-220: frames 594, 614.

14. Christian Limbaugh to Hawkins, August 9, 1815, and Hawkins to William H. Crawford, April 1, 1816, *M271*-1: frames 878, 1115; Hawkins to Kendal Lewis, September 4, 1815, in "Benjamin Hawkins—Kendal Lewis Correspondence."*Alabama Historical Quarterly* 21 (Spring 1959), 9; Extract from Report on Committee of Ways and Means, April 24, 1824, *M234*-219: frame 237; Opothleyohola to Secretary of War, April 24, 1826, and List of Friendly Creek Claims Liquidated at Fort Hawkins, July 1817, *M234*-220: frames 226, 230.

15. William McIntosh and Yohola Micco to Secretary of War, March 15, 1817, *M271*-2: frame 62.

16. McIntosh and Yohola Micco to Secretary of War, March 15, 1817, *M271*-2: frame 62.

17. Statement of John Winslett, April 13, 1832, Bill of Sale, May 22, 1820, *M234*-236: frames 337, 331.

It had been erroneously reported in the summer of 1813 that Grierson had lost seventy-three of his blacks to the hostiles. *American State Papers: Documents, Legislative and Executive of the Congress of the United States, from the First ot the Third Session of the Thirteenth Congress, Inclusive, Commencing March 3, 1789, and Ending March 3, 1815,* 38 vols. (Washington, D.C.: Gales and Seaton, 1832), Indian Affairs 1: 850.

18. Will of Robert Grierson, February 10, 1817, Will of Elizabeth Grierson, August 8, 1819, Statement of Elizabeth Grierson, September 13, 1819, *Records of Conveyance* (Montgomery County, Alabama, Courthouse), Book A-D: 2, 15, 16, 18, 19, 21; Robert Grierson's Estate, section 28, "Interesting Notes Upon the History of Alabama," Manuscripts Division, Alabama State Department of Archives and History, Montgomery; Inventory of Items Stolen, *M234-200*; frame 776.

In 1818, Elizabeth Grierson bought a slave named Abram. Bill of Sale for Abram, December 1, 1818, *Records of Conveyance,* Book A-D; 18. Grierson bought Nancy and her children Dan, Moses, and Dinah from his son Sandy Grierson in 1810 for $800. Bill of Sale, March 16, 1810, section 8, "Interesting Notes Upon the History of Alabama."

19. Daniel Hughes to McKenney, December 28, 1817, in *Territorial Papers* 18: 284; Commission of David B. Mitchell, October 3, 1816, National Archives Microfilm Publications, *Microcopy 15* (Letters Sent Relating to Indian Affairs, 1800-1824) 3: 433, hereafter cited as *M15,* followed by roll number.

20. E. P. Gaines to Secretary of War, January 12, 1818, Mitchell to John C. Calhoun, March 25, 1818, and February 3, 1818, Mitchell to William H. Crawford, December 25, 1817, *M271*-2: frames 630, 748, 741, 765.

21. Statement of John Oliphant, April 18, 1820, Bill of Sale, December 4, 1817, *M271*-3: frames 196, 144.

22. Mitchell to Calhoun, February 3, 1818, Statement of Mitchell, January 28, 1818, *M271*-2: frames 741, 539; Statement of Captain G. W. Melven, April 20, 1820. *M271*-3: frame 527.

23. Lieut. James Gadsden to Calhoun, May 7, 1818, *M271*-2: frame 650.

24. William H. Crawford to Mitchell, April 3, 1818, Mitchell to Crawford, April 28, 1818, Mitchell to Calhoun, February 18, 1818, *M271*-2: frames 766, 767, 731; House Resolution, November 16, 1818, *M271*-3: frame 136.

25. William Moore to John Clark, July 25, 1819, John Loving to Clark, September 27, 1819, *M271*-3: frames 140, 141.

26. Statement of Thomas S. Woodward, N.D., Statement of Moore, October 15, 1819, William Bowen to Mitchell, December 25, 1817, Statement of S. Rockwell, Z. Lamar, and L. Atkinson, November 2, 1818, *M271*-3: frames 142, 144, 146; Mitchell to Calhoun, November 12, 1819, *M271*-2: frame 1512.

27. Statement of John Oliphant, April 18, 1820, Clark to Mitchell, May 18, May 31, 1820, Richard W. Habersham to Clark, May 10, 1820, Mitchell to Secretary of War, July 27, 1820, William Wirt to President, October 17, 1820, Clark to John Q. Adams, December 18, 1820, *M271*-3: frames 196, 294, 299, 302, 557, 779, 804; Calhoun to Mitchell, February 16, 1821, *M15*-5:54.

28. R. S. Cotterill, *The Southern Indians: The Story of the Civilized Tribes before Removal* (Norman: University of Oklahoma Press, 1954), p. 209; William Rabun to Adams, February 17, 1819, *M271*-2: frame 1562; John Clark to Adams, January 19, 1820, *M271*-3: frame 123.

29. John Whitehead to Clark, January 26, 1820, *M271*-3: frame 164.

30. William Ball to Clark, January 22, 1820, *M271*-3: frame 153.

31. Statement of William Cabniss, January 6, 1820, *M271*-3: frame 153.

32. Cotterill, pp. 209, 213; Calhoun to Col. A. Pickens and Gen. Thomas Flournoy, August 8, 1820, Calhoun to Flournoy, October 19, 1820, and Extract of a letter . . .to General David Meriwether, November 22, 1820, *House Executive Document 91,* 20 Cong., 2 sess.,pp. 3-4, 5, hereafter cited as *Document 91.*

33. Copies of talks delivered by the Georgia Commissioners, December 27, December 28, 1820, *Document 91,* pp. 6-7.

34. Copy of the Answer to the Chiefs. . . , *Document 91,* pp. 7-8; *American State Papers,* Indian Affairs 2: 252-53.

35. Copy of a Talk Delivered by the Georgia Commissioners, December 29, 1820, *Document 91,* pp. 8-9; *American State Papers,* Indian Affairs 2: 253.

36. D. M. Forney and Meriwether to Calhoun, January 9, 1821, *Document 91,* pp. 10-11; Angie Debo, *The Road to Disappearance* (Norman: University of Oklahoma Press, 1941), p. 86; Memorial of the State of Georgia, December 12, 1823, *M234*-220; frame 492; Troup to Calhoun, January 6, 1824, David Glenn to Calhoun, July 28, 1824, and George Cary to Calhoun, February 19, 1825, *M234*-219: frames 176, 128, 662.

37. John Crowell to Calhoun, July 22, 1822, *M271*-4: frame 80; Crowell to Cal-

houn, August 20, 1821, *M271*-3: frame 905.

38. Crowell to McKenney, January 30, 1826, *M234*-220: frame 248; List of Persons, *M271*-4: frame 87; Crowell to Calhoun, August 20, 1821, *M271*-3: frame 905.

The names and ages of the fifty-nine blacks taken to the Creek agency are as fol'lows: Hector, 55; John, 55; Hector, Jr., 18; Patty, wife of Hector, 40, and three children: Affa, Juan, and Sarah; Tyrah, 22; Hannah, 24, and two children; Jeffery, 36; Frederick, 27; Bob, 21; Mag, 30; Nancy, 40; Billy, 45; Abner, 25; Nancy, 25; Dianna, 13; Lewis, 23; Mary, 25, and two children Flora and Hannah; Hannah, 46, mother of Mary; George, 65; Cato, 27; Caty, 28; John, 25; Rosa, 27; Hector, 50; Price, 35; Jim, 40; John, 39; John, 29; Charles, 35; Charles, 22; Capt. Bush, 45; Fillis, 40, and child; Mary. 30; Toby, 50; Augustine, 25; Manuel 36; Cabas, 30; Peter Maranda, 21; Valentine, 25; William, 22; Charles, 36; Lidia, 30; Cyrus, 27; Ned, 50; Nancy, 28, and two children. Crowell to Calhoun, August 20, 1821, *M271*-3: frame 905.

39. Secretary of War to Capt. John R. Bell, September 28, 1821, *Territorial Papers* 22: 220, 221, 221n; Calhoun to Crowell, September 29, 1821, November 8, 1821, and April 25, 1822, *M15*-5: 159, 187, 245; Crowell to Calhoun, January 22, 1822, and July 24, 1823, *M271*-4: frames 80, 386.

40. Crowell to Calhoun, April 6, 1824, *M234*-219: frame 77; Crowell to McKenney, January 30, 1826, *M234*-220: frame 248.

41. Charles J. Kappler, comp. and ed., *Indian Affairs: Laws Treaties,* 2nd ed., 4 vols. (Washington, D.C.: Government Printing Office, 1904), 2: 214-16, 264-68; Cotterill, pp. 219-22; *American State Papers,* Indian Affairs 2: 579.

42. Inventory of Items Stolen, *M234*-220: frames 711ff.

43. *Ibid.*; National Archives Microfilm Publications, *Microcopy 574* (Special Files of the Office of Indian Affairs, 1807-1904) 27: frames 991, 986, 1007, 1008, 885, hereafter cited as *M574,* followed by the roll number.

The blacks claimed by Chilly McIntosh were as follows: York, Winny, Miley, Hecto Caty, Sarah, Silvey, Sam, Binar, Billy, Sam, Hary, Dinar, Flora, Tom, Jack, Nanny, Ben Samson, Stephen, Jenny, Bettey, Lizar, Bob, Jake, Jackey, Eggy, Admon, Archa, Lizza, Bomby, Petter, St. John, Old Hector, Batty, Effa, Syrus, Tartar, Molinta, Binar, Coley, Nancy, Fanny, Toby, Jim Gaison, Campbell, Molly, Rose, Suffer, Gipter, Nelly, Rose, Brister, Mary, Jinny, Judah, Corinny, Sodo, Bardo, Sambo, Norris, Warner, Sarah and her child, Juice, Abram, Judah and her child, John Charley, Molly, Cindy, Lizer.

44. Inventory of Items Stolen, *M234*-220: frames 775, 776; *M574*-27: frames 854, 582, 1140, 1122, 991, 994, 1121.

45. *M574*-27: frames 852, 885, 969, 958. Blacks returned to Chilly McIntosh and Benjamin Hawkins were as follows: Abraham, Aggy, Edmond, Morey, Lucy, George, Judy and child, John Charles, Pompy, Rosa, Bristol, Jackey, Cintha, Limey, Warner, Luch, John, Jim, York, Winney, Caty, Silvey, Lizer, Sarah, Milley, Molley, Hector, Catey, Hector, Patty, Affa, Sarah, Jack, Sam, Biner, Billy, Sam, Harey, Diner, Tina, Tom, Jack, Nancy, Ben, Sampson, Stephen, Jinney, Bettey, Liza, Bob, Jake, Archie. *M234*-220: frame 770.

46. Inventory of Items Stolen, *M234*-220: frames 773-74; *M574*-27: frame 962.

47. Charles P. Tutt to James Barbour, October 13, 1826, *M234*-220: frame 674ff; Crowell to Porter, November 10, 1828, *M234*-221: frame 787.

48. L. M. Stone to Barbour, December 14, 1827, Crowell to Porter, November 10, 1828, *M234*-221: frames 523, 784; William Armstrong to C. A. Harris, February 3, 1837, *M234*-225: A123-37.

49. James A. Everett to John H. Eaton, May 25, 1829, McKenney to Porter, February 19, 1829, with enclosures, *M234*-222: frames 147, 206, 209, 212, 214.

50. Mitchell to Eaton, June 15, 1829, Opothleyohola to Mitchell, June 1, 1828, Mitchell to Andrew Jackson, June 21, December 30, 1829, *M234*-222: frames 216, 228, 234, 239.

51. James Moore to Lewis Cass, September 19, 1832, *M234*-223: frame 263.

chapter 5   REMOVAL

THE COMPACT OF 1802 between Georgia and the United States formed
the basis for what later became known in Indian affairs as removal policy. If
the Indians were to be removed from the limits of Georgia, there was need
for a place to relocate them. After the purchase of Louisiana, the lands
west of the Mississippi were looked at as the most likely place. In 1804,
the president was authorized by Congress to obtain cessions of Indian
lands in the East in exchange for Western lands. The great Creek cession
under the Treaty of Fort Jackson in 1814 apparently gratified momentarily
the Georgians' desire for more land, but by 1820, the whites were again
asking for cessions. United States negotiators urged the Creeks to consider
removal. In the Treaty of 1825, the McIntosh Creeks agreed to cede Creek
lands in the East in exchange for the same number of acres between the
Arkansas and Canadian rivers in the West. The Treaty of 1826, which
nullified the earlier treaty, ceded the lands formerly occupied by the Mc-
Intosh faction and provided for a deputation of them to go west to look
at the lands and to decide where to settle. They were given twenty-four
months to remove to the West, the government promising to pay their
expenses and to give them subsistence for twelve months after their arrival there. The McIntosh party chiefs were given $100,000 to divide
among no more than three thousand of their numbers, and the party
members were to be reimbursed by the Creek Nation for property they
had lost contrary to Creek laws.[1] Thus, the stage was set for the first
Creek removal, which resulted in a decline in the number of blacks
among the Creeks and in the return of some to slavery among the whites.
It also laid the foundation for nearly two decades of conflict between the
Creeks and Seminoles, conflict in which the issue was often slavery.

When, in early 1827, the McIntosh party sent a delegation to explore the western land, they decided on the land near the juncture of the Grand, Verdigris, and Arkansas rivers near Fort Gibson, which had been established in 1824. The first contingent of emigrants arrived there early in 1828, and by the end of that year their numbers had reached about 1,300. For the most part, they were the most prosperous of the McIntosh faction, who with their slaves began to lay out plantations. Others followed, and those who survived the rigors of the new land prospered so that by 1830, the agent reported that they had progressed in agriculture during the two years more than any other Indians within his knowledge and that they would have a surplus of corn of about 60,000 bushels. By that time, the Western Creeks numbered nearly 3,000, but their numbers diminished during the next three years because the country was "more unhealthy than usual." Yet the McIntosh Creeks with their blacks continued to emigrate in small parties. In 1831, eight blacks belonging to Susannah McIntosh emigrated, and twenty emigrated with Chilly McIntosh in 1831. When a census was taken in 1833, there were only 2,459, including 228 female slaves, 270 male slaves, four free black females, and nine free black males.[2]

Removal of the McIntosh party brought with it a number of slave controversies that had their bases in pre-removal events or in removal itself. One such claim was that of David Brearley, former agent to the McIntosh Creeks. In the spring of 1831, he asked the secretary of war to intervene on behalf of his claim for a family of slaves held by the Creeks. It appears that on October 26, 1827, Walter Grayson (Grierson) sold to Thomas Grayson a family of blacks—Jim and Jenny and their children Campbell, Molly, Rose, Dianna, Jupiter, Nelly, and Eady—for $1,500. That same year Thomas Grayson, who was ill, sent the family west with Benjamin Hawkins, who returned to Alabama with Brearley in 1828 to find that the blacks were claimed by Reuben Jordan, a white man who accused Hawkins of stealing them. Hawkins was arrested. Brearley, who needed Hawkins's aid in collecting the Indians for emigration, purchased Jordan's claim for $1,200, despite Hawkins's warning that there were Grayson and McIntosh claims for the same blacks. Brearley either ignored the warning or was unconcerned about it. Two or three months later, Brearley asked Hawkins to give bond for delivery of the blacks or be jailed. Terrified at the prospect of prison, Hawkins signed a paper, not intending, however, to give up the blacks. In the

West, Brearley's son claimed that Brearley did not want the slaves if
he could get the money back. Thomas Grayson offered to pay it and
try to collect from Hawkins, but Brearley's son asked for interest from
the time Brearley had originally paid the money. Grayson refused.
Brearley then convinced Hawkins's father, who had charge of the blacks,
that Brearley was to have them as payment for money he had advanced
to Benjamin Hawkins, which, of course, Hawkins later denied. Brearley
took the blacks and held them, except one who ran away and went to
Thomas Grayson.[3]

Brearley then set about trying to recover the lost slave through John
Campbell, the Creek agent. Thomas Grayson, insisting that his title
was good, tried to get the issue settled before a judicial tribunal, even
suggesting that the blacks be carried to Arkansas so the case could be
settled in the courts there. In the face of that threat, Brearley said that
he had no alternative but to sell the blacks for what they would bring
under the circumstances. He blamed Campbell for the situation, alleging
that there had been a bill of sale from Grayson to Hawkins (which would
have given Brearley a clear title to the claim), which Campbell had urged
Hawkins to destroy. In June 1832, Brearley took his charges against
Campbell to the secretary of war. Campbell denied the accusation and
pointed out that he had done all he could to assist Brearley in a case
which had, for the most part, worked itself out before he took office.
In 1834, Brearley still had not recovered the escaped black. Grayson
had taken him to Crawford County, Arkansas, to have the case tried
in the courts. When he returned to the Creek country, the agent had the
chiefs seize the black, but he escaped once more.[4]

Other slave claims grew out of the earlier settlement of claims among
the McIntosh party. In 1829 Rufus M. Farrington, who had married into
the McIntosh family, claimed twenty-two slaves in the Western Creek
Nation by virtue of his wife's right of inheritance. He instituted a suit
for the slaves in the Arkansas courts and enlisted the help of Agent
John Campbell, Sam Houston, and the Arkansas delegation to Congress
in an attempt to obtain the slaves. The Creek chiefs refused to recognize
the claim, but Farrington obtained judgment in the Arkansas courts.
The chiefs apparently prevailed, for in late spring of 1832, he was still
asking the War Department for help. Another McIntosh claim was that
of Susannah, the widow of William McIntosh, who in early 1832 claimed
the same slave family that Brearley claimed, except that now there were

two additional children, Betty and an infant whose name was not known. James and Jenny and their older children had been among those blacks whom William McIntosh had seized from Robert Grierson (Grayson) as payment for a judgment against Grierson in 1817. In 1820, McIntosh had willed them to Susannah and her children. After the seizure of the McIntosh property in 1825, the blacks fell into the hands of the Graysons, and Susannah claimed that they had not been paid for or returned as the Creek Nation had promised to do. She had gone before the chiefs several times, in both the East and the West, and they dismissed the case, maintaining that claims growing out of the McIntosh affair had all been settled. Others of the same blacks were claimed by both Delila McIntosh (now Drew) and Kendal Lewis. After McIntosh's death, Tartar, Malinda, Vina, Cloe, Nanny, Fanny, Betsy, Toby, and Ellic fell into the hands of Sandy Grayson, who had sold them to John G. Ross in the Eastern Cherokee Nation. Ross had then sold them to Lewis. Delila maintained that the property had not been returned nor paid for according to the Treaty of 1826. On May 21, 1832, the Western chiefs agreed that the blacks belonged to Delila but that Lewis should be paid out of the annuities. However, as late as 1838, the claim had not been paid.[5]

While these cases were being pursued in the West, events in the East had laid the groundwork for further removals. In the fall of 1828, the Eastern Creeks had sent an exploring party to the West, where they received a friendly greeting from the McIntosh Creeks, who formally invited their Eastern tribesmen to join them. Andrew Jackson had become president in 1829, and, dedicated to removal as Indian policy, he set about urging the Creeks and other tribes to remove. The same year the white Alabamans began to enforce their jurisdiction over the Creeks. Yet the Creeks refused to remove, and that fall they voted to remain in the East and come under state laws. Whites trespassed on Indian lands, took their slaves and other property, and embroiled them in lawsuits.[6] The Indian removal act was passed by Congress in 1830, but still the Creeks resisted removal.

However, harassment, trespass, violence, and a lack of redress finally forced the Creeks and other tribes to negotiate. Opothleyohola and other Creek chiefs signed a treaty on March 24, 1832, ceding all of their land in Alabama. They were given a choice of removing or staying. They could select homesteads to which they would receive patents after five years if they decided to remain. Provisions were made for providing the

Creeks who removed with subsistence stores, annuities, and reimburse-
ment for lost improvements. On May 9, 1832, the Seminoles signed the
Treaty of Payne's Landing, relinquishing their lands in Florida and agreeing to emigrate within three years and join the Creek Nation, the articles
to be binding only if a Seminole delegation found the Western lands
agreeable. Jumper, Fuckalusti Hadjo, Charles Emarthla, Coa Hadjo, Holati
Emarthla, Yaha Hajo, Sam Jones, and their black interpreter Abraham
went to the West. At Fort Gibson on February 14, 1833, the Western
Creeks agreed to receive the Seminoles as a constituent part of the Creek
Nation, located on some part of the Nation by themselves. On March 28,
the visiting Seminole delegation also signed a treaty at Fort Gibson,
later alleging that the treaty had been obtained by fraud, reaffirming
the Treaty of Payne's Landing and binding the entire tribe to removal.
It designated as their future home the Creek lands lying between the
the Canadian and the North Fork rivers west to a north-south line striking the forks of Little River, provided the western line did not extend
more than twenty-five miles from the mouth of Little River. Finally, a
treaty with the Apalachicola bands on June 18, 1833, relinquished the
reservations they had received in the Treaty of Moultrie Creek in 1823
and provided for their emigration to the Western lands of the Creeks
and Seminoles.[7]

As soon as the treaty of 1832 was signed, whites began to flock into
the Creek lands. They drove the Indians from their homes, plundered
them, and stole their livestock. Others perpetrated fraud upon them by
taking advantage of their ignorance of legal matters. Yet the Creeks
refused to remove despite the government's refusal to remove intruders
or to protect the Creeks.[8]

In the fall following the signing of the treaty, the government took a
census of the tribe, looking forward to removal or allotment of homesteads to the Creeks. Amalgamation presented a problem to the census
takers. They asked whether an Indian living with a black wife who was
his or someone else's slave was to be considered a head of a family and
to be enrolled as entitled to a reservation. They also wanted to know if
a half-Indian, half-black free person who kept a separate household and
had a black slave for a wife was to be enrolled as entitled to a reservation.
There were also a number of free blacks who differed from the Creeks
only in color, identifying with the Creeks in every other way. These
blacks, if admitted as members of the Creek Nation and if they had
families, were entitled to land under the treaty stipulations.[9]

The census listed 14,142 Upper Creeks, including 445 slaves, and 8,552 Lower Creeks, including 457 slaves, in the Eastern nation. The census figures reveal that there were no large slave holders left in the East in 1832. Most owned fewer than ten, and only a few owned more than twenty-five: William McGillivray, 25; William Walker, 32; Paddy Carr, 35; Fanny Lovett, 30. A number of free blacks were also enumerated with the Creeks. At Tuckabahchee were John McQueen, who listed two males and two females in his household, and Juba, who listed six males and four females. At Tuskeegee was Mary, who listed two males and three females, and at Eufaula was Hannah, the Widow of Eupolika, who listed three females. At Cheehaw was Sandy Perryman, who listed three males and two females. At Coweta were Meter, the wife of Nero, a free black, who listed four females; Polly, who was half-black and had a slave named John as a husband; and Billy Reddick, who listed one male and one female. At Broken Arrow were Lucy Prince, Jonathan Isaac, Jack, and Nancy, each of whom listed one male and one female in the household.[10]

When removal of these Creeks finally got under way, it was slow. In August 1833 a contingent of sixty-two McIntosh party Creeks emigrated under the direction of Chilly McIntosh and Benjamin Hawkins. Of them, twenty were slaves of Sally Harrod. Also among the group was Sally Grayson's "black boy." Upon their arrival in the West, the disbursing agent for Indian removal suspended payment of the party's expenses because he was unsure if he could pay the cost of removing slaves until he was informed that blacks were not allowed subsistence under the Treaty of January 1826.[11]

It was not until December 1834 that Creeks other than the McIntosh faction emigrated. The first contingent arrived in the West in March 1835. In the group were five slaves of Jelka Hadjo, three of David Marshall, three of Thomas Marshall, twenty-three of Sally Stidham, twenty-six of John Stidham, five of Chou-E-Hoc, and one of Whon Hoakey. There were blacks who emigrated without their owners: thirty-four belonging to Sampson Grayson; fifteen belonging to John Oponey, a sixteenth dying on the way; and four listed as "McIntosh's negroes." Finally, there was Charles, a mulatto, who had three in his party. In 1835 Benjamin Marshall took a small party, and Opothleyohola prepared the Tuckabahchees, Kealedjis, Thlopthloccos, Thlewarles, Autaugas, and Atasis to go. In December a party of 511 left Alabama. On December 19, after several days on the road, an Indian woman Ewoddy and her woman

slave joined the party. On the following day one of Benjamin Marshall's
blacks was reported very ill, but otherwise there had been "not much
sickness" on the trip. The man died on December 22. Chief Kotcher
Tustenugee had nine slaves, McInea six, Joseph Carr eight, Hannah
Carr four, Chofolwar two, Salaryee one, Viney Scott two, James
Marshall ten, William Marshall twenty-four, Benjamin Marshall thirty-
four. Also included in this contingent were twelve of Opothleyohola's
blacks and seven of Tuckabahchee Micco's, who had emigrated by
their own resources, four of Paddy Carr's blacks, and eleven in the
party of Lizzy Conrad, whose party contained no Indians.[12]

United States officials began to be afriad that emigration would
fail because of "embarrassments." Suits against the Indians multiplied.
Their blacks, horses, and other property were stolen, and they were
driven almost to desperation. It appeared that the only way to get them
out of Alabama was for the Creeks to pay the just demands against them
and for the government to protect them against those that were unjust.[13]

In May 1836, a few towns resisted the encroachments of whites and
began hostilities. General Thomas S. Jesup was sent to put down the
uprising, and Opothleyohola raised nearly 2,000 warriors to help him.
The hostiles, led by Eneah Micco, Jim McHenry, and Eneah Emarthla,
were quickly defeated. Neamathla, an old Red Stick who had returned
from Florida only a few years earlier, was captured in early June, and
a few days later about a thousand of his red, black, and white followers
surrendered. The other hostile chiefs were rounded up and, with their
people, taken west as prisoners.[14]

During 1836, an estimated 14,609 Creeks emigrated to the West. The
first contingent in June consisted of 2,498 persons, of whom only eleven
were blacks. Six of those belonged to Eneah Micco. The next contingent
of 3,022 was made up in August and contained forty-one slaves. Enumerated among the Indians was Lut-teen, a black, who headed a party of
twenty-one, which contained no Indians. Four contingents were made up
in September. The first contained 103 slaves. In the second were twelve
slaves out of the 1,975 total, and in the third only twenty of the 2,420
people were slaves. In the last contingent, thirty-three of the 1,170 were
slaves. These Creeks had either lost to whites or had divested themselves
of great numbers of slaves from the time of the 1832 census to their
removal. Whereas they had owned over 900 slaves in 1832, the great
body of Creeks removed with only 333 slaves in 1835 and 1836. Some

had previously removed, others were sold, and still others were retained in Alabama through suits, theft, or fraud.[15]

In November 1836 Opothleyohola, en route to the West, paused near Little Rock to write a friendly greeting to Governor James S. Conway and to ask that the ten to twelve thousand of his people then within the limits of Arkansas be allowed to halt while he conducted some "business" for them. The greeting was also signed by Little Doctor, Mad Blue, Tuckabahchee Micco, and Ned, Opothleyohola's black interpreter. Conway complained that the Indians had camped too long and accused them of killing livestock, burning fence rails, and stealing corn and asked that they move on as soon as possible.[16]

During the next few years, remnants of the tribe were rounded up or emigrated with the Cherokees and other tribes. A group of 543 arrived in the West in May of 1837, and another arrived in June. The latter included fourteen slaves of David Barnet and five of Simmehoke, or Widow Prince. Other small parties arrived, having emigrated by their own resources, including Josiah Fisher and A. J. Stidman, both with two slaves. A group of 297, containing no slaves, was removed in November 1837. In 1841 a group of eighteen contained one slave, and in 1846 a group of 104 included two slaves of William Moore and thirty-seven of Abraham Foster. In 1847, an emigration party included slaves Tom, Joe, Scipio, Louisiana, Polly Pierson, Judy, and Phillip, and a group the following year included Fien, Sarah, and Isaac. For the most part, then, the great mass of Creeks had been removed by the end of the third quarter of 1837, about 15,546 having emigrated by that time.[17] Of those who remained some were killed or enslaved by the Alabamans, and some fled to the Seminoles and Apalachicolas.

General Jesup had no sooner taken care of the Creek affair of 1836 than he was ordered to Florida to command the army against the Seminoles, who had been openly hostile to removal since December 1835. Before he left the Creek Nation, Jesup recruited a regiment of Creek warriors. In return for 600 to 1,000 warriors willing to go against the Seminoles, the Creeks were to receive an advancement of $31,900 to be applied against the debts of their bands. They were to receive as well the pay and emoluments of soldiers in the army of the United States and, most important, "such plunder as they may take from the Seminoles." If the Creeks remained in service after the Seminoles had been subdued, they were to receive $10,000. The agreement was entered

into on August 28, 1836, by Opothleyohola, Little Doctor, Tuckabahchee Micco, Mad Blue, Jim Boy, and Jelka Hadjo. Jesup would use
these warriors to advantage, expanding the term "plunder" to mean any
property of the Seminoles, including their slaves. The Creeks were to
have as the spoils of war any Seminole black they captured. Blacks who
belonged to whites and had run away or had been captured by the Seminoles were to be returned to their owners, but the Creeks were to receive a reward of twenty dollars for each one they captured. Jesup insisted on these measures, for by the time he assumed command, he was
convinced that he was engaged in "a negro not an Indian war."[18]

Both slave and free, the Seminole blacks had been the allies of the
Seminoles since the war had broken out. Their active participation in
that war has been well documented in other studies[19] which demonstrate that the blacks used their position as interpreters to maintain
a powerful influence over their Indian masters or allies and that they
gave the Indians persuasive council to resist removal to the West, which
the Seminoles had agreed to in the Treaty of Payne's Landing. It became apparent to General Jesup that defeat of the Seminoles depended
upon the defeat or surrender of the blacks, who represented some of
their fiercest and most intelligent warriors and leaders. The Creek warriors were effective in reducing the black fighting force.

The 776 Creek warriors served Jesup through his first campaign
during the fall of 1836 and the following winter, the principal battles
of which took place on the Withlacoochee River, near Lake Apopka,
and on Hatchelustee Creek, the latter battle occurring in January, 1837.
On June 2, 1837, Jesup ordered about ninety blacks, most of them
captured by the warriors, to be taken to New Orleans by Lieutenant
G. H. Terrett of the Marines, to be placed in the hands of Major Isaac
Clark at Fort Pike. Clark was ordered to confine them, and, if possible,
make them support themselves by their own labor. Besides these ninety,
seventeen remained at Tampa Bay. Jesup's troops had also captured
about ninety blacks who were the property of United States citizens.[20]

On June 13, Jesup sent part of the Creek volunteers to Mobile aboard
the steamer *Merchant* to be mustered out. The rest of the regiment remained in Florida until the fall, and as time to muster them out drew
near, Jesup faced the problem of disposing of the blacks that the Creeks
claimed by virtue of their contract with the government. He feared that
if the blacks were sent west as slave property of the Creeks, conflicts with

the Seminoles would arise over them. He therefore issued orders on September 6, 1937, taking the blacks on account of the government to be held subject to orders of the secretary of war. The sum of $8,000 was to be paid to the Creek chiefs and warriors in proportion to the number of captives taken by each battalion. The Creeks had also captured thirty-five of the slaves belonging to citizens of the United States, for which the Creeks were to receive a reward of twenty dollars each. A few days later, Jesup sent the last of the Creek warriors to Pass Christian, Mississippi, to be discharged and then taken to New Orleans to be paid for the captives and to prepare for emigration to the West. The families of many of the warriors had already emigrated and had suffered greatly. Left behind when their warriors went to Florida, they had been harassed by whites. In February 1837, for instance, whites attacked the home of Anne Curnell (Cornell) and carried away two free blacks and an Indian boy. There were also instances of robbery and rape. The Creeks were so harassed that they had to leave their property and flee down the Alabama. They had spent months at Mobile Point and Pass Christian. But that was not the end of their troubles. On their way from New Orleans to Fort Gibson, over 300, including four of Jim Boy's children, died when the steamboat *Monmouth* sank.[21]

Captain John Page, superintendent of the Creek removal, had been instructed not to take west the blacks captured by the Creek warriors. Jesup had purchased them to "end all difficulty" and asked Secretary of War Joel R. Poinsett to sanction the purchase, suggesting that the money be charged to the Seminole annuity. There still remained the matter of disposing of the blacks. He wrote, "It is highly important to the slave holding states that these negroes be sent out of the country; and I would strongly recommend that they be sent to one of our colonies in Africa. The sum paid to the Indians is entirely satisfactory to them though it is far less than the value of the negroes."[22]

Poinsett approved the purchase on October 7, but the agreement with the Creeks was not as solid as Jesup had thought. When they reached Pass Christian, they refused to take the $8,000 for their interest in the blacks. However, they emigrated without the blacks, who remained at Fort Pike, Louisiana, during the next several months. In April 1838 the Creek delegation to Washington, headed by Opothleyohola, appealed to the commissioner of Indian affairs for a settlement of their claim for the blacks.[23]

Commissioner of Indian Affairs C. A. Harris disagreed that the value of the slaves should be charged against the Seminole annuity. To do so would deprive the friendly Seminoles, who had already emigrated, as well as those who had been hostile. In another way, it would be paying the Creeks with their own money, for the treaty of May 9, 1832, had provided for the reunion of the Creeks and Seminoles. The treaty provided that the annuities granted to the Seminoles would be added to those of the Creeks, so that both Creeks and Seminoles would share equally as part of the Creek confederation. Jesup had also suggested that Congress appropriate the money to pay for the slaves and for their transportation to Africa, but public opinion in the United States was so sensitive toward the subject of slavery at that time that Harris thought such a course dangerous for the government to pursue. The alternative was to turn the blacks over to the Creeks. However, taking the blacks from their Seminole owners, with whom they were being held at New Orleans, would be a delicate matter. If they were to be turned over, Harris felt that the transfer should take place before they were taken to the western country, for seizure of the slaves there would likely cause difficulties between the Creeks and Seminoles.[24]

Acting Secretary of War Captain Samuel Cooper approved this latter suggestion and ordered the blacks to be placed at the disposal of the Creek delegation. By this time, the number of blacks at Fort Pike had been reduced by sickness to about eighty-five. It was necessary for the Creeks to identify the ones they captured and to eliminate those for whom whites had claims as stolen or runaway property. For these latter, the Creeks would be paid twenty dollars each, in accordance with Jesup's original agreement with the Creek warriors. Harris directed the Creeks to divest themselves of the slaves before they were removed west. Any arrangement they made respecting the property and submitted to the department would be approved. Above all, however, the blacks were not to be taken west.[25]

The Creek delegation appointed Nathaniel F. Collins of Tuskegee, Alabama, as their agent to receive the blacks for them and the warriors for delivery to James C. Watson of Columbus, Georgia, Collins's brother-in-law, to whom they sold the blacks on May 8, 1838, for $14,600. Harris secured approval of the sale from the secretary of war, and orders were issued to General Jesup and Major R. A. Zantzinger at Fort Pike to deliver the blacks to Collins at his request. There were certain stipulations, however. Collins was to hold the slaves, subject to the lawful claims of all white persons. The officers were cautioned to deliver only those captured by the Creeks. The problem handed Collins was a difficult one. Harris gave him a list of blacks captured by Jesup's troops and believed to be claimed by the Creeks. Harris supposed that all of those Collins sought were at Fort Pike, but it was for Collins to find them. No expense of any kind growing out of the matter would be borne by the United States.[26]

Meanwhile, because of the sickly condition of the Seminoles and blacks at Fort Pike, General Edmund P. Gaines, commander of the Western Military Division, had ordered Major Clark to move the prisoners to Fort Gibson as soon as possible, which order the department approved.[27] But Clark was unable to carry it out. The heirs of Hugh Love of Muscogee County, Georgia, filed claims for sixty-seven of the blacks, whom they claimed Love had purchased from the Creeks.

The blacks were claimed under a purchase allegedly made in 1835. On January 10 of that year, Hugh Love, a licensed trader among the Creeks in the West, was called on by a Creek woman named Gray, whose relatives several years earlier had left the Eastern Creek Nation, gone to Florida, and associated themselves with the Seminoles. She told Love that while she was still in Alabama she had a number of slaves, consisting of Pompy and Dolly and their children. About 1795, however, they were run off to Florida by her relatives and had remained there ever since. About 1815, Hicks, the Seminole chief, sent her word of the whereabouts of the blacks. She sent her son and a company of men to recover them. However, the blacks fought with and defeated the company, killing some and seriously wounding her son. Mrs. Gray never tried to recover them again. She agreed to sell them to Love for $5,000 in money and goods. Hugh Love agreed, and in the spring of 1835 started to Florida to capture the blacks, but he was thwarted by the Seminole agent. He died shortly thereafter.[28]

John Love, Hugh's brother, took up the claim. On May 2, 1838, he obtained a writ to prevent the Army from removing the slaves from the jurisdiction of the New Orleans court. Lieutenant John G. Reynolds, the Seminole emigration agent, was in Tampa Bay, and the Seminoles then at New Orleans, including Micanopy and other chiefs, were nearly in a state of mutiny. They claimed the blacks, and they believed that the government had brought them to New Orleans to rob them of their slaves.

The heirs of Love sued General Gaines for the recovery of the sixty-seven slaves or for damages of $67,000. On May 9, Gaines asked the court to set aside the order on two basic grounds: that the slaves were prisoners of war, taken in combat and therefore under the exclusive custody of the army, and that there was no proper defendant in the case since Gaines denied that he had command or control over the prisoners. The judge, however, held the opposite. He aptly pointed out that only a few days earlier the general had ordered the prisoners transported up river and that the officers at the barracks would have given up the prisoners if the general had so ordered. Finally, no witness could be found who could swear that he had seen any of the blacks carrying arms when they were captured; therefore, the judge ruled that the slaves were not prisoners of war but the property of prisoners. It was useless to argue, he said, that once the prisoners reached their destination and were released from military control the plaintiffs could prosecute their claim. It would be too difficult to get the Seminoles to relinquish the property. Therefore, he ruled that the jurisdiction of the court should be maintained and charged Gaines with the court costs.[29]

At this point Lieutenant Reynolds returned to New Orleans from Tampa Bay. He made immediate arrangements for the embarkation of all of the emigrants, now totalling 1,160, except those blacks for whom claims had been made. Like Gaines, he felt that the claims were fraudulent, but on advice of the district attorney he decided to leave the sixty-seven blacks, their Indian owners, and witnesses in the case. Meanwhile, Love's heirs dropped their suit against Gaines and filed another, this time for thirty-one of the original sixty-seven because upon his arrival at New Orleans, John Love had found Pompy, Dolly, about thirty of their descendants, and others in one camp and had them secured. The rest were in another camp, and when word reached there that Love was on his way, all of the blacks in the camp painted themselves so that none could be identified.[30]

Pompey subsequently died, leaving thirty-two in custody. Of these, most were the descendants of Pompey and his two wives, Melinda and Dolly, who was at the time about seventy-five years old. The old Mikasuki chief Kinhijah (or Capichee Micco) had bought Melinda and Dolly near St. Augustine during the English period in Florida. The women, not related, were purchased from different men, and both became Pompey's wives. From them came most of the slaves of whom Miccopotokee was guardian. He had inherited them from his uncle Kinhijah according to

Indian custom. At first, Miccopotokee refused to take them and told
Tuskeneehau and his sisters, the children of Kinhijah, to keep them. Tuskeneehau killed himself, and his sisters died. Then Miccopotokee took
charge of the blacks by virtue of his double claim of the will and of relationship. Later, it was claimed that he held them as guardian for Tuskeneehau's daughters. He had the matter investigated by Seminole Agent
Wiley Thompson in April 1835, and received a certificate of title. The
following captives at New Orleans were descendants of Pompey and
Melinda: Long Toney; Milly his sister; Tenna, their aunt; Mary and Nancy,
her daughters; and Mary's five children. The following were descendants
of Pompey and Dolly: Prince; Peggy, Scilla, Fanny, and Eliza, daughters
of Dolly; Hagar, daughter of Peggy; Hagar's baby; Bella, daughter of
Scilla; Charles, Margaret, and Silvia or Silba, the children of Fanny.[31]

Several of the others claimed by Love were considered the property
of Harriet Bowlegs, who had had repeated assurances from Jesup and
from Agent John C. Casey that all her slaves would be secured to her in
compliance with the treaty. Among her slaves detained by Love were
Flora, who was very old, her daughter Juba and Juba's daughter, Abbey
or Cumba. Fai or Fy, the mother of Flora, had been owned by Cow
Keeper, who bequeathed her to one of his female relatives, a sister of
Echo Fixico. From her, King Bowlegs (Eneah Micco) purchased Flora.
When he died, he left Flora and her offspring to his daughter Harriet.
Noble was the son of Beck, who had been bought by Bowlegs during
the English period at St. Augustine, before the birth of her first child
Polly. Polly became the mistress of old Bowlegs, and he freed her and
her children. The other children of Beck, including Noble, were be-
queathed to Harriet. Jacob and Daily, brothers, were the grandchildren
of Rose, whom Bowlegs had bought from a man named Forrester near
St. Augustine. Rose and her offspring were willed to Sanathlaih-Kee,
Harriet's sister, who had died in 1837, and the property passed to Harriet.[32]

Leaving the thirty-two blacks in the hands of civil authorities in New
Orleans, Reynolds started his party upstream. On the morning of May 19,
453 Indians embarked on board the steamer *Renown*, and three days
later, 674 embarked on the *South Alabama*. The Indians in this latter
party included the chiefs Micanopy, Coa Hadjo, and Philip. Reynolds,
on board the *South Alabama* was met at Vicksburg, Mississippi, by Collins, who had arrived at New Orleans on the day after Reynolds had left;

he had hurried to overtake Reynolds and demanded the slaves claimed
by the Creek warriors and now belonging to Watson. But Reynolds was
apprehensive because of the excitement among the Seminoles as a result
of the Love claim in New Orleans, and he did not want to lose any time
in the emigration. Thus, he persuaded Collins to travel with him as far
as Little Rock, Arkansas, feeling that before the party reached that point,
he could persuade the Seminoles to voluntarily give up the blacks.[33]

On the evening of May 26, Reynolds called a meeting of the chiefs and
others owning slaves and read the departmental orders directing the re-
linquishment of the slaves to Collins, telling them that the Creeks would
have the slaves anyway upon their arrival at Fort Gibson. Micanopy led
the Seminoles in their refusal, saying that the department's action was
contrary to the promise made to them by Jesup concerning the security
of their property if they agreed to emigrate. Reynolds did not again
broach the subject until they reached Little Rock on June 1, when they
were held up by low water. On that night, he again assembled the Seminoles, and they again refused, this time becoming more vexed than before. Reynolds, in exasperation, concluded that nothing short of force
could separate the slaves from the Indians.[34]

Therefore, he called on the governor of Arkansas to come to his aid
in taking the slaves. Acting Governor Sam C. Roane refused, and requested that Reynolds not attempt to turn over the blacks within the
state, especially in the vicinity of Little Rock. He urged Reynolds to
be on his way as soon as possible so that the citizens of Little Rock
might "be relieved from the annoyance of a hostile band of Indians and
savage negroes." The citizens of Arkansas had been concerned about
Indian hostilities ever since the government had begun to settle Indian
tribes on lands west of the state. There had been much agitation among
the settlers along the western border for the establishment of a fort near
the line. Roane felt that the government was inviting the massacre of
citizens by bringing the Indians to the West, provoking them, and then
turning them loose. So he visited the chiefs and assured them that their
blacks would not be taken from them; the chiefs, in turn, promised to go
to their new country peaceably.[35] The fact that the War Department had
hoped to avoid removing the blacks in question to the West was of little
consequence to Roane.

After such an unfriendly reception from the governor, Reynolds went
immediately to Fort Gibson, where he asked General Matthew Arbuckle,

commander of the Second Department of the Western Military Division, to use force to effect the surrender of the blacks. Arbuckle declined as Roane had done. First, it would be difficult to identify those claimed with certainty, since they were in company of such a large number of other Seminole blacks and since there was no one at Fort Gibson at the time who could point them out. Second, the Seminole chiefs remained adamant in their insistence that the slaves claimed by the Creek warriors came within Jesup's promise that they would retain their slave property if they emigrated. Arbuckle called a council with the chiefs, and each one voluntarily promised to give up the blacks if the president of the United States decided that they must.[36]

Action by the president was not likely, for the department considered itself rid of the problem of Watson's claim. As far as Commissioner Harris was concerned, the departmental action of placing the blacks at the disposal of the Creek delegation had relieved it of further obligation in the matter. In regard to other blacks captured by the United States troops and removed to the West he felt it "expedient" for the government not to interpose. Thwarted in his efforts to recover the slaves for Collins, Reynolds returned with Collins to New Orleans, where the matter of thirty-two blacks claimed by Love still remained to be settled.[37]

When Reynolds and Collins reached New Orleans, they found that the U.S. attorney had asked for an order to show cause why the thirty-two blacks being held by the Love claim should not be delivered to Gaines and Reynolds and the suit dropped. The order was issued on June 17, and ten days were allowed for Love's heirs to file an appeal. Collins evidently knew that the order was not absolute until the ten days were up and that the sheriff could not deliver the slaves until that time had expired, yet for some reason, on the day before the effective date, Collins left New Orleans for Alabama. On the following day, the blacks were turned over to Reynolds, and the Love claim was dropped. Since Collins nor any agent authorized by him was present, Reynolds immediately took the blacks to Fort Gibson.[38]

When Reynolds left Fort Gibson for New Orleans, little did he know that a furor awaited him downstream. Upon learning that he had taken the blacks to the West, Commissioner Harris had written Reynolds an urgent letter condemning the action. The object of delivering the slaves to the Creeks within the states was to prevent their being carried west, whereby contentions and difficulties between the Creeks and Seminoles would be avoided. Now it was likely that troubles would ensue, for Harris felt that the Creeks would not be satisfied with the Seminoles' retaining the blacks, nor could the Seminoles live in the same country and abide seeing their slaves in the hands of the Creeks. Finally, the secretary of war feared that the blacks would "form a dangerous population" in the new country, as they had in Florida. Thus, Harris ordered Reynolds to do all in his power to recover the blacks and deliver them to the Creek agent.[39]

But it was too late. When Reynolds answered Harris in early September, he expressed doubt whether the Creeks would have obtained the slaves anyway, since there were many persons ready with claims similar to Love's. He had sent them on to prevent further difficulties. Had Collins been in the city on the day the slaves were released to him, Reynolds protested, he would have turned over to him any that could be identified as captives of the Creeks. But Collins had not been there, nor had anyone else with authority to receive them, and since he had been ordered to incur no expense in regard to the Creek claims, he had not wanted to detain them.[40]

Reynolds's problem was aggravated by Collins who wrote to Harris late in July complaining because he had failed to obatin the blacks he sought from the first contingent, calling the entire episode a farce. He charged duplicity on the part of Reynolds regarding the second group. First, he claimed that the blacks were turned over to Reynolds while he, Collins, was still in New Orleans. Reynolds had then supposedly set about chartering a boat secretly, and when Collins talked with Reynolds, he had said nothing about it. Collins demanded the slaves, but Reynolds replied that the sheriff would not give them up. With the sickly season coming on, Collins had left New Orleans. Collins felt that the release of the slaves on the day following his departure and their immediate shipment from the city smacked of a plot to deprive him of the property.[41]

Commissioner Harris was convinced that there had been "a great disregard, if not violation" of the orders of the department and asked Reynolds for an explanation of his actions, reminding him that while he was on duty with the Indian department he was bound to obey the orders of no military officer who had not been placed under the commissioner's direction. Reynolds was surprised at this attack. He felt that he had done all he could to aid Collins. What object, Reynolds asked, could he have had in clandestinely sending the blacks to Arkansas?[42]

Reynolds was finally rid of the matter, which now lay in the hands of General Arbuckle at Fort Gibson. The matter was further complicated when Watson paid $14,600, the agreed sale price, to William Armstrong, the Western superintendent, who in turn paid it to the Creeks. Unaware that the money had been paid, the secretary of war directed Arbuckle to do the job which Reynolds had failed to do. But the prospects of obtaining the blacks seemed slight to Arbuckle. Now that the Creeks had been paid, they would not likely concern themselves with delivering the slaves to Watson's agent, and despite their promise the Seminole chiefs would not likely give them up to be taken from the country as servants for the white man. The Seminoles were as much under the influence of the black interpreters as they had been in Florida, and it was not likely that they would be surrendered without force. Even then, success was not likely, for the Seminoles and the other Seminole and Creek blacks would likely come to their aid, or they would bolt and leave the country. If they were taken, it would be difficult to keep them under proper guard. Arbuckle therefore felt that it would be best to convince the Seminoles to refund from their annuity the amount paid the Creeks and that the government, in turn, pay Watson for his claim. Yet he had his orders.[43]

He delayed action on the matter until September 26, when Jim Boy and several of the Creek warriors were at Fort Gibson on their return from a general Indian council at the Cherokee council house. Arbuckle hoped to enlist their help in having the blacks turned over to Watson's agent, but the Creeks said that they had been paid and did not wish anything further to do with the matter. Arbuckle also appealed to Micanopy, who was recognized as the principal chief of the Seminoles, but he refused to give up the blacks and told Arbuckle to consult the individuals who owned them. Since the owners and all of the blacks in the Seminole camp were opposed to the claim, it is not likely that Micanopy had the power to turn them over. The only resort left was force. Arbuckle viewed the influence of the blacks as insidious. In his opinion, the great number of "bad negroes" brought to the Creek country by the Seminoles would ultimately prove an injury to the tribe and to the states of Missouri and Arkansas by "furnishing a harbor for runaway negroes and horse-thieves."[44]

Collins began to doubt whether Arbuckle would be able to secure the blacks, and he asked Secretary Poinsett to see that the government paid for them if Arbuckle failed. The suggestion was welcomed by the secretary, who was reluctant to use military force in taking the blacks, for the resulting dissatisfaction would seriously interfere with the policy of the government in relation to the Indians. Therefore, William Armstrong and Arbuckle were directed to open negotiations with the Creeks to adjust all of their claims against the citizens or the government of the United States. If they found Watson's claim was just, they were directed to insert a provision in any agreement they reached which would allow the matter to be handled as the president might determine.[45]

Crawford and Arbuckle felt that nothing could be gained by calling the Creek chiefs together in light of their refusal so far to interfere with the blacks. Arbuckle felt that the best way for the matter to be settled was for the government to pay Watson for his loss, together with interest and a reasonable allowance for his time and expense in trying to recover the slaves. The matter was taken up in the House of Representatives, and on a motion of the Hon. Charles Downing a resolution was passed on January 28, 1839, calling for a complete report by the Department of War on the disposition of all slave property captured during the Seminole War.[46] There the matter rested for the time being.

Watson's purchase had been made at the insistence of Secretary Poinsett, and he and Commissioner C. A. Harris had done their best to prevent the slaves from reaching the West. A contemporary antislavery critic charged that they consciously attempted to return the blacks to a state of servitude,[47] and one historian has charged that Harris "emerges in the role of a public official working to obtain property for men of political influence at the expense of the Indians and to the detriment of the slaves."[48] Whatever their personal motives may have been, Harris officially justified their action by saying that turning the blacks over to the Creeks was the alternative to shipping the blacks to Africa, an action which would have proved unwise for the government to take "when the public mind here and elsewhere is so sensitive upon the subject of slavery."[49] In subsequent years both the Love and the Watson claims were revived several times, but after 1838, they were a Seminole, not a Creek problem.[50]

Removal and its accompanying problems were devastating to all of the Southeastern tribes. It was particularly so to the Creeks. Whereas in 1832 there were 21,792 in the East alone, in 1859 there were only 13,537 in all.[51] Many had died or were killed during the trek. Most, however, died of diseases contracted after removal. The weather was much colder in the Western lands, and the Indians suffered from respiratory diseases.

Besides life, the Creeks also lost vast quantities of property, their claims in 1838 amounting to $608,784.79. On November 23 of that year the Creeks settled all claims for property abandoned or lost in

consequence of removal in return for $50,000 worth of stock animals
to be distributed to the towns in proportion to the people's losses.
The United States as well invested $350,000 for the Creeks, the interest
to be paid annually, the first year in money and thereafter in money,
animals, and goods. The treaty as well made appropriations to settle
the claims of the McIntosh Creeks and the hostiles of the war of 1836.
Jim Boy and David Barnet wanted the settlement in money rather than
in stock animals, for the treaty did not take into account, they said,
the great personal losses suffered by many of the Creeks. They had
paid money for the blacks and goods they had lost and needed money
to replace them.[52]

Of particular concern to Jim Boy was property lost by the Creek
warriors in the sinking of the *Monmouth* in the Mississippi. Over three
hundred people drowned, and property valued at $71,615 was lost.
Among the casualties was one of Opothleyohola's blacks who had been
used as an interpreter with the Creek warriors in Florida. Opothleyohola
had hired out Sam, Thomas, and Pairo in September of 1836. Two of
them were returned to him. Which one was drowned is uncertain. Jim
Boy and Yargee as well lost blacks during the Seminole War. Each had
a black used as an interpreter and guide killed by the Seminoles.[53]

There were other Creek blacks, such as the well-known Cow Tom
and Caesar Bruner, who had served as interpreters in Florida. Caesar suffered losses of his own. A free man, he had been under the guardian-
ship of Billy Walker, who attended to his business. While Caesar was in
Florida Walker died, and Caesar could obtain no word of his family or
property. His wife Amy and four children belonged to Walker. When he
left Alabama in 1836, he left his money and property with his wife, but
sent his "free papers" on to Arkansas with his sister Sukey. In 1837,
Caesar made a pathetic appeal to General Jesup to help him find his
family and regain his property.[54]

Other Creek blacks had claims for property lost or abandoned in the
East. At Coweta were Sam, Long Billy, Rinty, Arfrie, Sam Jr., Cudjo,
Aggy, Lucy, Clory, Sarah, Abram, Big Jack, Kitto, George, Joseph, March,
Anny, Caty, Molly, Molly (second), Marian, Milly, Billy, and Indy. At
Wochohoy were Sharper, William, Manual, Darcus, and Affie. At Eufaula
were Colly, Bob, Dick, Sam, Sandy, Jacob, Dean, Tommy, Simon, Pat-
ty, and Dinah. At Hitchata (Hichiti) were Lizey, Nisey, and Charles.
And at Big Spring was Billy.[55]

Material losses and a declining population made economic recovery slow during the decade following removal. Rebuilding the Creek Nation was made even more difficult by the development of slave controversies between the Creeks and Seminoles. While most of the controversies were local, they were played out against the backdrop of the larger national controversy over slavery, which was later to engulf not only the Creeks but the other tribes of the Indian Territory as well.

NOTES

1. Charles J. Kappler, comp. and ed., *Indian Affairs: Laws and Treaties,* 2nd ed., 4 vols. (Washington, D.C.: Government Printing Office, 1904-29), 2: 214, 266.

2. David Brearley to James Barbour, May 28, 1827, Muster Rolls, National Archives Microfilm Publications, *Microcopy M234* (Office of Indian Affairs, Letters Received) 237: frames 29, 417, 421, hereafter cited as *M234,* followed by the roll number; Angie Debo, *The Road to Disappearance* (Norman: University of Oklahoma Press, 1941), p. 95; Luther Blake to John H. Eaton, July 3, 1830, John Campbell to Elbert Herring, November 20, 1833, *M234*-236: frames 135, 370.

3. Brearley to Eaton, May 2, 1831, Bill of Sale, October 26, 1827, Statement of Benjamin Hawkins, August 23, 1832, Campbell to Lewis Cass, October 27, 1832, *M234*-236: frames 217, 294, 296, 287.

4. Brearley to Cass, January 5, 1832, *M234*-233: frame 18; Statement of Hawkins, August 23, 1832, Campbell to Cass, October 27, 1832, Brearley to Cass, June 20, 1832, Campbell to Herring, February 25, 1834, *M234*-236: frames 296, 287, 291, 403.

5. Rufus M. Farrington to Campbell, December 10, 1830, Campbell to Cass, March 28, 1832, Statement of Susannah McIntosh, January 12, 1832, Wiley Thompson to Herring, April 16, 1832, Statement of Fushache Micco et al., January 12, 1832, Susannah McIntosh to Thompson, January 11, 1832, Statement of John Winslett, April 13, 1832, *M234*-236: frames 262, 259, 322, 325, 330, 331, 334, 337; A. H. Sevier to Cass, May 29, 1832, enclosing Farrington to Cass, April 1, 1832, *M234*-233: frame 320; William Armstrong to C. A. Harris, February 3, 1837, with enclosures, *M234*-225: A123-37.

6. Debo, pp. 96, 97, 98; Brearley to Peter B. Porter, December 12, 1828, *M234*-236; frame 233; Lower Creek Chiefs to the President, January 21, 1830, John Crowell to Thomas L. McKenney, May 5, 1830, *M234*-222: frames 274, 312.

7. Kappler, 2: 344-45.

8. Details of the Creek troubles with whites appear in Grant Foreman, *Indian Removal* (Norman: University of Oklahoma Press, 1932), pp. 129-39.

9. B. S. Parsons and Thomas J. Abbott to Cass, September 7, 1832, *M234*-223: frame 306; Parsons to Cass, October 16, 1832, in J. H. Johnston,

"Documentary Evidence and the Relations of Negroes and Indians," *The Journal of Negro History* 14 (January 1929), 37.

10. Debo, p. 99; Census Roll, 1833, National Archives Record Group 75 (Records of the Bureau of Indian Affairs), *Creek Removal Records; Senate Document 512,* 23 Cong., 1 sess., pp. 239-394.

11. Muster Roll of Emigrants, J. Brown to George Gibson, January 3, 1834, and D. Kurtz to Gibson, November 10, 1834, National Archives Record Group 75, *Letters Received,* Records of the Commissary General of Subsistence: Creek.

12. Debo, p. 100; Muster Roll of a Company of Creek Indians . . . 28th March 1835, *Letters Received*; Creek Muster Roll No. 8, National Archives Record Group 75, *Emigration Lists, 1836-38;* Muster Roll and Muster Roll . . . 3rd day of February 1836, *M234*-237: frames 653, 646, 655; Gaston Litton, ed., "The Journal of a Party of Emigrating Creek Indians, 1835-1836," *The Journal of Southern History* 7 (May 1941), 228, 232, 233.

13. Bvt. Maj. Gen. Thomas S. Jesup to Cass, August 30, 1836, *M234*-225: frame 75; Foreman, p. 141.

14. Capt. F. S. Belton's Journal of Occurrences, *M234*-237: frame 519; Debo, pp. 101-02; Foreman, pp. 145-48, 151; Cass to Jesup, May 19, 1836, *M234*-255: frame 26.

15. Debo, p. 102; Muster Rolls 1-8, *Emigration Lists, 1836-38;* Foreman, pp. 153-54, 160, 162-63, 180-81; Thomas S. Woodward, *Woodward's Reminiscences of the Creek, or Muskogee Indians, Contained in Letters to Friends in Georgia and Alabama* (Montgomery: Barrett & Wimbash, 1859; reprint ed., Mobile: Southern University Press for Graphics, Inc., 1965), pp. 92, 93-94; Ethan Allen Hitchcock, *A Traveler in Indian Territory: The Journal of Ethan Allen Hitchcock, late Major-General in the United States Army,* ed. Grant Foreman (Cedar Rapids, Iowa: The Torch Press, 1930), p. 147.

16. Opothleyohola to James S. Conway, November 7, 1836, National Archives Record Group 94 (Records of the Office of the Adjutant General), *General Jesup's Papers,* Letters Received, box 12 (hereafter cited as *JPLR*); Conway to Lieut. Edward Deas, December 6, 1836, *M234*-237: frame 564.

17. Debo, pp. 102-103; Creek Muster Roll No. 7, *Emigration Lists, 1836-38;* Blake to T. Hartley Crawford, August 27, 1839, *M234*-239; B808-39; Crawford to Armstrong, September 27, 1846, National Archives Microfilm Publications, *Microcopy M21* (Office of Indian Affairs, Letters Sent) 36: 157, hereafter cited as *M21,* followed by the roll number; Muster Rolls, *M234*-238: D79-37, S499-37, S689-37; *M234*-240: R550-48, L2546-46, L162-47, R289-48.

18. *House Executive Document 381,* 25 Cong., 2 sess., pp. 1-2, and *JPLR,* box 12; Harris to Capt. Samuel Cooper, May 2, 1838, *House Document 225,* 25 Cong., 3 sess., pp. 44 (hereafter cited as *Document 225*); John K. Mahon, *History of the Second Seminole War, 1835-1842* (Gainesville: University of Florida Press, 1967), p. 196.

19. Mahon; Kenneth Wiggins Porter, *The Negro on the American Frontier* (New York: Arno Press and The New York Times, 1971).

20. T. B. Linnard to Maj. Isaac Clark, June 2, 1837, Linnard to Lieut. G. H. Terrett, June 2, 1837, Jesup to Col. J. Gadsden, June 14, 1837, and Jesup to Brig. Gen. Roger Jones, July 20, 1837, *Gen. Jesup's Papers,* Letters Sent, hereafter cited as *JPLS.*

21. List of Creek Volunteers. . ., June 13, 1837, *JPLR,* box 12; Orders No. 175, September 6, 1837, Jesup to W. G. Freeman, September 9, 1837, *Document 225,* pp. 4, 72; Foreman, pp. 180-81; Jesup to Joel R. Poinsett, April 11, 1837, *M234*-238: J85-37; Carolyn Thomas Foreman, "The Brave Major Moniac and the Creek Volunteers," *The Chronicles of Oklahoma* 23 (Summer 1945), 106.

22. Jesup to Frederick Searle, September 9, 1837, Linnard to Capt. John Page, September 22, 1837, Jesup to Poinsett, September 23, 1837, *JPLS.*

23. Lieut. T. T. Sloan to Harris, May 6, 1838, *Document 225,* pp. 91, 43; Armstrong to Harris, April 23, 1838, *M234*-225: A362-38.

24. Harris to Cooper, May 1, 1838, National Archives Record Group 393 (Records of the United States Army Continental Commands, 1821-1920); *Second and Seventh Military Departments,* Letters Received, box 2 (hereafter cited as *2nd and 7th LR*); and *Document 225,* p. 43.

25. Harris to Armstrong, May 5, 1838, *Document 225,* p. 44.

26. Opothleyohola et al. to Harris, May 8, 1838, *2nd and 7th LR,* box 2; U. S., Congress, House, Committee on Indian Affairs, 30 Cong., 1 sess., April 12, 1842, *House Report* 724, p. 2; Harris to Cooper, May 9, 1838, Harris to Maj. Gen. Alexander Macomb, May 9, 1838, Harris to Bvt. Maj. R. A. Zantzinger, May 19, 1838, and Harris to Nathaniel Collins, May 9, 1838, *Document 225,* pp. 28, 46, 48.

27. Special Orders 8, April 29, 1838, and Harris to Lieut. J. G. Reynolds, May 11, 1838, *Document 225,* p. 90.

28. John H. Love to James Logan, July 3, 1840, *M234*-923; A899-40.

29. Heirs of Love vs. E. P. Gaines (Judgment on Rule), n.d., Clark to Harris, May 3, 1838, *Document 225,* p. 31.

30. Reynolds to Harris, May 15, 1838, Reynolds to Harris, May 21, 1838, *Document 225,* pp. 92, 97; Grant Foreman, pp. 364-65; Love to Logan, July 3, 1840, *M234*-923: A899-40.

31. Casey to Clark, July 11, 1838, *Document 225,* pp. 119-20; List of Seminole Negroe Prisoners turned over at Fort Pike, March 21, 1838, National Archives Record Group 75, *Miscellaneous Muster Rolls, 1832-46;* List of Slaves Owned by Miccopotokee or Copiah Yahola, April 29, 1835, in *M234*-802: D153-56.

32. See note 31.

33. Reynolds to Harris, May 26, 1838, Muster Roll, May 1838, and Collins to Harris, July 29, 1838, *Document 225,* pp. 97, 99; Grant Foreman, p. 366.

34. Reynolds to Harris, June 2, 1838, *2nd and 7th LR,* box 2; *Document 225,* p. 100; Grant Foreman, p. 366.

35. Reynolds to Governor of Arkansas, June 3, 1838, Sam C. Roane, to Reynolds, June 4, 1838, *Document 225,* p. 102; Grant Foreman, p. 366.

36. Reynolds to Arbuckle, June 12, 1838, Reynolds to Harris, June 18, 1838, *Document 225,* pp. 101, 103; Muster Roll of Seminoles Emigrated June 1838, Conducted by Lt. J. G. Reynolds, *Miscellaneous Muster Rolls, 1832-1846;* Arbuckle

to Reynolds, June 13, 1838, National Archives Record Group 393, *Secondary Military Department,* Letters Sent (hereafter cited as *2nd LS*), *M234*-255: A 692-38, *Document 225,* p. 103; Arbuckle to Jones, June 13, 1838, *M234*-255: A692-38.

37. Harris to Cooper, May 25, 1838, Collins to Harris, July 29, 1838, *Document 225,* pp. 48, 124.

38. Collins to Harris, July 29, 1838, Tod Robinson to Reynolds, October 2, 1838, Reynolds to Harris, June 28, 1838, *Document 225,* pp. 124, 104; Collins to Reynolds, June 25, 1838, *2nd and 7th LR,* box 2.

39. Harris to Reynolds, July 6, 1838, *M234*-291: R415-39; *Document 225,* p. 49.

40. Reynolds to Harris, September 7, 1838, *M234*-291: R415-39; Edwin C. Mc-Reynolds, *The Seminoles* (Norman: University of Oklahoma Press, 1957), p. 213.

41. Collins to Harris, July 29, August 8, 1838, *M234*-225: C761-38, C764-38; *Document 225,* pp. 111, 112.

42. Harris to Reynolds, August 27, 1838, Reynolds to Harris, September 20, 1838, *M234*-291: R415-39.

43. *House Report 724,* p. 2; Arbuckle to Armstrong, August 27, 1838, and Arbuckle to Poinsett, August 27, 1838, *2nd LS; Document 225,* p. 114.

44. Arbuckle to Poinsett, September 28, 1838, *2nd LS; M234*-225: A470-38; *Document 225,* p. 126.

45. Collins to Poinsett, September 28, 1838, *M234*-225: C838-38, Crawford to Armstrong and Arbuckle, November 15, 1838, Crawford to Collins, November 15, 1838, *Document 225,* pp. 126, 51.

46. Arbuckle to Crawford, January 12, 1839, *2nd LS; Document 225,* p. 1.

47. Joshua R. Giddings, *The Exiles of Florida* (Columbus, Ohio: Follett, Foster and Company, 1858), pp. 194-213.

48. McReynolds, p. 212.

49. Harris to Cooper, May 1, 1838, *2nd and 7th LR,* box 2; *Document 225,* p. 43.

50. The following sources relate to Watson's claim: J. C. Watson to Poinsett, November 22, 1839, Watson to Crawford, December 6, 1839, Richard W. Habersham et al. to Poinsett, July 2, 1840, E. A. Nisbet to Poinsett, July 2, 1840, Watson to Poinsett, July 25, 1840, Watson to Crawford, February 18, 1842, *M234*-289: W1099-39, W1010-39, H727-40, N83-40, W1226-40, W1715-42; Crawford to Poinsett, April 8, July 1, July 9, 1840, Crawford to John Bell, August 10, 1841, National Archives Microfilm Publications, *Microcopy M348* (Office of Indian Affairs, Report Books) 2: 59, 141, 143, 476 (hereafter cited as *M348,* followed by the roll number); Crawford to John C. Spencer, January 19, 1842, *M348*-3: 83; James Dawson to Commissioner of Indian Affairs, June 30, 1840, Watson to Poinsett, January 11, 1841, John H. Watson to Poinsett, February 24, 1841, A. Iverson to Crawford, February 27, 1841, Bell to Crawford, April 29, 1841, J. C. Watson to Bell, July 7, 1841, *M234*-226; D475-40, W1351-41, W1372-41, I714-41, W1433-41, W1519-41; Crawford to Poinsett, February 27, 1841, Poinsett to Arbuckle, March 2, 1841, Bell to Armstrong, March 24, 1841, Crawford to Armstrong, April 29, 1841, *M21*-30: 143, 152, 184, 245; *House Report 724,* p. 2; Giddings, pp. 243-50.

For a recent account of the Watson case as part of the national debate over slavery, see James E. Sefton, "Black Slaves, Red Masters, White Middlemen: A Congressional Debate of 1852," *Florida Historical Quarterly* 51 (October 1972), 113-28.

The following sources relate to the Love claim: Arbuckle to Roley McIntosh, June 8, 1840, and Arbuckle to Logan, July 19, 1840, *2nd LS;* Love to Logan, July 3, 1840, Armstrong to Crawford, October 17, 1840, Mark A. Cooper to Bell, May 17, 1841, *M234*-923; A899-40, C1411-41; T. F. Foster to Secretary of War, January 7, 1842, *M234*-226: F251-42; W. T. Colquitt to Spencer, *M234*-289: C1710-42; Crawford to Bell, June 7, 1841, *M348*-2: 420; Crawford to Spencer, May 13, 1842, *M348*-3: 142; Crawford to Foster, January 21, 1841, *M21*-31: 389.

51. Debo, p. 103.

52. Arbuckle to Crawford, January 10, 1839, Treaty Concluded November 23, 1838, Jim Boy and David Barnet to Armstrong and Arbuckle, November 22, 1838, National Archives Microfilm Publications, *Microcopy T494* Documents Relating to the Negotiation of Ratified and Unratified Treaties with Various Indian Tribes, 1801-1869) 9: Frames 82, 90, 86.

53. Debo, p. 102; Armstrong to Harris, April 14, 1838, *M234*-225; A346-38; Joseph Bryan to William Medill, December 22, 1846, *M234*-801: B2799-46; Medill to Bryan, December 30, 1846, Medill to Armstrong, December 30, 1846, *M21*-39: 86, 87; Medill to Benjamin Marshall et al., June 22, 1848, *M21*-41:2.

54. Statement of Jim Boy, June 11, 1837, *JPLS*; Caesar Bruner to Jesup, April 9, 1837, *JPLR,* box 12.

55. List of Claims for Property Lost and Left in the Old Creek Nation, October 24, 1836, *M234*-255: frame 208; Marshall et al. to Medill, April 27, 1848, *M234*-228: M215-48.

chapter 6

SLAVERY IN
THE NEW LAND

THE FIRST FEW years following removal were troubled times for the Creeks. They found the western land unhealthy, and, in a weakened condition upon arrival, great numbers died before they could adjust to the new climate. In 1831, for instance, 500 of the McIntosh Creeks died from fever, influenza, and other diseases. There were cholera and smallpox epidemics in the winter of 1833-34. During the year following the great migration of 1836, many were sick. At least 3,500 died, and the Creeks were disheartened. By 1838, the Creeks were reported enjoying better health, but there were still bad years to come. Floods occurred in the spring of 1845, destroying homes and crops in the river bottoms and leaving unhealthy conditions in their wake. Sickness prevailed in the summer, and many Creeks died. Their numbers continued to decline steadily because of prevailing diseases such as pneumonia. The census of 1857 listed 14,888 in the tribe, a loss of 10,000 since removal. A census of 1859 listed 13,550 persons, a decline of 43 percent in the Creek population after removal.[1] Despite health problems, the Creeks set about rebuilding their society. Shortly after removal they were able to reduce their factionalism and make significant changes in their government as well as in their manners and customs, including the institution of slavery.

Although it ultimately delcined, factionalism persisted during the early years of the tribe's reunion in the West. The Creeks were divided into the Upper and Lower towns once more. Roley McIntosh was chief of the Lower Creeks. Several men served as chief of the Upper Creeks, but the influence of Opothleyohola was paramount. The tribe was nearly equally divided between the two, and all towns adhered to these two chiefs. Each town had a chief, and the town chiefs, with the principal chief, held councils and passed laws. The Lower Creek settlements extended up the Verdigris River and between it and the Arkansas, as well as along both banks of the Arkansas up to the Red Fork (about eighty miles). They were separated from the Upper Creeks by a prairie that extended south from the bottoms of the Arkansas to the bottoms of the North Fork (about forty miles away) and west between the Deep Fork, North Fork, and the Canadian to Little River.[2]

In 1840 it was reported that the Creeks had adjusted their differences. They met in general council and elected McIntosh as principal chief and then began building a general council house at which town chiefs from the whole nation met annually to pass laws for the government of the people. By 1845, it was reported that the political differences between the Upper and Lower Creeks were disappearing and that all cheerfully submitted to Roley McIntosh as principal chief.[3] This report was probably an exaggeration of the facts, but there is no doubt that the factionalism was waning.

The national council's deliberations were restricted to national matters affecting the Upper and Lower Creeks in common. Problems relating to either group only were dealt with in their own councils, held separately and not interfered with by the other party. The councils were conducted similarly, composed of the chiefs of different towns. The chiefs, usually older citizens with some exceptions, were described as "extremely ignorant" and "noted for their superstitious bigotry, for their old customs and ceremonies, and most bitter prejudices against all measures calculated to reform the condition or enlighten the minds of their people."[4]

In 1839 the Creeks were still working by towns. All who were attached to a chief lived together and cultivated a town field, all sharing in the labor. Individuals had plots of their own as well. By 1841, however, many were farming separate fields. By 1845, the Lower Creeks had given up the practice of town fields altogether. They had given up the wearing of ornaments and paint except for festivals or ball plays; they generally copied the dress of the whites, and many understood English. The Upper Creeks, more isolated from contact with the whites, maintained more of their aboriginal dress, manners, and farming methods.[5]

The Creeks were excellent farmers, producing corn, rice, cotton, pumpkins, melons, potatoes, and beans. They raised large quantities of corn, most years producing a surplus which they at first sold to the military at

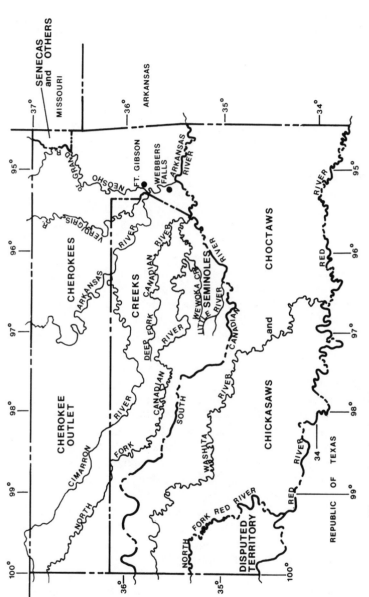

Western Lands of the Five Civilized Tribes, 1840

Fort Gibson and later exported to Ireland and other foreign countries. In 1840, the government provided large quantities of stock animals from which they developed great herds.[6]

Much of the labor was done by blacks, who helped form the financial base for the wealthier Creeks. In 1845, for instance, the McIntosh family's estimated worth was $150,000, and Benjamin Marshall was supposedly worth $50,000. Marshall's plantation on the Verdigris was one of the best known in the Nation, noted for its fields and orchards. Chilly McIntosh established his plantation near the mouth of the Verdigris, and Roley McIntosh, half-brother of William, built his plantation in the forks of the Arkansas and the Verdigris.[7]

The slave usually performed a certain amount of service for his master and supported himself and his family during his free time.[8] In 1845, William Quesenbury, an Arkansan, wrote of the Creek slaves: "I have been told that three of their negroes can perform as much work as one of ours. The negroes have to support themselves with clothing and food. To do this they are allowed the Saturday of every week, and after their master's crop is laid by in July, from that time to September, or harvest time."[9]

The blacks lived on little individual farms and did not have to be under an overseer as did the slaves of the Cherokees and Choctaws. Sometimes, slaves of different masters were married and lived apart from either master. Their houses were as good as those of the poor Creeks, usually one or two rooms made of logs chinked with mud and animal hair and chimneys of mud and sticks. During the early years in the West the cabins were sometimes clustered together for protection against intrusion by wild Indians. The blacks farmed cotton, carded and spun the fiber, and wove cloth for their own clothes. They tanned hides for harness and shoes. They raised vegetables, rice, and corn, the latter being used to make sofkee, their main dish. The Indians had few native mechanics. Whites or blacks—both slave and free—were the artisans and smiths. And some owners apparently did not care if their slaves learned to read and write.[10]

Historian Angie Debo has stated that slavery "rested very lightly" upon the slaves in the Creek country and that possession of slaves was "a great convenience," free of the exploitation and degradation that marked slavery among the whites. Despite the growing severity of the Creek slave code during the decade preceding removal, the comparative laxity of the code and the social practices regarding free blacks still allowed blacks to accumulate property with which they could purchase their own freedom or that of others.[11] Instances of such transactions are common in the official records. In 1845, for instance, the free black Hope purchased a fifteen-year-old boy Flem for $290. In 1847, Robin purchased himself from William Grierson (Grayson). Lina was purchased by her husband Nero, who was free. According to Chilly McIntosh, Governor Nero (who died about 1854) bought all of his family, some of the money for which he had borrowed on a promissory note. At his death, he owned a wagon, oxen, and ten ponies. The Creeks often used blacks as interpreters in dealing with the whites and rewarded them for their efforts, again providing a means by which the blacks could purchase their freedom. Caesar, who had been an interpreter in Florida, left $400 with his wife, who belonged to Billy Walker, when he left Alabama for Florida. Walker died and left his property to Ned Hendrick of Montgomery, who in 1842 had Caesar's wife and his money. The money he left and what he earned in Florida was to be used to buy his wife, but Caesar had not been allowed to return to Alabama from Florida, and in 1842 Hendrick was asking $3,500 for Caesar's wife and three children.[12]

In February 1842 Lieutenant Colonel Ethan Allen Hitchcock used an old black interpreter to talk to the Tuckabahchee Micco about his religious beliefs, and Yargee's black Tom interpreted for Hitchcock in his conversations with Yargee. Hitchcock traveled from the Upper Creek settlements to Edwards's trading post near old Fort Holmes at the mouth of Little River. His guide was Hughes, a black, with whom he lodged en route at the home of a family named Connor. He wrote, "I and the nigger have taken dinner together. If Maj. Downing could say 'I and the General' then *I and the nigger.* . . . We had some meat so fried out of countenance that I could not tell what it was for some time. . . . We had some native corn bread. . . . There were just four fried eggs and I must commend the delicacy of the nigger who considerately left his for me and I left one 'for manners.' Then we had a cup of very good coffee with sugar, but there is no milk in this country."[13]

Blacks were relatively free in their social lives during the early years in the West. They were allowed to visit one another and were often sent on errands. They attended the ball plays and dances, or "bangas" as they called them. William Quesenbury attended a dance at "old Salley's" in the Lower Creek country in the summer of 1845. He wrote, "We found a goodly number of red and black of both sexes already assembled, and a continual increase was also pouring in. . . . Soloman the fiddler

sometimes played too fast, and he was often told that he needn't be put-
tin' on airs, that he was nothing but a sofka raised nigger." Quesenbury
lodged with Constantine Perkins, at whose house the next morning an
Indian woman called bringing an old letter from a man named Stanley
concerning a petrified mammoth bone. "The squaw very gravely told
C. that John, a negro, had given her the letter last night at the party and
said that Mr. Perkins had given it to John as a draft for a jug of whiskey
John deserved a good hickory withe. He had bought nearly half the liquor
the poor squaw had with Stanley's old letter."[14]

Perhaps the most rigid social restrictions on the Creek blacks concerned
their tendency to embrace Christianity. In pre-removal days, the Upper
Creeks had not tolerated Christian services among the blacks, and they
brought their intolerance with them to the West. As Indian officials said,
they were more bitterly "prejudiced against all measures calculated to
reform the condition or enlighten the minds of their people." At first,
the McIntosh Creeks had felt no animosity toward the missionaries. In
1830 the American Board of Commissioners for Foreign Missions organized
a Presbyterian Church with thirty members, mostly blacks, in the Creek
Nation. In December of that year the Baptist Board of Missions arrived,
finding five or six Baptists in the Creek country. All were slaves except
for a Creek named John Davis and one other. They had not been congregated into a church. Davis had been preaching, and the board took him
under its patronage. In 1832, the Reverend Isaac McCoy, representing the
board, arrived in the Creek Nation to check on the progress of the Baptist
work. A great number of slaves came forward to be baptized, but to Mc-
Coy's dismay few could give anything like a satisfactory account of "a
work of grace upon their souls." The first ten who offered themselves
were turned away. McCoy dismissed the meeting and advised the native
preachers not to admit to fellowship in the church "any who could not
give satisfactory evidence of conversion to God." In 1832 the Methodists
arrived, and by the end of that year they and the Baptists had 200 and 65
members, respectively, while the Presbyterians had 81. A majority of the
members were black.[15]

In 1836 one of the Methodist missionaries was charged with preaching
abolitionism. Although there was now some Creek opposition to missionaries, a council on August 31 failed to vote to expel them. However,
the missionaries left the Nation anyway, believing that the situation was
unsafe. Although there had been no overt abolitionism among the missionaries, some of the slaveholders did not like the missionaries' work

among the blacks. About this time, the hostile Creeks from the "war" of 1836 arrived in the West from Alabama. When the McIntosh Creeks met the new arrivals in council at Fort Gibson, they agreed formally, apparently to appease the immigrants, to expel the missionaries, whom the hostile Creeks particularly disliked and viewed as a threat to the chiefs' power. Removal of the missionaries left the preaching to "a few ignorant negroes in the Arkansas settlement." The chiefs imposed a penalty of fifty or one hundred lashes upon blacks and Indians who attended Christian services. The punishment was more often applied among the Upper Creeks than elsewhere. Still, small groups met secretly, sang spirituals in English and hymns in Creek, and listened to the black preachers.[16]

At North Fork Town in January 1842, Colonel Hitchcock observed at a private home a meeting of "Creeks, half-breeds and negroes engaged in prayer and singing psalms." He wrote:

They commenced by singing a hymn in Creek to Creek music. It was rather more plaintive than solemn; after that several hymns in English were sung to Methodist or Baptist tunes; words were simple and apparently made by themselves: "Farewell Father," with a chorus and then "Farewell, Mother" and so on sister, brother, preacher, "I'm bound to go on," was about all I could hear of one hymn. I went into the room just a moment. A negro after I came out made a prayer with considerable energy. The feelings were the same that I have seen exhibited in New York and elsewhere.

Hitchcock's description is most revealing: the language and the music were those of the Creeks and the whites, and the lyrics that he heard were apparently those of the old slave spiritual. The Tuckabahchee Micco asked Hitchcock if he could explain the meaning of the black people's holding meetings (i.e., becoming Christians), for the Creeks neither understood nor liked it.[17] The chief's comments suggest that the Upper Creeks' objections to Christianity were general and not specific. However, the cultural borrowing was plain, and Christianity, because it was foreign, was a threat to the chiefs' authority.

John D. Lang and Samuel Taylor, Jr., Quakers who visited the Creeks in the fall of 1842, wrote:

Many of the slaves and Indians appear sober and religious. Some of the slaves are approved preachers and hold meetings regular on first-days. We attended one of these meetings, which was conducted in a moderate and becoming manner. It

was composed of Indians and slaves and their masters; their minister was an un-
educated slave. All seemed interested in the meeting, and several much affected,
even to tears. A slave-holder told us that he was willing his slaves should go to
these meetings for it made them better men and women. The Creeks have long
been slave holders, and appear insensible on the subject of this great evil.[18]

As early as 1838, it was reported that prejudices against the missionaries were giving way. After 1842 the hostility to the missionaries
began to decrease rapidly, even among the Upper Creeks. That year,
Robert M. Loughridge of the Presbyterian Board of Foreign Missions
was allowed to enter the Nation. He could preach only at his mission
station at Coweta. Methodist missionaries arrived in the fall of 1842.
There was still some opposition, and Indians were whipped. In 1843
the Creek council passed a law forbidding both Indians and blacks
to attend preaching, apparently unless authorized by the council. In
1845, it was a standing law that anyone preaching or holding religious
meetings would receive fifty lashes for the first offense and one hundred
for the second, and lashes were still given to blacks for attending such
meetings. To maintain their authority, the chiefs paid out of the annuity
a number of enforcers called light horse men, who executed this and other
laws. Yet at the same time, it was reported that the Creeks were less opposed to missionaries, and religious societies were openly extending their
operations in the Nation.[19]

In 1848, in the vicinity of the Creek agency, there were four Baptist
churches that had been served by Joseph and William Islands and a black
preacher named Jacobs until a mission had been established in January
of that year by Americus L. Hay. Later that year, the chiefs ended their
formal opposition to Christianity. At that time, three of the eight Baptist
preachers were black, and thirty-nine of the Methodist members were
black.[20]

The Creeks had begun to codify their laws regarding blacks soon after
their arrival in the West. In operation among the Lower Creeks was the
code adopted in 1825, an expansion of a code of 1818. After removal,
the Upper Creeks began to record their laws, and the general council
in 1840 collected the laws into a code of laws for the whole Nation.[21]

The early laws were essentially those that had been in force before
removal. If a black killed an Indian, the black would suffer death. If an
Indian killed a black, the Indian would pay the owner his value or suffer death. If a slave killed another slave, he would receive one hundred

lashes, and his owner would pay the owner of the dead black one-half of that black's value. It was unlawful for any black to abuse an Indian citizen. It was unlawful for an Indian man to take a black for a wife, and any black, slave or free, convicted of having intercourse with a Creek woman was given a hundred lashes. Any Creek woman found guilty of the charge was given fifty lashes. Any citizen found guilty of harboring runaway slaves was punished by a fine of fifty dollars or one hundred lashes. Blacks guilty of the same offense were given one hundred lashes. Any person capturing a runaway slave was entitled to a reward of twenty-five dollars to be paid by the Creek owner. If the owner did not reside within the Nation, the reward was fifty dollars. Slaveholders were not responsible for the debts of their slaves.[22]

Historian Angie Debo has written that the Creek slave code "increased in severity as the aristocratic mixed bloods sought to change the easy and tolerant slavery of the primitive Indian to the real servitude practiced by the neighboring states." It is granted that the code increased in severity, but only in the two or three years before the outbreak of the Civil War did it approach the severity of the codes in the slave states and even then it did not approach very closely. Rather, and particularly regarding free blacks, the Creeks seemed to be reacting to the increasing severity of codes in the neighboring Indian nations, particularly that of the Cherokees, which caused free blacks to flee those nations and come to the Creek country. In January of 1847 the Creek chiefs complained that the number of blacks claiming to be free had multiplied to such an extent that it was "truly alarming." Some of them from outside the Creek Nation had settled among the Seminole blacks who had congregated on the Fort Gibson reserve, and others had settled among the Seminole blacks on Little River. This latter settlement worried the Creeks, who wanted to break it up and expel the free blacks from their nation.[23] In fact, the Creeks wanted to do what the neighboring tribes, particularly the Cherokees, had done.

Between 1839, when they adopted their constitution in the West, and 1843, the Cherokees wrote a rather strict code concerning slaves and free blacks. On November 15, 1842, apparently more under the influence of Seminole blacks in the Cherokee Nation than in response to the drafting of a slave code, a group of Cherokee slaves from plantations near Webbers Falls stole horses, burglarized a store, taking supplies, guns, and ammunition, and started for the Mexican country. The Cherokees trailed the slaves southwest into the Creek Nation where the runaways were apparently joined by slaves from the Bruner and Marshall plantations, bringing their number to about thirty-five. A party of Creeks organized to go in pursuit of the Creek slaves and, joining forces with the Cherokees, overtook the blacks about ten miles beyond the Canadian River. The blacks entrenched themselves, and a battle ensued in which two of them were killed, twelve were captured, and the rest escaped. The pursuing parties returned home for reinforcements.[24]

Rumors exaggerated the number of slaves involved. Lang and Taylor wrote: "A few days prior to our arriving there, about 200 slaves ran away from their masters. They belonged in the Creek and Cherokee nations. This caused great excitement, and a posse was sent after them from both nations."[25] The blacks met with and murdered two travelers on the plains and were finally captured by a company of Cherokees nearly three hundred miles southwest of Fort Gibson. Most were returned to their owners, and two were sent to Arkansas to stand trial for murder. It is likely that the Creek slaves involved were recipients of the same kinds of influences that had caused the Cherokee slaves to run away. Wrote Lang and Taylor: "Both Church and State seemed aroused on account of these desertions, and ready to make every possible effort to recover them at all hazards, and in the future to enact more rigid laws for the government of their slaves, and for binding their chains more strongly upon them."[26]

One way the Creeks made their laws more restrictive was to try to control the emancipation of blacks. The laws at first provided for the emancipation of slaves, who would be recognized as freemen of the Nation without condition. Later, freed blacks over twelve years of age were required to pay the Nation an annual tax of three dollars, except those who were recognized as citizens of the Nation. Freed blacks were also taxed twenty-five cents per head for cattle, horses, and sheep and five dollars for wagons. Martin Vann and D. N. McIntosh of Arkansas District and Jim Smith and Espakok Yohola were appointed to take a census of the free blacks and to collect the tax. Still later, an owner was prohibited from emancipating his slaves unless he took them out of the Nation.[27]

After the Seminoles became a part of the Creek Nation under the Treaty of 1845, the Creeks passed a law putting their laws in full effect over the Seminoles. Creek slaves had apparently been allowed to accumulate some property although there had been a law against it since 1840. The Seminoles, however, allowed their blacks to accumulate as much property as they wished. In an apparent attempt to bring the Seminole blacks into conformity with their practices the Creeks passed a law prohibiting slaves from owning or possessing horses, cattle, or guns. The light horse men were authorized to take any such property they found to be sold and the money to be placed in the national treasury.[28]

Other laws regarding blacks were passed during the 1850s. In 1856 a school law forbade the hiring of abolitionists as teachers. On May 8, 1859, the Creek council made "bona fide members and citizens" all free-born persons, except those of African descent, who had theretofore been received and acknowledged as citizens of the Creek Nation. Persons of not more than half African blood, if their mothers were Creeks, were considered Creek citizens.[29]

The law regarding citizenship reflects a growing racial consciousness. Historians, however, have disagreed concerning the extent of racial prejudice among the Creeks. John Walton Caughey has written that "The Creeks seem to have entertained race prejudice against Negroes," in contrast to their "very complaisant attitude" toward the Europeans. On the other extreme is Annie Heloise Abel, who did the first significant work on slavery among the Indians. She says that "the Creeks had no aversion whatever to race mixtures and intermarriages between the negroes and Indians was rather common. The half-breeds resulting from such unions were accepted as bona fide members of the tribe by the Indians in the distribution of annuities, but not by the United States courts." Abel says elsewhere that at the time of her writing in 1915, the Creeks presented "a very curious spectacle of an almost complete mixture." Kenneth Wiggins Porter echoes these statements by saying that the Creeks lacked racial prejudice and differed from the Cherokees, Chickasaws, and Choctaws in their attitudes toward blacks. And Angie Debo has said that except for a few mixed bloods, there was little prejudice against intermarriage with blacks, and the children were adopted without prejudice into the tribes.[30]

The evidence, however, suggests that racial prejudice was more widespread than indicated here, especially in post-removal days and particularly among the Lower Creeks. One of the pre-removal laws had denied the right of inheritance to the offspring of blacks and Indians and had called it a "disgrace" to the Nation for Creeks to marry blacks. The law against intermarriage had been reinstated in the West. Some people interpreted this law to forbid copulation with blacks. If an Indian kept one of his black women, she was taken away from him and given to his nearest relative. If it was proved that an Indian woman copulated with a black, each received lashes. There were other evidences of racial prejudice. In 1842, Davy Grayson complained to Colonel Hitchcock that he had received no provisions "of any account," nor had he received any annuity money since he arrived in the West. When asked the reason, "he said he didn't know, but he has colored blood in him he says, and some have told him that was the reason, yet Jim Boy a colored mixed is a Chief."[31]

In his synthetic study of slavery among the Indians, William G. Mc-Loughlin hypothesizes that the Indians arrived at an understanding of racial differences in an attempt to maintain their identity. Forced to admit the superiority of the whites because of their technology, the Indians saved themselves from "total degradation," McLoughlin says, by reserving for themselves a position above that of the black man. The threat of annihilation forced the Indian to develop a theory of polygenesis to explain his position.[32]

Regardless of the reason for such theories, they existed among the Creeks. One was told by the Tuckabahchee Micco in 1842. According to him, "the old people" believed that at first there were only red men. The Creator decided to make some white men so He told three red men to go into the river and wash. The first went in and stayed a long time and came out white. The second stayed only a short time. The water had been soiled, and his color was not changed. When the third went into the water, it was more soiled, and he came out black. At first people of all colors were one people; then the Creator offered them a choice. He showed the red man a piece of paper (signifying the ability to read and write), but the red man could make nothing of it and took up, instead, the bow and arrow and lived in the woods by hunting and digging roots. When the white man looked at the paper, he kept it. The Tuckabahchee Micco said that nothing was said of the black people. Before the world ends, he said, there will be peace among all people, white and red. Again, there was no mention of the blacks.[33]

Another theory was attributed to Neamathla, the old Red Stick who had returned to the Creeks in 1826 and had been a leader in the Creek "war" of 1836. According to this theory, the Great Spirit created three races and assigned duties to each, never intending the three to mingle. The Great Spirit took up some dust and blew it from His hand, and a white man stood up in front of Him. The Great Spirit was sorry, for the feeble and sickly man was not what He had intended to make. But the Great Spirit spared him. The Great Spirit tried again and this time created a black man. That grieved the Great Spirit, for the man was black and ugly. On the third attempt, He created a red man, at whom He smiled. The Great Spirit then gave each a choice from three boxes containing tools necessary for supporting themselves. Although the white man was not the Creator's favorite, he was the first created and therefore got first choice. The white man looked into the boxes and chose the one containing "pens and ink and paper and all the things you white people use." The black man, although created second, did not get second choice; that went, instead, to the Great Spirit's favorite. The red man chose the box containing "beaver traps, bows and arrows and all the kinds of things the Indians use." The black man was given a box containing "hoes and axes—plainly showing that the black man was made to labor for both the white and red man."[34]

There can be little doubt that, as the national debate over slavery heated up and the nation moved toward war, racial prejudice increased among the Creeks. The increasing severity of the Creek slave code can be explained in part, too, by Creek reaction to the increasing debate over slavery in the West. The Compromise of 1820, while admitting Missouri as a slave state, had prohibited slavery "forever" in the remaining territory purchased from France north of 36° 30', the parallel which formed the southern boundary of Missouri. The slaveholding Indians had been settled south of that parallel, with the exception of the Cherokees, who owned lands north to the 37th parallel and had a tract of 800,000 acres called the Neutral Lands in the southeastern corner of present-day Kansas. There were, as well, slaves held by traders, missionaries, and other whites among the northern tribes.[35] It was not, however, until the Mexican cession in 1848 that the American debate over slavery began to affect significantly the slaveholding Indians. The debate concerning whether the new territory would be slave or free focused attention on the West and resulted in the Compromise of 1850, which admitted California as a free state, created the territories of Utah and New Mexico with their people's having a choice regarding slavery, prohibited the slave trade in the District of Columbia, and, most significantly, passed a severe fugitive slave law.

There then arose the question of whether this latter law applied to the Indian Territory. In 1838 Attorney General B. F. Butler rendered a decision concerning that part of Article 4 of the U.S. Constitution which said, in part, that "no person held to service or labor in one state under laws thereof, escaping into another, shall, in consequence of any law or regulation therein, be discharged from such service or labor; but shall be delivered up on claim of the party to whom such service or labor may be due." In Butler's opinion, the clause referred exclusively to those parts of the Union which were duly organized as separate states. Until specifically provided for by legislation from Congress, the Indian Territory was excluded from the clause.[36]

The case Butler decided involved a family of free blacks named Beams, who lived in the Choctaw Nation and were claimed by a white Mississippian, John B. Davis. In 1853, through the influence of Secretary of War Jefferson Davis, John Davis sought to have the fugitive slave law of 1850 enforced regarding the Beams family, a number of whom by that time had moved to the Creek Nation. Early in 1854, Attorney General Caleb Cushing overturned Butler's decision of 1838 and said that Davis could lawfully enter the Indian Territory to claim any person who owed his service under the laws of Mississippi. In the wake of this decision, Davis's agents entered the Indian Territory and captured members of the Beams family in both the Choctaw and the Creek Nations.[37] As a later chapter of this work will reveal, the instances of white slave hunters entering the territory and taking slaves increased dramatically after 1854.

That same year the Kansas-Nebraska Act was passed. Under that act questions regarding slavery in the territories and new states were to be decided by the people residing there through their representatives. The Missouri Compromise was also repealed, effectively denying Congress the right to exclude slavery from the territories. The sectional struggle which earned the name of "Bleeding Kansas" brought the slave controversy even nearer to the Indian Territory.

There was a marked increase in abolitionist activity in the territory.[38] The debate between proslavery and free-soil partisans became an open one. Choctaw Agent Douglas H. Cooper believed in 1854 that within five years the abolitionist missionaries to the Indians would have the ascendency. Cooper believed that they had to be stopped: "Otherwise we shall have a great run-away harbor, a sort of Canada—with 'underground rail-roads' leading to & through it adjoining Arkansas and Texas." The federal government could not stop the abolitionism because it was "paralized by the abolition strength of the North." Said Cooper, "I see no way except secretly to induce the Choctaws & Cherokees & Creeks to allow slave-holders to settle among their people & control the movement now going on to abolish slavery among them."[39]

The debate over slavery was carried on mainly by the missionaries among the Indians. Representatives of the American Board of Foreign Missions were split in sympathy in 1855, and an open rift developed in 1859, with Samuel Austin Worcester in the Cherokee Nation the most important antislavery spokesman and Cyrus Kingsbury in the Choctaw Nation the most important proslavery spokesman. When the rift developed in 1859, the Presbyterian Board of Foreign Missions stepped in.[40]

As abolitionist activities increased in the Indian Territory, the Creeks became more restrictive than ever before concerning the activities of their blacks, and controls were placed on the free blacks as well. In early 1861 the Creeks passed a series of laws aimed at rigidly controlling the black population. Slave owners were required to keep their slaves "immediately around their improvements." No slave was permitted to go more than two miles from his owner's premises without a written pass; if caught violating the law, the slave received twenty-five lashes for every offense. No slave was permitted to go any distance from his master's premises at night; the penalty was twenty-five lashes. Whereas slaves had formerly been denied the right to own or carry guns, they were prohibited from having or carrying weapons of any kind after March 1, 1861. The penalty was twenty-five lashes. Any citizen of the Nation could enforce these laws. Slave owners were also responsible for the activities of their slaves. In issuing passes to their slaves, owners were required to specify in the pass the point or points to which the slave was going. If the owners violated this law, they were fined ten dollars for each offense. Slaves were also prohibited from hiring out during their free time from their owners. Violation brought a fine of fifty dollars for each offense. Neither could slaves engage in mercantile business if the goods were their own. If caught, the slaves forfeited their goods to the Nation to be sold to the highest bidder. The proceeds went into the national treasury except for 25 percent, which was divided between the informer and the light horse men who executed the law.[41]

Also effective on March 1, 1861, was a law prohibiting blacks from preaching to an Indian congregation. However, blacks could attend religious worship within two miles of their owners' premises only if a free person not of African origin was present to oversee the proceedings. Another

law prohibited persons from giving passes to slaves who did not belong
to them. If convicted, such a person was fined one hundred dollars and
given one hundred lashes. If he could not pay the fine, he received an
additional one hundred lashes. If the slave receiving such an illegal pass
escaped, the person giving the pass was required to pay the owner the full
value of the slave and received a hundred lashes as well. If he was unable
to pay, he suffered death.[42]

Free blacks who were in the Nation legally were given until March 10,
1861, to choose Indian owners. Any black failing to do so would be sold
by the Nation to the highest bidder. Blacks were expressly forbidden to
choose white persons as owners, and whites were prohibited from bidding
for any free black. The term of bondage was not to exceed one year. If
any person took control of a free black by the latter's consent and then
disposed of the black, he was to pay double the value of the black and
receive one hundred lashes. If he was unable to pay, he suffered death.
The free blacks were allowed to dispose of their property as they deemed
proper. The light horse men were charged with enforcing these laws.[43]

Despite the growing severity of the Creek slave code, it was recognized
at the time of the Civil War that the institution of slavery as it existed
among the Creeks and other tribes differed significantly from the institution in the white South. Wiley Britton, who was with the Union Army
in the Indian Territory during the Civil War, said that slavery among the
Cherokees, Choctaws, Chickasaws, and Creeks, though generations old,
had

never existed in the form that characterized it in the slave states of the Union,
particularly in the Southern states. The worst features of slavery, such as the hard
treatment imposed upon the slaves of the South was hardly known to the slaves
of these Indians prior to the war. Indeed, the negroes brought up among the
Indians were under such feeble restraint from infancy up that the owners and
dealers in slaves in Missouri and Arkansas did not hesitate to acknowledge that
Indian Negroes were undesirable because of the difficulty of controlling them.[44]

In a recent attempt to synthesize the study of African slavery among
the Indians, William G. McLoughlin concludes that we do not know how
much easier life for the blacks was because the information is conflicting
and that the unraveling of the contradictions will come only after detailed
studies are made of each tribe.[45] Those studies, of course, will have to take
into account, as this study of the Creeks attempts to do, the historical,

cultural, and economic circumstances of each tribe at the time of its adoption of the institution of slavery.[46]

The question arises in the case of the Creeks concerning whether their slave code and laws regarding free blacks, while passed on a national level, were strictly enforced on the local level. There is evidence to indicate that they were not. It should be remembered that the pre-removal slave codes were written by the Lower Creeks and that it was they who had led the way in codifying national laws in the West. There had always been some local control over slave matters, especially among the Upper Creeks. The Upper and Lower chiefs in their respective councils had settled debates over slave titles and determined the disposition of slave property. In the West, the council served as a court to determine titles, interpret wills, and sanction sales of slaves. It had the power to call out the light horse police to catch blacks, if necessary, and to enforce its decisions in slave cases.[47]

Evidence indicates, however, that the light horse police did not enforce the slave code but that it was left to individuals. As indicated above, for instance, some slave owners did not object to their slaves' attending religious services, while the Upper Creek chiefs opposed it bitterly. Also the law against slaves' owning weapons seems to have been generally enforced, but there is some evidence that some McIntosh Creeks, while not allowing the blacks to keep guns in their cabins, at least in the early years in the West, maintained arsenals to which the blacks had access during times of threat by the wild Indians to the west.[48] The Lower Creeks had also written laws forbidding amalgamation, a law which was also written in the West. However, cohabitation and amalgamation continued, even among the McIntosh Creeks in the West. For instance, on his return from the prairies in 1832, Washington Irving and some of his half-starved companions stopped at a log farm house in the western part of the Creek lands. Near the house were a stable, a barn, and granaries about which were hogs, chickens, and turkeys. The owner of the house was apparently a mixed-blood Creek, whom Irving referred to as a white man. His spouse was a "fat good-humored negress," who served boiled beef and turnips from an iron pot in the fireplace onto "a brown earthen dish" and who seated Irving and his friends "around a three-legged table" to enjoy their repast.[49] Other instances of amalgamation and cohabitation were apparent in the removal records.[50]

There is evidence, too, that the law against ownership of property was

Paro Bruner, a Former Creek Freed Black, Photographed circa 1900.
Courtesy of Research Library, Oklahoma Historical Society,
Oklahoma City.

Martin Nance or Nancey, a Former Creek Slave, Photographed circa
1891. Courtesy of Research Library, Oklahoma Historical Society,
Oklahoma City.

not strictly enforced. The Treaty of 1866, for instance, between the Creeks and the United States provided for the payment of claims for losses sustained by the loyal Creeks and blacks during the war. The blacks—formerly both slave and free, but mainly from the Upper Creek settlements—submitted and were paid claims for sizable amounts of property. Official records indicate that the former slaves owned large herds of hogs, cattle, and sheep. They also owned large numbers of horses, and a few owned guns, both of which Creek laws expressly forbade. They owned oxen teams and wagons and agricultural, brick-laying, carpentry, and cabinet-making tools as well as musical instruments and household goods. They also held large quantities of corn, rice, potatoes, and other goods. Similar claims for property were submitted by former free blacks. There were also free blacks in business in the Creek Nation. Sarah Davis, for instance, lost her boardinghouse and house of entertainment for traders and government and other employees at the agency. She owned a building with seven large rooms. Monday Durant lost a general store near the mouth of Little River, and Scipio Barnett also lost his store and merchandise.[51] The strictness with which the property law and others regarding blacks were enforced apparently had much to do with the degree to which the town system had broken down in local areas. It had obviously degenerated to a greater degree among the Lower than among the Upper Creeks.

As with slavery elsewhere, slaves were unequally distributed among the Creeks. In 1860, there were 1,651 slaves in the Creek Nation held by only 267 Creek slaveholders. Two owners held over seventy-five each, and ten owners held a total of 433. The average of slaves per slaveholder was about six, while the number of Indians in the tribe per black was nine.[52]

The slaves represented, at most at any given time, about 10 percent of the Creek Nation's population during the years preceding the Civil War. Yet the impact they had on Creek history during the years following removal was great in relation to their numbers. Although the code of laws regarding them became stricter as time passed, the greater severity was apparently a reaction to events in the Indian Territory, especially the acts of the neighboring tribal groups. The most significant were the Seminoles, who, from the beginning of their removal in 1838 until a separate nation was established for them in 1856, were a part

of the Creek Nation. The differences between the characteristics of
the institution of slavery in each nation as well as between the social
practices of each regarding blacks were a constant source of irritation
between the two peoples.

NOTES

1. Grant Foreman, *The Five Civilized Tribes* (Norman: University of Oklahoma
Press, 1934), pp. 150, 178, 211, 216; *Senate Document 1*, 26 Cong., 1 sess., p. 471;
Senate Document 1, 25 Cong., 3 sess., p. 511; *Executive Document 2*, 29 Cong.,
1 sess., p. 514; Michael F. Doran, "Population Statistics of Nineteenth Century
Indian Territory," *The Chronicles of Oklahoma* 53 (Winter 1975-76), 498, 501.

2. *Senate Document 1*, 26 Cong., 1 sess., p. 471; *Senate Document 1*, 25
Cong., 3 sess., p. 512; *Executive Document 2*, 29 Cong., 1 sess., pp. 516-17.

3. *Executive Document 2,* 26 Cong., 2 sess., p. 314; *Executive Document 2*,
28 Cong., 1 sess., p. 415.

4. *Executive Document 2*, 29 Cong., 1 sess., p. 515.

5. *Senate Document 1*, 26 Cong., 1 sess., p. 471; *Executive Document 2*, 27
Cong., 2 sess., p. 315; *Executive Document 2,* 29 Cong., 1 sess., p. 517.

6. *Senate Document 1,* 25 Cong., 3 sess., p. 511; *Executive Document 2,* 26
Cong., 2 sess., p. 313; *Executive Document 2,* 27 Cong., 2 sess., p. 315; *Executive
Document 2,* 27 Cong., 3 sess., p. 443.

7. *Executive Document 2,* 29 Cong., 1 sess., p. 517; John Bartlett Meserve, "The
MacIntoshes," *The Chronicles of Oklahoma* 10 (September 1932), 318, 319; Carolyn
Thomas Foreman, "Marshalltown, Creek Nation," *The Chronicles of Oklahoma* 32
(Spring 1954), 52. Marshall, whose father was an Englishman, was a prominent man
among the Lower Creeks. He had signed the Treaty of 1825 but had escaped the fate
of McIntosh. He had been interpreter at the negotiations of the Treaty of 1827 and
had signed the Treaty of 1832.

8. Angie Debo, *The Road to Disappearance* (Norman: University of Oklahoma
Press, 1941), p. 115; George P. Rawick, ed., *The American Slave: A Composite Autobiography,* 19 vols. (Westport, Conn.: Greenwood Publishing Company, 1972), 7:
55, 115, 157.

9. *Arkansas Intelligencer,* August 2, 1845; Grant Foreman, p. 174.

10. Rawick, 7: 8, 157, 117, 55-57; George McIntosh (Interview), *Indian-Pioneer
History,* 116 vols. (Indian Archives Division, Oklahoma Historical Society), 7: 73;
Debo, pp. 110, 115. When Washington Irving visited the Creek agency in 1832, he
noted that a black was shoeing horses there. See also his references to "negro huts."
Irving, *A Tour on the Prairies,* author's rev. ed. (New York: G. P. Putnam's Sons,
1910), pp. 30, 33.

11. Debo, p. 115.

12. Statement of Elizabeth Perry, March 8, 1845, Statement of William Grierson, December 27, 1847, National Archives Record Group 393 (Records of the

United States Army Continental Commands, 1821-1920), *Fort Gibson,* Volume "Indian Affairs," pp. 50, 30; Francis N. Page to P. H. Raiford, March 10, 1851, National Archives Record Group 393, *Second and Seventh Military Departments, Letters Sent;* Debo, p. 115; Ethan Allen Hitchcock, *A Traveler in Indian Territory: The Journal of Ethan Allen Hitchcock, late Major-General in the United States Army,* ed. Grant Foreman (Cedar Rapids, Iowa: The Torch Press, 1930), pp. 149-50.

13. Hitchcock, pp. 116-17, 123, 145, 152-54.

14. Grant Foreman, pp. 201-03; Rawick, 7: 58, 117; *Arkansas Intelligencer,* August 2, 1845.

15. Isaac McCoy, *History of Baptist Indian Missions: Embracing Remarks on the Former and Present Condition of the Aboriginal Tribes; Their Settlement Within the Indian Territory, and Their Future Prospects* (Washington, D.C.: William M. Morrison; New York: H. and S. Raynor, 1840), pp. 425, 452, 453; Debo, p. 116.

16. Debo, pp. 117-18; *Executive Document 2,* 29 Cong., 1 sess., p. 515; McCoy, pp. 507-09; *Arkansas Intelligencer,* June 14, 1845.

17. Hitchcock, pp. 109-10, 127.

18. John D. Lang and Samuel Taylor, Jr., *Report of a Visit to Some of the Tribes of Indians Located West of the Mississippi River* (Providence: Knowles and Vose, 1843), pp. 40-41.

19. *Senate Document 1,* 25 Cong., 3 sess., pp. 511, 512; *Senate Document 1,* 26 Cong., 1 sess., p. 471; Debo, p. 119; Grant Foreman, pp. 179, 181; *Executive Document 2,* 29 Cong., 1 sess., pp. 515, 519; *Arkansas Intelligencer,* June 14, 1845.

20. Grant Foreman, p. 195; Debo, p. 120.

21. Debo, p. 125.

22. Laws 4, 5, 29, 30, 31, 32, 33, 37, 48, "Laws of the Creek Nation," *Creek— Laws,* Grant Foreman Collection, Indian Archives Division, Oklahoma Historical Society; Grant Foreman, pp. 213, 214; Debo, pp. 126, 127.

23. Debo, p. 126; James Logan to William Medill, January 12, 1847, National Archives Microfilm Publications, *Microcopy M234* (Office of Indian Affairs, Letters Received) 227: G18-47, hereafter cited as *M234,* followed by the roll number.

24. *Laws of the Cherokee Nation: Adopted by the Council at Various Periods* (Tahlequah, Cherokee Nation: Cherokee Advocate Office, 1852), pt. 2: 18, 19, 37, 44, 53, 55; Daniel F. Littlefield, Jr., and Lonnie E. Underhill, "The Cherokee Slave 'Revolt' of 1842," *American Indian Quarterly* 3 (Summer 1977), 121-31; Statement of John Drew, January 3, 1843, *M234*-87: S3322-43; *Arkansas State Gazette,* December 21, 1842; *Fort Smith Elevator,* February 12, 1897; Captain J. Brown to Captain W. W. S. Bliss, November 20, 1842, *Second and Seventh Military Departments,* Letters Received, box 4.

25. Lang and Taylor, p. 41. The number of participants is established in contemporary documents cited above. A recent article gives the exaggerated number, without substantiation, as "too hundred or more." The same writer says, "The runaways were found and returned without serious incident," ignoring a pitched battle related above and the later murder of two men. See R. Halliburton, Jr., "Black Slave

Control in the Cherokee Nation," *The Journal of Ethnic Studies* 3 (Summer 1975), 29.

26. Statement of Drew, January 3, 1843, *M234*-87: S3322-43; *Arkansas Intelligencer,* April 29, 1843; Lang and Taylor, p. 41.

27. Laws 24-28, 49, "Laws of the Creek Nation"; Grant Foreman, p. 213; Debo, p. 127.

28. Matthew Arbuckle to Mic-ca-nup-pa and other Seminole Chiefs, May 11, 1840, National Archives Record Group 393, *Second Military Department,* Letters Sent; Grant Foreman, p. 215; Debo, p. 127; Laws 55, 73-74, "Laws of the Creek Nation."

29. Laws 110-111, "Laws of the Creek Nation"; Debo, p. 127.

30. John Walton Caughey, *McGillivray of the Creeks* (Norman: University of Oklahoma Press, 1938), p. 5; Annie Heloise Abel, *The American Indian as Slaveholder and Secessionist* (Cleveland: The Arthur H. Clark Company, 1915), pp. 23n, 20n; Kenneth Wiggins Porter, *The Negro on the American Frontier* (New York: Arno Press and The New York Times, 1971), p. 44; Debo, p. 116.

31. Antonio J. Waring, ed., *Laws of the Creek Nation,* University of Georgia Libraries Miscellaneous Publications, no. 1 (Athens: University of Georgia Press, 1960), pp. 20-21; Hitchcock, pp. 151-52.

32. William G. McLoughlin, "Red Indians, Black Slavery and White Racism: America's Slaveholding Indians," *American Quarterly* 24 (October 1974), 374, 378-79.

33. Hitchcock, pp. 126, 124-25.

34. Cited in McLoughlin, pp. 384-85. Washington Irving recorded Neamathla's legend in his essay "The Seminoles." See Irving, *Wolfert's Roost,* author's rev. ed. (New York: G. P. Putnam's Sons, 1910), pp. 247-50.

35. Abel, pp. 21-22.

36. B. F. Butler to Joel R. Poinsett, August 30, 1838, *M234*-922: A556-39.

37. Opinion of C. Cushing, February 18, 1854, Jefferson Davis to S. A. Worcester, October 7, 1854, National Archives Microfilm Publications, *Microcopy M574* (Special Files of the Office of Indian Affairs, 1807-1904) 75: frame 1482, Choctaw 1727-54; S. Cooper to Commanding Officer, Fort Gibson, May 4, 1854, *Fort Gibson,* Letters Received, box 4. For a detailed history of the Beams family, see Daniel F. Littlefield, Jr. and Mary Ann Littlefield, "The Beams Family: Free Blacks in Indian Territory," *The Journal of Negro History* 61 (January 1976); 16-35.

38. Abel, p. 23.

39. Cited in Abel, pp. 41-42.

40. Abel, pp. 41-42; William G. McLoughlin, "The Choctaw Slave Burning: A Crisis in Mission Work among the Indians," *Journal of the West* 13 (January 1975), 113-27; "Indian Slaveholders and Presbyterian Missionaries, 1837-1861," *Church History* 42 (December 1973), 535-51.

41. Laws 112-119 and 110-112, new series, "Laws of the Creek Nation"; Grant Foreman, p. 215; Rawick, p. 117.

42. Laws 113-118, new series, "Laws of the Creek Nation"; Grant Foreman, p. 216; Debo, p. 127.

43. Laws 119-122, new series, "Laws of the Creek Nation."

44. Wiley Britton, *The Civil War on the Border,* 2 vols. (New York: G. P. Putnam's Sons, 1890-1904), 2: 24-25.

45. McLoughlin, "Red Indians, Black Slavery and White Racism," pp. 368-69.

46. Since McLoughlin's writing, R. Halliburton, Jr., has published *Red over Black: Black Slavery among the Cherokee Indians* (Westport, Conn.: Greenwood Press, 1977), and I have published *Africans and Seminoles: From Removal to Emancipation* (Westport, Conn.: Greenwood Press, 1977).

47. Statement of David Barnet, February 2, 1842, *M234*-226: H1047-42; Solon Borland to Orlando Brown, June 10, 1850, John Drennen to Luke Lea, March 31, 1852, *M234*-228: B702-50, D78-52; Brown to Borland, June 15, 1850, National Archives Microfilm Publications, *Microcopy M21* (Office of Indian Affairs, Letters Sent) 43: 260: D. B. Aspberry to E. B. Bright, February 16, 1854, Aspberry to R.G. Atkins and Tommy Hay, n.d., *M234*-802: M383-57.

48. McIntosh, 7:73.

49. Irving, *A Tour on the Prairies,* pp. 239, 247-48.

50. B. S. Parsons and Thomas J. Abbott to Lewis Cass, September 7, 1832, *M234*-223: frame 306; Parsons to Cass, October 16, 1832, in J. H. Johnston, "Documentary Evidence and the Relations of Negroes and Indians," *The Journal of Negro History* 14 (January 1929), 37; Census Roll, 1833, National Archives Record Group 75 (Records of the Bureau of Indian Affairs), *Creek Removal Records.*

51. Various claims, especially Claims 55, 113, 117, and 969, National Archives Record Group 75, *Records Relating to Loyal Creek Claims, 1869-70.*

52. Ohland Morton, "Confederate Government Relations with The Five Civilized Tribes," *The Chronicles of Oklahoma* 31 (Summer 1953), 199; U.S. Department of the Interior, Census Office, *Eighth Census of the United States, 1860* (Washington, D.C.: Government Printing Office, 1864), book 1: xv; U. S., Department of Commerce, Bureau of the Census, *Negro Population, 1790-1915* (Washington, D.C.: Government Printing Office, 1918; reprint ed., New York: Arno Press and The New York Times, 1968), p. 56..

Those Creeks owning ten or more slaves were as follows: Sally McLish (13), David Bruner (11), Heirs of Doyle Hopoine (23), Heirs of Kotcher Tustennuggee (10), Billy Islands (10), Peter Yargee (13), John Yargee (16), Milly Yargee (28), Hotiche Herrod (10), Moty Kinnard (12), Opothleyohola (25), Abram Foster (12), John Sells (15), Roley McIntosh (62), Daniel N. McIntosh (29), George W. Drew (10), Lafayette Marshall (12), Heirs of Vicey Lands (11), Catharine Vann (13), Moses Perryman (37), Phillip Marshall (10), James Butler (10), Benjamin Marshall (76), Eliza Gooding (12), Vicey Barnwell (20), Jane Hawkins (76), Hunter (14), Lucinda Bruner (11), Timothy Barnett (19), Henry Perryman (11), Hannah Stidham (10), Absalom Cornells (10), Roseanna Sells (15), George Anderson (10), Joseph Smith (18), George W. Stidham (42), Susan Cornells (32), Malinda Hawkins (18), Kendal Lewis (17), Eliza Smith (11), Tallassee Yargee (10), and Halputta Harjo (20). National Archives Microfilm Publications, *Microcopy M653* (Population Census Schedules) 54: Creek Nation.

CREEK CLAIMS AND SEMINOLE RESISTANCE

chapter 7

BESIDES THE FEW hundred blacks taken west by the Creeks, nearly five persons of African descent removed with the Seminoles between 1838 and 1843. Besides those captured by the Creek warriors were those who had surrendered under an agreement with General Thomas S. Jesup at Fort Dade on March 6, 1837; those who were captured by or voluntarily surrendered to United States troops; those who surrendered with Alligator and his band in April 1838; those who were brought in by their owners and sent west with them; those who belonged to white owners but who were not returned to them before removal; and those who claimed to be free by virtue of their partisan action on behalf of the United States during the Seminole War.[1] With such large numbers of blacks in the Creek country, conflict between the Creeks and Seminoles was inevitable. Among the Seminole blacks were a number claimed by Creek citizens, some of the claims predating the Red Stick War. Whereas the Seminoles were disorganized for a number of years following removal, the Creeks had begun to centralize their government, thus making for a more "efficient" handling of slave matters and ensuring a stronger leadership by the chiefs in such issues. It also resulted in the development of a more severe slave code while the Seminoles had none and, at least for the first few years following removal, maintained a semblance of the loose alliance that had existed between them and their blacks before removal. Issues regarding blacks would pervade Creek-Seminole affairs for several years following removal. Slave claims and trends in Creek civil and political affairs simply confirmed the Seminoles' fear that, once in the West, the Creeks would dominate them and take their property.

Although the Treaty of Payne's Landing (1832) had provided for Seminole resettlement on Creek lands, the Seminoles were afraid that union with the Creeks would result in the loss of their tribal existence and interests. The Creeks, because of their numbers, would control Seminole internal regulations and police and would make and execute laws that were partial to the Creeks. In short, they were afraid of becoming a powerless, oppressed minority. Of particular concern were their blacks, many of whom were claimed by Creeks who charged that the blacks had absconded to the Seminoles while they were still east of the Mississippi. Others they claimed had been captured by the Seminoles or had surrendered under General Jesup's promises of freedom to those blacks who would surrender and, as a result, had emigrated with the Seminoles. Over the years, the Seminoles had come to look upon the blacks as their property. The Seminoles feared that if they united with the Creeks, the blacks would be taken from them by force or by laws enacted by the Creeks. For that reason, most of them under Alligator, Holatoochee, Wild Cat, Concharte Micco, and other head men settled with Cherokee permission on Cherokee lands in the river bottoms near Fort Gibson. Only Micanopy's and Black Dirt's bands went to the western part of the Creek Nation and settled respectively on the Deep Fork and Little River. By 1839, there were about 2,000 Seminoles on Cherokee lands, but it was assumed that when they gathered their crops, they would remove to the Creek country. But time passed, and they remained near the fort, evidently content to take government rations, and showed little desire to farm.[2] The Creeks did not want the Seminoles to unite and settle in one area, ostensibly because they did not feel that the Seminoles were ready to settle in a body and become quiet and orderly neighbors. Among them were too many blacks who had participated in the war and who would now "exercise an improper influence" over the Seminoles.

The Treaty of Fort Gibson (1833) had reaffirmed the Treaty of Payne's Landing by designating for the Seminoles a tract between the Canadian and the North Fork, west to a line running north and south between the two and striking the forks of Little River, provided the western line did not extend more than twenty-five miles west from the mouth of Little River, but when Opothleyohola and his followers arrived in the West, they settled in the eastern part of this tract near the confluence of the North Fork with the Canadian. The Seminoles used this as an excuse not to remove from Cherokee lands. In the fall of 1838 the chiefs wrote General Jesup that they liked the land, but that they would not settle among the Creeks, who looked upon them "as runaways, and would treat us just as they would so many dogs."[3]

Commissioner of Indian Affairs T. Hartley Crawford was convinced in early 1839 that a forced union of the tribes would be fatal to the weakened Seminoles. Seminole determination not to unite with the Creeks and other factors made Crawford recommend the assignment of another tract with which the Seminoles would be satisfied. At the request of President Martin Van Buren, on February 18, 1839, Congress designated a tract "between the Deep Fork or Little Fork and the North Fork of the Canadian so as to embrace a country equal in extent to the one the Seminoles were to have had in the Creek Nation between the main and the North Fork of the Canadian." Many of the Seminoles removed from the Cherokee Nation in the spring of 1839, but Alligator objected and dissuaded others from going.[4]

Crawford, like the Creeks, saw the blacks as a dangerous element among the Seminoles. He wrote of them in his annual report of 1839: "They are indisposed to labor; their negroes are equally so, who, unfortunately, have great control over them. It is to be deeply regretted that their slaves were ever permitted to enter the Indian country." The following year, Western Superintendent William Armstrong made a similar comment. He found the Seminoles lazy and much under the influence of the blacks, concerning whom they had "many difficulties." He wrote, "It is to be regretted that they were ever permiteed to bring a negro with them; they exercise an improper influence over them, and show a bad example to other slaves."[5]

The difficulties of which Armstrong spoke resulted in part from Creek action. Numerous Creeks claimed blacks among the Seminoles. For example, Milly Francis, the daughter of the Red Stick prophet Josiah Francis, had a claim for eight blacks among the Seminoles. She told Lieutenant Colonel Ethan Allen Hitchcock in 1842 that before her father had gone to England in 1815 he had divided his blacks among his children. Milly's sister sent the blacks to Florida, intending to follow with her family, but the family did not go. When the Seminoles were sent west, the blacks were with them. Rose, the only one who had been given to Milly by her father, recognized Milly and admitted her ownership. Rose had seven children, whom Milly claimed. Rose's husband did not belong to

Milly. The Love claim had also been revived and had almost resulted in armed conflict between the Creeks and the Seminole blacks. Also, the Creeks had begun to codify their laws, among which was one taking horses, guns, and other property from their slaves. Micanopy and the other Seminole chiefs feared that the Creeks would try to apply their laws to the Seminole slaves, who were allowed to own weapons and to accumulate property. They asked General Matthew Arbuckle at Fort Gibson to prevent any interference, and he assured them that the Creeks would not interfere as long as the Seminoles did not encourage or permit their blacks to harbor runaways.[6]

Creek concern over slave issues manifested itself on other fronts. Whites continued to claim slaves among the Creeks. In 1838, Joseph B. Cleveland of Alabama claimed slaves Ben, Frank, Will, Robin, Suckey, her daughters Delila, Ardomer, Rose, and Charlotte, and Delila's children Sancho and Claris on the basis of a bill of sale from Sally Redmouth, Cleveland's mother-in-law, who had inherited the blacks from her father Choakchot Hadjo. Cleveland had taken the blacks in 1836 and had used them to make a crop of corn, but Cleveland had fallen ill, and they were taken to the West by a black man named Joe Bruner. The Indians claimed that the bill of sale was fraudulent, that Sally thought that she was marking a power of attorney, not a bill of sale.[7]

Another case raised in 1838 was that of Lucy Mims, a Creek who had sent a family of blacks to the West by Thomas Hawkins, a white man, who had sold them to a Cherokee. Lucy appealed for help to War Department officials, who denied that they had power to enforce the return of property under those cirucmstances and told her to apply to the Cherokee agent or the courts of the Cherokee Nation.[8]

In 1840, the Creeks pushed claims for blacks among the Seminoles, one of whom was Toney Barnet, captured among the Seminoles in 1837. When he was captured, Toney, aged 36, was said "to be a good soldier, and an intrepid leader. He is the most cunning and intelligent negro we have here. He is married to the widow of the former chief of the nation." Toney, his wife Polly, and children Beckey, Grace, Lydia, Mary Ann, and Martinas, claimed to be free.[9] Toney was claimed by David Barnet, a half-blood Creek. Toney had apparently been, at one time, the property of Barnet's uncle Michee Barnet, who lived on the Flint River in Georgia. About 1822, Toney had run away to Florida, where he joined the band of Jumper, who claimed him. In 1826, Seminole Agent Gad Humphreys hired James Hard-ridge from the Creek Nation as an interpreter. At the Seminole agency, Hardridge recognized Toney and a year or two later went to the Creek country where he obtained a bill of sale for Toney from Michee Barnet. Hardridge presented his claim for Toney to Jumper, who recognized it without hesitation and turned Toney over to Hardridge, who stayed two years longer with Humphreys. When Hardridge prepared to leave Florida, Toney begged to be allowed to find a purchaser for himself so he could remain in Florida. Humphreys bought Toney, who stayed with him for a number of years, after which Toney's wife, described as a mulatto and the widow of old Chief Bowlegs, bought him and freed him.[10]

Toney had served as an interpreter and guide for a time during the war in Florida and then had emigrated in 1839, joining Micanopy's settle-ment on the Deep Fork, where he remained until David Barnet seized him as a slave. The Barnets claimed that the sales in Florida which led to Toney's claim to freedom were invalid. The Creek council had decided that Toney belonged to Singiche Barnet, who exchanged him for another black belonging to David Barnet, who wanted to use Toney as an inter-preter. When Toney was seized, his wife went to Fort Gibson for help. General Arbuckle demanded Toney's release and insisted that he was free. Barnet freed him, and he went back to the Seminoles.[11]

Shortly after this event, Captain John Page organized a delegation of Seminole chiefs to go to Florida to try to persuade the remaining Semi-noles to emigrate. Holatoochee, one of the delegates, chose Toney as his interpreter. Page maintained that during the selection of the delegation, Barnet had said nothing about Toney, who Page assumed was free. Bar-net told a different story. He claimed that when word came that Page wanted Toney to go to Florida, he went to Fort Gibson and told Page not to take his slave away. Page then allegedly told Barnet that he was going to take him no farther than Fort Smith, but, suspecting something different, Barnet had chief Roley McIntosh ask Arbuckle not to let Page take Toney away. Barnet claimed that he interpreted McIntosh's speech and that Arbuckle promised that he would not let Page take the black. Page denied that Barnet had ever spoken to him on the matter and claimed to be unaware of Barnet's appeal to Arbuckle.[12] Over Barnet's objections, in October 1840, Toney accompanied the delegation to Florida.

The Western Creeks were as good slave hunters as they had been in the East. In November 1840 they captured two blacks, Billy and Grandison, on the Arkansas River about twenty miles above Fort Gibson. The blacks were armed with guns and had run away from their Cherokee owners. A few days later five blacks were in custody. One had arrived on the Arkansas River in late August, and the others in October. The latter were accompanied by two young Cherokees named Harlin, who apparently had persuaded the blacks to run away. The Creeks, according to their law, collected a fifty-dollar reward for the return of each slave.[13]

Shrewd slave hunters and traders themselves, the Creeks were always alert to white slave hunters who came into their lands. In early 1841, the chiefs called before them Warren R. Foster, whom they considered "a suspisous character." Foster had with him a black whom he claimed to have purchased in Little Rock from Nelson W. Hill but who the chiefs believed, from talking to the black, belonged to W. E. Woodruff, editor of the *Arkansas Gazette*.[14]

Another source of irritation for the Creeks came from the tribes to the west. They developed the practice of buying blacks from the Comanches who had stolen them, primarily in Texas. In December 1840, the chargé d'affaires of the Republic of Texas informed American officials that a captive had returned from the Caddoes with news that there were Kickapoos, Shawnees, Cherokees, Choctaws, and a "considerable number of Negro slaves, men, women, and children" from the United States among the Caddoes. American officials also learned of a Comanche raid on the Colorado River plantation (Bastrop County) of Joseph W. Robertson on February 18, 1839. The Indians had carried off a number of Robertson's slaves, and in 1841 he learned that two of them were held by citizens of the Creek Nation. Adjutant General Roger Jones instructed General Zachary Taylor, who commanded the Second Military Division at Fort Smith, to find out if any United States Indians had been involved in the raids.[15]

Robertson claimed that Manuel and Aaron were held on the Canadian by James Edwards, a white man who had married a Creek, and his son-in-law Jesse Chisholm. In December 1840 Robertson went to Edwards, but, he claimed, a party of Cherokees who had been expelled from Texas and were encamped at Chisholm's place learned his business and ran him off. It was later charged that he had been chased away because he had tried to steal the blacks. General Taylor was skeptical of the whole affair for he could not understand why Robertson, after going to great expense to travel to the Indian Territory, did not get in touch with the military authorities at Fort Gibson or Fort Smith. Taylor also doubted if there were any escaped blacks among the Caddoes for no one had applied for their return. Nevertheless, Taylor asked Creek Agent James Logan to investigate.[16]

One of the blacks had been bought by Jesse Chisholm. Chisholm, a part-Cherokee trader who knew the languages of many of the Western tribes, was often relied upon as a liaison between the government and those tribes. In 1839, on his return from California, he bought the boy, whom he called Sambo, from the Comanches for $150 and apparently agreed to sell him to Lucinda Edwards. In January 1841, after Robertson had tried to recover his blacks, Chisholm made a bill of sale for Sambo to Lucinda Edwards. George Brinton and two Cherokees had bought the other black, whom they called Abram, from Comanches on the Colorado River in 1839. They sold the fifteen-year-old black to Lucinda Edwards in early 1840. In November 1841, Colonel Richard B. Mason, commander at Fort Gibson, sent a detachment to the Canadian to bring the two blacks to the fort. They admitted that they belonged to Robertson and that they had been stolen by the Comanches who, alone, had made the raid.[17]

Meanwhile, the Creeks had continued to wrangle with the Seminoles over slave property. General Taylor took a firm stand regarding those claims. When the Seminoles were removed, the government had assured them that they would not be deprived of their blacks by the Creeks or anyone else. Until he received direction from the War Department, Taylor would honor that promise. He told Creek Agent James Logan that he would not allow them to be deprived of a single slave without their consent and directed Logan to put a stop, if possible, "even to the discussion of this subject as no good can result from the same."[18]

Because of their fear that the Creeks would take their property, the Seminoles remained in the Cherokee Nation despite efforts in 1840 and 1841 to get them to remove to the Creek country. Only with the promise of a country of their own would they feel secure. However, the Creeks continued to oppose the union of the Seminoles as a group. In January 1842, Roley McIntosh, Harlock Harjo, Sam Miller, and others drafted a memorial to the government protesting the designation of a separate part of the Creek lands for the Seminoles; instead, the Creeks would share what they had with the Seminoles, scattered throughout the region. The Creeks gave their memorial to S. C. Stambaugh at Washington, who held the memorial until late March, when he learned that a subagent had been sent to the Seminoles and that steps were being taken to get them to remove to the country assigned to them according to treaty. Stambaugh felt that the Creeks were justified because they felt that it was their understanding with the United States commissioners who had negotiated the Treaty of 1833 that the Seminoles would not be recognized as a separate and independent nation after removal but would merge with the Creeks. In the West, General Taylor called a halt to attempts to remove the Seminoles to the Deep Fork until he could visit Fort Gibson in early May, and parties of emigrant Seminoles and blacks arriving in the territory from Florida were landed in Creek territory south of the Arkansas to avoid adding numbers to the hundreds already on Cherokee lands.[19]

In his annual report for 1842, Superintendent William Armstrong blamed the Seminole disunion on fear of Creek domination. While he granted that the Creeks should rightly fear the influence of the blacks over the Seminoles, he also granted that the Seminoles should fear oppression by the Creeks, especially when difficulty arose over the right to property. Most disputes over property rights had arisen concerning blacks, particularly those who the Creeks claimed had absconded before or during the Seminole War and had emigrated with the Seminoles. Armstrong felt that the title to those blacks should be settled as soon as possible, for it was a problem "calculated to produce and keep up a bad state of feeling." Armstrong was now more kindly disposed to the blacks than he had been in his earlier reports. The Seminoles on the Deep Fork had raised a surplus of corn, beans, pumpkins, and melons, and a few had raised small patches of rice that year. "The labor, however," he said, "is principally performed by the Seminole negroes, who have thus far conducted themselves with great propriety."[20]

Besides the Seminole problem, two slave claims were dominant in 1842. One was the claim that D. B. Mitchell, the former agent, had tried to settle before the Creeks emigrated. Mitchell, as heir of his brother, claimed Biner and her two children, whom his brother had sold to James Moore. The slaves had not been paid for. Opothleyohola had taken the blacks, assumed the debt in 1827, and had thwarted Mitchell's efforts to collect. Moore had then died, and in 1842 Mitchell tried to retrieve the blacks from Opothleyohola. Commissioner T. Hartley Crawford ruled that it was not within the authority of the War Department to interfere summarily and instructed the agent to make inquiry. Superintendent William Armstrong called on Opothleyohola in May 1842 and asked the chief for any papers he had relating to the case. The chief said that he did not want to be bothered with Mitchell any more and would have nothing more to say about it. Although Armstrong told him that the order to investigate came from the secretary of war, the chief still would not discuss it. He insisted that he had bought the blacks and would keep them and their increase. The chief warned Mitchell to cease bothering him, and Armstrong encouraged Mitchell to drop the subject because he could not see how "the Negroes are to be got at." It was regrettable, he said, that slave claims should be left open to settlement in the Indian country. [21]

The Robertson case was also continued in 1842. Early that year, the two disputed blacks were at Fort Gibson where they were clothed and put to work for the quartermaster and other officers at jobs where there was no risk of their escape. When Secretary of War J. C. Spencer learned that the blacks had been seized and brought to the post, he was clearly angry and ordered them returned to Lucinda Edwards, from whom they had been taken. They had been taken in warfare by the Comanches outside the United States, and Spencer believed that the United States had no obligation to deliver to the inhabitants of Texas any type of property captured in war. The United States was not responsible for the acts of those Indians, he said. [22]

In early 1842, the Creeks had also begun pursuing the case of Toney Barnet once more. David Barnet applied for Toney's return to the Indian Territory from Florida and for payment for his services as interpreter in Florida since October of 1840. The matter was forwarded for explanation to Captain John Page, who was then at Fort Cross, Florida. Page maintained that Barnet had made no protest at the time he organized the delegation. Also, he felt that Toney was a free black, having known him in Florida since 1825, and that he would have a "poor chance" when his claims were decided by the Indians. [23]

In 1842, Toney was at Cedar Keys, Florida, acting as interpreter for Colonel Jenkins I. Worth. Said Page, "I promised him he should return to Arkansas when Ho-la-too-chee left but Col. Worth could not spare him. Consequently, he is detained here contrary to his wishes." Toney finally reached New Orleans with a contingent of Seminoles in early March 1843 and arrived in the Indian country on April 26.[24]

About forty miles below Fort Gibson, as the emigration party neared its destination, the Seminoles threatened to kill Toney, who fled to Fort Gibson for safety. They evidently blamed him for their having been taken to the West, for at Webbers Falls in the Cherokee Nation, they murdered another black interpreter, apparently as they had agreed to do when they reached the Indian country.[25]

Toney remained at Fort Gibson until June, when Chief Roley McIntosh demanded his return to David Barnet. Colonel William Davenport, commander of the post, consulted General Taylor, who was convinced that the sale of Toney in Florida had been valid and that the Creek council decision giving him to Barnet was therefore invalid. Second, to Taylor, Toney came under General Jesup's promises of freedom. Third, the Seminoles had been promised the security of their property in the West. Therefore, Taylor directed Davenport not to turn Toney over to the Creeks until he received different orders from Washington. To the force of Taylor's statement, were added those of James and William Barnet, the sons of Michee Barnet, the original owner of Toney in the East. According to them, their father had sold Toney and received pay for him from James Hardridge, who in turn had sold Toney to Gad Humphreys. According to the Barnets, their uncle Casena Barnet and some of the chiefs of the tribe knew well that the sale had been made.[26]

The Creeks were angry at the army's interference in what they considered an internal affair which they had assumed had been settled by their courts. They therefore appealed to the secretary of war. When Creek Agent James L. Dawson forwarded the complaint to the commissioner, he said that he had been much troubled by the slave question arising between the Creeks and Seminoles on account of General Jesup's proclamation. He asked for a ruling on whether the claim of the blacks to freedom, emanating from Jesup's order, would be regarded as valid and sufficient in all cases arising under it.[27]

By this time, it was apparent to some officials that the issue of slave property was the major barrier to Seminole unification in the western part of the Creek Nation. According to Armstrong, if the matter of slave property remained unsettled, it might, and probably would, lead "to unpleasant collisions between the parties." Also, he felt that the matter of settling the Seminoles among the Creeks needed revision in order to resolve the differences between the two. Thomas L. Judge, the Seminole subagent, while admitting that the slave question had generated some excitement, did not apprehend any serious consequences from it. He had discussed it with the Creek chiefs who had told him that the Nation had no claims against the Seminoles but that some of their people had. They insisted, however, that they would resort only to legal measures. Judge was inclined to believe them. For that reason, he had little patience with the Seminoles who remained in the Cherokee Nation and suggested that the government cut off all annuities to them until they agreed to remove.[28]

A few weeks later, however, Judge decided that the slave question was more serious than he had thought. In October, 1843, the Creeks and Seminoles met in council, and those in the Cherokee Nation agreed to remove if a parcel of land could be found for them on the North Fork. The slave question, among other claims, came up. Judge, who was present, said that he found that the question "was like to be attended with more serious consequences than I had apprehended." To ward off trouble, he took a firm stand in favor of the Seminoles and against the Creeks: the Seminoles would be secure in their property if they removed. Judge felt that the Seminoles would never submit to the Creek laws, especially those concerning their blacks, such as the law forbidding blacks to carry weapons or to own horses. At a recent council, the Creeks had passed another law forbidding preaching to and by blacks.[29]

Judge's position concerning the slave property of the Seminoles was supported by Commissioner T. Hartley Crawford who believed that the security of the Seminoles in their slave property was necessary for the peace and security of the Creek country. Then on November 18, 1843, he recommended to the secretary of war that a commission consisting of Armstrong, the different agents of the tribes, and the subagents of the territory be appointed to meet with the Creeks and Seminoles and settle the dispute concerning the blacks and the occupancy of the land and that in the meantime there be no removal of the Seminoles from the Cherokee lands until the matter was settled. Secretary J. M. Porter approved the recommendation.[30] However, no instructions were forthcoming from the recommendations until the spring of 1844.

In January 1844, Crawford ruled in the case of Toney Barnet that the progress made by the government through its officers must be sustained against all who would interfere and disturb what it had guaranteed. The preponderance of evidence was in favor of Toney's freedom. This ruling and a statement by Casena Barnet that his brother had indeed sold Toney to James Hardridge in Georgia resulted in the issuing of free papers to Toney.[31] Crawford's decision meant, no doubt, that the Creeks would have to take matters into their own hands. Thus, once more, trouble erupted between the Creeks and Seminoles over slave titles, and the first of a long series of raids by Creek slave hunters on the Seminole blacks began.

The first serious confrontation occurred when Siah Hardridge, a Creek, claimed some thirty blacks held by Sally Factor, a Creek woman living with the Seminoles. Hardridge had purchased what was called the "Burrows claim," which predated emigration. In an effort to compromise with Sally Factor, he had agreed to pay her $2,000 for the blacks, but the blacks themselves opposed the sale and prevailed upon the Seminole chiefs, who induced the Seminole subagent and Chief McIntosh to have Hardridge relinquish Sally Factor's bill of sale. Hardridge, of course, denied McIntosh's right to cancel the sale and brought Sally Factor before him to repeat her trade with Hardridge. Before McIntosh and Benjamin Marshall, she testified that she had sold the blacks to Hardridge and that the Seminole chiefs had then said that she had got too little for them and induced her to apply to McIntosh to cancel the sale. She also testified that she had an absolute title to only ten of the blacks. The rest belonged to her deceased sister's children, of whom she was guardian. It was her desire, she said, for Hardridge to have the slaves and those of her sister's children if the Creek and Seminole chiefs decided she had the right to sell them.[32]

When Hardridge left the Creek agency, Agent James L. Dawson and McIntosh directed him to leave the slaves alone until the Creek and Seminole chiefs had decided the rights of the parties. Hardridge agreed, but on April 3, 1844, Wild Cat reported that Hardridge had stolen a black named Dembo Factor from Osiah Hadjo's town on the Deep Fork. Micanopy, the principal chief of the Seminoles, sent Wild Cat to Fort Gibson to enlist the army's aid. The Seminoles believed that Dembo had been taken to the mouth of the Canadian to be sent downstream and sold. They wanted General Taylor to have searched all boats passing Fort Smith. According to Wild Cat, the incident enraged the Seminoles, and they feared an outbreak of difficulties between the Seminoles and the Creeks if Hardridge and others like him were not punished for kidnapping slaves.[33]

Dawson heard that Dembo was in irons at North Fork Town. He pledged that if Dembo was in the Nation, he would be returned to the Seminoles and, if taken out, the property of Hardridge would be held liable. The Creeks apparently wanted to avoid a clash with the Seminoles, for there was a movement afoot among them at that time to urge the government during the approaching summer to help them unite with the Seminoles as one people. They disavowed any national claim against the slaves of the Seminoles and declared themselves perfectly willing to have the United States decide between their people and the individual claimants. On the Seminole side, Micanopy himself appealed to the military officials at Fort Gibson to write Chief McIntosh concerning the return of the blacks, stressing that it was his wish to "live brotherly" with the Creeks.[34]

When word of Dembo's abduction reached General Taylor, he reacted in a manner that might have been predicted. It was his view that the faith of the government had been pledged by General Jesup in Florida and that the emigrating Seminoles should not be harassed by claims for their blacks. On two previous occasions, he had told the Creeks that he would tolerate no "forcible irregular prosecution of such claims." Taylor reaffirmed that stand. He also had a warning for Hardridge. If he tried to gain possession of Seminole blacks except by application to the chiefs of the tribe, Taylor would have him placed in irons to await the pleasure of the government. Taylor was determined not to allow the harmony between the Creeks and Seminoles to be jeopardized by the kidnapping attempts of a scoundrel such as he believed Hardridge to be.[35] Pressure from the military officials and from the Creeks finally resulted in Dembo's release.

It became apparent that strong pressure from the government would be necessary in resolving the Seminoles' unsettled condition, settling their difficulties with the Creeks, and removing the obstacles to their settlement on the land assured them by treaty. Only then could the tribe make progress toward "civilization." Thus, on April 10, 1844, Commissioner T. Hartley Crawford established a commission composed of William Armstrong, the agents to the Chickasaws, Choctaws, Cherokees, and Creeks, and the Neosho and Seminole subagents to treat with the two tribes. The commission's greatest challenge was to prevail on the Seminoles in the Cherokee country to remove to the Creek Nation, for they feared Creek domination more than ever. However, according to Judge, they would settle on the North Fork of the Canadian if they could be guaranteed the safety of their property.[36] Thus, the commission was given broad powers to secure their removal and secure the peace of the Indian country.

Crawford insisted on an agreement which would contain certain points.

First, because the Creeks were the larger tribe, their government and laws would prevail over both nations, to be altered or repealed as the two tribes saw fit. Second, the Creeks should agree that the property brought with the Seminoles from Florida or from their present position into the Creek country, or any property acquired thereafter should not be liable to attachment or be taken from them on any claim that predated emigration, unless the action had the sanction of the president. In other words, the assurances given the Seminoles in Florida that they would retain the blacks sent west with them should be guaranteed. Third, the Seminoles should be made to understand that if they could come to no arrangement with the Creeks, the government would force them to go into the Creek country and come under Creek laws anyway. Finally, the Creeks should be reminded that their treaty obligations included receiving the Seminoles on their land and that the obligation carried no condition concerning the property brought with them or the ownership of that property based on title acquired before their emigration.[37]

As a result of conferences with a Seminole delegation headed by Alligator in Washington, the commissioners' authority was extended to negotiate an agreement, if possible, whereby the land designated for the Seminoles by the act of Congress on February 18, 1839, would be set apart for their exclusive use. Crawford felt that this concession by the Creeks might result in the reunification of the Seminoles and was therefore worth a try.[38]

The department's sympathy for the Seminole position was disapproved of by the Creeks, who called it a "one sided business." In a letter to the agent, Roley McIntosh, Eufaula Harjo, and Benjamin Marshall insisted that the Creeks wanted the Creeks and Seminoles to become one people, that they would never consent to a separate country for the latter. Again they denied that the Creek Nation had any claims against the Seminoles for any of their blacks but stated that some individual Creeks had claims which would be "impartially investigated."[39]

Crawford pointed out to Armstrong that the first obstacle to overcome in obtaining a separate land for the Seminoles would be Creek hostility to the idea. Crawford wanted Armstrong to obtain concessions from them without any cost to the government or to the Seminoles. As a last resort, he was to allow the Creeks, with approval of the Seminoles, a part of the $15,400 due the Seminoles under the Treaty of Payne's Landing. Other small amounts could be allowed the Seminoles for property they had abandoned in Florida and for the costs of removing the Seminoles from the Cherokee Nation to the Creek country.[40]

To Crawford, the letter of protest from the Creek chiefs had placed "their controversy about slave property in a rather more favorable position" than before. However, by this time Judge was fully convinced that the Seminoles could not and should not ever be a constituent part of the Creek Nation and had realized that the two peoples had "no community of interest or feeling, and never can have." The farther apart they were the better. Judge had learned in the council of October 1843 that the distrust between the two peoples concerning slave claims and other matters was too deep to be overcome. When he filed his annual report in August 1844, he was convinced that the recent stress on the relations between the Creeks and Seminoles made it "highly impolitic and improper" for the Seminoles to settle among the Creeks or for the government to make them do so.[41]

When negotiations began with the Creeks and Seminoles, the blacks were of foremost concern to the Seminoles. The chiefs drafted a memorial in which they submitted "propositions to avoid unpleasant feelings on the part of the Creeks," asking that, in view of the excitement between the Seminoles and some Creeks over slave claims, the Creeks not allow their citizens to interfere with any of the Seminole blacks. The Seminoles maintained that the blacks had been put under their protection by the government and could not be taken away without the government's consent. Any case arising over title should be settled by the president. The Seminoles also asked for a separate country of their own, subsistence upon settlement in their country, and an agent of their own.[42]

While the Seminoles insisted that they would not submit to the Creek laws, the Creeks at first would not have them on any other terms. But the commission—consisting of Armstrong, Cherokee Agent Pierce M. Butler, and James Logan—held out monetary inducements and found a compromise. The annuity guaranteed by the Treaty of Payne's Landing was increased from $3,000 to $5,000, the increase to be paid in goods. The Creeks were given an additional $3,000 for educational purposes, and their annuity already granted was extended for thirteen years.

The treaty, agreed to on January 4, 1845, was as follows. First, the Seminoles could settle in a body or separately as they saw fit in any part of the Creek country. They could make their own town regulations, subject to the general control of the Creek council, in which the Seminoles would be represented. There was to be no distinction between the members of the tribes except in their monetary affairs, in which neither could interfere with the other. Second, all Seminoles who had not done so would immediately remove and settle in the Creek country. Third, all contested cases between the two tribes concerning the right to property, growing out of sales before the ratification of the treaty, were subject to the decision of the president. The Seminoles expressed a desire to settle in a body on Little River, some distance west of the residence of the greater part of those in the Creek Nation. Therefore, rations would be issued to those who removed to Little River while on their way, and after the emigration was completed, the tribe would receive six months' subsistence rations. Those who were not in the Creek country before the issue of rations began were to be excluded, except those in Florida who were given twelve months to remove and re-join the tribe. Finally, the Seminoles were to receive $1,000 per year for five years, to be paid in agricultural implements to replace the property they had left in Florida.[43]

The treaty was ratified on March 6, 1845, and most of the Seminoles removed to the Creek country, where they settled in twenty-five towns. Each town had its own head men and town laws. A general council of the tribe had supervisory control over all of the towns. A majority of the head men, with approval of Micanopy, could pass laws to govern all of the Seminoles, provided the laws did not conflict with the laws passed by the Creek general council. Besides the principal chief, the following chiefs made up what was known as the executive council: Wild Cat, who was Micanopy's "counsellor and organ" and assisted him in making decisions, Tussekiah, Octiarche, Pascofar, Echo Emathla, and Passockee Yahola. Indian officials naively expressed the belief that the treaty would resolve the differences between the tribes regarding slave property.[44]

While the treaty may have preserved the Seminoles' social integrity, it left much to be desired concerning their political identity. Like so many treaties, it was simply words on a page. It did not remove the fear of oppression in the hearts of the Seminoles nor the Creeks' distrust concerning the blacks' influence over the Seminoles. Neither did it remove the major source of difficulty between the Seminoles and the Creeks: the title to and control of the blacks in the Nation. In fact, bringing the

Seminoles under the general control of Creek laws in many ways served only to aggravate the issue which often flared into violence.

NOTES

1. *Official Opinions of the Attorneys General of the United States,* 25 vols. (Washington, D.C.: Government Printing Office, 1852-1906), 4: 725.
Schedules of the Seminole blacks appear in *Executive Document 225,* 25 Cong., 3 sess., pp. 66-69, 74-78, 79, 95-96; National Archives Record Group 94 (Records of the Office of the Adjutant General); *General Jesup's Papers,* Letters Received, box 12; National Archives Record Group 75 (Records of the Bureau of Indian Affairs); *Miscellaneous Muster Rolls, 1832-46;* National Archives Microfilm Publications, *Microcopy M234* (Office of Indian Affairs, Letters Received) 802: D153-56, hereafter cited as *M234,* followed by the roll number; *Microcopy M574* (Special Files of the Office of Indian Affairs, 1807-1904) 13: special file 96, hereafter cited as *M574,* followed by the roll number.

2. William Armstrong to T. Hartley Crawford, September 10, 1842, *Executive Document 2,* 27 Cong., 3 sess., pp. 443-44, 445; Crawford to Armstrong, April 10, 1844, *M574*-13: frame 246; Charles J. Kappler, comp. and ed., *Indian Affairs: Laws and Treaties,* 2nd ed., 4 vols. (Washington, D.C.: Government Printing Office, 1904), 2:344-45; Grant Foreman, *Indian Removal* (Norman: University of Oklahoma Press, 1932), p. 380; Edwin C. McReynolds, *The Seminoles* (Norman: University of Oklahoma Press, 1957), p. 234; Ethan Allen Hitchcock, *A Traveler in Indian Territory: The Journal of Ethan Allen Hitchcock, late Major-General in the United States Army,* ed. Grant Foreman (Cedar Rapids, Iowa: The Torch Press, 1930), p. 92.

3. Kappler, 2: 388-91; Angie Debo, *The Road to Disappearance* (Norman University of Oklahoma Press, 1941), pp. 101-02; Crawford to Joel R. Poinsett, January 14, 1839, *Senate Document 88,* 25 Cong., 3 sess., p. 2.

4. Crawford to Poinsett, January 14, 1839, *Senate Document 88,* 25 Cong., 3 sess., pp. 2-3; Crawford to Armstrong, April 10, 1844, *M574*-13: frame 246.

5. *Senate Document 1,* 26 Cong., 1 sess., p. 472; Armstrong to Crawford, October 1, 1840, *Executive Document 2,* p. 314.

6. Hitchcock, pp. 102-03; Brig. Gen. Matthew Arbuckle to Roley McIntosh, June 7, June 8, 1840, Arbuckle to Mic-ca-nup-pa and other Seminole Chiefs, May 11, 1840, National Archives Record Group 393 (Records of the United States Army Continental Commands, 1821-1920), *Second Military Department,* Letters Sent, hereafter cited as *2nd LS.*

7. Bill of Sale, February 29, 1836, and Will of Choakchot Hadjo, Ebenezer Pond Papers, Manuscripts Division, Alabama Department of Archives and History, Montgomery; D. H. Lewis to J. C. Spencer, June 27, 1842, with enclosures, *M234*-226: L1674-42; James Logan to Poinsett, November 21, November 24, 1838, Samuel J. Cook to Poinsett, December 3, 1838, Cook to William S. Fulton, December 2, 1838, *M234*-225: L621-38, L622-38, C881-38, F109-38.

8. Arbuckle to Logan, August 9, 1838, *2nd LS*; McIntosh to Spencer, January 13, 1842, *M234*-226: M1295-42; Crawford to McIntosh, February 19, 1842, National Archives Microfilm Publications, *Microcopy M21* (Office of Indian Affairs, Letters Sent) 31: 476, hereafter cited as *M21*, followed by the roll number.

9. Registry of Negro Prisoners, *House Executive Document 225,* 25 Cong., 3 sess., p. 69.

10. Gad Humphreys to Col. R. B. Mason, December 5, 1845, National Archives Record Group 393, *Fort Gibson,* Volume "Indian Affairs," p. 15; Statement of David Barnet, February 2, 1842, *M234*-226: H1047-42.

11. Statement of Barnet, February 2, 1842, *M234*-226: H1047-42; Head Men and Warriors to Secretary of War, July 25, 1843, *M234*-227: D830-43; Arbuckle to McIntosh, May 10, 1840, *2nd LS.*

12. Capt. John Page to Crawford, September 6, 1842, *M234*-289: P1158-42; Statement of Barnet, February 2, 1842, *M234*-226: H1047-42.

13. Robert McIntosh to Arbuckle, November 6, 1840, Fort Gibson, *Letters Received,* box 1, hereafter cited as *Gibson L R*; Arbuckle to Capt. George W. Allen, November 12, 1840, *2nd LS.*

14. Roley McIntosh et al. to Arbuckle, February 1, 1841, National Archives Record Group 393, *Second and Seventh Military Departments,* Letters Received, box 3, hereafter cited as *2nd and 7th LR.*

15. Hitchcock, p. 28; Brig. Gen. Roger Jones to Brig. Gen. Zachary Taylor, September 29, 1841, *Gibson L R,* box 1.

16. Joseph W. Robertson to James S. Mayfield, April 7, 1841, *2nd and 7th LR,* box 3; Taylor to Jones, October 24, 1841, *Second and Seventh Military Departments,* Letters Sent, hereafter cited as *2nd and 7th LS;* Mason to Logan, October 29, 1841, *Gibson L R,* box 1.

17. Statement of Jesse Chisholm, September 17, 1845, Bill of Sale, January 24, 1841, Statement of George Brinton, September 19, 1845, Bill of Sale, March 10, 1840, *M234*-227: A1914-45; Mason to Jones, November 24, 1841, *2nd and 7th LS.*

18. Taylor to Logan, September 9, 1841, *2nd and 7th LS.*

19. S. C. Stambaugh to Crawford, March 30, 1842, *M234*-226: S3148-42; W. W. J. Bliss to Mason, April 11, 1842, Bliss to Colonel S. W. Kearny, May 13, 1842, *Gibson L R,* box 1.

20. Armstrong to Crawford, September 10, 1842, *Executive Document 2,* 27 Cong., 3 sess., p. 445.

21. Crawford to H. M. Waterton, April 7, 1842, *M21*-32: 88, *M234*-226: W1766-42; Crawford to Spencer, March 25, 1842, National Archives Microfilm Publication, *Microcopy M348* (Office of Indian Affairs, Report Books) 3: 124; Testimony of Joseph Burnet (Bruner?), May 16, 1842, Mitchell to Crawford, June 1, 1842, Armstrong to Crawford, June 4, 1842, *M234*-226: W1883-42, A1259-42. Mitchell raised the claim again in 1847, but the Commissioner again ruled that the department could offer him no relief. It was raised again in 1850, but the department simply answered requests for information on the status of the case from Mitchell and congressmen. William Medill to D. J. Bishop, May 15, 1847, *M21*-39: 357; V. E. Howard to Com-

missioner, March 8, 1850, Howard to Orlando Brown, March 14, 1850, *M234*-228: H1154-50, H1157-50; Brown to Howard, March 11, 15, 1850, *M21*-43: 70, 78.

22. Bliss to Mason, February 28, 1842, *Gibson LR,* box 1, and *2nd and 7th LS*; Jones to Taylor, June 8, 1842, *M234*-443: A1581-42; Bliss to Mason, July 7, 1842, Jones to Mason, July 29, 1842, *Gibson LR,* box 1.

23. Maj. Ethan Allen Hitchcock to Spencer, June 1, 1842, *M234*-226: H1047-42; Crawford to Page, July 30, 1842, *M21*-32: 358; Page to Crawford, September 6, 1842, *M234*-289: P1158-42.

24. Page to Crawford, September 6, 1842, *M234*-289: P1158-42; LeGrand Capers to Crawford, March 4, 1843, *M234*-806: C1923-43; Foreman, p. 384. In 1842, Worth offered Toney a reward of $500 if he would persuade the warriors of Octiarche's band to come in and emigrate. He was shown the money, and it was put in a box with his name on it and left with LeGrand Capers, the emigration officer. The money was to be paid upon the contingency that Toney would be faithful at all times. But Worth soon found that Toney was up to "his old tricks of duplicity and double dealing" and as an example to the other interpreters ordered him whipped in their presence. J. B. Luce to Armstrong, March 7, 1845, *M234*-806: A1789-45. At New Orleans, Toney had applied for his money and was promised it, but the boat left before he could collect it. Upon reaching the Indian country, he again applied for the money. It was not paid, and when he applied for it again in 1845, he was again denied. At that time General Worth wrote, "In respect to that scoundrel *Toney,* I only regretted that it was not lawful to have had him shot instead of emigrating him." Judge to Taylor, July 28, 1843, *Gibson LR,* box 2; Crawford to Armstrong, April 3, 1845, Crawford to Jenkins I. Worth, April 3, 1845, and Crawford to Armstrong, April 29, 1845, *M21*-36: 277, 331; Worth to Crawford, April 12, 1845, *M234*-806: W2623-45.

25. Head Men and Warriors of the Upper Towns to Secretary, July 25, 1843, *M234*-227: D830-43; Armstrong to Crawford, May 22, 1843, *M234*-800: A1457-43.

26. Col. William Davenport to Taylor, June 15, 1843, *2nd and 7th LR,* box 5; Bliss to Davenport, June 21, 1843, *Gibson LR,* box 1; Davenport to McIntosh, July 5, 1843, *Fort Gibson,* Letters Sent, hereafter cited as *Gibson LS.*

27. James L. Dawson to Crawford, August 5, 1843, *M234*-227: D830-43.

28. Armstrong to Crawford, September 30, 1843, Judge to Armstrong, September 15, 1843, *Executive Document 2,* 28 Cong., 1 sess., pp. 415, 424-25.

29. Judge to Crawford, October 22, 1843, *M234*-800: J1350-43.

30. Crawford to Armstrong, April 10, 1844, *M574*-13: frame 246.

31. Crawford to Armstrong, January 24, 1844, Armstrong to Dawson, January 24, 1844, *M21*-34: 446, 457; Statement of Judge, February 21, 1844, *2nd and 7th LR,* box 5; Judge to Crawford, April 23, 1844, *M234*-800: I1449-44.

32. Dawson to Capt. Nathan Boone, April 10, 1844, *Gibson LR,* box 2. Siah Hardridge, who was one of the most persistent slave hunters among the Creeks, was probably the same man as Joseph Siah Hardridge, a brother-in-law of the well-known Creek leader George Stidham. Joseph Siah Hardridge was reputedly among those who had killed William McIntosh. He died at present Yaholo, Oklahoma, in 1868. Loney Hardridge (Interview), March 24, 1937, *Indian-Pioneer History,* 116 vols.

(Indian Archives Division, Oklahoma Historical Society), 2:316.

33. Dawson to Boone, April 10, 1844, *Gibson LR,* box 2; J. N. Belger to Col. Gustavus Loomis, April 3, 1844, *Gibson LS.*

34. Dawson to Boone, April 10, 1844, *Gibson LR,* box 2; Boone to Dawson, April 8, 1844, *2nd and 7th LR,* box 5.

35. Bliss to Dawson, May 13, 1844, *2nd and 7th LS.*

36. Crawford to Armstrong, April 10, 1844, *M574*-13: frame 246; *House Executive Document 2,* 28 Cong., 2 sess., pp. 323-25.

37. *Ibid.*

38. Crawford to William Wilkins, May 20, 1844, *House Executive Document 2,* 28 Cong., 2 sess., p. 325.

39. McIntosh et al. to Dawson, received June 8, 1844, *M234*-800: M1973-44.

40. Crawford to Armstrong, June 17, 1844, *House Executive Document 2,* 28 Cong 2 sess., pp. 326-27.

41. Judge to Armstrong, August 26, 1844, *House Executive Document 2,* 28th Cong., 2 sess., p. 471.

42. Seminole Memorial, December 28, 1844, *M234*-800: frame 626.

43. Ratified Treaty No. 244, Documents Relating to the Negotiation of the Treaty of January 4, 1845, with the Creek and Seminole Indians, National Archives Microfilm Publications, *Microcopy T494* (Documents Relating to the Negotiation of Ratified and Unratified Treaties with Various Indian Tribes, 1801-1869) 9: frames 235-43; Kappler, 2: 550-52.

44. R. W. Kirkham to Gen. Thomas S. Jesup, August 20, 1846, *Fort Gibson* Volume "Indian Affairs," p. 18; Jesup to Medill, June 13, 1848, *M234*-801: J96-48; Marcellus Duval to Crawford, September 30, 1845, Armstrong to Crawford, September 30, 1845, *House Executive Document 2,* 29 Cong., 1 sess., pp. 530-31, 506; Duval to Medill, October 15, 1846, *House Executive Document 4,* 29 Cong., 2 sess., p. 278. Not all of the Seminoles removed. Some remained in the Cherokee Nation in the bottoms of the Grand and Illinois rivers. In April 1846, the Cherokees complained that they were killing Cherokee livestock. Some were still in the Cherokee Nation a year later. Duval to Loomis, April 29, 1846, *Gibson LR,* box 2; Loomis to James McKisick, May 18, 1847, *Fort Gibson* Volume "Indian Affairs," p. 25.

SLAVE HUNTERS
AND TRIBAL
chapter **8** DIFFICULTIES

THE TREATY OF 1845 did not, as government officials had hoped, end the slave controversies between the Creeks and Seminoles. The Seminoles and their blacks were placed under the general control of the Creek laws, but the Seminoles' social practices differed radically from the Creek slave code. The Seminole blacks still lived separately from their owners and had begun to accumulate property and herds. They owned horses and carried weapons. Creek law expressly forbade all of those practices. The Creeks distrusted the enclaves of blacks, which they saw as a possible source of mischief as they had been in Florida. The Creek chiefs wanted to make the Seminole blacks conform to Creek law, and Creek slave hunters and opportunists were quick to see the possibilities of profit to be made in raiding the Seminole blacks. Thus, the next five years witnessed a marked increase in slaving activities in the Creek Nation.

No sooner was the treaty ratified than slaving activities began. In early March 1845, Dembo Factor came to Fort Gibson and complained that Siah Hardridge was after him again, this time trying to run him off to Texas and sell him. He claimed protection under General Jesup's promise of freedom to blacks who surrendered in Florida. At the same time Hardy, a former slave of Nelly Factor's who claimed freedom under Jesup's proclamation, was being claimed as a slave, presumably by Hardridge. Colonel Richard B. Mason issued a paper stating that Hardy was under the protection of the post until his case could be heard and that all were forbidden to molest him.[1]

Mason appealed to Adjutant General Roger Jones that something should be done promptly for the Seminole blacks to whom the government had pledged its protection. They were harassed by their various claimants—

white, Seminole, and Creek. They lived in uncertainty and suspense, running and skulking about to evade their pursuers. Mason called for an end to the harassment and recommended severe punishment for anyone who pursued the blacks. But no one seemed to know exactly which of the blacks really fell under the protection of General Jesup's promises in Florida. Mason suggested that the "free papers" of all those entitled to them be sent to Fort Gibson and that the commanding officers of the military posts in the area be instructed to apprehend any person interfering with those holding papers.[2]

In May 1845, Rose (the widow of Plenty) and August, who claimed freedom under Jesup's promises, complained of being pursued by Hardridge, who was trying to take them as slaves. Rose also claimed that several of her children were being pursued by Hardridge and asked that Mason intervene. Rose was apparently not considered free by the Seminoles, for in March 1840, Micanopy, Coa Hadjo, and Black Dirt had declared Rose and her children the property of Polly, a niece of Coa Hadjo, who had inherited the blacks from her grandmother Nancy Brown. Nevertheless, Mason was sympathetic to Rose's pleas. He felt that something should be done promptly to fulfill the pledge the United States had made through General Jesup in order to save the Seminole blacks from being "hunted like wolves." As far as Hardridge was concerned, Mason wanted General Arbuckle to place Hardridge in irons. Arbuckle chose, instead, simply to warn Hardridge to stop his slave-hunting practices. Creek Agent James L. Dawson was directed to inform the Creeks that measures would be taken against Hardridge unless he did so.[3] The warning was apparently sufficient, at least for the time being.

In July 1845, an event occurred which profoundly affected the status of the "free" Seminole blacks and created discontent among both the Creeks and the Seminoles. General Jesup, now Quartermaster General, visited Fort Gibson concerning the construction of stone buildings. From the post, Jesup sent word to the Seminole blacks, most of whom the Seminoles still claimed as slaves, that they were free under his promises in Florida. He asked them to come to Fort Gibson to talk with him, but he left before they arrived. However, he left a list of those who had surrendered under his promises. That summer, the blacks stopped working for the Indians who claimed to be their owners, and nearly all of the men, many of them with their families, went to the military reserve at Fort Gibson, where they sought the protection of the government and

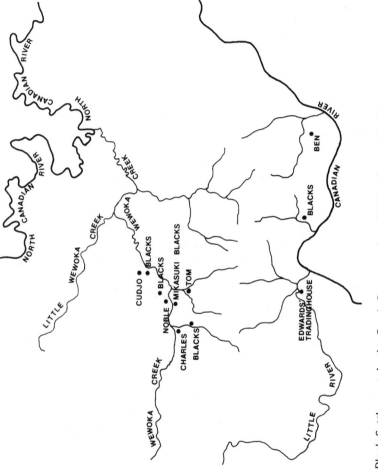

Black Settlements in the Creek Country, circa 1845. After Annie Heloise Abel, *The American Indian as Slaveholder and Secessionist.*

worked at what jobs the army could offer them. Sixty or seventy were set to work on the new stone buildings being erected. The situation displeased the Indians and became more disagreeable to the Creeks as during the next few months the blacks on the reserve were joined by others from the surrounding countryside who obviously had no right to protection by the government.[4]

Meanwhile, the Joseph W. Robertson case, which had arisen in 1841, was finally brought to a close. In early 1844, the new secretary of war, J. M. Porter, had reversed earlier decisions, saying that since the two blacks had been stolen by the Comanches, the sales were not valid. In response to a request by the Texas government, Porter ordered them delivered to Robertson. However, Creek Agent James Dawson failed to have them delivered, and in the summer of 1845 the new agent James Logan was directed to do so. Roley McIntosh and the other chiefs protested that the blacks had been honestly purchased during a trading expedition to the Comanches. They asked that the blacks be retained in the Creek Nation until further facts could be obtained. The chiefs' efforts were futile. Another order came to surrender the blacks, and in September 1845 Edwards gave them up. Logan believed that the blacks belonged to Edwards and, like the Seminole blacks, were the spoils of war. Nevertheless, on December 25, 1845, Logan turned the two blacks over to Cherokee Agent P. M. Butler, who was acting in Robertson's behalf.[5]

In March 1846, Seminole Subagent Marcellus Duval reported that complaints about the Seminole blacks on the Fort Gibson reserve were brought to his attention almost daily. The Seminoles felt that their understanding at the time of removal had been violated. Like Mason, Duval suggested that the papers of the legitimate claimants to freedom be sent to him so that he would have a certain base for action. Duval's motives were not as altruistic as Mason's. Strongly proslavery in sentiment, Duval was interested in finding which blacks were free so that the rest could be returned to the Indians as slaves. On April 8, 1846, General Jesup informed General Arbuckle that he had succeeded in getting the case of the blacks presented to the president, who would decide whether they were to be separated from the Seminoles and removed to another country or be allowed to occupy, as they had in Florida, a separate village in the Seminole country. The latter was what Jesup said he had promised them, although the idea was vehemently opposed by the Creeks and Seminoles. Jesup asked Arbuckle to protect them at Fort Gibson until the president made a decision.[6]

Arbuckle ordered the post commander to extend protection to those on the military reserve, merely as a favor to General Jesup. In response, Duval applied to Commissioner William Medill for instructions. He said that the Indians who claimed to own the blacks wanted action. If they were not the Indians' property, Duval thought that they should be removed from the Indian country "as they are most certainly under present circumstances, a nuisance to adjoining tribes, and will be eventually to the people of Arkansas as a harbor for runaway slaves." Not all of the blacks, however, were on the reserve. Some remained in the villages on the Deep Fork and Little River. Those blacks as well as those on the reserve, despite government protection, were subjected to raids by slave hunters.[7]

Wannah's two children Limus and Sarah were sold by the Seminole Jim to Siah Hardridge, who treated them badly. In July 1846, Colonel Gustavus Loomis, the new commander at Fort Gibson, appealed to Chief Roley McIntosh to return them until Loomis could find out on what terms Hardridge would relinquish his claim. However, by the following December, Chief McIntosh had not surrendered them. Hardridge had followed a typical pattern of confusing the issue by selling them to another Creek, who, it was learned, intended to send them downstream to be sold in Arkansas. Loomis protested that no sale was legal and warned that if they were found, they would be returned to their parents, who were then on the Deep Fork, until the case was decided. Loomis again appealed to McIntosh to have the children returned.[8]

Other blacks appealed to Loomis for protection. In February 1847, he issued a proclamation for the protection of Latty (or Lemo) and his family from a group of Creeks who had been trying to buy them from the Seminole who claimed them. Meanwhile, Marcellus Duval, who was in Washington, had taken the complaints of the Seminoles to the president. Duval foresaw what he considered dangers in confirming Jesup's promises to the blacks. If they were free, they had no right in the Creek country, and those Indians, joined by the Cherokees, would drive the blacks out. Arkansans, too, would object to a colony of free blacks so close to their boundary. What would the government do with them? What Northern state would receive three hundred free blacks, and would the blacks want to go north? Could the government afford to go into the colonization business of its own accord and ship them to Africa? Duval concluded, "The consequences of the subject going into Congress anyone can foresee, and I desire to avert the calamitous excitement which it would cause, shaking the Union to its center—a perfect 'firebrand' to be thrown among the discordant & combustible materials on the floor of Congress."[9]

In January 1847, Duval presented the case of Harriet Bowlegs to Commissioner William Medill, who had just been asked for a report on the Seminole blacks. Duval told the commissioner, rather condescendingly, that the blacks were a problem "of more importance than probably you are aware of, having a direct bearing on the feelings and conduct of the Seminoles, not to say anything of the ultimate condition of the negroes." When he learned that William Armstrong, the Western superintendent, had been requested to report on the matter, Duval said that he felt "confident in saying that he can give no information which is not already before the department."[10] From this point on, Duval tried to keep other officials from investigating the situation and to maintain his authority in the matter; his reason, as subsequently became apparent, was his interest and his brother's in some of the slaves.

There had been a steadily growing uneasiness in the Creek Nation concerning the increasing numbers of free blacks within its bounds. In the preceding January, the chiefs had complained that the number of blacks claiming to be free had multiplied to such an extent that it was "truly alarming." The neighboring tribes had expelled all free blacks from their country, the Creeks charged, and the blacks had flocked to the Creek Nation. Besides those at Fort Gibson and on Little River, a number who claimed freedom under Jesup's promises had congregated and formed a place of refuge for runaways from the states and the neighboring Indian nations. The Creeks maintained that they wanted to act in accordance with the wishes of the government, but they were determined to break up the settlement on Little River and to expel all free blacks from their country.[11]

By "neighboring tribes" the Creeks meant the Cherokees. In the aftermath of the slave "revolt" of 1842, they had passed an act ordering all free blacks not freed by Cherokee citizens to leave the Nation by January 1, 1843. The Choctaws excluded free blacks from their annuity in 1844 but did not expel them. The Chickasaws did not expel their free blacks until the late 1850s.[12]

The problem of the blacks on the reserve became more complex daily. Speculators were trying to get the names of those protected and made claims whether they had a true claim or not, as in the case of Wannah's children. The Creeks grew more excited about the blacks, and in the summer of 1847 there was much talk among them of seizing all of the blacks and making slaves of them. Then, they thought, the government would be forced to act and decide the question at once.[13] In June, it was learned that Wannah's children had been run off to Fort Smith and sold for whiskey. Angered, Colonel Loomis asked General Arbuckle to investigate, and if they had been sold, he suggested that unless they were returned, $2,000 be deducted from the next annuity payment to the Creeks, since it was Hardridge who had taken them in the first place.[14] Such suggestions, no doubt, accounted in part for the Creeks' desire to put a swift end to the controversy. But the end was several months in the future.

During the fall of 1847, Colonel Loomis continued to extend protection to blacks who came to the post. In November, for instance, he extended protection to sixteen blacks who claimed to be free persons in the Creek Nation. They had been the property of Sally Stidham until July 3, 1841, when she made a will giving them their freedom and recorded it in the Crawford County Courthouse in Arkansas. In 1847, some of her distant relatives were trying to break the will, and a Creek named Potostee was trying to capture the blacks as slaves. The matter of the will was pending before the chiefs. The blacks left all of their property and fled to the post. There Loomis gave them a room and sought permission to issue rations to them, for it was the opinion of James Logan, the Creek agent, that they were free because he had written the will.[15]

At about the same time, an event occurred which further angered the Creeks. Kibbet, a Seminole black living at Fort Gibson, went into the Creek Nation to the home of Tustenuggee Micco to find the name of the person who had informed on some of his former misdemeanors. Tustenuggee Micco gave him the name of Joseph Smith, to whose house Kibbett went. There he abused and threatened Smith with a gun, and he threatened other Creeks, especially anyone who tried to apprehend him. He stole a mare from Smith and returned to the military reserve. James Logan asked Colonel Loomis to turn Kibbett over to the Creeks for trial. Kibbett admitted that he had taken the mare but claimed that he was justified because Smith had taken one of his and that he merely meant to hold the mare until Smith returned his horse. Loomis refused to turn him over without General Arbuckle's permission because he was not sure that the Creeks had jurisdiction in the case.[16]

McIntosh and the other Creek chiefs were angry at Loomis's decision.

The only reason they had allowed the Seminole blacks to remain in their country, they said, was that General Jesup had promised them that they had the right to try any of the blacks who committed crimes. Logan was alarmed, for by the second week in December, the Creek chiefs were in "an ill humor" about the Seminole blacks. Logan was afraid that trouble would grow out of anything that looked as if the army was screening the blacks from trial. Arbuckle evidently saw the danger in a refusal to turn Kibbett over, for he was delivered the following week.[17]

During the spring of 1848, raids continued on the settlement of blacks on the military reserve at Fort Gibson. In late April, the Creeks even raided the military reserve at Fort Smith, Arkansas, where some of the Seminole blacks had hired out as free laborers. Newman McIntosh sent his overseer to Fort Smith, where he thought Joe, a Seminole black he claimed, was working. But finding Joe employed in the quarters of Arbuckle's aide-de-camp, Lieutenant F. F. Flint, the overseer sent a constable, who took Joe away, despite Flint's protests that Joe was under the protection of the government.[18]

By this time, officials in Washington were preparing to make a decision concerning the status of blacks on the military reserve. In December 1847, Marcellus Duval had urged President James K. Polk to act. It had been nearly a year since he had written the president, and nothing had been done: "Why the matter was allowed to slumber in a pigeonhole I can't say but believe it was because being a subject which most of the northern men are afraid of, it was thought to be easiest to let it pass with as slight a notice as possible inasmuch as there could be legally no other decision than that the negroes were slaves and subject to the Indians." After his return from Washington earlier in the year, Duval had been urged by friends to seize the blacks as fugitives, but he had refused because he feared that if he did and the military opposed him the Indians would be "very apt to commit some unlawful act" because they would feel that they had their agent's backing. Duval did not want to attempt anything he could not carry out for he would lose his authority among the Indians. Again, Duval returned to the national significance of the situation: "By emancipating these slaves, (had we the right to do so) an inducement would be held out to all slaves in our southern community in time of war to take part with our enemies—until some *General* should see proper to *buy them off by promises of freedom.*" He asked President Polk to order the blacks returned to the Seminoles.[19] Polk referred it to Secretary of War William L. Marcy for investigation.

The Creek delegation to Washington also pressed for action. On April 6, 1848, Benjamin Marshall, Tuckabahchee Micco, George Scott, and George W. Stidham complained to Commissioner Medill that the large number of blacks who were in the Creek country and who claimed to be free exercised "a most pernicious influence" on the blacks in the region as well as upon "the lower and more ignorant class" of Indians. Most of the blacks were claimed by the Seminoles and were "a positive nuisance to the Creeks." If they belonged to the Seminoles, the Creeks wanted them returned to the Seminoles, and if they did not, the Creeks wanted the government to "insure their speedy removal from the Creek Country."[20]

Again on April 26, the Creek delegation complained about the blacks at Fort Gibson and Little River. The Creeks did not want to argue whether Jesup had the right to free the blacks by proclamation; they simply wanted the question of title examined so that the blacks would be removed from the Creek country or placed under the control of Creek laws. According to the Creeks, they were apparently subject to no controls and violated the laws of the United States and of the Creek Nation with impunity. The Creeks considered them "idle and worthless" and claimed that they brought whiskey into the Nation, stole, and offered inducements to the slaves in the surrounding areas to run away. A black who committed a crime ran to the post and received protection, they said. Many of the blacks were claimed by whites, whom the Creeks believed should be given the opportunity to send their agents to the Creek Nation to establish their claims and, if successful, should be assisted in removing their property from the Indian country. They asked the government to establish a tribunal before which the whites could process their claims. If the blacks were declared free under Jesup's proclamation, the Creeks wanted to know if they would then come under the jurisdiction of the Creek laws as other free blacks did.[21] By the time the Creeks made their complaint, the matter had been referred to John Y. Mason, the acting attorney general, for a decision.

In Mason's opinion, Jesup's promises of freedom to the blacks were not valid, and the blacks were the slave property of the Seminoles. Military authorities, he said, should be instructed to restore the blacks to the condition that existed before Jesup's letter to Arbuckle on April 8, 1846, asking that the army intervene for the protection of the blacks.[22]

In early August 1848, Secretary Marcy informed Arbuckle of Mason's decision and instructed him to deliver the blacks, in Duval's presence, to the chiefs, who were to deliver them to their proper owners. Those

who were not apparently the property of the Seminoles were to be reported to the department along with any claims made for them. The
Creek delegation to Washington was also informed of the decision,
Commissioner William Medill expressing the hope that the decision would
bring an end to the longstanding contention that had existed between the
Creeks and Seminoles concerning the blacks.[23] There remained the task
of carrying out the orders, which were no doubt disappointing to General
Jesup and catastrophic to the blacks who for nearly a decade had lived
with the illusory hope of freedom.

Less than a month after Mason's decision became known in the West,
slave speculators began to plot the capture of some of the blacks. During
the first week in September a party of fifteen Cherokees led by Bill Drew
and some Creeks, including Newman McIntosh and Joe Smith, raided the
Seminole country and succeeded in carrying off Clary and her children
Pussy, Rose, Caesar, Sarah, and Tenny, all claimed by Micanopy. They
claimed to have done so on orders of Chief Roley McIntosh. Captain W. S.
Ketchum, commander at Fort Gibson, appealed to McIntosh to hold the
blacks until Duval returned to the territory with orders for the settlement of the title and warned that any sale made before the settlement
would not be recognized. Micanopy also appealed for a settlement of the
matter in council.[24]

Chief McIntosh claimed that a Creek citizen was simply trying to regain his property and had hired a company of men to go to the Seminole
lands to get the slaves. The stolen blacks were then near his place, and he
assured Ketchum that they would be kept in the country until the title
could be settled. Not satisfied, Captain Ketchum sent troops for Pussy,
Rose, and Caesar, who were at Newman McIntosh's farm and for Sarah
at the residence of William Whitfield, son-in-law of the Creek agent. Since
first learning of the raid, Ketchum found that the Indians had beaten
Clary during the raid, had taken a gun from Thomas, Clary's husband, and
had taken a horse, saddle, and bridle from Margaret, a free black. Ketchum
demanded the return of those items.[25]

By the middle of September, Ketchum had all of the family except
Sarah inside the pickets at Fort Gibson. Sarah was still at Whitfield's,
supposedly ill and "under the operation of medicine" for fever, but
Whitfield promised to bring her in at the first opportunity. However,
Thomas's property was still at Newman McIntosh's farm, and Margaret's
was still at Whitfield's. Ketchum still insisted that it be returned, but

he was quick to assert that the show of military strength was simply
to ensure that the blacks would not be run off and therefore should not
alarm the Creeks.[26]

The property in question was significant because it exemplified one
of the important bases of contention between the Creeks and Seminoles.
Laws of the Creek Nation were in effect in the Seminole country. Among
these laws were those prohibiting blacks from owning horses and weapons.
Yet it was the Seminoles' practice to allow their blacks to hold such property. The Seminoles were unwilling to yield to the Creeks on this point;
hence, their insistence on the return of the property.[27]

Ketchum also felt it necessary to reassure the Seminoles that the army
would not allow raids to continue in their country. He assured Micanopy
that he would keep Clary and her children inside the garrison and give
them rations until "the Negro business" was settled. To ease tensions between the Creeks and Seminoles, he assured the Seminole chief that Roley
McIntosh was sincere when he said that the Creeks had no intention of
running the blacks off and selling them out of the territory. Furthermore,
Ketchum promised to continue giving refuge to those who came to the
post. Only a few days earlier, Jesse, Silla, and their four children from the
Seminole country had asked for and received protection from slave speculators.[28]

Despite Ketchum's efforts, tensions still existed between the Creeks
and Seminoles over the property which had been taken during the raid.
Late in September the gun and shot pouch of Thomas remained at Newman McIntosh's and Margaret's horse was in the possession of Constantine
Perkins. Micanopy sent Wild Cat to Ketchum with a message for Roley
McIntosh, saying that if McIntosh would have the property returned, when
"the Seminoles see the restored property, they will all be pleased."[29]

Occurring at a time when harmony between the tribes was desperately
needed, this episode caused concern to General Arbuckle. In order to prevent another such occurrence, he directed Ketchum to keep on the reserve all of the blacks reported free on Jesup's list filed at Fort Gibson.
They were not to leave without instructions from "proper authority,"
presumably Arbuckle himself. Others, not on the list and not claimed
by the Seminoles, were either blacks or runaways who had emigrated
with the Seminoles and continued to reside among them. Some of them
did not reside on the reservation, and Arbuckle ordered Ketchum to have
them come in to be kept on the reserve until the matter was settled.[30]

The task of turning the blacks over to the Seminole chiefs fell to Brigadier General William G. Belknap. The Creek authorities were expected to object, but according to the decision of the attorney general provisions for the settlement of claims between the two tribes had been made in the Treaty of 1845. As Arbuckle had expected, the Creeks sought to delay the transfer. McIntosh, Benjamin Marshall, and other chiefs asked Belknap to arrange an interview with the Seminoles in council before the blacks were turned over. No meeting was held, and on January 2, 1849, over 250 blacks were officially turned over to the Seminoles. Of that number, over half were on the military reservation, and the remainder were mainly at the Deep Fork and Little River with a few at the North Fork and Arkansas rivers. The government list also contained the names of fourteen free blacks, sixteen blacks who had been sold out of the Indian country, and thirty-four who had died.[31]

Surprisingly, the transfer went smoothly, especially in light of rumors that the blacks would be distributed among the different claimants as soon as they were delivered to the chiefs. In consequence, they had vowed to die where they were rather than to assent to being given up. Arbuckle had anticipated an escape attempt or at least some difficulty in making the transfer. However, the blacks were told that they would be permitted to live in towns as they had formerly done and that they would not be sold or otherwise disposed of to either white men or Indians without their consent. The Seminole chiefs were told that the blacks would be turned over with this expectation, to which the chiefs did not object, thereby virtually making a promise to that effect. The chiefs tried to allay the blacks' fears by telling them that they would remain with the Seminoles and be treated kindly. With that assurance, the blacks were willing to live with the Indians as they had previously done. In Arbuckle's opinion, these understandings were the basis of the smooth transfer and the reason why the blacks, though armed, did not resist.[32]

When preparations were being made for the blacks' transfer to the Seminoles, the military authorities had told the blacks that if any armed parties of claimants tried to seize them while they were en route to the Seminole country they were to defend themselves. However, they were warned to act properly and to be guilty of nothing that would tend to create any disturbance. In all cases, however, where they felt themselves to be wronged, they were to submit their case to the agent. During the weeks following the transfer, this advice was transformed by rumor to a mandate to kill, if possible, any Creeks who might attempt to execute their claims. On April 2, 1849, Wildcat appeared "quite drunk" at Arbuckle's office in Fort Smith, complaining that the blacks had been given some improper and unfriendly council.[33]

Arbuckle was skeptical but felt the need to have the matter clarified. Belknap, in fact, had told the blacks that in case of attack by whites on their way to the Seminole country they could defend themselves. However, on April 3, he informed them in the presence of Duval, Seminole chief Jim Jumper, and others that if any wrong was done them by the Indians on their arrival in the Nation, they must not attempt to right it themselves but must appeal to the chiefs and finally to the agent who would see that justice was done. Belknap directed his words to both the slaves and the free men.[34]

When the blacks reached the Seminole country, they began to resist the Indians' authority. At the Deep Fork, they were slow in removing from there to the place where the Seminoles had decided to settle them, even though Chief Jim Jumper continued to urge them to remove. When they finally did so, most of them did not settle where the Indians wanted them to, twelve miles from the agency, but settled instead on Wewoka Creek thirty miles from the agency, a place which was particularly objectionable to Chiefs Jumper and Passochee Yohola. However, the Seminoles decided to allow the blacks to settle after their own fashion until it was decided in council who the various families' owners were, making it known that when the decisions were made the blacks would be turned over.[35] Thus, the blacks formed small towns in the Seminole country, mainly at Deep Fork and Wewoka, most of them at the latter under the leadership of Gopher John. They retained their arms and lived with no control from their Indian masters, resolved to protect themselves from slaving activities.

As this chapter in Creek-Seminole relations was drawing to a close, the Creeks had domestic problems of their own. Early in 1840, several charges were filed against Creek Agent James Logan. Among them were some that related to slaves or the slave trade. Charges were made by T. H. Wolfe, a jewelry peddler from Philadelphia, who had come to the Creek country in 1841. Logan had taken him in, and he had lived in the Logan household until 1844. Logan later set Wolfe up in business as a silversmith. In 1848 Wolfe was the mail rider between the Creek agency and Fort Gibson. On May 27, Wolfe informed the Postmaster General that Logan and one B. W. Booker had intercepted the mail and had taken from it a packet bound for Napoleon, Arkansas. In apparent retaliation, Logan ordered Wolfe out of the Nation, but Wolfe, by virtue of having married a Creek, had been admitted to Creek citizenship by an act of the council. In October 1848, Wolfe made the additional charge that Logan used one of his own slaves as striker at the public blacksmith and arranged to have another man sign the receipts to make it appear that the latter was the striker, while Logan pocketed the money.[36]

Wolfe later charged that in 1847 Logan was stirring up trouble by denouncing Jesup's promises to the blacks as an imposition upon the Creeks. After it became known that the Seminole blacks would be returned to the Indians, Logan had supposedly worked to induce the Seminoles to sell their blacks rather than let them run at large. Through his assistance, a well-known slave trader named Nordheimer was able to buy for $500 seven slaves well worth $2,500 to $3,000. It was also rumored, said Wolfe, that through the efforts of Nordheimer, William Whitfield (Logan's son-in-law), and Logan, slave speculators had bought one hundred blacks from Billy Factor, a "young Seminole" who had been under Logan's care for over two years.[37]

Billy Factor may have been part Seminole, but he was generally considered a free black, the son of Rose Sena Factor, the black widow of an Apalachicola named Samuel Factor. Rose had escaped to the Seminoles from her Spanish master, Matteo Solano, in 1821, and later she and Billy were taken during Captain William Miller's raid and carried to the Creek Nation. She was purchased by the Black Factor, who gave her to his son as a wife. When the Seminole War broke out, the Factors owned a great deal of personal property in herds and crops. Billy served as army herdsman and later as interpreter, becoming one of the better known interpreters during the war.[38]

The plan of Factor, Logan, and the others was to run the blacks out of the Creek Nation to Memphis, Tennessee, to be sold down the river as Tennessee blacks. Logan was accused of having planned to send a half-blood Creek to a Seminole and ask to buy a certain black or family of blacks. If the Seminole said that he did not own them, the agent was to pay him to make a bill of sale anyway. The Creek would then make a bill of sale to a white man who would take the blacks out of the territory and sell them to another man who would take them to Memphis, sufficiently confusing the title.[39]

Logan was also accused of having committed fraud in the administra-

tion of the estate of Milley Francis by selling her seven or eight slaves
for "a paltry sum" in goods to his son-in-law Whitfield, and he was accused of lending money to slave speculators from the Indian annuity
funds. He was also accused of licentiousness. It seems that Logan took
in one B. W. Booker, who had fled the Cherokee Nation because he stole
a black man's wife. With his "fine Bright mulatto," he lived on the agency
reserve. Every afternoon he would allegedly go out for a ride "with his
fair one in the company with the agent's yellow mistress," Pauline.
Pauline would supposedly give dinners attended by Booker and his mistress. The foursome would read dispatches from Washington so that
"Anything of importance was always known by the negroes before any
other person in the country." According to Wolfe, not just the young
but the old—black, white, and red—fell prey to Logan's "licivious apetite."
He allegedly even allowed one of his blacks named Mate to keep a white
mistress, who supposedly had a child by Mate. The public blacksmith kept
by Logan supposedly had a white wife on the agency reserve, an Indian
family about two miles from the agency, and two or three children as
well by black women. Finally, about 1843 or 1844, Logan was alleged
to have hired "a free yellow man" named Pero to furnish coal for the
public blacksmith shops. Pero, who was considered an Indian because
his mother was an Indian, supplied the coal but received none of the
money.[40]

When Logan answered the charges early in 1849, he admitted inter-
cepting the mail "to save from sacrifice the property of a total stranger,
which would have been taken from him by an unprincipled speculator."
He had removed Wolfe because he had "slandered and abused" Logan.
Logan accused Wolfe of being ungrateful and angry because Logan
had refused to hire him as a blacksmith. Logan said that the charges
against him were not the work of Wolfe alone but were "a combined
effort" of all of his enemies. It is interesting to note that Logan did
not answer any of the charges relating to his slave speculation and
personal misconduct. Logan did say that he told Wolfe all of his "private
concerns which he has been base enough to expose to all who would listen
to him."[41] Logan did not answer the charges to the satisfaction of the officials in Washington, for he was replaced as Creek agent in the spring of
1849 by Philip H. Raiford.

By the time Raiford took office, there was little doubt that the Treaty
of 1845 had failed. The years since its negotiation had been marked by

slave raids, slave controversies, and charges of the involvement of public officials in slaving activities. Those events, however, would seem minor to citizens of the Creek Nation in comparison with events of the summer and fall of 1849.

The return of the Seminole blacks to a state of slavery ultimately created the most serious difficulties between the Creeks and Seminoles up to that time. The blacks had developed a strong sense of independence. There were the years of thinking that they were free under Jesup's proclamation and the three years of protection by military authorities at Fort Gibson. Then upon their removal to the Seminole country, the chiefs had made a verbal agreement with General Belknap not to sell the blacks without their consent. Also, they had been told to protect themselves against slaving activities. Thus, they evidently considered themselves free and merely wards of the Indians.[42] Finally, for the most part, they settled apart in towns of their own. Armed and living independently, the blacks caused difficulties not only between the blacks and Seminoles but between the Seminoles and Creeks as well.

Difficulties first arose between the blacks and Seminoles when, in June 1849, two Seminoles went to Gopher John's town at Wewoka to arrest "Walking Joe" for horse stealing. The black men, armed with knives and pistols, threatened the Indians, set Joe free, and warned the Seminoles not to come to their town again without first consulting their head men.[43]

Proslavery in philosophy as he was, Seminole Subagent Marcellus Duval saw a potential danger in the situation: "It must be decided whether the negroes govern or the Seminoles. Should the Seminoles allow the negroes to go on the Creeks will protest first and finally interfere which they have a right to do to keep order in the country." Also, if an Indian should be hurt in a confrontation with the blacks, Duval said that he could not "answer for the number of negroes who would suffer." More than all of this, however, Duval obviously feared the presence of an enclave of free or independent blacks in a slaveholding territory. He insisted that the blacks had committed acts for "which the lives of the ringleaders would be forfeited if committed in a slave state." He felt that the blacks must be brought into subjection to their masters. While he wished "to see them taught their proper place," he said that he would see that they were not "unnecessarily interrupted" and would protect them "from interference from all persons but their owners & the authorities of the nation."[44]

Duval blamed the situation on the military authorities, who he felt had encouraged the blacks' resistance to authority by protecting blacks on the reserve from unauthorized persons and legitimate owners alike. Duval cited the example of the family of Thomas who had been taken by their Creek owner D. N. McIntosh from the black town of Deep Fork. When the act was reported the blacks were taken from him and placed in the garrison. The military officers had allowed the blacks to keep their weapons in violation of the Creek law, and criminals had been given up only when the commanders were ordered to do so by Arbuckle. While at the garrison, the blacks were allowed to run their livestock in the Indian country, but the blacks rendered no service to their owners. Finally, Duval thought bad the advice Belknap had given the blacks at the time they were turned over. While Duval thought it was not good to squander slaves and to sell parents from children and husbands from wives, he felt that Belknap should never have told the Indians not to sell the blacks or scatter them unless the blacks wanted to go—at least, not in the presence of the blacks. For the latter had construed the advice to mean that they were still protected by the military, and they now used military force as a threat against the Indians.[45] Under these circumstances, Duval felt that if the military showed the least disposition to support the blacks, there would be trouble between them and the Indians.

Of course, Duval's complaint against the army had been longstanding because the officers would not let him have his way with the blacks. General Arbuckle, in reality, felt that many of the blacks had been separated from the Seminoles for so long that they would never be "very serviceable" to them or to anyone else as slaves. They were too independent and insubordinate. He wrote, "In their present position, I regard them as a nuisance in the Seminole country. They were counselled to conduct themselves properly when they were turned over, and assured that if they did so, they should not be cruelly or illegally treated. But it seems they have acted otherwise."[46]

When, in July, the Seminoles met in council and decided who were the blacks' owners under Seminole laws, the blacks refused to be separated or to allow their towns to be broken up. The chiefs, mindful of the fighting ability the blacks had demonstrated during the Florida war, were reluctant to confront the blacks and force their compliance with the decrees of council. Thus, the owners turned to Duval to secure their property and to avoid bloodshed.[47]

The Creeks had been watching these developments very carefully and now began to assert their right to disarm the blacks in accordance with their laws, which did not permit blacks to live in separate towns or to bear arms. However, in this instance, the Creeks were apparently influenced by speculatòrs who wanted the blacks returned to their Indian owners, who had sold them to the speculators. The Creeks' taking the matter into their hands would force a confrontation with the Seminoles, who vehemently disliked any interference of the Creeks in their affairs, even though they themselves would like to see the blacks disarmed. There was no doubt that the blacks would resist the Creeks by force if they should come to disarm them. In view of the danger of the situation, Duval called on Arbuckle to send troops to disarm the blacks so that they could be brought into subjection. His request was endorsed by John Drennen, the superintendent of Indian affairs for the Western Territory.[48]

Arbuckle denied Duval's request for troops. The general knew that Duval and the Seminoles wanted the army to disarm the blacks to save themselves risk and trouble, for he knew that they feared armed resistance by the blacks if the Indians tried to separate and dispose of them. But Arbuckle questioned Duval's motives. He had learned that about one-third of the blacks had been promised to William J. Duval, the brother of Marcellus, for his services as attorney in getting the blacks turned over to the Seminoles. He learned that about as many more had been sold or otherwise disposed of to the Cherokees and Creeks, with some United States citizens having an interest in the transactions. The blacks knew it, too, and they would resist rather than be disarmed.[49]

Arbuckle's suspicions of Duval were heightened when Belknap reported that it was the general impression in the Seminole country "that the agent takes a deep interest in obtaining for his brother one third of the negroes provided him by the Indians for his agency in having them restored to the Seminoles by the government." Belknap also learned that on his way back to the Seminole country from Fort Smith, Duval was accompanied by P. N. White and a man named Johnson, trader and lawyer of Van Buren, and that these two men proposed to the Creek subchief Benjamin Marshall to disarm the blacks. Marshall refused. Belknap expected no trouble from the Creeks, "in fact no trouble at all unless from the agents."[50]

Duval's credibility was further eroded on September 7 and 8, 1849, when the Seminole chiefs Wild Cat, Passockee Yohola, and George Cloud denied that the Seminoles had had any complaints against the blacks and said that the blacks were settled in three towns sufficiently convenient to them, that they wished the blacks to keep their arms so they might hunt to feed their poor families, and that they hoped the blacks might not be disturbed in any way. They charged Duval with asking Chief Roley Mc-Intosh to send some of the Creeks to meet the Seminoles in council, tel-ling him that if the Creeks approved of disarming the blacks, the Semi-noles would help them do it. The Creek chief Jim Boy was to be at the head of the council which was to have met on September 3 near the black settlements; however, the Seminoles were opposed to any interference by the Creeks, refused to attend, informed the Creeks that they would not meet them, and sent the delegation to General Arbuckle. The general be-lieved that the subagent's action would probably lead to difficulties be-tween the Creeks and Seminoles and instructed Drennen to warn his agents about actions that might cause trouble. Duval had made his over-tures to the Creeks in the absence of Philip H. Raiford, the Creek agent, whom Arbuckle asked to keep the Creeks from interfering until the government could act. Finally, to the Adjutant General Roger Jones, Arbuckle wrote that if an investigation was conducted, "it will be easily ascertained who are the persons most directly and deeply interested in carrying into execution the plan proposed by the Seminole sub-agent and urgently recommended by the acting superintendent."[51]

Meanwhile, some of the bolder Seminole blacks had drifted back to the vicinity of Fort Gibson, much to the dissatisfaction of the Creeks, who considered them "a worthless, lazy set of vagabonds," who would "give much trouble sooner or later." Other free blacks of the Creek Na-tion lived in the vicinity. In early October, General Belknap went on an inspection tour, and the slave hunters took the opportunity to make raids on the blacks. On October 9, 1849, a man named Myers from Fort Smith stole a woman and her three children. They were free, the wom-an considered an Indian by virtue of her mother's having been a full-blood Yuchi. Soldiers recovered the blacks. Investigation showed that Myers had been misled in his purchase, and he was released. On October 11, Siah Hardridge presented a claim for some blacks he had purchased from Nel-ly Factor in 1843. He claimed that they were in the Cherokee Nation near the post. Hardridge was reminded that no claim dated before the return of the blacks to the Seminoles was valid. Nevertheless, Hardridge attempted to take Dembo Factor, who drew a pistol and a knife and was wounded by a shotgun fired by Hardridge's brother. Hardridge was forbidden to further molest the blacks, but that night he made another attempt to take them. However, the blacks drove him off.[52]

Dembo was taken to the post hospital where the surgeon pronounced his wound mortal. Later that day, Hardridge took him from the hospital and into the Creek Nation, and by the end of the month Dembo was reported to be recovering. A few days after the raid, a man named Tyrell from the Cherokee Nation and apparently employed by Hardridge came late at night to the quarters of one of the officers and tried to carry off a Seminole woman, swearing "that he would have her if he was compelled to cut off her head." The ferries across the Arkansas were watched to prevent the Seminole blacks from escaping to the Seminole country. Upon learning of these activities in his absence, General Belknap was convinced that the slave traders had taken advantage of his absence to make the raids, and he felt that Hardridge was simply the agent for some trader and had no claim whatever to Dembo. He therefore asked General Arbuckle to press the Creek authorities for Dembo's return. However, Arbuckle was reluctant to act because nothing could prevent the Seminoles from selling their slaves even though they had promised not to do so without the blacks' consent. Therefore, he suggested that if Dembo had been taken illegally, the owner should demand his return from the Creeks. If any attempt were made to seize blacks near the garrison, Belknap was not to allow them to be taken unless the claimant could satisfactorily prove the validity of his title and unless no other satisfactory course could be pursued.[53]

Shortly after the raids, Wild Cat delivered a talk at the North Fork and asked Duval to forward it to the president of the United States. He asked the government to remove his people from the Creek Nation to a place near the Rio Grande. His people were tired of living among the Creeks, he said, and the country would suit them better in the south. He also believed that he could induce Billy Bowlegs and all of the remaining Seminoles in Florida to go willingly to the Rio Grande, whereas they would always object to being removed to lands near the Creeks.[54]

Wild Cat's dissatisfaction with affairs in the West had been long-standing. Although he had signed the Treaty of 1845, he smarted under the Creek dominance established by the pact. For some time he had been a chief advisor to Micanopy, and for over a decade had been expected to succeed the latter as principal chief of the Seminoles. He laid plans for a confederacy of the Seminoles and the Southwestern tribes with

himself at the head. However, his plans were thwarted, and he had to
take his followers to join the tribes of the southwest. Wild Cat evidently
got his idea in 1845 and 1846 when he traveled in the Southwest on peace
and trading missions to the Comanches. During his travels, he met the
Kickapoos, Lipans, Tonkawas, and Comanches. In 1847, he sent a message
to the secretary of war, complaining that the Indian Territory was not a
better land than Florida, and in 1848 he sent representatives to the tribes
he had met in his earlier travels, as well as to the Kichai and Wacos, urging
them to come to the Indian Territory and join the Seminoles.[55]

However, matters did not go as he had expected on the home front.
Micanopy died on the night of his arrival at Fort Gibson to receive the
blacks from General Belknap. The election of principal chief did not fall
to Wild Cat but to Jim Jumper. Thus, Wild Cat could not ask the wild
tribes to join one who was not a chief. Therefore, he decided to lead his
people south of the Rio Grande and there establish a colony for refugees
including Indians and blacks from Texas, the Indian Territory, and Arkansas. Wild Cat persuaded some of his people and a few Creeks, with a combined strength of twenty to twenty-five warriors, to leave the Indian
country and make treaties with the Western tribes and with Mexico.
Using a hunting pass given him by Duval, he claimed he had permission
to go to look for new lands. When in late October the party left the
Seminole country, they were accompanied by Gopher John and about
twenty other black men and their families. Also in the group were a few
slaves belonging to Creeks and Cherokees. Numbering about two hundred,
they encamped in the spring of 1850 on Cow Bayou on the Brazos so
the blacks could make a corn crop, and in the summer of 1850 they
went on to Mexico, where they asked admission as settlers.[56]

Slaving activities in the early summer of 1850 pointed more certainly
to the duplicity of Duval, who, with other claimants, capitalized on the
absence of Wild Cat, the blacks' strongest Indian defender, and Gopher
John, their strongest leader. Without these two figures, the blacks who
remained were at the mercy of the Indians. In early June, a party of
slave hunters from the Creek Nation entered the Seminole country,
taking three slaves. Two of the men were Siah Hardridge and his son,
who shot a slave belonging to Gopher John and took him away. D. N.
McIntosh captured Jim Bowlegs and Stephen but had a bill of sale for
only the latter. They were rescued, however, by General Belknap. Belknap sent an officer to Chief Roley McIntosh in protest against the ac-

tion. McIntosh was angry. He sympathized with Hardridge, for Gopher John had "decoyed off a number of negroes" belonging to Hardridge. According to McIntosh, the Seminole chiefs had given Hardridge permission to take all of the property left by Gopher John in the Nation. Even if Hardridge had no claim to the black, the Creeks would have supported him in his action because the black resisted and tried to take a gun from Hardridge's son, who shot him. As for Jim Bowlegs, he was a slave and had arms and a horse, both of which were prohibited by Creek law. D. N. McIntosh had a bill of sale for Stephen, and thus had the right to take his property anywhere he found it. After defending the Creeks' actions, McIntosh then attacked Belknap, who he said had earlier told him in the presence of Benjamin Marshall and Kendal Lewis that he would have nothing more to do with the Seminole blacks but now said that he would offer them protection. To McIntosh, the blacks had repeatedly broken the laws of the Creek Nation, but the military had asked the Creeks to suspend the laws when it came to the Seminole blacks. If the Creeks had no right to make and enforce laws regarding those people, McIntosh wanted to know so that the Creek delegation to Washington could work at getting the matter settled.[57]

The events which followed the departure of Wild Cat and Gopher John resulted in nearly three hundred blacks leaving the Indian country for Mexico, including 180 who left with Jim Bowlegs in the summer of 1850. This group was pursued by a party of Creeks and white slave traders, who overtook them near Fort Arbuckle. The blacks resisted, and some were killed. A few escaped, but most of them were captured and brought back to the Seminole country.[58]

This attempted escape was caused by great excitement that erupted in the Seminole country on June 24, when a party of armed and equipped men arrived in the vicinity of Wewoka. Among them were Creeks, headed by Newman McIntosh and including Hardridge, Tom Carr, Joe Smith, John Sells, and others. There were Cherokees, including William Drew, Dick Drew, and Martin Vann, and there were four white men, P.H. White of Van Buren, J. M. Smith of Fort Smith, a trader near the Creek agency named Mathews, and Gabriel Duval of Montgomery, Alabama. Duval was the brother of Marcellus Duval and had taken over the claim of their brother William, who had recently died. The Seminoles at first became excited because they did not know the object of the party, and when they learned that they intended to attack the blacks' town, many became determined to assist the blacks in defending themselves.[59]

Captain F. T. Dent of the Fifth Infantry was in the vicinity and intervened to prevent a confrontation. He sent word to Marcellus Duval, asking him to come to the scene, pointed out to Newman McIntosh that the
action the group intended to take would likely start a war between the
Creeks and Seminoles, and warned that he would interfere to prevent it.
Dent persuaded McIntosh to try to arrive at some understanding with the
Seminole chiefs. When Duval arrived the following day, he told McIntosh
and his party to remove to the north side of the North Fork into the
Creek country, and they did so. Duval then called a council of the Seminole chiefs, and McIntosh and four other Creeks came to meet them.
The chiefs agreed to admit the Creek party and to help them in taking
and delivering a number of blacks, the number Dent did not learn. As
soon as the Seminoles came to the decision, Dent retired from the
scene.[60]

He later learned that those of Jim Bowlegs' followers who had been
taken were kept as prisoners for a short time to keep them from giving
information to and supporting those who had fled. All of those taken
were still at the Seminole agency on July 15, some apparently to be
turned over to the Creeks who had camped about six miles from the
black town and another thirty-four to satisfy the claim of William J.
Duval.[61]

Wild Cat returned to the Indian Territory in September of 1850.
He, Gopher John, a chief of the Kickapoo, and their followers had
received tentative approval to settle in Mexico. Wild Cat returned to
gather more of his people. On the way he visited the Comanche, Caddo,
and Waco, but had little success in getting them to join him. However,
he was more successful with the Kicapoo, a large group of them agreeing to join him.[62]

The Kickapoos from among whom Wild Cat recruited had lived for
years on the Canadian and had carried on a rather steady trade with
the Creeks, buying principally powder and lead from the trading houses
on the Little River. In mid-September 1850, they came in for more supplies and brought news that Wild Cat was on his way and wanted the
Seminoles to meet him and as many as possible to prepare to join him.
These events, plus rumors in Eastern newspapers that Wild Cat had recruited eight hundred Indians for the purpose of raiding the whites,
caused the Creeks to become uneasy. Echo Hadjo and Billy Hadjo, Creek
head and second chief of Canadian District, reported Wild Cat's return
to Belknap and directed the merchants on Little River to sell no more

powder to the Kickapoos or other Indians. On September 20, it was reported that Wild Cat was in the Indian country, and all of the chiefs and head men of Canadian District, including Echo Hadjo, Billy Hadjo, Jimmy Chopco, Tustanug Chopco, and Arlock Fixico, asked Chief McIntosh to "censure the people of this country in his remaining in their midst, as harboring men guilty of outrages on other citizens."[63]

On September 23, McIntosh wrote to General Belknap:

The messenger came in last night that Wild Cat got back, and brought in a news that he went on and talk with Mexican, and they agreed to give him land and subsistence if he come in and settle in the country. Now he come back with enticing news, and want to carry his people in that nation; and the negroes, he told them if they emigrate to that country, they will all be free by the government. This is good news to the negroes. I am told some are preparing to go. He further states that he had four hundred men with him when he was traveling, but he came in by himself, one woman, and a young man. What come of this four hundred men we have not learned. Wild Cat held council with his people—had this talk with them. When I was with you last, when I got a true talk of Wild Cat I would let you know; this is a true talk I send you."[64]

From about the time of Wild Cat's return to the Indian country, rumors of depredations upon whites in Texas began to circulate in the western part of the Creek Nation. J. C. Gibson, a white man who lived there, heard that Wild Cat and a small party of his people and a band of Comanches crossed into Texas and killed a hundred people. Wild Cat himself added to the rumors by changing his stories. At one time he claimed to have recruited 1,600 Kickapoos and at another only 600. The result was a great deal of excitement among the Creeks, who began to feel the need to check his influence with his people. They had called one council on September 23, and they met again on September 30 at Tuckabahchee to adopt some measure to stop him.[65]

A few days later, Chief McIntosh sent 300 Creek warriors into the Seminole country to prevent any blacks from leaving with Wild Cat and to detain him until the Creeks could find what his mission was. McIntosh wrote the Seminole chiefs, stressing that the object of the invasion was not to deprive the Seminoles of their blacks but to prevent their escape. The party went as far as Wewoka, where they learned that Wild Cat was still in the Seminole country and that a number of blacks were preparing to leave. The party returned to the Creek country without accomplishing anything. Nevertheless, Wild Cat left the Seminole country to keep from being taken. He succeeded in persuading about thirty or forty Indians to go with him.[66]

With the departure of Wild Cat and Gopher John and their followers, the blacks in the Seminole country lost their protectors. The way was now open for the Creeks to fulfill one of their long-time objectives: to break up the remaining enclaves of blacks in the Seminole country. During the next few years, Creek raiding parties concentrated their efforts in that direction.

NOTES

1. Colonel R. B. Mason to Brigadier General Roger Jones, March 5, 1845, National Archives Record Group 393 (Records of the United States Army Continental Commands, 1821-1920), *Fort Gibson,* Letters Sent, hereafter cited as *Gibson LS.*

2. *Ibid.*

3. Mason to James H. Prentiss, May 21, 1845, *Gibson LS*; Statement of Micanopy and others, March 16, 1840, *Fort Gibson,* Letters Received, box 1 (hereafter cited as *Gibson LR*); Prentiss to Mason, May 28, 1845, National Archives Record Group 393, *Second and Seventh Military Departments,* Letters Sent, hereafter cited as *2nd and 7th LS.*

4. Marcellus Duval to William Medill, March 24, 1846, National Archives Microfilm Publications, *Microcopy M234* (Office of Indian Affairs, Letters Received) 801: D1059-46, hereafter cited as *M234,* followed by the roll number; Duval to James K. Polk, December 21, 1846, National Archives Microfilm Publications, *M574* (Special Files of the Office of Indian Affairs, 1807-1904) 13: frame 191, hereafter cited as *M574,* followed by the roll number; Edwin C. McReynolds, *The Seminoles* (Norman: University of Oklahoma Press, 1957), p. 246.

5. P. M. Butler to J. M. Porter, August 18, 1843, *M234*-442: B1864-43; Decision of Porter, February 1, 1844, Butler to T. Hartley Crawford, March 21, 1844, *M234*-443: W2365-44, B2004-44; James Dawson to Crawford, June 5, 1844, Commissioner to James Logan, July 29, 1845, A. P. Upshaw to Commissioner, September 13, 1843, Logan to Medill, April 1, 1846, with enclosures, *M234*-227: D969-44, A1914-46, L2553-46; Crawford to David S. Kaufman, September 26, 1845, Crawford to William Armstrong, September 26, 1845, National Archives Microfilm Publications, *Microcopy M21* (Office of Indian Affairs, Letters Sent) 37: 154, 155, hereafter cited as *M21,* followed by the roll number; Medill to William L. Marcy, February 18, 1846, with enclosures, National Archives Microfilm Publications, *Microcopy M348* (Office of Indian Affairs, Report Books) 4: 581, hereafter cited as *M348,* followed by the roll number.

6. Duval to Medill, March 24, 1846, *M234*-801: D1059-46; Major General

Thomas S. Jesup to Brigadier General Matthew Arbuckle, April 3, 1846, *M574*-13: frame 91; *Official Opinions of the Attorneys General of the United States* (Washington, 1852-), 4: 723-24.

7. Duval to Commissioner, July 10, 1846, *M234*-801: D1091-46; Lieutenant R. W. Kirkham to Jesup, August 20, 1846, *Fort Gibson,* Volume "Indian Affairs," p. 18, hereafter cited as *Gibson Indian Affairs.*

8. Captain A. Cady to Jones, March 18, 1846, *Gibson LS*; Colonel Gustavus Loomis to Roley McIntosh, July 20, 1846, December 17, 1846, *Gibson Indian Affairs,* pp. 18, 24.

9. Statement of Loomis, February 4, 1847, *Gibson Indian Affairs,* p. 24; Duval to Polk, December 21, 1846, *M234*-801: P5-47, and *M574*-13: frame 191.

10. Duval to Medill, January 26, 1847, *M574*-13: D9-47.

11. Logan to Medill, January 12, 1847, *M234*-227: G18-47.

12. *Laws of the Cherokee Nation: Adopted by the Council at Various Periods* (Tahlequah, Cherokee Nation: Cherokee Advocate Office, 1852), p. 71; Arrell M. Gibson, *The Chickasaws* (Norman: University of Oklahoma Press, 1971), p. 226; Wyatt F. Jeltz, "The Relations of the Negroes and Choctaw and Chickasaw Indians," *The Journal of Negro History* 33 (January 1948), 31-32; *Constitution, Laws, and Treaties of the Chickasaws* (Tishomingo City, Chickasaw Nation: E. J. Foster, 1860), p. 115.

13. Loomis to Lieutenant F. F. Flint, July 20, 1847, *Gibson Indian Affairs,* p. 26.

14. Loomis to Flint, July 20, 1847, *Gibson Indian Affairs,* p. 26.

15. Loomis to Mrs. Leonard, October 25, 1847, Loomis to Logan, November 23, 1847, *Gibson Indian Affairs,* p. 31; Logan to Loomis, November 23, 1847, *Gibson LR,* box 3.

16. Statement of Tustenuggee Micco, December 9, 1847, Logan to Loomis, December 6, 1874, Loomis to Flint, December 8, 1847, Loomis to Logan, December 8, 1847, *Gibson LR,* box 3; Loomis to Logan, December 10, 1847, *Gibson Indian Affairs,* p. 33.

17. Logan to Loomis, December 9, 11, 15, 1847, *Gibson LR,* box 3.

18. Loomis to Jesup, January 21, 1848, Jesup to Loomis, Feburary 17, 1848, *Gibson Indian Affairs,* pp. 34, 35; Captain B. L. E. Bonneville to Flint, April 21, 1848, *Second and Seventh Military Department,* Letters Received, box 7, hereafter cited as *2nd and 7th LR;* Flint to Bonneville, April 23, May 1, 1848, *Gibson LR,* box 3. Bonneville described Joe as twenty years old, five feet seven inches tall, having a thin, sharp face, yellow complexion, "bright," "quick," "smart," and speaking good English. He had waited on several officers at Fort Gibson. Joe was the son of Primus and Hannah, both claiming to be free under Jesup's proclamation. Bonneville had a file containing their "free papers," signed by General Zachary Taylor on April 30, 1840, after their surrender. In Bonneville's opinion, Joe was entitled to protection by the government. Bonneville to Flint, May 3, 1848 *2nd and 7th LR,* box 7.

19. Duval to Polk, December 1, 1847, *M547*-13: frame 202; *Official Opinions of the Attorneys General,* 4: 723.

20. Benjamin Marshall et al. to Medill, April 6, 1848, *M574*-13: Creek M216-48.

21. *Ibid.*

22. *Official Opinions of the Attorneys General,* 4: 720-29; President Polk approved the opinion on July 8, 1848.

23. William Marcy to Arbuckle, August 5, 1848, and Medill to Duval, August 5, 1848, *Gibson LR,* box 3; Medill to Marshall et al., August 10, 1848, *M21*-41: 157, and *M574*-13: frame 136.

24. Flint to Captain W. S. Ketchum, September 4, 1848, *Gibson LR,* box 3; Ketchum to McIntosh, September 8, 1848, *Gibson Indian Affairs,* p. 38.

25. McIntosh to Ketchum, September 9, 1848, *Gibson LR,* box 3; Ketchum to McIntosh, September 11, 1848, *Gibson Indian Affairs,* p. 39. Margaret may have been the daughter of Polly Barnet, the wife of Toney, and was free by virtue of her manumission by old Chief Bowlegs in 1819. Statement of J. W. Washbourne, October 14, 1854, *M234*-801: D709-54.

26. Ketchum to McIntosh, September 13, 1848, *Gibson Indian Affairs,* p. 39; William Whitfield to Ketchum, September 14, 1848, *Gibson LR,* box 3.

27. Ketchum to McIntosh, September 28, 1848, *Gibson Indian Affairs,* p. 41.

28. Ketchum to Micanopy, September 24, 1848, *Gibson Indian Affairs,* p. 40.

29. Ketchum to McIntosh, September 28, 1848, *Gibson Indian Affairs,* p. 41. The property in question had not been returned in January 1849. Logan to General William K. Belknap, January 30, 1849, *Gibson LR,* box 3.

30. Flint to Ketchum, September 25, 1848, *Gibson LR,* box 3.

31. Flint to Belknap, December 19, 1848, and McIntosh et al. to Belknap, December 27, 1848, *Gibson LR,* box 3; List of Negroes Turned Over to the Seminole Chiefs at Fort Gibson, C. N., Jan'y 2nd 1849, *M574*-13: Seminole J143-49.

32. Arbuckle to Jones, January 8, 1849, *M574*-13: Seminole J143-49; Arbuckle to Jones, July 31, 1849, and Flint to John Drennen, August 13, 1849, *House Executive Document 15,* 33 Cong., 2 sess., pp. 22, 26, hereafter cited as *Document 15.*

33. Flint to Belknap, April 2, 1849, *Gibson LR,* box 3.

34. Belknap to Flint, April 4, 1849, *2nd and 7th LR,* box 7.

35. Duval to Belknap, June 7, 1849, *Gibson LR,* box 3; Duval to Arbuckle, July 16, 1849, *M574*-13: Seminole W359-49; Arbuckle to Jones, July 31, 1849, *Document 15,* p. 22.

36. S. M. Rutherford to Medill, February 1, 1849, Logan to Rutherford, February 23, 1849, T. H. Wolfe to Cave Johnson, May 27, 1848, McIntosh to Wolfe, July 27, 1848, Wolfe to Medill, October 26, 1848, *M234*-228: R436-49, R510-49, B349-49.

37. Solon Borland to Medill, February 6, 1849, with enclosures, *M234*-228: B349-49.

38. Decision of the Chiefs, June 15, 1827, William DuVal to Jenkins I. Worth, December 22, 1842, Statement of Nelly Factor, September 4, 1828, Statement of DuVal, September 10, 1828, *M234*-289: S3398-43; W. K. Sebastian to Commissioner,

May 1, 1852, *M234*-801: S90-52; M. Thompson to Jacob Thompson, December 6, 1858, *M234*-802: T346-58.

39. Borland to Medill, February 6, 1849, with enclosures, *M234*-228: B349-49.

40. *Ibid.*

41. Logan to Rutherford, February 23, 1849, *M234*-228: R510-49.

42. Francis N. Page to Assistant Adjutant General, November 18, 1854, *Document 15*, pp. 10-11.

43. Duval to Belknap, June 7, 1849, *Gibson LR*, box 3. Gopher John was a free black who had been a leader among the black hostile forces during the Seminole War. He had often served as interpreter in and around Fort Gibson. Jesup to Marcy, April 3 and July 1, 1848, *M574*-13; Statement of Butler, April 16, 1845, *M234*-800: B2452-45.

44. Duval to Belknap, June 7, 1849, *Gibson LR,* box 3.

45. *Ibid.*; Duval to Medill, June 9, 1849, in M234-801: R519-49.

46. Arbuckle to Adjutant General, July 31, 1849, *Document 15*, p. 23.

47. Duval to Arbuckle, July 16, 1849, *M574*-13: W359-49; and *Gibson LR*, box 3.

48. *Ibid.*; Drennen to Arbuckle, July 20, 1849, *2nd and 7th LR,* box 7; *Document 15*, p. 20; Francis N. Page to Assistant Adjutant General, November 18, 1854, *Document 15*, p. 11.

49. Arbuckle to Adjutant General, July 31, 1849, *M574*-13: Seminole W359-49; *Document 15*, pp. 21-22; Page to Assistant Adjutant General, November 18, 1854, *Document 15*, p. 11.

50. Belknap to Flint, August 8, 1849, *2nd and 7th LR*, box 7.

51. Flint to Drennen, September 10, 1849, *2nd and 7th LR*, box 7, *M574*-13: frame 237; *Document 15*, pp. 28-29; Flint to Philip H. Raiford, September 10, 1849, Arbuckle to Jones, September 14, 1849, *Document 15*, pp. 29-30, 31.

52. Captain J. Lynde to Flint, October 12, 1849, *2nd and 7th LR,* box 7.

53. Belknap to Flint, October 31, 1849, *2nd and 7th LR*, box 7; Flint to Belknap, November 9, 1849, *Gibson LR*, box 3.

54. Duval to Orlando Brown, November 5, 1849, *M234*-289: D247-49.

55. Duval to Medill, October 15, 1846, *House Executive Document 4,* 29 Cong., 2 sess., p. 279; McReynolds, pp. 256-57; Grant Foreman, *The Five Civilized Tribes* (Norman: University of Oklahoma Press, 1934), pp. 244-45; Wild Cat to Secretary of War, March 17, 1847, *M234*-801: C82-47; Kenneth Wiggins Porter, *The Negro on the American Frontier* (New York: Arno Press and The New York Times, 1971), p. 426.

56. Duval to Medill, June 9, 1849, Duval to Brown, May 30, 1850, *M234*-801: R519-49, D392-50; Page to Assistant Adjutant General, November 18, 1854, *Document 15*, pp. 10-11; McReynolds, pp. 260, 261-62; Porter, pp. 424, 427; Muriel Wright, "Seal of the Seminole Nation," *The Chronicles of Oklahoma* 34 (Autumn 1956), 266; Carolyn Thomas Foreman, "The Jumper Family of the Seminole Nation," *The Chronicles of Oklahoma* 34 (Autumn 1956), 283. For an authoritative treatment of Wild Cat's activities in Mexico, see Porter, pp. 424-59.

57. McIntosh to Belknap, June 12, 1850, *2nd and 7th LR*, box 8; *Document 15*, pp. 16-17.

58. Porter, p. 428; Page to Assistant Adjutant General, November 18, 1854, *Document 15,* pp. 12, 17-18.

59. Dent to Flint, July 15, 1850, *2nd and 7th L R,* box 8; *Document 15,* pp. 17-18.

60. *Ibid.*

61. Dent to Flint, July 15, 1850, Statement of Molly, July 15, 1850, *2nd and 7th L R,* box 8; Washbourne to Thomas S. Drew, January 5, 1855, *M234*-802: D153-56.

62. Porter, pp. 427-28.

63. Echo Hadjo and Billy Hadjo to Belknap, September 18, 1850, Echo Hadjo et al. to McIntosh, September 20, 1850, *Gibson L R,* box 3; *Document 15,* pp. 31-32.

64. McIntosh to Belknap, September 23, 1850, *Gibson L R,* box 3; *Document 15,* p. 32; Duval to Luke Lea, September 25, 1850, *M234*-801: D451-50.

65. C. J. Atkins to Commandant at Fort Gibson, September 30, 1850, McIntosh to Belknap, September 23, 1850, *Gibson L R,* box 3; Duval to Lea, September 30, 1850, *M234*-801: D455-50.

66. Belknap to Brevet Major Page, October 15, 1850, *2nd and 7th L R,* box 8; *Document 15,* pp. 32-33; Duval to Lea, December 9, 1850, *M234*-801: D481-50; Duval to Lea, October 25, 1851, *House Executive Document 2,* 32 Cong., 1 sess., p. 405.

THE LAST DECADE OF SLAVERY

chapter **9**

THE DECADE OF the 1850s was a period of great slaving activity in the Creek country. Much of the activity was generated by the Creeks themselves, especially against the blacks owned by the Seminoles. There was, however, a great increase in the instances of slave hunting by whites, particularly from Arkansas. As the decade progressed, they became bolder in their intrusion into the Indian Territory, for they found that some of the Indians, especially the Creeks, were willing to trade with them and to help them capture the blacks they claimed.

The Creek national officials were not cooperative regarding slave claims against the Nation itself. In 1850, Thomas E. Wilson of Van Buren, Arkansas, sought payment for a slave he had bought from Wiley Connard (Kinnard), the sale having been sanctioned by the Creek council. Dean, the black, was later declared free by the courts of Arkansas. The newly formed Department of the Interior declined to interfere, saying that it was a matter between Wilson and the Indians. In 1852, Edward Hanrick of Tallapoosa County, Alabama, sought payment from the Nation for a note due him for having cleared the title to slaves owned by Yargee. On the eve of removal in 1836, Yargee's blacks were apparently attached for debts in the amount of $16,506.26 charged against the estate of Big Warrior. The Upper Creek chiefs, including Little Doctor, Mad Blue, Opothleyohola, Tuckabahchee Micco, Tustanuggee Chopco, and several others told Hanrick that if he would pay the debts, they would give him $8,500 immediately and a draft for the rest against the 1838 annuity. The note had not been paid, and Western Superintendent John Drennen believed it a legitimate debt.[1]

The Creeks themselves created other slave controversies by selling blacks to whom they had doubtful title or no title at all. Their victims quite often were women, either black or Indian. The black women were usually those who were without husbands or anyone else to help protect them. A good example was Lina, who with her children was free by virtue of her husband's having purchased them. Her husband, a free black who had formerly belonged to the Creek Paddy Carr, had been allowed to purchase himself. Lina's husband had died, and her "free" papers were taken by Nero, who later gave them to Hotoochee Horod, who, in turn, gave them to Daniel Aspberry, a half-blood Creek who kept a store in the Nation. Since she had no papers, Paddy Carr tried on occasion to sell her and the children, but he was unsuccessful in the Nation because they were generally recognized as free. Therefore, in the spring of 1851, Carr took Lina and five of her seven children, placed them aboard a steamboat at the Verdigris landing, sent them to Fort Smith, Arkansas, and put them up for sale with his brother Joe and Sam Brown as his agents. Lina's oldest daughter Jenny, about fourteen or fifteen, was kept at Paddy Carr's, and her oldest son Zedick or Aleck was given to Chilly McIntosh. "Title" to him was transferred several times, and he was finally sold by Newman McIntosh to a white man and was supposedly taken to Missouri. Lina contended that her intent to bring her case before the chiefs had prompted Carr to ship her out of the country, and she named several whites in the Creek Nation who could support her claim. It was, in fact, supported by the Creek agent, Philip H. Raiford.[2]

Other victims of the Creek slave speculators were blacks belonging to women or children who had guardians assigned to them or were vulnerable because they had no family. The decade was dominated by one large but significant case, commonly called the Pryor Case. It involved the slaves of two Seminole women Molly and her sister. Thirty-four of Molly's blacks had been promised by the Seminole chiefs to satisfy the claim of William J. Duval for attorney's fees. These women's slaves had also been the object of the Love claims during the 1830s and 1840s. In 1850, Molly claimed to own seventy-nine grown slaves "besides many infant children," who were slaves or their descendants inherited from her grandfather. Molly was the daughter of Tuskeneehau, a Mikasuki chief, and granddaughter of Kinhijah (Capichee Micco), a Mikasuki chief. At her death, the property was to go to her sister. She claimed that when her father died, Miccopotokee was made guardian of the slave property, at which time a half-blood Creek named Archie Gray began selling the slaves, without apparent title, to Hugh Love of Georgia. Miccopotokee

had not yet removed to the West, so the claim was settled in his favor
in the East. Then in 1844 or 1845, the Creek council decided the slaves
belonged to Molly and her sister.[3]

On April 7, 1853, Molly's sister sold her right to the slaves to Daniel
Boone Aspberry, a half-blood Creek, for $1,000. At the time, she was
very old. Her slaves were only nominally in a state of servitude. They
did not work regularly, nor did they pay her for the liberty of disposing
of their own time and labor. They refused to support her in a separate
residence and to cultivate fields separately for her. But if she would live
with any of them, they would support her, so she went from slave family
to slave family. As time passed, she became less satisfied with the arrangement and looked for a way to control her slaves and to force them to support her. Aspberry convinced her to place the title in his name so he could
have legal control over them. They made a bill of sale with the understanding that Aspberry would capture as many as he could, sell them, and pay
her $100 for each one caught. The slaves named in this sale were Lucy and
her five children, Nar-see-chop-see and her six children, and Nancy and
her six children. Molly's sister died the following summer, and her slaves
passed to Molly, who on September 30 sold that interest to Aspberry for
$2,000. Slaves named in this sale were Bob, Susan and her ten children, Wil-
liam, Nelly and her three children (Scipio, Sandy, and Nero), Billy, and
ten others not named.[4]

However, before Aspberry could capture a single black or, therefore,
pay her any money, Molly died. Since Aspberry had a bill of sale, he decided to claim them all. The only problem was that the blacks knew the
circumstances of the title. They did not put up a claim to freedom, but
neither would they recognize him as their master and sent him word that
they would resist unto death any attempt to capture them. Apparently
some of the Seminoles backed them in their defiance of Aspberry. Aspberry then offered to certain citizens of the United States an equal share
in the blacks if they would bring their influence to bear on authorities in
the Creek and Seminole Nations. Aspberry took the matter before the
Creek council, who decided that the sale was valid. The chiefs ordered
the Creek light horse police to deliver them.[5]

In November 1853, Aspberry, thirty other Creeks of the light horse,
and a few whites went to the Seminole country, captured over a score of
the blacks, and killed one youth who tried to help his mother escape. Although the Seminole chiefs had a claim to them, since the two women died

without issue, the Creeks insisted that their laws were the only ones in force and that the Seminoles had no say in the matter. The Creeks had recognized Aspberry's title. A few days later, Seminole Agent B. H. Smithson learned that Aspberry had sold the blacks to a white Arkansan who was expected in the Nation daily to claim them. Smithson feared trouble would result.[6]

Those captured were taken to Arkansas. Alarm spread to other slaves in the area. Aspberry and his group, who remained in the Seminole country to try to take the rest of the blacks he claimed, found it necessary to leave in haste because of the excitement that prevailed among the Seminoles and blacks. Aspberry's associates refused to aid him further. He then made offers to others for assistance, but to no avail.[7]

Aspberry had made arrangements to sell twenty-five of the blacks to E. B. Bright and Constantine Perkins, two white men who had helped him to capture them. Bright and Perkins took twelve and left ten with Aspberry, including Scipio, William, Bob, Betty, Lucy and her four children. Some of these and others whom Aspberry claimed remained at large in the Seminole country: Scipio, Betsey, Hetty, Patty, Rhoda, July, Flora, Guide, Pompe, Sanches, Ishmael, Lucy and child, Betsey (second by that name), Ben, and William. After the slave-hunting party had been run out of the Seminole country and Aspberry could not persuade anyone else to assist him, he decided that Bright and Perkins had given up the idea of taking any more. He offered to sell the claim to Cornelius D. Pryor, a U. S. citizen and trader at North Fork, Creek Nation. Pryor studied the offer and, thinking that Bright and Perkins had withdrawn from the business, accepted the proposition.[8]

Archibald H. Rutherford, a clerk in the office of the superintendent of Indian affairs at Fort Smith, hearing that Aspberry had settled the claim, wrote for his share of the profits. He was apparently one of the officials who had helped bring pressure to bear in the Indian country to help Aspberry get his claim. There is some implication that Smithson, the Seminole agent, knew of the relationship between the two, for Rutherford wanted Aspberry to give his pay for "services" to Smithson. Or, if Aspberry found a slave worth $350, he was to deliver the slave to George M. Aird for Rutherford. In response to Rutherford's request, Aspberry made out a bill of sale for a black named Willie Bob, aged about eighteen.[9]

In February 1854, the matter became complicated when Perkins saw Pryor and insisted on keeping his interest in the slaves. Pryor had spent a great deal of effort in trying to obtain the slaves, so he asked Aspberry for indemnification for his losses and release from the agreement. That would have meant a great loss to Aspberry, who proposed to turn over to Perkins all of the slaves he had except one and to let Pryor have the sixteen yet to be captured in the Seminole country. The proposition apparently satisfied all concerned, and Aspberry hired agents to collect the money due him from Pryor when Pryor succeeded in getting possession of the blacks. He empowered them to call on the Creek light horse to keep the blacks in the country until they were paid for.[10]

With this claim apparently settled, Aspberry continued other slaving activities. He was responsible for at least one raid in the spring of 1854. About the middle of April, a group of Creeks came by night and attacked the home of George Noble, a free black in the Seminole country, killing Noble's oldest son and carrying the rest of his family away. They also destroyed fifty bushels of corn, killed a brood sow, and stole a horse and three ponies. Noble, who had been freed by Harriett Bowlegs, was away in Florida at the time. In December 1853, Lieutenant John Gibbons of the army and Agent Smithson had urged Noble to go with the Seminole delegation to Florida to try to induce the remaining Seminoles to emigrate. Noble refused at first because he had feared trouble for his family who were reported to have been purchased by Aspberry. Aspberry had threatened to seize them. Gibbons and Smith assured Noble that they would interpose on his behalf and promised that his family would not be molested. They wrote the Creek authorities regarding Aspberry, who allegedly claimed title. Under those circumstances, Noble agreed to go. After he had gone, Aspberry sold the claim to another Creek; Noble's family was stolen, taken to Louisiana, and sold. When Noble returned and found his family gone, he appealed to Superintendent Thomas S. Drew at Fort Smith for aid in recovering his family, but his appeal was fruitless.[11]

There were more raids on the Creek and Seminole blacks during the following summer. One raid was against a well-known family of free blacks named Beams. Descendants of William Beams and his slave Nelly, the Beams family had removed from the Old Choctaw Nation in Mississippi to the western Choctaw Nation in 1833. Although they had been emancipated by Beams, his two Choctaw children sold them to John B. Davis of Mississippi, who sent agents to the western Choctaw Nation to secure the family in 1836, 1839, and 1840. In the latter

year, a raid on the family near Fort Towson had resulted in the death
of one and the capture of four others who were sold into slavery in
Texas.[12]

During the next few years, attempts were made to obtain the Beams
family legally. In the late 1840s, apparently in order to protect themselves against future slaving raids, they separated, part of them going
to the Creek Nation, where they were allowed to live as free blacks.
This group included Mary and her child Katy, Mitchell, Martin, Nelly
and her children, David, Girt, Ezekiel, Mary (a second by that name),
Eliza and her six or seven children, and two other women.[13] It was
seven members of this group who were taken in the summer of 1854.

In late 1853, Davis had applied to have the Fugitive Slave Law of
1850 executed on the Beams family. Through the influence of Secretary
of War Jefferson Davis, the application reached Attorney General Caleb
Cushing, who, on February 18, 1854, ruled that John B. Davis or his
agents could lawfully enter the Choctaw Nation to claim any persons who
owed him service under the laws of Mississippi. If he met with obstacles, he
could call on the United States authorities for help in apprehending such
persons. President Franklin Pierce approved the decision on March 6. On
May 19, Jefferson Davis informed Davis's attorney that the fugitive slave
laws applied to the Choctaw Nation and that the Department of the Interior would so instruct its agents in the territory. The adjutant general informed the commander at Fort Gibson of the decision and said that Davis's
evidence was prima facie sufficient to establish his right to the Beams
family. However, he stressed that if contending rights were claimed, either
by other persons or the Beams family on their own part, the question of
rights would have to be determined by a court of law.[14]

During the spring and summer of 1854, William Houser, an attorney
at Van Buren, Arkansas, and agent for Davis, frequently applied to Thomas
S. Drew, the superintendent of Indian affairs at Fort Smith, for an extra-
dition order for the Beams family, which Drew denied because he had not
received any instructions from the Department of the Interior. On July 23,
Choctaw Agent Douglas H. Cooper asked for such instructions, but the
secretary of the interior did not answer until September 11, telling Cooper
that if the Beams family were really fugitive slaves, it might be proper to
give them up. Above all, however, before anything was done, Cooper was
to investigate the facts fully and thoroughly. The secretary also directed
Drew to take no steps until further instructions came. The delay in answer-

ing Cooper's letter was critical. By the time it was answered, several members of the Beams family had been captured. On July 27, in the absence of Creek Agent William H. Garrett, Drew had issued an order to the Creek chiefs, to give all due assistance to Davis in capturing the Beams family living in the Creek Nation so that military force would not be necessary. The order named Martin, Nelly, Becky, Gilbert, Lotty and her children, Rhody and her children, Abe, Nancy and her children, Rhoda (a second by that name) and her children, and Mitchell. Armed with that order, William Houser, James Woosly, Ephraim B. Bishop, Washington Duval, John Latta, and Alexander McKisick—all of Van Buren—entered the Indian Territory.[15]

They went first to the Choctaw agency where they showed the order to Cooper and produced the letter from Jefferson Davis to John Davis's attorney, stating that the attorney general had decided that the Fugitive Slave Law applied to the Indian Territory. Cooper refused to assist them because he had not yet received any instructions from the commissioner of Indian affairs. However, he did offer to bring suit to test Davis's case in court; Houser implicitly promised to do so. Despite Cooper's refusal to help, Houser and his party captured William, the son of Nancy Beams, and Silas, the son of Lotty, and sent them to Van Buren. From the Choctaw Nation, Houser went to the Creek Nation where he took Martin (about twenty-eight years old) and Mary Beams—both children of Nancy— Mary's daughter Katy, Ellen (the daughter of Rhody), and David Beams. Martin was shot in the breast and badly wounded. Mitchell Beams (about thirty-five years old), who had hid out, was sold on credit to Roley McIntosh for $1,000. Houser also took a bond of E. B. Bright for the delivery at any time of another of the Beams women and three of her children.[16] Bright, it will be recalled, was also involved in the Aspberry-Pryor case in the Creek Nation.

On his return to Van Buren, Houser stopped at Tahlequah, Cherokee Nation, and offered the blacks for sale. It happened that Samuel Austin Worcester, a missionary of antislavery sentiment among the Cherokees, was in town and recognized the Beams family, having at one time hired one of the men as a free hired man. Worcester knew that the Beams family had been recognized as free blacks, so he appealed to the Cherokees, who refused to interfere, and then complained to Jefferson Davis and asked for an investigation. Superintendent Thomas S. Drew was asked to explain his having given Houser the letter that had permitted capture of the blacks without authorization from the Interior Department. Drew at first denied

having given the letter, but in the face of evidence, he made a full statement on the matter. He had denied the repeated requests of Houser and
Bishop for orders to secure the Beams family. But on July 27, he was
preparing to leave for southeastern Arkansas to visit his family, some
of whom were ill; he planned to be gone a month. Houser and Bishop repeated their request on that day. They expected daily the instructions
from the department which would allow them to enter the Indian Territory and arrest the blacks. If the order came, they could operate through
the Choctaw agent concerning the blacks there, but those in the Creek
Nation were a different matter. The Creek agent was gone, and there was
no indication of when he would return; Drew, too, would be gone. If the
order came in the absence of both of them, Houser and Bishop would
have no means to capture the blacks in the Creek Nation, and they would
likely flee when they heard of the capture of those in the Choctaw country.
Drew then wrote the letter to the Creek chiefs, but he claimed that it was
understood by Houser that the document was to be used only when the
expected instructions came from Washington. Drew said that although
the document was written on that contingency, it was written officially
without any conditions on its face. No copy was retained in his office,
and Drew claimed that he merely forgot about it. When he heard that
Davis had taken the Beams family, he assumed that the proper orders had
come down from the department. Drew offered the weak defense of his
preoccupation at the time with family matters and of the villainy of
Houser.[17]

Douglas H. Cooper was indignant. He had no doubts that the Beams
family were free. The Fugitive Slave Law of 1850 had provided that any
blacks claimed as runaway slaves might be carried before the United
States commissioner for examination, but it created great expense and
hardship in the Indian Territory to send people hundreds of miles for
preliminary investigation. Cooper therefore asked the secretary of the
interior to work toward having the Indian agents act as commissioners
under the Fugitive Slave Law and do the work of preliminary investigation. Otherwise, he said, "the door will be opened wide for fraud and
wrong to the free colored persons, within the Indian country."[18]

Meanwhile, the situation of the captured members of the Beams
family had become more desperate, except for David who had escaped
en route to Van Buren and had returned to the Creek Nation. Houser
and his associates had told the blacks and the officers who had helped

capture them that the blacks would have a fair and impartial hearing
concerning their claims to freedom upon reaching Van Buren. But once
there, they found Davis waiting for them and decided to divide the property. Woosly, a slave trader at Van Buren, claimed a fourth interest and
took Ellen and Silas, buying Davis's claim to them. Houser took Martin
and William. He sold Martin to Phineas H. White and Thomas B. Emerson,
business partners, paying Davis his share of the proceeds, and sold William down the Arkansas River, beyond the jurisdiction of the Circuit
Court at Van Buren. Bishop took Mary and her daughter Katy and paid
Davis his share.[19]

When news of these transactions reached the Choctaw Nation, Cyrus
Kingsbury, a missionary to the Choctaws, Sampson Folsom, and others—
all friends of the Beams family—hired Josephus Dotson, an attorney from
Mississippi then living with Cooper, to go to Van Buren and institute
proceedings to establish the family's freedom. Cooper had supposed that
the matter would be summarily disposed of in the courts of Arkansas
"under a writ of Habeas Corpus," but found that under Arkansas law
the question of freedom could not be determined under that process.
Too, the Beams family were in the possession of men of means who
would make every effort to retain possession so that they would not lose
the money they had invested. When Dotson reached Van Buren in October
1854, he found that suit had already been brought for the freedom of two
of the blacks by two local attorneys, William Walker and Joseph James
Green. When the authorities would not issue a writ of habeas corpus in
the case, Dotson filed suit for the freedom of Ellen and Silas Beams,
then in the hands of Woosly. He also sent a messenger to the circuit
judge, then in Clarksville some fifty miles away, with a petition for the
remaining members of the Beams family to sue as poor persons under
Arkansas law. Walker and Green succeeded in obtaining restraining
orders to prevent the removal of the blacks beyond the jurisdiction of
the court. William had already been sold by William Houser to S. D.
Strayhorne of Dardanelle, Arkansas. Strayhorne, in turn, had sold William to William Fowler, then in the southern part of Arkansas. Walker
and Green, with Dotson's help, succeeded in getting the authorities
to pursue him and in having him brought back.[20]

The Beams family fared badly with their captors. Most of them had
been born free and were not used to the hard labor to which they were
put by their "owners." Thus, Walker succeeded in getting them released
from their captors while their cases were pending and hired them out at

a dollar a month. However, Mary and her child Katy were ill and were boarded and put under the care of a doctor.[21]

Kingsbury and Folsom appealed for justice. They said of the Beams family: "It is not surprising that a family living for sixty years among the Indians, and intermarrying with them, should become allied and attached to an extensive connection, both by blood & by the ties of friendship. Several of them bear strikingly the lineaments of the Red People, and speak but imperfectly any other language." The result of the appeal was that Superintendent Drew was instructed to hire the necessary counsel and to make every effort to recover the members of the family who had been sold and carried away. Reasonable expenses would be defrayed by the government.[22]

The cases were docketed for the February 1855 term of the circuit court at Van Buren, but because of the heavy docket, the cases were not reached and were continued. Meanwhile, in January, there had begun a movement designed to effect Drew's removal from office. Whether it resulted from his administrative error is uncertain. Drew left office on April 17, 1855, and on the day before, he removed from the office files of the Western superintendency most of the correspondence relating to the Beams cases. He said that he did so to maintain his "individual rights & public standing" since he had been summarily dismissed "without notice."[23] Drew, at least, related his dismissal to the case. He was replaced by Charles W. Dean.

While the Beams cases were going on in Van Buren, other slaving activities continued in the Creek Nation. In the fall of 1854, reports circulated that a large number of Creek and Seminole blacks were preparing to run off the following spring, one group proposing to go to Mexico and another to Canada. However, the military informed the chiefs of both tribes of the rumors and pledged to cut off any attempt to escape. About this time, some of the blacks who had been claimed by Aspberry appealed to Pryor to purchase all of them from Aspberry. They proposed to find buyers for themselves from Pryor in the Creek and Seminole lands; some of them had relatives who were free and would assist in paying Pryor a fair price for their freedom. Pryor went to see Aspberry, who agreed to the purchase apparently thinking that if the sales could be made, all parties involved would be paid and, therefore, satisfied. On November 24, 1854, Aspberry made out a bill of sale and took Pryor's promissory note for $7,800.[24]

Pryor then went to the Seminole country to try to dispose of the blacks to persons there. J. W. Washbourne, the Seminole agent, was absent, and Pryor ran into difficulties. He saw some of the blacks and told them of his purchase, saying that he was willing to let each one select a purchaser that he was willing to live with and to liberate those who could pay a fair price for freedom. They were satisfied, but told him that some of the Seminoles objected to the arrangement and disputed Aspberry's title. One of those who objected was Halleck Tustenuggee, whom Pryor sought out. He found Halleck Tustennuggee drunk and argued the matter with him to no avail. The Indian asked Pryor to meet him at the home of F. A. Cummings, a trader, and he would come the next day to discuss it further. Halleck Tustennuggee did not show up and sent word that he would meet Pryor at the Creek council in December and have the matter submitted for decision.[25]

During his discussions with Halleck Tustenuggee, Pryor learned that Halleck Tustenuggee and Necksucky claimed to be guardians of the blacks but made no claim to ownership. Therefore, Pryor was willing to let the Creek council consider the matter. But when the council met at the Creek agency on December 26, 1854, Halleck Tustenuggee failed to appear. Pryor applied to Washbourne to have the blacks delivered to the nearest point within reach of the civil process so Pryor might establish his title in court of law, but Washbourne only referred the matter to Superintendent Drew.[26]

On January 6, 1855, Pryor appealed for aid from Drew. He claimed title to Scipio and Sancho (about twenty-one years old), William (about twenty-five), Prince (about twelve), Cyrus (about fifteen), Lucy and her four children, Betsy and her four children, Thamar and her seven children, and Rhody and her infant, all of whom were under the control of Necksucky and Halleck Tustenuggee, as well as five others who were in the Creek country. Pryor's appeal was supported by a letter from Agent Washbourne, a former business partner of Pryor. Drew, in turn, forwarded Pryor's complaint to the commissioner of Indian affairs, George W. Manypenny. However, he had little favorable to say about Pryor's claim. He had received many complaints during the previous year about the disruption of peace and harmony of the Seminole tribe by raiding parties from the Creek Nation. From what he could learn, Aspberry had never paid anything when he "purchased" the blacks, and he therefore doubted the legality of the claim. Washbourne had written to Drew, favoring Pryor's claim, but Drew dismissed the endorsement: "I am compelled, however, to make many allowances for his kindly disposition towards Pryor for his utter ignorance of the local affairs of these people as he has not been among them but for a few weeks at a time since his appointment." Since the claim had caused much disturbance between the Creeks and Seminoles, Drew felt that it should be fully investigated.[27]

Drew told Pryor that he would take no action until he heard from the commissioner of Indian affairs and advised Pryor to go see the Seminoles again. Pryor attended the annuity payment at the Seminole agency. He saw Halleck Tustenuggee and asked that the matter be investigated before the chiefs and the agent. The Seminole agreed and called a council the next day, at which time Pryor learned that the Seminoles did not dispute the title but were offended at the manner in which part of the blacks had been taken from the country. In other words, they resented the interference by the Creeks. Pryor then left the Seminole country, asking Halleck Tustenuggee to meet him at the Creek council then in session at Tuckabahchee, where Creek Agent W. H. Garrett, Washbourne, and the chiefs would investigate. Halleck Tustenuggee refused. Pryor then obtained a certificate that stated that the violence perpetrated during the capture of the blacks was an act of officers of the Creek Nation. Armed with that statement, he went to see Drew again in March 1855.[28]

Pryor was convinced that Halleck Tustenuggee and the other Seminoles planned to sell the blacks, and he feared that when the grass came up, the blacks would leave for the Rio Grande and attempt to join Wild Cat's band. Therefore, Drew wrote to Halleck Tustenuggee and the other chiefs, instructing them to see that the blacks were not taken out of the country by traders nor allowed to leave for the plains until Pryor's claim could be settled.[29]

Pryor was supported in his claim by Agent Garrett. He held that Aspberry's claim had been upheld by the Creek chiefs, that they had issued an order to the light horse to capture the blacks for Aspberry, and that the rumors of violence and disorder in the capture were not substantiated by his investigation. Garrett felt that there was no reason why the blacks should be kept in the Seminole country and that the government was obligated to take "prompt and decisive steps in breaking up the settlement of negroes in that country which for years past has been notorious as a safe refuge and harbor for every fugitive slave for hundreds of miles around." If Pryor had a title to the blacks, he should be offered an opportunity to prove it, said Garrett.[30]

Drew again wrote for instructions and presented a further complication for Commissioner Manypenny. It was the custom of the Seminole chiefs to levy a tribute upon large estates in the Seminole country; upon the extinction of heirs, as in the present case, the town chiefs claimed the property and, in cases of minors, became guardians of the property. Halleck Tustenuggee now claimed $100 tribute for each black before he would permit his removal. Pryor said that he could not pay the tribute; the Creeks, however, were willing to send their light horse to take the blacks. Drew directed Garrett not to permit any such act by the Creeks until instructions came from Washington.[31]

In March 1855, Pryor went to the Seminole country, where John Jumper and Pascofar affirmed the title of Molly and her sister and said that they had tried to prevent the latter from selling the blacks to Aspberry. Jumper asked Pryor to stay until the Seminole council met, at which time he would appoint some men to tend to the matter. At the council, the chiefs debated, finally agreeing that Pryor was right. What they found objectionable was the woman's failure to follow the old custom of obtaining the consent of the chiefs to sell her slaves. At the time of her grandfather's death, he had asked the town chiefs to keep the property together so that the slaves could "make corn for his children." Since she had sold them despite Jumper's advice, the chiefs felt that they had done their duty.[32]

Washbourne was at that time away from the agency. The chiefs told Pryor that when the agent returned, he could come with his papers, point out the blacks, and take them. They would hold the Nation bound for their safekeeping. They gave him Robert or Bob, whom Pryor had agreed to liberate for $300. Robert paid Pryor, who gave him his "free papers." The act was approved by the council. Then the chiefs named Halleck Tustenuggee and Passockee Yohola to aid Pryor. He was to meet them at Billy Harjo's and there receive the blacks. When Pryor went to meet them, they failed to show up. By their action in relation to Bob, the Seminole chiefs had in effect recognized Pryor's claim to all of the blacks. But at this point, they began to hesitate. When Halleck Tustenuggee and Passockee Yohola failed to meet him, he returned to Jumper with a list of the blacks and asked the chief for a copy of the proceedings of the council. Jumper refused, saying that he did not like to sign papers in the name of the chiefs. He told Pryor that Passockee Yohola was under subpoena to appear in federal court and that he would be in Van Buren in a few days and could make a statement before the superintendent. Pryor returned to Arkansas, found Passockee Yohola at Van Buren, but found the superintendent gone. Pryor decided to have him make the statement before A. M. Wilson, the U. S. district attorney. At that time Washbourne appeared, angry at the letter Drew had written in January concerning Washbourne's ignorance of Seminole affairs. He also was angry at Garrett, whom he felt Drew had instructed to act in the matter without Washbourne's approval. Washbourne said that if any council was held and Garrett presided, he would tell the Seminoles not to attend, and he sent Passockee Yohola home, telling him to make no statements.[33]

Pryor convinced Washbourne that he had had nothing to do with Drew's action. Washbourne finally agreed to call a council and to investigate, but because of poor communications Pryor missed the council. Pryor alleged that at the council Halleck Tustenuggee and Passockee Yohola had been bribed by parties who wished to purchase the blacks from them to swear that the blacks belonged to the minor children of Charley Brown who had died a few years before, that Brown was the original Capichee Micco, the real owner, and that Molly was only acting as guardian for him while his children were in the West and he remained in Florida. Pryor charged that Halleck Tustenuggee and Passockee Yohola were to be paid to get the matter taken before the Creek council and that Chilly McIntosh and Watt Grayson, both Creeks, would get the blacks. It was agreed at the council that the matter was entirely under Creek laws.[34]

When Pryor showed up a few days later, he showed Washbourne a copy of the statement that Molly had made before the military authorities in 1850, alleging that Duval and Jumper were trying to deprive her of her slaves. Washbourne had referred the whole matter to the Creek council on the basis of a paper signed by Marcellus Duval saying that the blacks belonged to Capichee Micco. He now became convinced that he had been deceived.[35]

Pryor attended the Creek council, though protesting that the case should be settled not by the Indians but by the agents. In conversation, the Seminoles denied having said that Charley Brown was Capichee Micco, for the latter had died many years before in Florida and had appointed Miccopotokee as guardian of his property. When the council met, the Seminoles showed that Capichee Micco had died in Florida, that Tuskeneehau was his son, that Miccopotokee was the guardian of the property until his death in the West when he turned the property over to Micanopy as guardian of the property for Molly and her sister. Charley Brown was only distantly related to Capichee Micco and had no right to the property. At that point the Seminoles stopped the investigation and denied having given Washbourne instructions to have it presented to the council, saying that they would not be bound by a decision of the Creek council. The proper place, they said, was before the Seminole agent and Seminole council.[36]

Meanwhile, Jumper had sold one of the blacks. Washbourne instructed the Seminoles not to sell any more and called a council, asking that all papers in the case be brought in. Halleck Tuskenuggee left to get them and held up the council for two days, returning without them, bringing only two papers which he said he had found in an old trunk upon Charley Brown's death. At this time the Seminoles insisted that there were other heirs of Capichee Micco who would contend for part of the estate. Halleck Tustenuggee said that they were the grandchildren of Capichee Micco and were jointly entitled with the children of Tuskeneehau. Halleck Tustenuggee told the council that Capiche Micco had eight children and then named fourteen. Creeks Chilly McIntosh and Watt Grayson were also on hand and contested the right of the two sisters to sell the blacks. The chiefs thereupon declined to decide the question and asked that the matter be sent back to the Creek council. Washbourne decided to do so, and the Seminoles said that they would abide by the decision at Hilibi Square twenty days from then. Pryor accused Chilly McIntosh of bribing Halleck Tustenuggee to suppress the papers and asked Bob, the black who had purchased his freedom from Pryor, to find out what Halleck Tustenuggee had done with the papers given him at Molly's death.[37] Pryor attended the Creek council at Hilibi Square, but the Seminoles failed to attend. No further action was taken until the meeting of the Creek council in December of that year, when the Seminoles requested an investigation. Meanwhile, Robert made a statement before Washbourne that he had belonged to Molly, who had died about two years earlier. On the day she died, Chitto Lorny, a distant relative, took some papers from Molly's trunk, but a black woman took them away from him and gave them to Bob. Bob took the papers to old Abraham, a well-known Seminole black, who kept them a while and then gave them back to Bob, who later gave them to Halleck Tustenuggee. That was the last time Bob saw them.[38]

By the time the Creek council met in December 1855, Chilly McIntosh had purchased the rights of all claimants adverse to Molly and her sister except one. Allahokee, Suffoh Yotee, Haste, Mut-char-kee, Nooksa Harjo, and Pahosee were supposedly equally entitled to a share of the estate of their grandfather as was Sharpkee, whom the Seminoles claimed had not received any share in Florida. Halleck Tustenuggee and Passockee Yohola were witnesses to all of this. Pascofar, George Cloud, Cochar Nacoofta, and others testified that none were living except Sharpkee and that no such persons were in the Seminole country. They also testified that when Capichee Micco had died, the property had been divided equally, the council rendering judgment; the property in question had belonged to the sisters. The council found in favor of the heirs, a decision which left the Seminoles dissatisfied.[39] That meant, in effect, that the council recognized McIntosh's claim.

In the spring of 1856, Pryor renewed efforts to acquire the blacks he claimed. If he had found little sympathy in Superintendent Drew, he found even less in Charles W. Dean, who had replaced Drew shortly after Pryor's second appeal to Drew in March of 1855. During the year following Dean's appointment, Pryor approached him several times with his claim, but Dean refused to act because he was not sure of Pryor's title. If it was good, Dean was not sure the department had the authority to put him in possession. On April 10, 1855, Pryor again asked for assistance in prosecuting his claim for thirty-seven blacks, including Sancho, Scipio, Ishmael, William, Billy, Cyrus, Sampson, Jim, Teanear or Tenny and her eight children, Hetty, Rhody, Thamar and her two children. Pryor had at no time before claimed that many. Undoubtedly the claim was based on a new agreement that he had negotiated with Aspberry on April 2, in which Aspberry relinquished all right and title to the blacks named in Aspberry's bill of sale to Pryor on November 24, 1854.[40]

This time, Dean forwarded the papers relating to the claim to Commissioner Manypenny for instructions. Of particular concern to Dean was the fact that the bill of sale from Molly's sister, although alleged to have been recorded in both the Seminole and Creek agencies, had never been produced. Also, it had not been shown that Aspberry had paid anything for the claim. As far as Pryor's financial circumstances were concerned, Dean wrote, "I would about as soon believe him were to assert that he had paid cash in hand—seven million dollars for the negroes as that he had paid seven thousand dollars for them." It was impossible for him to have raised that much; in fact, he had not paid Aspberry anything but had given him a promissory note.[41]

Embittered by his failure to get the blacks, Pryor turned on his former friend, Washbourne. Washbourne would not order the Seminoles to turn the blacks over to Pryor without instructions from the superintendent. Drew would not give such instructions, and Dean had told Washbourne not to comply with Pryor's wishes. As time passed, Pryor developed a "deadly enmity" toward Washbourne and began trying to find delinquencies in the agent's official capacity. He went to Washbourne and told him that he had evidence to support charges of misconduct in office but that he would suppress the information if Washbourne would have the blacks seized and turned over. Dean intervened for Washbourne, saying that he would not have his agent intimidated. Dean considered Pryor a man "destitute of honorable principles" and "prompted by a sentiment of vindictive malice." He no longer traded but remained in the Creek Nation for the sole purpose of speculation, causing much dissatisfaction among the Seminoles. Dean asked W. H. Garrett to have Pryor expelled, but the Creek agent could not since no complaint had been made against Pryor by the Creeks. In May, Pryor filed a formal complaint, charging Washbourne with being absent from his post, juggling accounts by overcharging, spending contingent funds for traveling, causing dissatisfaction among the Creeks and Seminoles, and mishandling annuity funds.[42]

Pryor's claim and the difficulty it had caused among the Indians as well as among officials of the United States in the Western Territory exemplified the growing interest of whites in the blacks in the Indian Territory. Slaving was a lucrative business, and the interest of slave hunters in the slaves of the Indians had grown as the risks involved had decreased after Wild Cat's departure. His departure, that of others who later followed him, and the activities of slave hunters greatly reduced the number of blacks in the Indian Territory between 1849 and 1855.

In the early summer of 1856, a number of Arkansans from the Van Buren area made plans to form a company for buying up claims against the Seminole slaves particularly and blacks generally in the Indian Territory. This proposed organization caused Dean to write to Commissioner Manypenny concerning the problem.[43]

Dean maintained that the government should take some action to control slave hunting in the Indian country to preserve peace and harmony there. One Arkansan, for instance, had recently "bought for a song" a claim to a family of Seminole free blacks who had lived in the country for years, were considered free, and could prove it. The head of the family had been employed by the government in both Florida and the West. It was only through influential friends that the family succeeded in keeping the purchaser from trying to enforce the claim.

According to Dean, when the Indians were isolated from the whites, there was no trouble among them about titles, but the whites were abetted by the shrewder Indians in getting possession of titles. Many times oppression resulted, especially of women and children who lost their property. The degraded position of Indian women and the relationship of the guardian as it existed in the Indian country were simply means "whereby the guardian, if so disposed, possesses himself of the property of the ward." This practice was increasing, Dean charged that many members of the Creek delegation to Washington were slave speculators. One of them was Chilly McIntosh, who had bought up the adverse claims in the Pryor case. Evidence showed that he could not have a shadow of a claim, yet he was "quietly and energetically prosecuting the claim." Dean asked Manypenny if the Indians' trade in slaves with the whites might not be checked or if Congress could render void all contracts for slaves with Indians.[44]

Perhaps no slave controversy demonstrated better than the Pryor case the complexities that had been typical of relations between the Creeks and Seminoles regarding slave property since the late 1830s. The Indian mode of property descent and title was not always understood by the whites who purchased slave claims. While they often entered such bargains in good faith, the Indians—and particularly the mixed bloods—who clearly understood the Indian mode of establishing titles sometimes took advantage of the whites by selling slaves to whom the titles were contested. The Pryor case also demonstrated the extent to which tribal rivalries confused the issues as the Creeks on the one hand sought to resist it and insisted on self-determinism regarding matters of property.

In 1854, Congress called for an investigation of the difficulties which had arisen between the two tribes since removal. Assistant Adjutant General Francis N. Page's report sounded as if it could have been written by Superintendent William Armstrong fifteen years earlier. He wrote of the Seminole blacks:

This system of trading for these negroes is still kept up, and, in my opinion, the sooner the Seminole nation gets rid of them, the better. All of the intelligent Creeks and licensed traders in the nation agree in the statement that these negroes exercise a most pernicious influence over the Seminoles. They endeavor to incite them to violate the laws of the Creeks, and, perfectly free from all restraint by the Seminoles, encourage them in riotous conduct and drunkenness. The conduct of the Creek nation to the Seminoles has been that of continued forbearance and non-inter-ference with them. The Seminoles maintain the principle that they are entirely inde-pendent of the Creeks, and not under the operation of their laws. The Creeks have foreborne compelling compliance with the treaty stipulations rather than create a disturbance, and they put up with daily violation of their laws, because they fear forcible resistance on the part of the Seminoles.[45]

The Treaty of 1845 had failed.

In the summer of 1856, the problem was finally settled. A treaty of August 7 dissolved the weak union between the two tribes and established a separate Seminole nation of over two million acres, the boundaries of which ran from the mouth of Pond Creek on the Canadian, north to the North Fork, up that stream to the southern boundary of the Cherokee Out-let, west to the hundredth meridian, south to the Canadian and along that stream to the mouth of Pond Creek.[46]

Meanwhile, the Beams cases had dragged on in Van Buren. At the August 1856 terms of the court, the cases of Mary and Katy Beams vs. E. B. Bishop and James Woosly and of William Beams vs. William Fowler were heard. Verdicts were rendered in favor of the Beams family. The attorneys for the family felt that the cases would be regarded as conclusive of the free-dom of the whole family since identical arguments and the same proofs were to be used in all. At the conclusion of these two cases, all of the Beams family were allowed to return to the Indian Territory. Attorneys Walker and Green acted as securities for the forthcoming of those whose cases were yet to be heard. Those cases were heard during the February 1857 term. Verdicts were given in favor of the family in the cases of Silas Beams vs. James Woosly and Benjamin Hartgraves and of Martin Beams vs. P. H. White and T. B. Emerson. The case of Ellen Beams vs. James Woosly and Benjamin Hartgraves never came to trial, for Ellen died before the case was finished.[47]

The Pryor case was not dead. Pryor evidently distrusted the superin-tendent in the matter of the claim, for early in 1857, he renewed it and the charges against Washbourne through Creek Agent William H. Garrett. Secretary of the Interior Jacob Thompson instructed Elias Rector, the new superintendent for the Western District, to investigate. Meanwhile, Pryor had appealed to Rector, who at first was inclined to support the claim. But when instructions came directing a full investigation, he held a public hearing, which Pryor attended. Pryor failed to show the kind of hard evidence which Rector wanted to see. There was some doubt concerning the clear title of Molly's sister, which was the foundation of the claim. No sufficient consideration ever passed from Aspberry to her. The Seminoles claimed that she had received three dollars, but there was no evidence that she received anything. At most, Aspberry could not have paid more than $1,500 for the twenty-three blacks he had forcibly taken and sold. Finally, there was no evidence that Pryor had ever paid anything for the claim. As far as Washbourne went, Rector could find no reason to censure him. Pryor raised the matter one last time in 1859. Through a lawyer in Washington, he asked the department to explain the status of his claim there. The answer was plain. Rector's findings had gone against Pryor, and the department concurred.[48]

The major slave claim during the last two years of the decade was that of former Creek Agent James Logan. The claim went back to 1840 when, according to Logan, John Ward of Scott County, Arkansas, sold some blacks to William Hull. Ward, who had a Creek wife and had lived in the Creek Nation, died shortly thereafter and four of the blacks—Nancy, Jeff, Linn, and Jack—ran off to the Creek Nation. Hull pursued them and, after paying the Creeks a reward of fifty dollars each, recovered two of them. Roley McIntosh recognized Hull's claim and advised the Creeks holding the others to give them up, but the Creeks would not. Hull sold the two he recovered to McIntosh's niece. Hull died in 1844, and the administrator of his estate sold the two remaining blacks to Logan in 1845. Logan demanded the blacks, but the chiefs took no action, and in 1848 Logan demanded payment for the blacks' service since 1840 and handed the chiefs a bill for $5,400, which they refused. Logan then turned the matter over to Senator R. W. Johnson of Arkansas, who put it before the commissioner of Indian affairs.[49] No action was taken.

In 1851 Agent Philip H. Raiford took the case to the Creek chiefs, who refused to act. The facts were most complicated. All four of the blacks had been seized by Tom and Elijah Carr in 1840. Nancy and Jeff had been apprehended by Hull. Linn and Jack remained at large. Linn had been sold by Thomas Carr to Opothleyoholoa's brother, who sold him to John Dillard of Arkansas. Jack was sold by Elijah Carr, and he was owned successively by the Cherokee James Thompson, Watt Grayson, Sandy Grayson, Watt Grayson again, and Elijah Carr again, who had

Jack in 1851. To these complications was added the testimony of Arkansans that Hull's title to the blacks was uncertain if not, in fact, canceled by agreements between Ward and Hull.[50]

Logan got his case reviewed in 1858 by Western Superintendent Elias Rector. Creek Agent W. H. Garrett supported Logan's claim against those of the Creeks, but at the chiefs' request submitted all of the evidence for a decision by the commissioner by which decision they agreed to abide. When Commissioner A. B. Greenwood reviewed the case in early 1860, he could find no evidence that the Creeks had "done any act which would make the nation responsible under the intercourse law of 1834," even though the evidence showed that the blacks were fugitive and were still in the Creek country. Greenwood refused to decide the issue and suggested that Logan secure the blacks under the fugitive slave law and then have the question of title settled in the courts.[51]

Thus, the last decade of slavery in the Creek Nation was one of importance for blacks in the Indian Territory, particularly in the Creek country. The constant wrangling between the Creeks and Seminoles—much of it related to slaving activities—had resulted in a final partition of the lands and a separate Seminole nation. But it had come too late. By 1856, whites and Creeks had divested the Seminoles of many of their slaves or had caused others to run away, principally to Mexico. In the Creek Nation proper, the number of slaves had increased during the decade, and the slave code had become more severe, as the influences of the American debate over slavery reached Creek territory. In 1860, the Creeks were on the verge of being drawn into the civil conflict that resulted when the debate broke down.

NOTES

1. Solon Borland to Orlando Brown, June 10, 1850, John Drennen to Luke Lea, March 31, 1852, National Archives Microfilm Publications, *Microcopy M234* (Office of Indian Affairs, Letters Received) 228: B702-50, D78-52, hereafter cited as *M234,* followed by the roll number; Brown to Borland, June 15, 1850, *Microcopy M21* (Office of Indian Affairs, Letters Sent) 43: 260, hereafter cited as *M21,* followed by the roll number.

2. Francis N. Page to Philip H. Raiford, March 10, 1851, National Archives Record Group 393 (Records of the United States Army Continental Commands, 1821-1920), *Second and Seventh Military Departments, Letters Sent,* hereafter cited as *2nd and 7th LS*; Raiford to Lieutenant F. F. Flint, March 17, 1851, *Second and*

Seventh Military Departments, Letters Received, box 8, hereafter cited as *2nd and 7th L R.*

3. Statement of Molly, July 15, 1850, *2nd and 7th L R,* box 8; J. W. Washbourne to Thomas S. Drew, January 5, 1855, *M234*-802: D153-56.

4. William H. Garrett to Commissioner of Indian Affairs, May 30, 1856, *M234*-229: G93-56; Charles W. Dean to George W. Manypenny, April 29, 1856, *M234*-802: D153-56; C. D. Pryor to Drew, January 6, 1855, *M234*-833: D782-55.

5. Dean to Manypenny, April 29, 1856, *M234*-802; D153-56; A. H. Rutherford to Manypenny, December 6, 1853, *M234*-801: D476-53.

6. Dean to Manypenny, April 29, 1856, *M234*-802: D153-56; B. H. Smithson to Manypenny, November 24 and 27, 1853, *M234*-801: D476-53.

7. Dean to Manypenny, April 29, 1856, *M234*-802: D153-56.

8. D. B. Aspberry to E. B. Bright, February 16, 1854, *M234*-802: M383-57.

9. Rutherford to D. B. Aspberry, January 27, 1854, *M234*-802: M383-57; Edwin C. McReynolds, *The Seminoles* (Norman: University of Oklahoma Press, 1957), p. 274.

10. Aspberry to Bright, February 16, 1854, Aspberry to R. G. Atkins and Tommy Hay, n.d., *M234*-802: M383-57; McReynolds, p. 274.

11. Drew to Manypenny, October 25, 1854, *M234*-801; D709-54; Carolyn Thomas Foreman, "The Jumper Family in the Seminole Nation," *The Chronicles of Oklahoma* 35 (Autumn 1956), 285.

12. Cyrus Kingsbury and Sampson Folsom to Manypenny, November 20, 1854, John B. Davis to Drew, n.d., National Archives Microfilm Publications, *Microcopy M574* (Special Files of the Office of Indian Affairs, 1807-1904) 75: Choctaw K59-54, Cherokee B463-54, hereafter cited as *M574*, followed by the roll number; W. H. Fowler to General Matthew Arbuckle, March 4, 1839, Arbuckle to Colonel Josiah Vose, March 5, 1839, Arbuckle to William Armstrong, March 6, 1839, Fowler to Commander at Fort Towson, March 28, 1840, L. N. Morris to Captain J. B. Clarke, March 29, 1840, Clarke to Armstrong, March 29, 1840, Morris to Clarke, March 29, 1840, John T. Camerin to Henry Cheatham, October 7, 1845, *M234*-171; A574-39, A778-40, A1976-46; Armstrong to T. Hartley Crawford, February 22, 1839, *M234*-922: A556-39.

13. Davis to Drew, n.d., *M574*-75: Cherokee B463-54.

14. Opinion of C. Cushing, February 18, 1854, Jefferson Davis to S. A. Worcester, October 7, 1854, *M574*-75: frame 1482, Choctaw 1727-54; S. Cooper to Commanding Officer, Fort Gibson, May 4, 1854, National Archives Record Group 393, *Fort Gibson,* Letters Received, box 3, hereafter cited as *Gibson L R.*

15. Drew to Robert McClelland, November 21, 1854, McClelland to Douglas H. Cooper, September 11, 1854, McClelland to Drew, September 11, 1854, Drew to Chief and Head Men of the Creek Nation, July 27, 1854, and George Butler to Worcester, November 22, 1854, *M574*-75: Choctaw 1786-54, Choctaw 1727-54, Cherokee B463-54, Choctaw W444-54.

Thomas Stevenson Drew (1802-79) had served as the third governor of Arkansas. A native of Tennessee, he had come to Clark County, Arkansas, in 1818 as a peddler. He married well and became a prosperous farmer. In 1844 he was elected governor, having held no other political office except as clerk of Clark County from 1823 to 1825. He was reelected in 1848 but resigned shortly thereafter because the salary was too small to support his family. He was appointed superintendent in 1853. At the time, he was farming in Desha County, Arkansas. See Lawrence Dalton, *History of Randolph County, Arkansas* (Little Rock, Ark.: Democrat Printing and Lithographing Company, [1946?]), pp. 47-49; *Arkansas Gazette,* April 7, 1853.

16. Kingsbury and Folsom to Manypenny, November 20, 1854, Cooper to McClelland, October 25, 1854, and List of Members of Beams Family Who Brought Suit for Freedom under Laws of Arkansas, *M574*-75: Choctaw K59-54, Choctaw C1111-54, Choctaw C1110-54.

Mitchell Beams lived in the Creek Nation until his death in 1892. In 1875, he voted as a tribal member in New Yorker Town, Creek Nation. At the time of his death, he was farming 130 acres in Muskogee District. He had three living children: Jacob Beams, Mrs. Sallie Grayson, and Mrs. Louisa Hutton. Beams was apparently married three times. Jacob Beams, born about 1850, was the child of Mitchell and Beck Beams, and Louisa, born about 1856, was the child of Mitchell and Tooka Beams. His third wife was Parthenia, the widow of Granderson Taylor. Indian Archives Division, Oklahoma Historical Society, Creek Records, 27227, 27666, 29349. See also, *Campbell's Abstract of Creek Indian Census Cards and Index* (Muskogee, Okla.: Phoenix Job Printing Co., 1915), pp. 77, 194, 219.

17. Worcester to Davis, September 6, 1854, Butler to Charles E. Mix, November 22, 1854, Davis to Worcester, October 7, 1854, Drew to McClelland, October 30, 1854, Butler to McClelland, November 22, 1854, Worcester to McClelland, November 25, 1854, Drew to McClelland, November 21, 1854, and Drew to Manypenny, November 21, 1854, *M574*-75: Choctaw 1727-54, Cherokee B463-54, Choctaw I272-54, Choctaw D738-54, Choctaw W444-54, Choctaw I786-54, Choctaw D729-54.

Worcester, born in Worcester, Massachusetts, was ordained a Congregationalist minister in 1825. He went in that year to Brainard Mission, Cherokee Nation East. Two years later, he went to New Echota as a missionary and translator of the Bible into Cherokee. He helped establish the Cherokee newspaper, the *Cherokee Phoenix.* In 1835, he went west where he established Park Hill Mission. He was still engaged there in 1854.

18. Cooper to McClelland, October 19, 1854, and October 25, 1854, *M574*-75: Choctaw C1109-54, Choctaw C1111-54.

19. Kingsbury and Folsom to Manypenny, November 20, 1854, List of Members of Beams Family, *M574*-75: Choctaw K59-54, Choctaw C1110-54.

20. Kingsbury and Folsom to Manypenny, November 20, 1854, Cooper to McClelland, October 30, 1854, Josephus Dotson to Cooper, October 15, 1854, William Walker and J. J. Green to Manypenny, January 17, 1855, and List of Members of Beams family, *M574*-75: Choctaw K59-54, Choctaw C1110-54, Choctaw C1109-54, Choctaw W461-55, Choctaw C1110-54.

21. Walker to Manypenny, September 6, 1856, and Walker to Jacob Thompson, June 13, 1857, *M574*-75: Choctaw W178-56, Choctaw W375-57.

22. Kingsbury and Folsom to Manypenny, November 20, 1854, McClelland to

Commissioner of Indian Affairs, December 18, 1854, and February 12, 1855, *M574*-75: Choctaw K59-54, Choctaw I-776-55, Choctaw I873-55.

23. Cooper to Manypenny, March 18, 1855, Franklin Pierce to McClelland, January 6, 1855, and Statement of Drew, April 16, 1855, *M574*-75: Choctaw C1262-55, Western Superintendency I813-55, Choctaw D930-55.

24. Major G. W. Andrews to Post Adjutant, Fort Gibson, November 23, 1854, *Gibson LR,* box 3; Pryor to Dean, April 10, 1856, *M234*-802: D153-56; *Foreman Transcripts* (Indian Archives Division, Oklahoma Historical Society), 7: 71.

25. Pryor to Dean, April 10, 1856, *M234*-802: D153-56.

26. Pryor to Drew, January 6, 1855, *M234*-833: D782-55.

27. Pryor to Drew, January 6, 1855, Drew to Manypenny, January 29, 1855, *M234*-833: D782-55; Washbourne to Drew, January 5, 1855, *M234*-802: D153-56.

28. Pryor to Dean, April 10, 1856, *M234*-802: D153-56.

29. *Ibid.*; Drew to Manypenny, March 14, 1855, *M234*-833: D816-55.

30. W. H. Garrett to Drew, February 12, 1855, *M234*-833: D816-55.

31. Drew to Manypenny, March 14, 1855, *M234*-833: D816-55.

32. Pryor to Dean, April 10, 1856, in *M234*-802: D153-56.

33. *Ibid.*

34. *Ibid.*

35. *Ibid.*

36. *Ibid.*

37. *Ibid.*

38. Statement of Robert, October 6, 1855, *M234*-802: D153-56.

39. Pryor to Dean, April 10, 1856, *M234*-802: D153-56.

40. *Ibid.; Foreman Transcripts,* 7: 71.

41. Dean to Manypenny, April 29, 1856, *M234*-802: D153-56.

42. Dean to Manypenny, May 30, 1856, Washbourne to Manypenny, May 8, 1856, *M234*-802: D171-56, W64-56.

43. Dean to Manypenny, June 24, 1856, *M234*-802: D180-56.

44. *Ibid.*

45. *House Executive Document 15,* 33 Cong., 2 sess., pp. 12-13.

46. Charles J. Kappler, comp. and ed., *Indian Affairs: Laws and Treaties,* 2nd ed., 4 vols. (Washington, D.C.: Government Printing Office, 1904-29), 2:756-63; McReynolds, pp. 227-81.

47. Dean to Manypenny, August 23, 1855, February 20, 1856, August 18, 1856, Cooper to Mix, June 11, 1857, Dotson to Commissioner of Indian Affairs, August 18, 1856, February 25, 1857, Walker to Manypenny, September 6, 1856, *M574*-75: Choctaw D930-55, D74-56, D215-56, C933-57, D377-57, D216-56, W178-56.

48. Pryor to R. W. Johnson, February 14, 1857, Thompson to Acting Commissioner, June 12, 1857, Elias Rector to Commissioner, June 24, 1857, Rector to J. W. Denver, July 7, September 17, 1857, *M234*-802: I503-57, I596-57, R270-57, R274-57, R341-57; Mix to Jacob Thompson, June 6, 1857, National Archives Microfilm Publications, *Microcopy M348* (Office of Indian Affairs, Report Books) 10:224;

Denver to Rector, June 17, 1857, *M21*-57: 57; Mix to M. Thompson, April 7, 1859, *M21*-60: 415.

49. Statement of James Logan, *M234*-230: R858-58.

50. Logan to Philip H. Raiford, January 12, 1851, Statement of Watt Grayson, October 26, 1851, Statement of William Hull, December 18, 1841, Statements of R. J. Cook, December 19, 1856, October 28, 1857, *M234*-230: R858-58, R383-59.

51. Rector to A. B. Greenwood, November 16, 1859, with enclosures, *M234*-230: R383-59; Greenwood to Johnson K. Rogers, February 15, 1860, *M21*-63: 21.

CIVIL WAR AND
EMANCIPATION

chapter 10

FROM THE REVOLUTIONARY WAR until the outbreak of the Civil War, the blacks had played an important role in Creek Affairs. Since tribal politics had been dominated by the slaveholding class of Creeks, the tribe was destined to become involved in the American Civil War. Many slaveholding Creeks assumed a pro-Confederate posture, but others remained loyal to the Union. Thus, once more, the Creeks found themselves split into factions along traditional lines and pitted against each other in war as they had sometimes found themselves in earlier times.

As a result of political events of 1860, by late January 1861, South Carolina, Alabama, Florida, Mississippi, Georgia, and Louisiana had seceded from the Union, and Arkansas was contemplating doing the same. At that time, Governor Henry M. Rector wrote to John Ross, principal chief of the Cherokees, appealing for his support of Arkansas in its action. His comments about the Indian Territory had application to the Creeks as well as to the other slaveholding tribes:

Your people, in their institutions, productions, latitude, and natural sympathies are allied to the common brotherhood of the slaveholding States. Our people and yours are natural allies in war, and friends in peace. Your country is salubrious and fertile, and possesses the highest capacity for future progress and development by the application of 'slave labor.'. . . It is well established that the Indian country west of Arkansas is looked to by the incoming administration of Mr. Lincoln as fruitful fields ripe for the harvest of abolitionism, free-soilers, and northern montebanks. We hope to find in you friends willing to co-operate with the south in defence of her institutions, her honor, and her firesides, and with whom the slave-holding States are willing to share a common future, and to afford protection commensurate with your exposed condition and your subsisting monetary interests with the general government.[1]

A large element in each of the so-called Five Civilized Tribes, including the Creeks, was responsive to such arguments and receptive to Confederate overtures.

In retrospect, John T. Cox, special Indian agent in the Indian Territory in 1864, assessed the causes of the Indian defection of the South. During the Buchanan administration people of Southern sympathy had secured appointments to or had gained the favor of every governmental office within the limits of the Southern Superintendency of Indian Affairs. Douglas H. Cooper, the Choctaw agent, had been so concerned about the missionaries, whom he charged with having systematically tried "to abolitionize the Indian country," that he suggested that officials of the Southern Superintendency induce the Choctaws, Chickasaws, and Creeks to allow slaveholders to settle among them to control the abolitionist movement. Such men as Cooper influenced all sources of information in 1861. Postmasters early claimed that the United States government had fallen. Indian agents and others discouraged the Indians and destroyed their confidence in the United States. Fort Gibson had been abandoned, military necessity had led to the abandonment of other posts, government stores, and ordnance depots in the West, and the government was unfortunately late in recognizing the need to assist the Indians in resisting Confederate overtures. The Indians felt abandoned. Commissioner of Indian Affairs William P. Dole blamed the defection of the Indians on the withdrawal of military support and on the Lincoln administration's failure to explain to the Indians the policy it intended to pursue regarding slavery.[2]

Albert Pike of Arkansas was sent by the Confederate Department of State as a commissioner to the Indian Territory to explain to the Five Civilized Tribes the organization of the Confederate government and to offer the hand of peace. Before the end of the year, he had concluded a treaty with each of the tribes.[3] The Cherokees were initially stubborn, and Pike first secured treaties with the other tribes.

In June a council of mainly Southern-sympathizing Choctaws, Chickasaws, Seminoles, and Creeks was held at North Fork Town in the Creek Nation. On July 1, they formed a "United Nations of the Indian Territory," and among the provisions of their constitution was the right of the Grand Council of Delegates to raise Indian troops to oppose "invading forces of Abolition hordes under Abraham Lincoln." On July 10, the Creeks, among whom there was much loyal sentiment, signed a treaty with the Confederacy. Apparently through bribery and other means, Pike was able to obtain the signatures of Motey Canard (Kinnard), who had been elected principal chief, Echo Harjo, Chilly McIntosh, D. N. McIntosh, and others.[4]

It is generally conceded that the treaties were more favorable to the Indians than any they had signed with the United States, particularly regarding self-determination of the tribes. Besides guaranteeing the territory, the self-determination of the Creeks, the right to define their own citizenship and to regulate trade in their lands, and access to the state courts, the Confederate States of America took over financial matters that had theretofore rested with the United States. Among other things, the treaty recognized African slavery and titles according to Creek laws, applied the fugitive slave law to the Creek Nation, and provided for Confederate Indian troops.[5]

While Pike was negotiating with the Creeks, many of the full-blood Creek leaders, such as Oktarharsars Harjo, who opposed the Confederacy, were on a mission of peace to the prairie tribes, apparently sent away to make Pike's mission easier. When they returned home and found that Motey Canard, the McIntoshes, and other chiefs had made a treaty, they refused to sign it, avowing their allegiance to the United States. The loyal Creeks met on August 5, declared the treaty void and the office of chief vacant, and named Oktarharsars Harjo chief. The disloyal faction then put a $5,000 bounty on his head. Under threats against their lives and of impressment into rebel service, some of the loyal Creeks under Oktarharsars Harjo and others began to move their families west, away from the disloyal faction, and sent a delegation to Washington to explain their situation.[6]

The Creeks were nearly evenly divided in sympathies. The pro-Confederate element, of course, was strongest among the mixed bloods, who operated large plantations and held more slaves than did the full bloods. There were, however, many slaveholders among the pro-Union faction. The slavery issue, while important, was apparently not central to the split among the Creeks, but the division was, rather, along traditional lines. Once more, the old division between the Lower Creeks and the Upper Creeks emerged, the former generally following the Confederacy and the latter generally remaining loyal. The division had been reflected in the political developments in the Nation. In 1859, the aging Roley McIntosh had relinquished leadership of the Nation. Motey Canard and Jacob Derrisaw (Dereseaux) had been elected first and second chiefs of the Lower Creeks, while Echo Harjo and Oktarharsars Harjo had been elected in the Upper

Creeks.[7] Although Canard was considered the principal chief of the Nation, he did not represent the unifying force that Roley McIntosh had represented.

With Oktarharsars Harjo gone, the loyal Creeks and some of the Seminoles rallied around the aged Opothleyohola, who had resisted all inducements by the Confederate agents and his fellow Creeks to join the Confederacy. Douglas H. Cooper, the former Choctaw agent, had been directed by the Confederate War Department to raise troops among the Choctaws and Chickasaws. He went to the Canadian River to try to persuade the loyal Creeks and Seminoles to defect, but he failed. Therefore, in the fall of 1861, he mounted an armed force of Choctaws, Chickasaws, and Texans, as well as Creeks under D. N. McIntosh and Creeks and Seminoles under Chilly McIntosh and John Jumper, and marched on Opothleyohola's camp, reaching North Fork Town on November 15. However, Opothleyohola had departed.[8]

Upon receiving news of Cooper's approach, Opothleyohola had decided to leave the Creek Nation, pass through the Cherokee country, and take refuge in Kansas. In his party were Seminoles under Halleck Tustenuggee, John Chupco, and Billy Bowlegs and several hundred Creek and Seminole blacks, whom he promised, if they would be faithful to the government, that they would be free as the Creeks. The exact number of blacks in the group is uncertain. Writers have accepted official records of 200 to 300 blacks in Opothleyohola's force in the fighting that ensued. The escape of these people has been treated often, and their struggle has been described in terms all but epic. They were overtaken three times and fought battles with Confederate troops at Round Mountain on November 19, at Chustolasah on December 9, and at Chustenalah on December 26. The last battle was costly. The Confederates captured about 160 women and children, and the loyal Indians lost nearly all of their goods and livestock. The weather was bitter, and snow was on the ground. In their retreat before the Confederate army, the loyal party suffered greatly. Many froze to death, and the trail was marked by bodies.[9]

Creeks and blacks both were killed and captured in these battles. Captured slaves were taken back to their masters. Some of those captured were free blacks. The Confederate Creeks passed a law providing for their sale and confiscated the property of Opothleyohola's followers.[10]

When they arrived in Kansas, the Creeks, once comfortable, and some even wealthy, were now poor and had nothing. Encamped at the Sac and

Fox agency, they were tired but anxious to fight the rebels, although the president had not called on the Indians to take up arms. During the winter of 1861 and the following spring and summer, thousands of Indians and blacks were driven from their homes because of their loyalty to the government. They were ineffectual in their resistance to the disloyal Indians and to the white troops from Texas and elsewhere who sought to hold the Indian Territory for the Confederacy and in the process destroyed the Indians' improvements, farms, and herds. Other Creek blacks, left behind by Opothleyohola, took refuge in the Cherokee country and later sought protection at Fort Gibson where, by 1863, blacks numbered about a thousand. At that time there were about 3,200 Creeks and blacks at the Sac and Fox agency in Kansas.[11]

Some of the blacks, however, were less fortunate. On February 29, 1861, the Creeks had passed a law giving the free blacks ten days to select an Indian master. Those not doing so would be sold to the highest bidder for a period of twelve months. New owners who sold the blacks to non-citizens received a fine of twice the value of the black, one hundred lashes, and the loss of an ear. The blacks were given the right to dispose of their property as they saw fit. Cooper's army, as well, took a number of blacks as captives. Others were later captured and sent south, and there were many instances of families being separated, husbands from wives and parents from children. Later, when the Union army began activities in the Indian Territory, some Southern Creeks such as Mose Perryman and Benjamin Marshall took their slaves to the Red River in the Choctaw and Chickasaw Nations to prevent them from escaping to the North, and others, including several of the McIntosh family, went to east Texas with their blacks. It was there, near Jefferson, that Roley McIntosh died in 1863.[12]

In the winter months of early 1862, Opothleyohola and his followers camped on the upper waters of the Verdigris in Kansas. There were 3,168 Creeks, 53 of their slaves, and 38 of their free blacks, as well as 777 Seminoles (probably including a number of blacks) and some Cherokees, Chickasaws, Quapaws, and Kickapoos. All were destitute, and many suffered from disease and frostbite. In the spring they were moved to the Neosho River, and the Creeks encamped at Leroy, Kansas, where an insufficient subsistence allowance for them was begun by the government.[13]

The disloyal Creeks remained at home and fared much better than did the refugees, but by late 1862, the Confederates were not able to keep all of the promises made in treaties with the Five Civilized Tribes. S. S. Scott,

The Confederate commissioner of Indian affairs, felt it necessary, at Jefferson Davis's insistence, to visit the Indian Territory and then later assure the tribes that even though the exigencies of war had prevented the Confederate States from fully complying with the treaties, there was no doubt that they would. In a follow-up letter after his visit, Scott wrote to the Five Civilized Tribes:

Slavery with you is as obnoxious to the fanaticism of the north as it is in the Confederate States, and could that government subjugate them and deprive them of their slaves, it would not be long in taking yours from you also. But this is not all. After having dispossessed you of your slaves, it would fasten upon your rich and fertile lands and distribute them among its surplus and poverty-stricken population, who have been looking toward them with longing hearts for years.[14]

The refugee blacks who accompanied the Creeks to Kansas suffered greatly along with the Indians. They have inadequate medical attention, food, shelter, and clothing. In the fall of 1862, they were removed to the Sac and Fox agency, where they spent the cold Kansas winter of 1862-63. After the spring of 1863, the refugee blacks were mainly women, children, and old men, for most of the able-bodied men joined the Union forces.[15]

In early 1863, a regiment was organized in Kansas from among the black refugees from Missouri and Arkansas. Known as the First Kansas Colored Infantry, the unit was joined by some of the blacks from the Creek Nation. When Col. W. A. Phillips occupied Fort Gibson with his loyal Indian troops in the spring of 1863, General James G. Blunt decided to place the 1,000 men of the First Kansas at his disposal as reinforcements. They participated in the battle of Honey Springs and the battle of Cabin Creek, the two most important engagements in the Indian Territory. In early 1864, blacks were mustered out of the Indian regiments and into black regiments. The interpreters in the Indian regiments, especially the Creek, were almost exclusively black, residents of the Indian country; some officers considered them indispensable for the maintenance of discipline and good service. Those of the most active and efficient First Regiment were mustered out first. The First Kansas was stationed at Roseville, Arkansas, throughout most of 1864. It was reorganized as the Seventy-Ninth U. S. Colored Troops and on February 1, 1865, was put in the Second Brigade of the Seventh Army Corps with headquarters in Little Rock. Brigade General John McNeil, commanding the District of the

Frontier, wrote of the First Kansas at Fort Smith in November of 1863: "The negro regiment is a triumph of drill and discipline, and reflects great honor on Colonel Williams, in command. Few volunteer regiments that I have seen make a better appearance. I regard them as first-rate infantry."[16]

Creek blacks who served in the First Kansas Colored Infantry included Saucer Bradley, Jacob Bernard, and Snow Sells. Creek blacks who served in the Seventy-Ninth included Henry Deer, Sampson Sells, August Deer, Morris Kernell (Cornell), Scipio Sancho, Scipio George, Redmond Kurnell (Cornell), and Bully Kurnell. Those who fought with the Second Kansas Colored Infantry included Adam Dyle, Robert Benjamin, John Cooks, James Quabner, and John Kernell. The Second was reorganized into the Eighty-third U. S. Colored Infantry, in whose ranks served Abe Prince, Billy Caesar, Tony Dyle, William Peter, Gabriel Jimison, Stephen Barnett, Simon Renty, Aaron Grayson, Safe Barnwell, and Sam Renty. Many other Creek blacks served as soldiers in the First Indian Home Guards Regiment, established in June of 1862. They included Samuel Barnett, Green McGillivray, Hardy Stidham, Simon Brown, William Hawkins, Joe Reese, Louden Marshall, Love Jimboy, Tolly Lewis, Thomas Ab, Pickett Renty, Chales Renty, Texas Bruner, James Kernell, and Sam Nero. Others, such as Thomas Bruner, served as interpreters for the regiment. There were, of course, other free blacks and former slaves from the Creek Nation in these units. The records relating to these men clearly demonstrate that they numbered among the killed, wounded, and maimed. Other blacks not serving as soldiers served as teamsters in the quartermaster corps.[17]

Early in 1863, the United States took advantage of the weakened condition of the loyal Creeks in Kansas to secure a treaty. It was not until after the death of Opothleyohola in the spring that they made progress. Through the Creek black interpreter Harry Island, they negotiated a treaty, signed in September, which recognized, among other things, the "Necessity, justice, and humanity" of the Emancipation Proclamation, and the Creeks agreed that slavery should cease and that they would set aside a portion of their lands for occupancy by the freedmen and "all others of the African race who shall be permitted to settle among them." The treaty provided as well for compensation for the loyal Creeks for losses of property, other than slaves, suffered during the war. The Creeks rejected the treaty in 1864 because of amendments made to it during its ratification by the Senate.[18]

Meanwhile, the Southern refugees were encamped along Red River above the Washita and on the Washita below Fort Washita. They, too, now suffered greatly and were discouraged. The slave owners among the Indians, on both sides of the Red River, during February and March of 1864 had run their slaves to the Brazos in Texas, and the rebels were less concerned with repossessing the Indian Territory than with holding the Red River valley, "as the slaves of the refugees are drifting in the direction of the Brazos."[19] For by that time, the Union forces were clearly regaining control of the Indian Territory.

One official wrote that the army at Fort Gibson in 1864 was

greatly incumbered by the colored race, (who have fled to our lines for protection, and must have support;) and notwithstanding every inducement is presented them to remove north, yet their attachment to the Indian race and the Indian country, together with the discouragements presented by those who express apprehension that the north will be overrun by a dependent no-producing class, render it almost impossible to shake them off, and as a consequence large amounts of supplies, that might be made available for the support of the Indians, must of necessity be used to subsist colored refugees.

In February, it had been estimated that there were 500 blacks from various tribes, all of them destitute, at the fort.[20]

To complicate the matter, an act passed on May 3, 1864, appropriated funds to remove the refugee Indians from Kansas to their homes in the Indian Territory. They were delayed so that they did not arrive at Fort Gibson until June 15, too late to raise a crop, even if they could have left the safety of Fort Gibson to do so, for the country was infested by guerrillas and bushwhackers. They added their numbers to the destitute refugees already in the Indian Territory. In the fall of 1864, there were from fifteen to seventeen thousand of the latter in the territory. Isaac Coleman, the Creek agent, reported that while the Cherokees were in their own country and could scatter among their friends, the Creeks, Seminoles, Yuchis, Chickasaws, and Choctaws were compelled to camp in the vicinity of Fort Gibson, entirely dependent on the government for support. They wanted protection, and if the government could secure that, they could do much towards supporting themselves by hunting and fishing. At that time there were about 6,000 Creeks and Yuchis at the fort. Through their black interpreter Harry Island, the Creek chiefs appealed to the commissioner of Indian affairs to sustain them until the next planting season. Also serving as an interpreter for the refugee Creeks was the well-known Cow Tom The Creeks and their blacks remained near the post until the war was over.[21]

As the area became safer, the blacks settled in the fertile Arkansas-Verdigris valley and opened small farms of their own where the plantations of some of their former masters had stood. In early August, 1865, the loyal Creeks passed a law making them members of the tribe.[22]

When the war was over, the United States government was exacting regarding terms of peace with the Five Civilized Tribes. In the fall of 1865, a board of commissioners was sent to meet with them at Fort Smith, Arkansas. The board consisted of D. N. Cooley, the commissioner of Indian affairs; Elijah Sells, the superintendent for the Southern Superintendency; Thomas Wistar, a leader among the Society of Friends; Brigadier General W. S. Harney of the United States Army; and Colonel Ely S. Parker of General Grant's staff.[23]

The disloyal Indians had not yet arrived when the council convened at Fort Smith on September 9, 1865. Nevertheless, D. N. Cooley called the meeting to order, presenting the president's wishes to renew alliances with the Indians. By aligning themselves with the Confederacy, the Indians were told, they had forfeited all rights due them under the treaties with the United States and must consider themselves at the mercy of the government. This applied to the loyal factions as well, but the commissioners assured them that they would recognize the loyalty of those who had fought for the Union and had suffered on its behalf.[24]

The loyal Creeks, numbering about 6,000, were represented by Oktarharsars Harjo, Micco Hutke, Coweto Micco, Cotchoche, Thlocos Yohola, and several others. Their interpreter was Harry Island, a black. The blacks among the Creeks and Yuchis were represented by Ketch Barnett, John McIntosh, Scipio Barnett, Jack Brown, and Cow Tom. Micco Hutke expressed surprise at the call for treaty negotiations, the Creeks having supposed, he said, that they had come to settle their differences with their rebel brothers.[25]

On the second day, Cooley reviewed the fact that the various tribes had made treaties with the Confederate States. Those treaties had destroyed those previously made with the United States, thereby forfeiting all rights to annuities and lands. The president was anxious to renew relations with the Indians, but in the new treaties to be negotiated, the president insisted on certain stipulations , among them that the institution of slavery be abolished, that steps be taken for the unconditional emancipation of all persons held in bondage, and that the blacks be incorporated into the tribes on an equal footing with the original members or that they be otherwise provided for. A further stipulation would abolish slavery or involuntary servitude in the tribes except as punishment of a crime. However, Cooley insisted that those who had remained loyal, even though their nation may have gone over to the enemy, would be liberally provided for.[26]

The third day of the council was used in hearing anything that the assembled delegates had to say about their position in the negotiations. The Creeks were not prepared to say anything.[27]

On the fourth day, the loyal Creeks accused the former chief of the Nation of having made the treaty with the Confederates while several of them were on a mission to the wild Indians and claimed that their names had been put on the treaty without their knowledge.[28] The chiefs expressed a desire for a new treaty, but would not accept the alterations the Senate had made in the treaty of 1863.

After a few days of the council, the commissioners became convinced that no final treaties could be concluded at that time, at least until the differences between the loyal and disloyal factions were resolved. Therefore, they drafted a preliminary treaty to be signed by those delegates present, rejecting treaties with all other parties, reaffirming their allegiance to the United States, and agreeing to reestablish peace with them.[29]

The fifth day of the council was spent in reading the treaty of peace. After some hesitation, the Creeks signed it on the following day.[30]

On the eighth day, delegations from the Southern factions arrived, and the treaty of peace was interpreted to them. On the following day, the Southern Creeks signed the treaty, and the Creek agent announced that the Creeks had "buried the tomahawk . . . beyond resurrection" and would work out their differences upon reaching home. The loyal Creek delegation then read a statement which said, in part, "We are willing to provide for the abolishing of slavery and settlement of the blacks who were among us at the breaking out of the rebellion, as slaves or otherwise, as citizens entitled to all the rights and privileges that we are."[31]

The council lasted two days longer and accomplished little more than making arrangements for delegations from both factions to go to Washington at a later date and work out a treaty.

In early November the two factions of Creeks met to work at reunification of the tribe. Oktaharsars Harjo (Sand) was affirmed as principal chief, and word was sent for the disloyal Creeks still in the Red River country to return home.[32]

At the time of the Fort Smith conference, the loyal Creeks were living on Cherokee lands as well as their own in the vicinity of Fort Gibson, awaiting harvest time so that they could remove to their old homes. In October 1865, Southern Superintendent Elijah Sells reported that living with the Creeks and Seminoles were large numbers of blacks, whom Sells claimed the Indians desired to have incorporated into the tribe "as citizens, with equal rights." For the most part, they remained in the Arkansas-Verdigris valley, which area the Creeks apparently agreed to assign the blacks for their exclusive use. The former plantation owners in the region refused to return and live among the blacks and settled, for the most part, in the region surrounding North Fork Town.[33]

But the condition of many blacks in the Indian Territory was "one of great hardship, resulting from the fact that a portion of the people refused to recognize the result of the war in making them free." It became apparent to the government that the freedmen of all tribes must be protected until their status was firmly and clearly established. Thus, late in October 1865, the Adjutant General's Office assigned Brevet Major General John B. Sanborn, of the United States Volunteers to the duty of "regulating the relations between the Freedmen in the Indian Territory and their former masters as the Secretary of the Interior may indicate," and the War Department directed post commanders and officers of the quartermaster's department to furnish Sanborn with such escorts, transportation, and supplies as might be necessary for him to carry out his duties.[34]

Orders were issued to Sanborn on November 20. Where he found relations between the freedmen and their former masters amicable and satisfactory to both, he was not to interfere or disturb them. But where he found rights denied or abuses existing, he was to give immediate relief. He was to discourage idleness among the freedmen and encourage them in their own support by urging them to make contracts with persons who were willing to hire them as laborers either for wages or as sharecroppers. The contracts were to be in writing, duly filed, and to cover a period of no more than one year. The Indian agents were to cooperate with Sanborn in seeing that the freedmen were allowed to occupy lands of their own so that they could realize the profits of their own labor. Sanborn was also to stress upon the Indians the justice of admitting the freedmen to rights of persons and property and to the equal enjoyment of the bounty that might thereafter be bestowed by the national government. He was also to broach the idea of the Indians' granting to the freedmen an equal enjoyment of civil rights, using the argument that in doing so the Indians would be following the example of the whites as well as increasing the strength of their nations.[35]

At the time of Sanborn's appointment, rumors were rife in the Indian Territory that murder and other violence were being perpetrated upon the freedmen. Some of them complained to General H. J. Hunt at the Headquarters for the Frontier District of the Department of Arkansas at Fort Smith, yet they were not able to testify first-hand to the murders. Hunt ascribed the rumors to the general feeling of uneasiness that gripped the freedmen. Some Indians told them that they were free, while others told them that they were still slaves. In answering them, Hunt took the safe route, telling them that they would certainly be freed, for the treaties being negotiated would ensure that. Meanwhile, he told them, they must support themselves and continue quietly at their work with their present owners, making contracts for wages when offers of suitable wages were made to them. Further, they must "keep quiet and bear the evils that attend their change of condition as well as possible." Hunt found that they were very reasonable concerning what he told them and seemed contented with the prospects held out to them. Upon his inquiry concerning official views of the freedmen's status, Hunt was informed by Commissioner Cooley that "the constitutional number of states having ratified the antislavery amendment, there is not, in fact, a slave within the limits of the United States."[36]

Sanborn arrived at Fort Smith on December 24, and he brought with him certain preconceived ideas concerning the status of the freedmen of the Indian Territory. These views differed significantly from those of General Hunt, who believed that the Emancipation Proclamation did not apply to the Indian Territory and that slavery would exist there until otherwise provided by law. Sanborn believed, mistakenly, that the blacks of the Indian Territory were not legally slaves before the war but that they were voluntary slaves who had the right to leave their masters and go anywhere. If they escaped to a free state, he reasoned, they could not have been returned by process of court. Sanborn disagreed with Hunt's idea that it would be disastrous to inform the blacks that they were free. Hunt believed that they would abandon their old homes and go to the military posts and become dependent on the government. Sanborn believed that if their proposed rights among the Indians were explained to them, the freedmen would remain where they were. They would have to be told sometime, he argued, and the sooner, the better. To Sanborn, the best course for the government to pursue was to consider the blacks as part of the tribes to which they belonged and to give them freedom of choice of staying or leaving. Those who remained should have all the rights, interests, and annuities that were given to the Indians. It was important at once to confer upon the freedmen the right to hold and acquire real estate, which would make them feel responsible for the contracts they made, making their property liable to loss if the contracts were broken.[37]

Sanborn established his headquarters at Fort Smith and made his policies known through circulars, the first of which he released on January 1, 1866. It contained his orders from the department and directed the agents to explain to the Indians the new relation which existed between them and their former slaves and to stress to the freedmen that they were now invested with all the rights of free men. It emphasized the government's commitment to protect the freedmen in their persons; an outrage committed upon a freedman would be considered an outrage upon the United States. It instructed the agents to see that contracts were made and that fair wages were paid for labor; all contracts for periods longer than a month were to be in writing.

The circular also outlawed the system of polygamy that had always existed to some extent among the Indians and therefore had been practiced by some of the freedmen. No freedman thereafter would be allowed to take more than one wife; those cohabitating at that time would be considered legally married. Marriages which had been solemnized by Indian custom were considered binding and valid, and until provision was made the agent could take the mutual pledges of a couple and give them a certificate. Finally, Sanborn's first circular stressed that every effort was to be made to remove all prejudice on the part of the Indians against the freedmen.[38] This latter point reflected the obvious naivete of the department in pretending that the absorption of the freedmen into the Indian tribes could be effected without any discrimination or social or racial prejudice.

Sanborn issued Circular No. 2 on the following day. It authorized Indian agents to sign ration returns for destitute freedmen of their respective tribes and authorized commissaries of subsistence to issue rations "in cases of great destitution."[39]

On his first visit to the Indian country, Sanborn visited the Creeks, Seminoles, Cherokees, and loyal Chickasaws, and found the freedmen "the most industrious, economical, and, in many respects, the more intelligent" segment of the population. It was their desire, he found, to remain in the Indian country on land set apart for their exclusive use. The matter of segregated lands had been much discussed in the Indian Territory, and the freedmen were therefore inclined to do no more work than was necessary in improving the lands they occupied because they expected to be relocated. Sanborn urged that some decision be made before spring, for plowing and planting would begin as early as the first of March. If they were not to be resettled, they should know at once. Sanborn believed that they could survive by themselves because most of them had ox teams, and among their numbers were blacksmiths, carpenters, and wheelwrights. He found that the Creeks looked upon the freedmen as their equals in rights and were in favor of incorporating them into their tribe with all the rights and privileges of native Indians.[40] He no doubt referred to the loyal faction of Creeks for, as subsequent events would show, the Southern faction was opposed to incorporation of the blacks.

A few days later, Sanborn made another tour of the Indian country and from what he saw there concluded that land should be set aside for the exclusive use of the freedmen. Each male over twenty-one should be able to enter a homestead of 160 acres, with no power to sell the property. There were a large number of freedwomen who had from one to several children during slavery but had never had a husband. It would be difficult for them under freedom to find husbands, so Sanborn recommended that they be allowed to enter 160 acres as a head of a household. He also recommended that four sections in every township of freedman land be set aside for school lands for freedman children.[41]

Circular No. 4 authorized the freedmen to remain in the Indian nations and to cultivate the lands they occupied and instructed Major Pinkney Lugenbeel at Fort Gibson to report the name of every Indian who denied those rights or whose conduct indicated an unwillingness to allow the freedmen to hold and cultivate land during the present season. The right of the freedmen to remain on the farms where their cabins were built and where they had been held as slaves would be maintained in all cases where their masters had abandoned the farms during the war and had gone south.[42]

Circular No. 6 stated that since negotiation of the treaty at Washington had been delayed and it was important that as large a crop of corn and other cereals as possible be produced that year, the freedmen should take up any unoccupied land that was not likely to be occupied by any Indians during the season and make a crop. Sanborn directed the army to protect any freedmen who thus settled and to enforce contracts in which freedmen owed part of the crop to Indians.[43]

By April, Sanborn considered the existing relations between freedmen and Indians as "generally satisfactory." The rights of the freedmen were acknowledged by all, fair compensation was paid for their labor, a fair part of crops to be raised on the old plantations was being allowed, there was plenty of labor for the freedmen, and nearly all of them were self-supporting. Only 150 in the entire Indian Territory applied to Sanborn for assistance during April, and much of that was rendered to those who had been taken south by their masters and who were just returning to their old homes. Things were going so well that he saw little reason to continue his commission beyond the tenth of May. There might be a few abuses that would need correction, but a general supervision of freedman matters would be more necessary at harvest time when contracts were due. Sanborn believed that the agents, under proper instructions, could carry out the duties of his office. Sanborn was mustered out of service on April 30, 1866.[44] The matter of freedman relations was put in the hands of Elijah Sells, the superintendent of Indian affairs for the Southern Superintendency.

Meanwhile, a delegation of loyal Creeks—Oktarharsars Harjo, Coweta Micco, and Cotchoche—accompanied by their black interpreter Harry Island, had been in Washington since January.[45] They negotiated a treaty which, among other points, recognized the rights of the freedmen to full equality in the Creek Nation. However, a delegation of the Southern faction had also come to Washington, hired an attorney, and, representing about half of the Creeks, strongly opposed the treaty because of its provision regarding the blacks. They were willing to set aside land for the blacks, but they were unwilling to adopt them into the tribe. As a result, the president returned the treaty for revision. For a time it appeared that the negotiations might fail altogether. The United States commission urged the loyal delegation to yield temporarily on the point. They refused:

they held out firmly for their freedmen, urging that when the brave old Opothleyo-holo, resisting all the blandishments of the rebel emissaries, and of his Indian friends, stood out for the government, and led a large number of his people out of the country, fighting as they went, abandoning their homes, they promised their slaves that if they would remain also faithful to the government they should be free as themselves. Under these circumstances the delegates declined to yield, but insisted that the sacred pledge should be fulfilled, declaring that they would sooner go home and fight and suffer again with their faithful friends than abandon the point.[46]

A treaty was finally signed on June 14 and proclaimed August 11. The Treaty of 1866, among other things, restored peace and friendship between the Creeks and the United States, granted amnesty to all members of the tribe, ceded over three million acres of land, guaranteed payment for losses sustained by the loyal Creeks, and granted railroad right of way through the Nation. Of most significance to the blacks was Article 2, which abolished slavery or involuntary servitude except as punishment for a crime for which a person was convicted according to the laws that applied uniformly to all members of the tribe. The article goes on as follows:

And inasmuch as there are among the Creeks many persons of African descent, who have no interest in the soil, it is stipulated that hereafter these persons lawfully residing in said Creek country under their laws and usages, or who have been thus residing in said country, and may return within one year from the ratification of this treaty, and their descendants and such others of the same race as may be permitted by the laws of the said nation to settle within the limits of the jurisdiction of the Creek Nations as citizens [thereof,] shall have and enjoy all the rights and privileges of native citizens, including an equal interest in the soil and national funds, and the laws of the said nation shall be equally binding upon and give equal protection to all such persons, and all others of whatever race or color, who may be adopted as citizens or members of said tribe.

The treaty also provided for $100,000 of the funds from the land cession to be used in reimbursing the loyal Creeks and freedmen for the losses they had sustained when they were driven from their homes by the rebels.[47] The treaty was signed by Harry Island, United States interpreter for the Creek Nation.

During 1866, the inhabitants of the Creek Nation tried to improve their condition, but dry weather and the resulting scanty crops, sickness, and grasshoppers made dismal their prospects for the coming winter. In his annual report, Creek Agent J. W. Dunn wrote:

There is less prejudice towards the negroes than I had feared. The Indians generally are a people of exceedingly strong passions and prejudices, having little sympathy

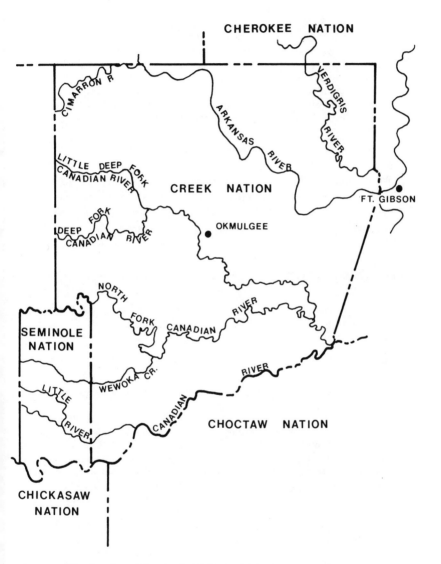

The Creek and Seminole Nations, 1866

with new ideas that usurp their established customs, but they have taken this pro-
vidential result of the war with so much calmness as our most peaceful citizens at
home. In my conversation with several intelligent Creeks, aside from active prejudice,
I have ever heard the opinion expressed that the negroes would prove the most
capable, intelligent, and industrious citizens; certainly, they promise well. This is
the first season on which to form a comparison. With all their disadvantages, the
freedmen have planned larger crops, have attended them more faithfully, and are
to-day further from want than are their former masters.[48]

Throughout the following few months, the blacks who had been with
the Southern Creeks straggled back into the Creek country. Some were
brought back by their former owners, but others were abandoned by their
owners or were mustered out of military service and had to find their own
means of returning. Still others who had taken up residence in other Indian
nations lingered too long and failed to return within the time limitation set
by the treaty and were later rejected as citizens.[49] Those who did return in
time were organized by 1869 into three towns—Arkansas Colored, North
Fork Colored, and Canadian Colored—where they began their lives as free
people. Their interests were looked after by their representatives in the
Creek National Council, several of whom were destined to rise to positions
of power and esteem in the Creek national government.

NOTES

1. Henry M. Rector to John Ross, January 29, 1861, *House Executive Document 1,* 38 Cong., 1 sess., pt. 3:345.

2. John T. Cox to W. G. Coffin, March 18, 1864, *House Executive Document
1,* 38 Cong., 2 sess., p. 477; Ohland Morton, "Confederate Government Relations
with the Five Civilized Tribes," *The Chronicles of Oklahoma* 31 (Summer 1953), 202;
Dean Trickett, "The Civil War in the Indian Territory," *The Chronicles of Oklahoma*
18 (December 1940), 267; U. S., Department of the Interior, *Report of the Secretary
of the Interior* (Washington, D.C.: Government Printing Office, 1861), p. 627.

3. S. S. Scott to Choctaws et al., December 26, 1862, *House Executive Document 1,* 38 Cong., 1 sess., pt. 3: 342; Morton, pp. 301-02.

4. Angie Debo, *The Road to Disappearance* (Norman: University of Oklahoma
Press, 1941), pp. 144, 145.

5. U. S., Department of War, *The War of the Rebellion: A Compilation of the
Official Records of the Union and Confederate Armies,* 70 vols. (Washington, D.C.:
Government Printing Office, 1880-1901), series iv, 1:426-43, hereafter cited as
Official Records; Morton, pp. 304-05; Debo, p. 145.

6. "Official Report of the Proceedings of the Council with the Indians of the
West and Southwest Held at Fort Smith, Arkansas, in September, 1865," *House*

Executive Document 1, 29 Cong., 1 sess., pp. 512-13 (hereafter cited as *Official Report*); John Bartlett Meserve, "Chief Opothleyahola," *The Chronicles of Oklahoma* 9 (December 1931), 445; Debo, pp. 144, 147, 148-49.

7. Morton, pp. 299, 307-08; Andre Paul DuChateau, "The Creek Nation on the Eve of the Civil War," *The Chronicles of Oklahoma* 52 (Fall 1974), 296; Meserve, p. 446.

8. Trickett, p. 268; Morton, p. 302; Debo, p. 150.

9. Trickett, pp. 268-69, 270; *Official Records,* i, 8: 6; Meserve, pp. 446-50; U. S., Department of the Interior, *Report of the Secretary of the Interior* (Washington, D.C.: Government Printing Office, 1866), pp. 10, 513; Debo, pp. 150-52.

The Battle of Round Mountain was fought south of the Cimarron River near Keystone, Oklahoma; the Battle of Chustolasah occurred about three and one-half miles southeast of Sperry, Oklahoma; and the Battle of Chustenahlah occurred on Hominy Creek west of Skiatook, Oklahoma. See "Oklahoma Historic Sites," *The Chronicles of Oklahoma* 36 (Autumn 1858), 291.

10. Laws 124-133, "Laws of the Creek Nation," *Creek—Laws,* Grant Foreman Collection, Indian Archives Division, Oklahoma Historical Society; George P. Rawick, ed., *The American Slave: A Composite Autobiography,* 19 vols. (Westport, Conn.: Greenwood Publishing Company, 1972), 7:8.

11. *Official Report,* p. 512; *Report of the Secretary of the Interior* (1863), *House Executive Document 1,* 38 Cong., 1 sess., pt. 3: 145, 294, 296, 299, 320; Freedman affidavits in National Archives Record Group 75 (Records of the Bureau of Indian Affairs), *Records Relating to Loyal Creek Claims, 1869-70* attest to the later escape of Creek blacks.

12. George Reynolds to Elijah Sells, December 5, 1865, National Archives Microfilm Publications, *Microcopy M234* (Records of the Office of Indian Affairs, Letters Received) 837: S13-66, hereafter cited as *M234,* followed by the roll number; Claims 43, 45, 62, 68, 75, 126, *Records Relating to Loyal Creek Claims, 1869-70*; Debo, pp. 143, 156-57; Laws 119-22, "Laws of the Creek Nation"; Rawick, 9: 120-21; Carolyn Thomas Foreman, "A Creek Pioneer: Notes Concerning 'Aunt Sue' Rogers and Her Family," *The Chronicles of Oklahoma* 21 (September 1943), 273, and "Marshalltown, Creek Nation," *The Chronicles of Oklahoma* 32 (Spring 1954), 54; *Indian-Pioneer History,* 116 vols. (Indian Archives Division, Oklahoma Historical Society), 72: 153-54.

Evidence of Cooper's intent to capture slaves can be found in the affidavits in *Records Relating to Loyal Creek Claims* and Edwin C. McReynolds, *The Seminoles* (Norman: University of Oklahoma Press, 1957), p. 311.

13. Debo, p. 152.

14. Scott to Choctaws et al., December 26, 1862, *House Executive Document 1,* 38 Cong., 1 sess., pt. 3: 342-43.

15. *Report of the Secretary of the Interior* (1863), pt. 3: 294, 299; *Report of the Secretary of the Interior* (1864), *House Executive Document 1,* 38 Cong., 2 sess., p. 174.

16. McReynolds, p. 311; Brig. Gen. James G. Blunt to Col. W. A. Phillips, April 30. 1863, May 30, 1863, Blunt to Maj. Gen. John M. Schofield, June 26, 1863, and Brig. Gen. John McNeil to Schofield, November 2, 1863, *Official Records,* i, 22: pt. 2, 262,

297-98, 337, 292; Cox to Coffin, March 26, 1864, *House Executive Document 1,* 38 Cong., 2 sess., p. 476; *Official Records,* i, 48: pt. 1, 258-59, iii, 5:660.

Details of the battle of Honey Springs can be found in *Official Records,* i, 22: pt. 1, 447-56; Wiley Britton, *Memoirs of the Rebellion on the Border, 1863* (Chicago: Cushing, Thomas & Co., Publishers, 1882), p. 154; McReynolds, pp. 309-11.

Details of the battle of Cabin Creek can be found in *Official Records,* i, 22: pt. 1, 378-82; Britton, pp. 316-26; MacReynolds, pp. 307-08.

17. Various Claims, *Records Relating to the Loyal Creek Claims, 1869-70*; S. W. Marston to J. Q. Smith, August 29, 1877, *M234*-868: Union A249-77.

18. *Report of the Secretary of the Interior* (1863), pt. 3: 145, 316; *Report of the Secretary of the Interior* (1864), p. 456; Debo, pp. 160-61.

19. Col. W. A. Phillips to W. P. Dole, March 22, 1864, Phillips to Maj. Gen. S. R. Curtis, March 17, 1864, Cox to Coffin, March 16, 1864, *House Executive Document 1,* 38 Cong., 2 sess., pp. 472-73, 476; Debo, p. 162.

20. Cox to Coffin, March 16, 1864, *House Executive Document 1*, 38 Cong., 2 sess., p. 476; Annie Heloise Abel, *The American Indian Under Reconstruction* (Cleveland: The Arthur H. Clark Company, 1925), p. 272.

21. *Report of the Secretary of the Interior* (1864), pp. 175, 176, 448; Isaac Coleman to Coffin, September 1, 1864, Ok-ta-ha-sus-hur-gah et al. to Commissioner of Indian Affairs, July 16, 1864, *House Executive Document 1,* 38 Cong., 2 sess., pp. 456, 458, 487-88; Claim 160, *Records Relating to Loyal Creek Claims, 1869-70.*

22. Debo, p. 167.

23. *Report of the Secretary of the Interior* (1865), *House Executive Document 1,* 39 Cong., 1 sess., p. 202.

24. Report of D. N. Cooley, October 30, 1865, *House Executive Document 1,* 39 Cong., 1 sess., p. 482; *Report of the Secretary of the Interior* (1865), p. 202; Abel, p. 189.

25. *Report of the Secretary of the Interior* (1865), p. 483; *Official Report,* pp. 497, 500.

26. *Report of the Secretary of the Interior* (1865), p. 202; Report of Cooley, October 30, 1865, 482-83; *Official Report,* pp. 502-503; Abel, p. 189.

27. *Official Report,* p. 503.

28. *Ibid.,* pp. 512-13.

29. *Report of the Secretary of the Interior* (1865), p. 203.

30. *Official Report,* p. 518.

31. *Ibid.,* pp. 522, 525.

32. Gail Balman, "The Creek Treaty of 1866," *The Chronicles of Oklahoma* 48 (Summer 1970); 194; Debo, p. 169.

33. J. W. Dunn to Elijah Sells, September 20, 1865, Sells to Cooley, October 15, 1865, *House Executive Document 1, 39* Cong., 1 sess., p. 440; Debo, pp. 170-71; *Report of the Secretary of the Interior* (1866), p. 56.

34. James Harlan to Cooley, November 18, 1865, *M234*-836: H1382-65.

35. Circular No. 1, January 1, 1866, *M234*-836: 156-66.

36. Gen. H. J. Hunt to Cooley, November 28, 1865, *M234*-836: H1323-65; Cooley to Hunt, December 15, 1865, National Archives Record Group 393 (Records

of the United States Army Continental Commands, 1821-1920), *Frontier District,* Seventh Army Corps and Department of Arkansas, Letters Received, 1865-66.

37. Bvt. Maj. Gen. John B. Sanborn to Cooley, December 26, 1865, *M234*-837: S101-66.

38. Circular No. 1, January 1, 1866, *M234*-838: 156-66.

39. Sanborn to Harlan, January 10, 1866, *M234*-837: S91-66.

40. *Report of the Secretary of the Interior* (1866), 283-84.

41. *Ibid.,* 286.

42. Sanborn to Maj. Pinkney Lugenbeel, April 7, 1866, in *M234*-837: S216-66.

43. Circular No. 6, March 27, 1866. *M234*-837: S203-66.

44. Sanborn to Cooley, April 13, 1866, in *Report of the Secretary of the Interior* (1866), p. 287; E. D. Townsend to Sanborn, April 11, 1866, *M234*-837: I237-66.

45. Balman, p. 194.

46. *Report of the Secretary of the Interior* (1866), p. 10; Debo, pp. 171-72.

47. Charles J. Kappler, comp. and ed., *Indian Affairs: Laws and Treaties,* 2nd ed., 4 vols. (Washington, D.C.: Government Printing Office, 1904), 2: 932-34.

48. *Report of the Secretary of the Interior* (1866), p. 318-19.

49. C. T. Foreman, "A Creek Pioneer," p. 274, and "Marshalltown, Creek Nation," p. 54; Rawick, 7: 121; Lipscom McGilvery (McGillivray) to Marston, February 28, 1877, *M234*-870; M1332-77.

chapter 11   CONCLUSION

DURING THE CENTURY preceding 1866, the Creeks had gone full circle. In the 1760s, blacks were present in the Creek country, either as runaways or as the property of white traders. But there is presently no evidence that the Creeks then held or even considered blacks as property. The tribe emerged from the Revolutionary War as holders of blacks as property, but they had not developed an economic system that called for a labor force. This came with the rise of a mixed-blood class of Creeks and with a government policy of encouraging the Creeks to undertake farming and the domestic arts. In the 1790s, the Creeks adopted an institution of slavery, but one that little resembled that in the nearby states. As Grant Foreman has observed, emerging as it did at the time when the Creeks were moving from a hunting to an agricultural society, the institution created a disparity in Creek society. The slaveholding class did not work, and the disparity widened in dress, manners, education, and wealth.[1]

The class that imitated the whites consisted mainly of mixed bloods among the Lower Creeks. After a time they dominated the leadership of the Nation, especially following their removal to the West. Under their leadership, the Creeks developed a system of slavery, replete with racial generalizations which, as time passed, more and more resembled that in the Anglo-dominated society. With the signing of the Treaty of 1866, the Creeks agreed not to hold Africans in a state of servitude. Thus the circle was complete. As a result of pressure from American governmental officials, they had adopted slavery as an institution; as a result of pressure from the same source, they had given it up.

The number of blacks among the Creeks had never been great. In 1832, there were only 902 slaves among the 21,762 Eastern Creeks. The slaves were held by only 162 Creeks, or only an estimated .75 percent of the population. How many slaves were held by the Western Creeks at the same time is uncertain. By 1860 the number of slaves among the Creeks had increased to only 1,532, but the Indian population had declined so that the slaves now represented 10 percent of the population.[2] Despite their small numbers in proportion to the Creek population, the Africans had played a significant role in Creek affairs.

From the conclusion of the Revolutionary War, slaves were a constant source of irritation in Creek-Georgia relations. The Georgians accused the Creeks of harboring runaways and of retaining blacks they had stolen from the plantations. The return of slaves and other property was a major point of negotiation before the Treaties of New York (1790) and Colerain (1794) as witnessed by articles in the treaties providing for the return of such property. Never satisfied with the attempts to settle property claims, the Georgians pressed for land cessions by the Creeks to pay for lost property. The political pressure the Georgians exerted ultimately resulted in the Creeks' removal. Thus, the presence of blacks in the Creek lands contributed directly to effecting the removal of the Creeks from their lands east of the Mississippi.

Blacks had also figured prominently in development of the posture the Creeks assumed toward the Seminoles before removal. From the Revolutionary War until 1823, the Seminoles were considered a loosely affiliated arm of the Creek Nation. During that period, however, the two groups grew farther apart in their social development and in their attitudes toward the United States. One of the points of greatest disparity concerned the blacks among each tribe. While the Seminoles developed a military alliance with their blacks, allowed them great freedom in accumulating property, and listened to their counsel, the Creeks did not develop such close relations with their blacks. When the Red Stick Creeks fled to the Seminoles in 1814, a wedge was driven between the two tribes, and the gap was ever widened. The Creeks as well as the Americans lost slaves who escaped to Florida. Hence the Creeks did not hesitate, particularly in 1816 and 1821, to assist the Americans in breaking up the black settlements in Florida and to launch slave-hunting raids into Florida.

The rupture between the tribes as a result of the Seminole-Red Stick union was transferred to the West at removal. Fearing the influence of blacks over the Seminoles, the Creeks viewed the blacks as a dangerous element of society and did their best to bring the Seminole blacks under control or to destroy them as a threat by processing claims for them or by launching raids against their settlements. Disputes over blacks were a major source of irritation between the tribes and finally, after a clear demonstration that they could not get along, contributed to the establishment of a separate Seminole Nation in 1856. Thus blacks played a significant role in undermining the Seminole Treaty of Payne's Landing (1832) and the Creek Treaty of Fort Gibson (1833), which called for a union of the Creeks and Seminoles.

The blacks among the Creeks also directly influenced their posture toward the American Civil War. Much of the power of the tribal government following removal rested in the hands of the wealthy Lower Creek slaveholders such as the McIntoshes, the Marshalls, the Stidhams, and others. That fact made them susceptible to the influence of proslavery governmental officials who dominated Indian affairs in the Indian Territory and to the overtures of emmisaries from the Southern states as war approached. Split loyalties reduced the Creeks to factionalism once more. Weakened by the war, they signed a treaty which not only ceded a great part of their western lands but, unknown to them at the time, laid the groundwork for the dissolution of their nation forty years later. Thus, directly or indirectly, the blacks had a profound influence upon the direction of Creek history.

Before removal, Creek attitudes and social practices regarding blacks stood in sharp contrast to the plantation slavery among the whites in the surrounding region. In the West, the situation was somewhat different. Distant from the slaveholding regions of Arkansas and Texas, the Creeks passed stricter slave laws as time passed, not in reaction to the stricter laws of the slave states but rather in reaction to political and cultural pressures from the other tribes, particularly the Cherokees and Choctaws and Chickasaws, whose laws regarding slaves became more and more like those of the white South. Cultural and political pressures from the Seminoles, as indicated above, were negative ones. A brief look at the attitudes toward slavery among those neighboring tribes is necessary.

The Cherokees held a greater number of slaves than any of the other tribes in the Indian Territory. In 1835 they owned 1,592, and by 1860 they had 2,511. Historians agree that slavery among the Cherokees was little different from that among the whites and that the status of blacks—both slave and free—declined in the Cherokee Nation after removal as laws became more severe. In 1839, by written constitution, the Cherokees admitted to citizenship the African offspring of Cherokee women but excluded the African offspring of African women and Cherokee men. All persons of "negro or mulatto parentage" were prohibited from holding public office. In 1839 the Cherokees passed a law prohibiting marriage of free citizens to "any slave or person of color" who was not a citizen. Punishment could not exceed fifty lashes. Convicted black males, however, received one hundred. In 1840, a law prohibited free blacks not of Cherokee blood and slaves from holding improvements and other property, and property then held was ordered seized and sold. Blacks were also prohibited from selling spirituous liquors. In 1841, "patrol companies" were created to capture and punish slaves caught off their masters' premises without a pass and to flog any black not entitled to Cherokee privileges and found carrying a weapon of any kind. That same year, a law prohibited the teaching of slaves and free blacks not of Cherokee blood to read or write. In the aftermath of the slave "revolt" of 1842, the council ordered all free blacks not freed by Cherokee citizens to leave the Nation by January 1, 1843, and passed a law that made any Cherokee citizen who freed his slaves responsible for their conduct. The law also stated that any free black found guilty of "aiding, abetting, or decoying" slaves to leave their owners was to receive one hundred lashes. An 1848 act prohibited the teaching of any black to read or write, and an 1855 law prohibited the hiring of teachers with abolitionist sentiments.[3]

The Choctaws also held large numbers of slaves. An 1831 census listed only 512 slaves and 11 free blacks, but by 1860, the Choctaws held 2,349 slaves. From removal until 1855, the Choctaws and Chickasaws lived under one government, the latter having settled on the western lands of the former. An 1838 law forbade cohabitation with a slave, the teaching of a slave to read or write without the owner's consent, and the council's emancipation of slaves without the owner's consent. In 1844, a law said "that no free negro unconnected with Choctaw blood should ever be allowed to draw any money from the Choctaw annuity." After 1855, when the tribes separated, Choctaw laws reaffirmed the laws against intermarriage and emancipation of slaves by the council. Other laws said that slaves brought to the Indian Territory would remain slaves, that owners should treat their slaves humanely, and that no person of African descent could hold public office.[4]

The Chickasaws acquired large numbers of slaves after removal to the West. Before removal, a few mixed-blood families owned large numbers, several more than twenty and one as many as 150. With the money received for their improvements and reservations at removal, many Chicksaws invested their money in slaves, whom they took to the West.   In

1860, Chickasaws held 975 slaves. Generally, relations between slave and master were relaxed, but there was little amalgamation. For the most part, they treated their slaves humanely, but the Chickasaws have been generally regarded as having held strong racial prejudices and having considered their slaves in the same manner as did white slaveholders.[5] In their constitution of 1855, the Chickasaws forbade emancipation of slaves by council without the owner's consent. In the late 1850s they assessed harsh penalties for harboring runaways and excluded free blacks from their nation. County judges were authorized to execute the latter law. Those who refused to go were sold into slavery to the highest bidder. They were sold for periods of one year until they agreed to leave the Nation.[6]

Estimates of the number of blacks among the Seminoles had varied before removal. However, nearly five hundred were removed with them. One estimate sets their number at 1,000 in 1860, but that number is far exaggerated when one takes into account the number who had fled to Mexico and those who were captured and sold by the Creeks and others. In 1867, there were only 333 of those who fled north during the war with the loyal Seminoles, who represented at least two-thirds of the tribe.[7]

There is a significant parallel between the attitudes of each tribe toward slavery and the population changes and trends toward acculturation. The tribes had suffered a great reduction in their numbers between removal and 1860. The Creeks declined by an estimated 43 percent, the Cherokees by 31 percent, the Choctaws by 27 percent, the Chickasaws by 18 percent, and the Seminoles by 53 percent. Meanwhile the number of whites and blacks had increased significantly in all tribes but the Seminoles. In the Cherokee Nation the whites represented 4 percent of the population while the slaves represented 15 percent. In the Choctaw Nation, the whites represented 5 percent while the slaves represented 14 percent. The percentages were 3 and 18, respectively, in the Chickasaw Nation, but in the Creek Nation, while the whites represented 4 percent of the population, the slaves represented only 10 percent.[8] The figures relating to the whites and blacks, when considered together, reflect the degree of acculturation taking place in the tribes, for there is a clear parallel between the increasing numbers of whites and slaves in the tribes and the increasing severity of the slave codes.

The degree of racial antipathy and of acculturation reached by each tribe before the Civil War directly affected the status of the blacks as free men in the Indian Territory. By the treaties negotiated with the five tribes in 1866, the United States secured provisions for the adoption of the blacks into the tribes. The Seminoles, who had been the least assimilated, had no slave code. They adopted their blacks immediately, and, in 1869, the Superintendent of Indian affairs for the Southern Superintendency wrote, "Accepting fully the results of the war, and granting to the freedman unconditional citizenship, the Seminoles are living in a state of more perfect peace than any other tribe within the superintendency."[9] In stark contrast, were the Chickasaws, who, as the most antipathetic of all towards the blacks, never adopted their freedmen. The Choctaws refused to adopt theirs until 1885. The Creeks and Cherokees, like the Seminoles, adopted their blacks immediately, the Creeks with less difficulty than the Cherokees. The rights enjoyed by the adopted freedmen varied to extremes. The Chickasaw freedmen had no rights except to occupy and improve small plots of land. Until their adoption, the Choctaw freedmen fared no better and only a little better after adoption. Many of the Cherokee freedmen were denied rights because they had failed to return to the Cherokee Nation within six months after the Cherokee treaty was proclaimed, and the freedmen were not able to participate fully in the political or educational life of the Nation.[10]

Despite the severity of their slave code, the Creeks had apparently lacked the racial antipathy of the Cherokees, Choctaws, and Chickasaws, and like the Seminoles made more provisions to insure the rights of the freedmen. The Creek freedmen settled for the most part in three towns—Arkansas Colored, Canadian Colored, and North Fork Colored—with representatives in both houses of the Creek National Council, and they enjoyed full rights as citizens. Their lives as free men in the Creek Nation spanned four decades. They became involved in the political factionalism that kept the Creek Nation unsettled for a number of years following the war.[11] Nevertheless, they produced a number of prominent leaders, among others, Supreme Court Judge Jesse Franklin; District Judge Henry C. Reed; tribal delegate to Washington Silas Jefferson; and tribal politicians Snow Sells, Scipio Sango, Monday Durant, John Kernel, and Sugar George. When the Creek Nation was dissolved in the early years of the twentieth century, the Creek freedmen, along with the Creeks, received allotments of land in severalty and became citizens of the United States.

NOTES

1. Grant Foreman, *The Five Civilized Tribes* (Norman: University of Oklahoma Press, 1934), pp. 207-08.

2. National Archives Record Group 75 (Records of the Bureau of Indian Affairs), *Creek Removal Records,* Census Roll, 1833; Michael F. Doran, "Population Statistics of Nineteenth Century Indian Territory," *The Chronicles of Oklahoma* 53 (Winter 1975-76), 501.

3. Kenneth Wiggins Porter, *The Negro on the American Frontier* (New York: Arno Press and The New York Times, 1971), p. 109; Foreman, pp. 54, 83, 420; William G. McLoughlin, "Red Indians, Black Slavery and White Racism: America's Slaveholding Indians," *American Quarterly* 24 (October 1974), 380-81; R. Halliburton, Jr., "Origins of Black Slavery Among the Cherokees," *The Chronicles of Oklahoma* 52 (Winter 1974-75), 496; *Laws of the Cherokee Nation: Adopted by the Council at Various Periods* (Tahlequah, Cherokee Nation: Cherokee Advocate Office, 1852), pt. 2: 7, 19, 44, 53, 55-56, 71, 173-74, 381; James W. Duncan, "Interesting Ante-Bellum Laws of the Cherokees, Now Oklahoma History," *The Chronicles of Oklahoma* 6 (June 1928), 179; J. B. Davis, "Slavery in the Cherokee Nation," *The Chronicles of Oklahoma* 11 (December 1933), 1066-67. A book-length study of slavery among the Cherokees is Halliburton, *Red over Black: Black Slavery among the Cherokee Indians* (Westport, Conn.: Greenwood Press, 1977).

4. National Archives Record Group 75, *Choctaw Removal Records,* Census Roll, 1831 (Census of North West District); Doran, p. 501; *Senate Report 1278,* 49 Cong., 1 sess., pt. 2; 493; Arrell M. Gibson, *The Chickasaws* (Norman: University of Oklahoma Press, 1971), p. 226; Wyatt F. Jeltz, "The Relations of the Negroes and Choctaw and Chickasaw Indians," *The Journal of Negro History* 33 (January 1948), 31-32.

5. National Archives Record Group 75, *Chickasaw Removal Records,* Census and Muster Rolls, 1837-39; *Senate Executive Document 166,* 50 Cong., 1 sess., p. 9; Jeltz, pp. 29-31; Gibson, pp. 125, 226; Doran, p. 501.

6. *Constitution, Laws, and Treaties of the Chickasaws* (Tishomingo City, Chickasaw Nation: E. J. Foster, 1860), 57-58, 115.

7. Doran, p. 501; a census of the loyal Seminole blacks and their descendants can be found in National Archives Microfilm Publications, *Microcopy M574* (Special Files of the Office of Indian Affairs, 1807-1904) 11, special file 87. A book-length treatment of slavery among the Seminoles is my *Africans and Seminoles: From Removal to Emancipation* (Westport, Conn.: Greenwood Press, 1977).

8. Doran, pp. 498, 501.

9. *House Executive Document 1*, 41 Cong., 2 sess., pt. 3: 842.

10. No adequate histories of the freedmen of these tribes exist except my work *The Cherokee Freedmen: From Emancipation to American Citizenship* (Westport, Conn: Greenwood Press, 1978). Porter (p. 527) points out the lack of scholarship. However, information can be gleaned from Angie Debo, *The Rise and Fall of the Choctaw Republic* (Norman: University of Oklahoma Press, 1934), and *The Road to Disappearance* (Norman: University of Oklahoma Press, 1941), and Gibson, *The Chickasaws.*

11. The best treatment of the Creek freedmen is to be found in Debo, *The Road to Disappearance.*

BIBLIOGRAPHY

I. MANUSCRIPTS AND TRANSCRIPTS

a. Alabama Department of Archives and History, Montgomery

A. B. Clanton Papers: Reminiscences of Fort Mims and Caleebe

J. D. Dreisbach Papers: Papers Presented to the Alabama Historical Society—Subject Indians, 1877-83

H. S. Halbert Papers: Battles of the Creek War (File 59)

A. B. Meek Papers: Notes

Albert J. Pickett Papers: Interesting Notes Upon the History of Alabama

Ebenezer Pond Papers

War of 1813-14: Benton and Fort Montgomery (Military Division, File 207)

War of 1813-14: Hawkins and Lower Creeks (Military Division, File 205)

War of 1813-14: Winchester Correspondence (Military Division, File 205)

b. National Archives, Washington, D.C.

Records of the Bureau of Census (National Archives Record Group 29). Population Census Schedules, 1860: Arkansas Slave Schedules (National Archives Microfilm Publications, *Microcopy M653*, Roll 54)

Records of the Bureau of Indian Affairs (National Archives Record Group 75).

   Chickasaw Removal Records: Census and Muster Rolls, 1837-39

   Choctaw Removal Records: Census Roll, 1831 (Census of North West District)

   Creek Removal Records: Census Roll, 1833

Documents Relating to the Negotiation of Ratified and Unratified Treaties with
    Various Indian Tribes, 1801-69 (National Archives Microfilm Publications,
    Microcopy T494, Roll 9)
Emigration Lists, 1836-37
Letters Received Relating to Indian Affairs, 1800-23 (National Archives Micro-
    film Publications, *Microcopy M271*, Rolls 1-4).
Letters Sent Relating to Indian Affairs, 1800-24 (National Archives Microfilm
    Publications, *Microcopy M15*, Rolls 3-5)
Miscellaneous Muster Rolls, 1832-46.
Records of the Commissary General of Subsistence: Letters Received
Records of the Creek Trading House, 1795-1816 (National Archives Microfilm
    Publications, *Microcopy M4,* Roll 1)
Records of the Office of Indian Affairs:
    Letters Received (National Archives Microfilm Publications, *Microcopy M234*,
        Rolls 87, 171, 219-23, 225-30, 236-40, 255, 289, 291, 442, 443, 800-02,
        806, 833, 836, 837, 870, 922, 923)
    Letters Sent (National Archives Microfilm Publications, *Microcopy M21*, Rolls
        30-32, 34, 36, 37, 41, 43, 57, 60, 63)
    Record Books (National Archives Microfilm Publications, *Microcopy M348*,
        Rolls 2-4, 10)
    Special Files, 1807-1904 (National Archives Microfilm Publications, *Micro-
        copy M574*, Rolls 11, 13, 75)
Records Relating to Loyal Creek Claims, 1869-70
Records of the Office of the Adjutant General (National Archives Record Group 94)
        General Jesup's Papers: Letters Received, Letters Sent.
Records of the United States Army Continental Commands, 1821-1920 (National
        Archives Record Group 393)
    Fort Gibson: Letters Received, Letters Sent, Volume "Indian Affairs"
    Second Military Department: Letters Received, Letters Sent
    Second and Seventh Military Departments: Letters Received, Letters Sent

c. Oklahoma Historical Society, Indian Archives Division, Oklahoma City

Creek Records: 27227, 27666, 29349
Foreman Transcripts. 7 Vols.
Grant Foreman Collection: Creek—Laws
Indian-Pioneer History. 116 Vols.

d. Other

Thomas H. Gage Papers, William Clements Library, University of Michigan, Ann Arbor.
Montgomery County Records, Montgomery, Alabama

II. FEDERAL DOCUMENTS

Carter, Clarence Edwin, comp. and ed., *The Territorial Papers of the United States.* 26 vols. Washington, D.C.: Government Printing Office, 1934-56; National Archives, 1958-62.

Hodge, Frederick Webb, ed., *Handbook of American Indians North of Mexico.* 2 pts. Washington, D.C.: Government Printing Office, 1907-10.

Kappler, Charles J., comp. and ed., *Indian Affairs: Laws and Treaties.* 2nd ed. 4 vols. Washington, D.C.: Government Printing Office, 1904-29.

Official Opinions of the Attorneys General of the United States. 25 vols. Washington, D.C.: Government Printing Office, 1852-1906.

Swanton, John R. *Early History of the Creek Indians and Their Neighbors.* Bureau of American Ethnology Bulletin, no. 73. Washington, D.C.: Government Printing Office, 1922.

———. *The Indians of the Southeastern United States.* Bureau of American Ethnology Bulletin, no. 137. Washington, D.C.: Government Printing Office, 1946.

United States Congress.

American State Papers: Documents, Legislative and Executive of the Congress of the United States, from the First Session of the First to the Third Session of the Thirteenth Congress, Inclusive, Commencing March 3, 1789, and Ending March 3, 1815. 38 vols. Washington, D.C.: Gales and Seaton, 1832-61.

20 Cong., 2 Sess., *House Executive Document 91.*

23 Cong., 1 Sess., *Senate Document 512.*

25 Cong., 3 Sess., *Executive Document 225.*

25 Cong., 3 Sess., *Senate Document 1.*

25 Cong., 3 Sess., *Senate Document 88.*

26 Cong., 1 Sess., *Senate Document 1.*

26 Cong., 2 Sess., *Executive Document 2.*

27 Cong., 2 Sess., *Executive Document 2.*

27 Cong., 3 Sess., *Executive Document 2.*

28 Cong., 1 Sess., *Executive Document 2.*

28 Cong., 2 Sess., *House Executive Document 2.*

29 Cong., 1 Sess., *House Executive Document 2.*

29 Cong., 2 Sess., *House Executive Document 4.*

30 Cong., 1 Sess., *House Report 724.*

33 Cong., 2 Sess., *House Executive Document 15.*

38 Cong., 1 Sess., *House Executive Document 1.*

38 Cong., 2 Sess., *House Executive Document 1.*

39 Cong., 1 Sess., *House Executive Document 1.*

41 Cong., 2 Sess., *House Executive Document 1.*

50 Cong., 1 Sess., *Senate Executive Document 166.*

United States Department of Commerce, Bureau of the Census. *Negro Population, 1790-1915.* Washington, D.C.: Government Printing Office, 1918. Reprint. New York: Arno Press and The New York Times, 1968.

United States Department of the Interior.

    Census Office. *Eighth Census of the United States, 1860.* Washington, D.C.:
        Government Printing Office, 1864.

    Report of the Secretary of the Interior. Washington, D.C.: Government Printing
        Office, 1861.

    Report of the Secretary of the Interior. Washington, D.C.: Government Printing
        Office, 1866.

United States Department of War. *The War of the Rebellion: A Compilation of the
        Official Records of the Union and Confederate Armies.* 70 vols. Washington,
        D.C.: Government Printing Office, 1880-1901.

III. COLONIAL AND STATE DOCUMENTS

Candler, Allen D., ed. *The Colonial Records of the State of Georgia.* 26 vols. Atlanta:
        The Franklin Printing and Publishing Company and The Franklin-Turner
        Company, 1904-26.

—— ed. *The Revolutionary Records of the State of Georgia.* 3 vols. Atlanta: The
        Franklin-Turner Company, 1908.

McDowell, William L., Jr., ed. *Colonial Records of South Carolina: Documents Relat-
        ing to Indian Affairs, May 21, 1750—August 7, 1754.* Columbia: South Carolina
        Archives Department, 1958.

—— ed. *Colonial Records of South Carolina: Documents Relating to Indian Affairs,
        1754-1765.* Columbia: University of South Carolina Press, 1970.

IV. INDIAN DOCUMENTS

Campbell's Abstract of Creek Indian Census Cards and Index. Muskogee, Okla.:
        Phoenix Job Printing Co., 1915.

Constitution, Laws, and Treaties of the Chickasaws. Tishomingo City, Chickasaw
        Nation: E. J. Foster, 1860.

Laws of the Cherokee Nation: Adopted by the Council at Various Periods. Tahlequah,
        Cherokee Nation: Cherokee Advocate Office, 1852.

Waring, Antonio J., ed. *Laws of the Creek Nation.* University of Georgia Libraries
        Miscellaneous Publications No. 1. Athens: University of Georgia Press, 1960.

V. MISCELLANEOUS DOCUMENTS AND LETTERS

Bassett, John Spencer, ed. *Correspondence of Andrew Jackson.* 7 vols. Washington,
        D.C.: Carnegie Institute, 1926. Reprint. New York: Kraus Reprint Co., 1969.

"Benjamin Hawkins—Kendal Lewis Correspondence," *Alabama Historical Quarterly*
        21 (Spring 1959); 7-9.

Caughey, John Walton. *McGillivray of the Creeks.* Norman: University of Oklahoma
        Press, 1938.

Claiborne, W. C. C. *Official Letter Books of W. C. C. Claiborne, 1801-1816.* Edited by
      Dunbar Rowland, 6 vols. Jackson, Miss.: State Department of Archives and
      History, 1917.

Corbitt, D. C., ed. "Papers Relating to the Georgia-Florida Frontier, 1784-1800,"
      Georgia Historical Quarterly 24 (June 1940); 150-57.

"Dispatches of Spanish Officials Bearing on the Free Negro Settlement of Gracia
      Real de Santa Teresa de Mose, Florida," *The Journal of Negro History* 9
      (April 1924); 144-95.

Doster, James F. "Letters Relating to the Tragedy at Fort Mims: August- September,
      1813," *The Alabama Review* 14 (October 1961); 269-85.

Hawes, Lilla M., ed. *The Papers of James Jackson, 1781-1798.* Collections of the
      Georgia Historical Society, vol. 11. Savannah: The Georgia Historical Society,
      1955.

Hawkins, Benjamin. *Letters of Benjamin Hawkins, 1796-1806.* Collections of the
      Georgia Historical Society, vol. 9. Savannah: The Morning News, 1916.

Johnson, Elmer D., and Sloan, Kathleen Lewis, eds. *South Carolina: A Documentary
      Profile of the Palmetto State.* Columbia: University of South Carolina Press,
      1971.

Johnston, J. H. "Documentary Evidence and the Relations of Negroes and Indians,"
      The Journal of Negro History 14 (January 1929); 21-41.

"Oglethorpe's Treaty with the Lower Creek Indians," *Georgia Historical Quarterly*
      4 (March 1920): 3-16.

VI. MEMOIRS, REMINISCENCES, AND TRAVEL NARRATIVES

Bourne, Edward Gaylord, ed. *Narratives of the Career of Hernando de Soto in the
      Conquest of Florida as told by a Knight of Elvas and in a relation by Luys
      Hernandez de Biedma, factor of the Expedition.* 2 vols. New York: Allerton
      Book Co., 1922.

Britton, Wiley. *The Civil War on the Border.* 2 vols. New York: G. P. Putnam's
      Sons, 1890-1904.

——. *Memoirs of the Rebellion on the Border, 1863.* Chicago: Cushing, Thomas &
      Co., Publishers, 1882.

Ellicott, Andrew. *The Journal of Andrew Ellicott, late commissioner on behalf
      of the United States during part of the year 1796, the years 1797, 1798,
      1799, and Part of the year 1800.* Philadelphia: Budd & Bartram, 1803.
      Reprint. Chicago: Quadrangle Books, 1962.

Feiler, Seymour, trans. and ed. *Jean-Bernard Bossu's Travels in the Interior of
      North America, 1751-1762.* Norman: University of Oklahoma Press, 1962.

Hawkins, Benjamin. *A Sketch of the Creek Country in the Years 1798 and 1799.*
      Collections of the Georgia Historical Society, vol. 2, pt. 1. New York: Wil-
      liam Van Norden Printer, 1848.

Hitchcock, Ethan Allen. *A Traveler in Indian Territory: The Journal of Ethan
      Allen Hitchcock, late Major-General in the United States Army.* Edited by
      Grant Foreman. Cedar Rapids, Iowa: The Torch Press, 1930.

Hodgson, Adam. *Remarks During a Journey Through North America in the Years 1819, 1820, and 1821 in a Series of Letters.* New York: Samuel Whiting, 1823.

Irving, Washington. *A Tour on the Prairies.* Author's rev. ed. New York: G. P. Putnam's Sons, 1910.

Lang, John D., and Taylor, Samuel, Jr. *Report of a Visit to Some of the Tribes of Indians Located West of the Mississippi River.* Providence: Knowles and Vose, 1843.

Litton, Gaston, ed. "The Journal of a Party of Emigrating Creek Indians, 1835-1836," *The Journal of Southern History* 7 (May 1941); 225-42.

Mereness, Newton D., ed. *Travels in the American Colonies.* New York: The Macmillan Company, 1916. Reprint. New York: Antiquarian Press, 1961.

Pope, John. *A Tour Through the Southern and Western Territories of the United States of North-America: the Spanish Dominions of the Mississippi, and the Floridas; the Countries of the Creek Nations; and Many Uninhabited Parts.* Richmond, Va.: John Dickson, 1792. Reprint. New York: Charles L. Woodward, 1888.

Rawick, George P., ed. *The American Slave: A Composite Autobiography.* 19 vols. Westport, Conn.: Greenwood Publishing Company, 1972.

Stuart, James. *Three Years in North America.* Edinburgh: Robert Cadell, 1833.

Van Doren, Mark, ed. *The Travels of William Bartram.* New York: Dover Publications, 1928.

Woodward, Thomas S. *Woodward's Reminiscences of the Creek, or Muskogee Indians, Contained in Letters to Friends in Georgia and Alabama.* Montgomery: Barrett & Wimbash, 1859. Reprint. Mobile: Southern University Press for Graphics, Inc., 1965.

VII. NEWSPAPERS

Arkansas Gazette (Little Rock), December 21, 1842, April 7, 1853.

Arkansas Intelligencer (Van Buren), April 29, 1843, June 14, 1845, August 2, 1845.

Fort Smith Elevator, February 12, 1897.

VIII. SECONDARY MATERIAL

a. Articles

Anderson, Robert L. "The End of an Idyll," *Florida Historical Quarterly* 42 (July 1963); 35-47.

Balman, Gail. "The Creek Treaty of 1866," *The Chronicles of Oklahoma* 48 (Summer 1970); 184-96.

Brannon, Peter A. "The Pensacola Indian Trade," *Florida Historical Society Quarterly* 31 (July 1952); 1-15.

Coulter, E. Merton. "Mary Musgrove, 'Queen of the Creeks': A Chapter of Early Georgia Troubles," *Georgia Historical Quarterly* 11 (March 1927); 1-30.

Davis, J. B. "Slavery in the Cherokee Nation," *The Chronicles of Oklahoma* 11 (December 1933); 1056-72.

Doran, Michael F. "Population Statistics of Nineteenth Century Indian Territory," *The Chronicles of Oklahoma* 53 (Winter 1975-76); 492-515.

DuChateau, Andre Paul. "The Creek Nation on the Eve of the Civil War," *The Chronicles of Oklahoma* 52 (Fall 1974); 296.

Duncan, James W. "Interesting Ante-Bellum Laws of the Cherokees, Now Oklahoma History," *The Chronicles of Oklahoma* 6 (June 1928); 178-80.

Foreman, Carolyn Thomas. "The Brave Major Moniac and the Creek Volunteers," *The Chronicles of Oklahoma* 23 (Summer 1945); 96-106.

——. "A Creek Pioneer: Notes Concerning 'Aunt Sue' Rogers and Her Family," *The Chronicles of Oklahoma* 21 (September 1943); 271-79.

——. "The Jumper Family of the Seminole Nation," *The Chronicles of Oklahoma* 34 (Autumn 1956); 272-85.

——. "Lee Compere and the Creek Indians," *The Chronicles of Oklahoma* 42 (Autumn 1964); 291-99.

——. "Marshalltown, Creek Nation," *The Chronicles of Oklahoma* 32 (Spring 1954); 52-57.

Greenslade, Marie Taylor. "William Panton," *Florida Historical Society Quarterly* 14 (October 1935); 107-29.

Hall, Arthur H. "The Red Stick War: Creek Indian Affairs during the War of 1812," *The Chronicles of Oklahoma* 12 (September 1934); 264-93.

Halliburton, R., Jr. "Black Slave Control in the Cherokee Nation," *The Journal of Ethnic Studies* 3 (Summer 1975); 23-35.

——. "Origins of Black Slavery among the Cherokees," *The Chronicles of Oklahoma* 52 (Winter 1974-75); 483-96.

Holland, James W., "Andrew Jackson and the Creek War: Victory at the Horseshoe," *The Alabama Review* 21 (October 1968); 243-75.

Jeltz, Wyatt F. "The Relations of the Negroes and Choctaw and Chickasaw Indians," *The Journal of Negro History* 33 (January 1948); 24-37.

"Jeremiah Austill," *The Alabama Historical Quarterly* 6 (Spring 1944); 81-91.

Johnson, Cecil. "Expansion in West Florida," *Mississippi Valley Historical Review* 20 (March 1934); 481-96.

Kinnaird, Lawrence. "International Rivalry in the Creek Country. Part I, The Ascendancy of Alexander McGillivray, 1783-1789," *Florida Historical Society Quarterly* 10 (October 1931); 59-85.

——. "The Significance of William August Bowles' Seizure of Panton's Apalachee Store in 1792," *Florida Historical Society Quarterly* 9 (January 1931); 156-92.

Littlefield, Daniel F., Jr., and Underhill, Lonnie E. "The Cherokee Slave 'Revolt' of 1842," *American Indian Quarterly* 3 (Summer 1977); 121-31.

Littlefield, Daniel F., Jr., and Littlefield, Mary Ann. "The Beams Family: Free Blacks in Indian Territory," *The Journal of Negro History* 61 (January 1976); 16-35.

McLoughlin, William G. "The Choctaw Slave Burning: A Crisis in Mission Work among the Indians," *Journal of the West* 13 (January 1974); 113-27.

——. "Indian Slaveholders and Presbyterian Missionaries, 1837-1861," *Church History* 42 (December 1973); 535-51.

——. "Red Indians, Black Slavery and White Racism: America's Slaveholding Indians," *American Quarterly* 24 (October 1974); 366-85.

Mahon, John K. "British Strategy and Southern Indians: War of 1812," *Florida Historical Quarterly* 44 (April 1966); 285-302.

Meserve, John Bartlett. "Chief Opothleyahola," *The Chronicles of Oklahoma* 9 (December 1931); 440-53.

——. "The MacIntoshes," *The Chronicles of Oklahoma* 10 (September 1932); 310-25.

Morton, Ohland. "Confederate Government Relations with the Five Civilized Tribes," *The Chronicles of Oklahoma* 31 (Summer 1953); 189-203.

Neeley, Mary Ann Oglesby. "Lachlan McGillivray: A Scot on the Alabama Frontier," *The Alabama Historical Quarterly* 36 (Spring 1974); 5-14.

Nunez, Theron A., Jr. "Creek Nativism and the Creek War of 1813-1814,"*Ethnohistory* 5 (Winter 1958-Summer 1959); 1-47, 131-75, 292-301.

O'Donnell, James H., III. "Alexander McGillivray: Training for Leadership, 1777-1783," *Georgia Historical Quarterly* 49 (June 1965); 172-86.

"Oklahoma Historic Sites," *The Chronicles of Oklahoma* 36 (Autumn 1958); 282-314.

Owsley, Frank L., Jr. "British and Indian Activities in Spanish West Florida During the War of 1812," *Florida Historical Quarterly* 46 (October 1967); 111-23.

——. "The Fort Mimms Massacre," *The Alabama Review* 24 (July 1971); 192-204.

Sefton, James E. "Black Slaves, Red Masters, White Middlemen: A Congressional Debate of 1852," *Florida Historical Quarterly* 51 (October 1972); 113-28.

Siebert, Wilbur H. "Slavery and White Servitude in East Florida, 1726-1776," *Florida Historical Society Quarterly* 10 (July 1931); 3-23.

Sturdevant, William C. "Creek into Seminole." in *North American Indians in Historical Perspective,* edited by Eleanor Burke Leacock and Nancy Oesterich Lurie. New York: Random House, 1971.

Swan, Caleb. "Position and State of Manners and Arts in the Creek, or Muscogee Nation in 1791." In *Information Respecting the History, Condition and Prospects of the Indian Tribes of the United States,* by Henry Rowe Schoolcraft. 6 vols. Philadelphia: J. B. Lippincott & Company, 1855. Reprint. New York: Paladin Press, 1969.

Tarvin, Marion Elisha. "The Muscogees or Creek Indians 1519 to 1893," *The Alabama Historical Quarterly* 17 (Fall 1955); 125-45.

Trickett, Dean. "The Civil War in the Indian Territory," *The Chronicles of Oklahoma* 18 (December 1940); 266-80.

West, Elizabeth Howard. "A Prelude to the Creek War of 1813-1814 in a Letter of John Innerarity to James Innerarity," *Florida Historical Quarterly* 18 (April 1940); 247-66.

Whitaker, Arthur Preston. "The South Carolina Yazoo Company," *Mississippi Valley Historical Review* 16 (December 1929); 383-94.

Willis, William S. "Divide and Rule: Red, White, and Black in the Southeast," *The Journal of Negro History* 48 (July 1963); 157-76.

Wright, J. Leitch, Jr. "A Note on the First Seminole War as Seen by the Indians,
    Negroes, and Their British Advisers," *Journal of Southern History* 34 (Novem-
    ber 1968); 565-75.
Wright, Muriel. "Seal of the Seminole Nation," *The Chronicles of Oklahoma* 34
    (Autumn 1956); 262-71.

b. Books

Abel, Annie Heloise. *The American Indian as Slaveholder and Secessionist.* Cleveland:
    The Arthur H. Clark Company, 1915.
——. *The American Indian under Reconstruction.* Cleveland: The Arthur H. Clarke
    Company, 1925.
Alden, John R. *John Stuart and the Southern Colonial Frontier: A Study of Indian
    Relations, War, Trade, and Land Problems in the Southern Wilderness, 1754-
    1775.* Ann Arbor: University of Michigan Press, 1944. Reprint. New York:
    Gordian Press, 1966.
Coe, Charles H. *Red Patriots: The Story of the Seminoles.* Cincinnati: Editor Pub-
    lishing Company, 1898. Reprint. Gainesville: University Presses of Florida,
    1974.
Coleman, Kenneth. *The American Revolution in Georgia, 1763-1789.* Athens: Uni-
    versity of Georgia Press, 1958.
——. *Colonial Georgia: A History.* New York: Charles Scribner's Sons, 1976.
Corkran, David H. *The Creek Frontier, 1540-1783.* Norman: University of Okla-
    homa Press, 1967.
Cotterill, R. S. *The Southern Indians: The Story of the Civilized Tribes before
    Removal.* Norman: University of Oklahoma Press, 1954.
Crane, Verner W. *The Southern Frontier, 1670-1732.* Ann Arbor: University of
    Michigan Press, 1956.
Dalton, Lawrence. *History of Randolph County, Arkansas.* Little Rock: Democrat
    Printing and Lithographing Company, [1946?].
Debo, Angie. *The Rise and Fall of the Choctaw Republic.* Norman: University of
    Oklahoma Press, 1934.
——. *The Road to Disappearance.* Norman University of Oklahoma Press, 1941.
Foreman, Grant. *The Five Civilized Tribes.* Norman: University of Oklahoma
    Press, 1934.
——. *Indian Removal.* Norman: University of Oklahoma Press, 1932.
Gibson, Arrell M. *The Chickasaws.* Norman: University of Oklahoma Press, 1971.
Giddings, Joshua R. *The Exiles of Florida.* Columbus, Ohio: Follett, Foster and
    Company, 1858.
Gray, Lewis Cecil. *History of Agriculture in the Southern United States to 1860.*
    Washington, D.C.: Carnegie Institution, 1932. Reprint. Gloucester, Mass.:
    Peter Smith, 1958.
Halbert, H. S., and Ball, T. H. *The Creek War of 1813 and 1814.* Chicago: Donohue
    & Henneberry, 1895. Reprint. Edited by Frank L. Owsley, Jr. University;
    University of Alabama Press, 1969.

Halliburton, R., Jr. *Red over Black: Black Slavery among the Cherokee Indians.*
    Westport, Conn.: Greenwood Press, 1977.
Irving, Washington. *Wolfert's Roost.* Author's rev. ed. New York: G. P. Putnam's
    Sons, 1910.
Littlefield, Daniel F., Jr. *Africans and Seminoles: From Removal to Emancipation.*
    Westport, Conn.: Greenwood Press, 1977.
    The Cherokee Freedmen: From Emancipation to American Citizenship. West-
    port, Conn.: Greenwood Press, 1978.
Loughridge, R. M., comp. *English and Muskokee Dictionary.* St. Louis: J. T. Smith,
    1890. Reprint. Okmulgee, Okla.: B. Frank Belvin, 1964.
McCoy, Isaac. *History of Baptist Indian Missions: Embracing Remarks on the
    Former and Present Condition of the Aboriginal Tribes; Their Settlement
    Within the Indian Territory, and Their Future Prospects.* Washington, D.C.
    William M. Morrison; New York: H. and S. Raynor, 1840.
McReynolds, Edwin C. *The Seminoles.* Norman: University of Oklahoma Press, 1957.
Mahon, John K. *History of the Second Seminole War, 1835-42.* Gainesville: University
    of Florida Press, 1967.
Meriwether, Robert Lee. *The Expansion of South Carolina, 1729-1765.* Kingsport,
    Tenn.: Southern Publishers, Inc., 1940. Reprint. Philadelphia: Porcupine
    Press, Inc., 1974.
Milling, Chapman J. *Red Carolinians.* Chapel Hill: University of North Carolina Press,
    1940.
O'Donnell, James H., III. *Southern Indians in the American Revolution.* Knoxville:
    University of Tennessee Press, 1973.
Perdue, Theda. *Slavery and the Evolution of Cherokee Society, 1540-1866.* Knox-
    ville: University of Tennessee Press, 1979.
Porter, Kenneth Wiggins. *The Negro on the American Frontier.* New York: Arno Press
    and The New York Times, 1971.
Pound, Merritt B. *Benjamin Hawkins—Indian Agent.* Athens: University of Georgia
    Press, 1951.
[Simmons, William Hayne.] *Notices of East Florida.* Charleston, S.C.: A. E. Miller,
    1822. Reprint. Gainesville: University of Florida Press, 1973.
Sirmans, M. Eugene. *Colonial South Carolina: A Political History, 1663-1763.* Chapel
    Hill: University of North Carolina Press, 1966.
Wardell, Morris L. *A Political History of the Cherokee Nation, 1838-1907.* Norman:
    University of Oklahoma Press, 1938.
Whitaker, Arthur Preston. *The Mississippi Question, 1795-1803: A Study in Trade,
    Politics, and Diplomacy.* New York: The American Historical Association,
    1934. Reprint. Gloucester, Mass.: Peter Smith, 1962.
Wright, J. Leitch, Jr. *William Augustus Bowles: Director General of the Creek Nation.*
    Athens: University of Georgia Press, 1967.

INDEX

Thomas (slave), 189; weapon taken from, 188
Thomas, Richard, 49
Thompson, Jacob, 226
Thompson, James, 227
Thompson, John, 49
Thompson, Joseph, 48, 49
Thompson, Louisa, 48
Thompson, Wiley, 123
Tom (free black), 90
Tom (slave): at Fort Mims, 62; escapes Fort Mims, 62; as interpreter, 139
Tombigbee River, settlements on, 60, 61
Tonkawa Indians, 199
Town system, breakdown of, 136
Towns, 139
Trade, attempts to regulate, 15
Treaty of August, 18, 20, 32
Treaty of Colerain, 36, 40, 57, 95, 96, 97, 98, 255
Treaty of 1845, 173-174, 193
Treaty of 1856, 226
Treaty of 1866, 247, 254
Treaty of Fort Gibson, 160, 256
Treaty of Fort Jackson, 66, 69, 89, 90, 110
Treaty of Galphinton, 32, 33, 34
Treaty of Indian Springs, 98
Treaty of Moultrie Creek, 76
Treaty of New York, 34, 36, 40, 57, 95, 96, 97, 98, 255; negotiated, 33
Treaty of Paris, 18
Treaty of Payne's Landing, 114, 118, 160, 256
Treaty of Shoulderbone, 32, 33, 34
Troup, George M., 98
Tuckabahchee, 35, 86; trader at, 20
Tuckabahchee Micco, 117, 118, 138, 141, 146, 187, 208; slaves of, 116
Tuskeneehau, 209, 222; Christianity opposed by, 86, 87; suicide of, 123
Tussekiah, 174
Tustanug Chopco, 202
Tustenuggee Chopco, 208
Tustenuggee Hopoie, 66
Tustenuggee Micco, 185
Tutt, Charles P., 102
Twiggs, David, 75

United Nations of the Indian Territory, 235
United States factory, 47, 56 n.67
Upper Creeks, 135; agriculture among, 37; location of, 3, 136; loyalty of, 235; McGillivray's influence among, 28; runaway slaves among, 17; slaving raids by, 17

Van Buren, Martin, 161
Vann, Martin, 144

Waco Indians, 199, 201
Walker, Billy, 139
Walker, Henry, 90, 91
Walker, John, 90
Walker, Taney, 64
Walker, William, 104, 115, 216
Walton, Robert, 30, 48
Wannah (slave), 183, 184
War of 1812, 97; Creek-Georgia relations before, 57
War of Jenkins' Ear, 39
War of the Spanish Succession, 13
Ward, John, 227
Washbourne, J. W., 218, 220, 221, 222, 224
Washington, George, 33
Watson, J. C., slave claim of, 120, 127, 128
Weapons: owned by free blacks, 49, 101; owned by Seminole blacks, 145; owned by slaves, 46, 154, 179
Weatherford, Charles, 30
Weatherford, Mrs. Charles, 43
Weatherford, William, 62, 65, 67; as Red Stick leader, 61
Weaving: by Creeks, 43; by slaves, 46, 137
Wewoka Creek, black settlement on, 191, 194
West Florida, creation of, 26
Whan (Juan), 41
Wheelwrights, 246
White, James, 33
White, P. H., 200
White, P. N., 196
White, Phineas H., 216
White Lieutenant, 37

About the Author

Daniel F. Littlefield, Jr., is Professor and Chairman of the English Department at the University of Arkansas at Little Rock. His previous books include *Hamlin Garland's Observations of the American Indian, 1895-1905, Africans and Seminoles* (Greenwood Press, 1977), and *The Cherokee Freedmen* (Greenwood Press, 1978).